UNEARTHING THE POLYNESIAN PAST

UNEARTHING THE POLYNESIAN PAST

Explorations and Adventures of
an Island Archaeologist

Patrick Vinton Kirch

University of Hawai'i Press
Honolulu

20 19 18 17 16 15   6 5 4 3 2 1

Library of Congress Cataloging-in-Publication Data

Kirch, Patrick Vinton, author.

Unearthing the Polynesian past : explorations and adventures of an island archaeologist / Patrick Vinton Kirch.

pages cm

Includes bibliographical references and index.

ISBN 978-0-8248-5345-7 (cloth : alk. paper)

1. Kirch, Patrick Vinton.   2. Polynesia—Antiquities.   3. Archaeologists—Biography. I. Title.

GN875.P64K57 2016

930.1092—dc23

[B]

2015013590

University of Hawai'i Press books are printed on acid-free paper and meet the guidelines for permanence and durability of the Council on Library Resources.

This is the road my body goes,
Lost in the foaming sea.
Aue! Aue! Aue!
Beneath the burning heat of the day,
Aue!

Old Tahitian Song

Contents

ILLUSTRATIONS

Figures

Maps

PREFACE

They were, in the words of the great Maori anthropologist Te Rangi Hiroa, the "Vikings of the Sunrise." One thousand years before Christ the Lapita ancestors of the Polynesians arrived in the sun-drenched archipelagoes of Tonga and Samoa, the ancestral homeland of Hawaiki. Over ensuing centuries, the descendants of these voyagers who were the first humans to explore the vast Pacific perfected the arts of non-instrumental navigation, sailing by the stars, winds, and currents. Their craftsmen carved large double-hulled canoes with sewn-plank timbers, propelled by sails of woven mats. In these deep-water craft, carrying everything needed to establish new colonies, they explored and settled every habitable island and archipelago across the untracked central and eastern Pacific, even reaching the shores of South America. They were truly, as Hiroa claimed, "the supreme navigators of history."

For nearly five decades I have pursued the history of these great seafarers who conquered the Pacific world even as Europe was mired in its Dark Ages. As an archaeologist and anthropologist of the Pacific and especially of Polynesia, my work has taken me from the Mussau Islands of Papua New Guinea in the west, to Mangareva in the east, to Hawai'i in the north. I have explored abandoned hilltop villages in the jungles of the Solomon Islands, dug through three thousand years of history in the sands of Tikopia, recovered the traces of South American sweet potato tubers brought back by Polynesian seafarers to Mangaia in the Cook Islands, and mapped ancient temples and agricultural fields on the windy slopes of Haleakalā on Maui. It has been an exhilarating quest.

Mostly, the fruits of my explorations of Polynesian archaeology have been published as academic books and monographs and in the more than three hundred articles and chapters I have written for scientific journals and edited collections, intended for the use of scholars and students. Archaeologists spend years in university and graduate school learning the arcane, technical language of our discipline: of stone tool and pottery typologies, of stratigraphic descriptions, of radiocarbon chronologies. The academic codes of tenure and promotion enforce our practices of writing and publication. To be sure, publication of the technical details of our research is essential if the knowledge we have painstakingly acquired is to be preserved for future generations of scholars.

But as I have grown older I realize more and more that what we archaeologists do and what we have learned are of immense interest to a larger public. We have an obligation to share our experiences and our knowledge as widely as possible, and not only because much of our research is funded by the public purse (in my case, largely through grants from the National Science Foundation). My book, *A Shark Going Inland Is My Chief: The Island Civilization of Ancient Hawai'i*, published in 2012, is one effort toward that goal of sharing my accumulated knowledge with those beyond my professional world.

Here, in *Unearthing the Polynesian Past*, I tell the stories of my many expeditions and fieldwork among the islands and peoples of the Pacific. In writing this book, I have kept three fundamental aims in mind. First, I want to convey the sheer adventure of doing archaeology in the islands of Polynesia and the Pacific: not just the work of digging into the stratified sands of Hālawa or Talepakemalai but also the experiences of living among traditional societies in Anuta and Tikopia, the setbacks when politics or personal animosities interfered with fieldwork, the discomfort of long voyages on inter-island boats, and the exhilaration of unexpected discoveries. Over the years, sometimes while sipping a whiskey after a long day of excavations, I have regaled my graduate students with tales of fieldwork on remote islands. But these stories, these adventures—these explorations of an island archaeologist—deserve to be shared more widely.

My second goal is to impart—in a manner free of academic jargon—what I and my students and colleagues have learned from these many expeditions to islands large and small. How has our work changed what we know about the Polynesian past? What difference does it make to our understanding not only of Pacific history but also of the nature of human societies generally and, specifically, of their complex interactions with the natural world? I have long advocated the view that the islands of the Pacific are "microcosms" of history, that by unraveling the course of cultural evolution on these islands we gain insights about the relationships between humans and nature that go beyond particular times and places. In these pages, I hope to share some of these insights.

Finally, over my academic career of fifty years, the discipline of archaeology has grown and changed immensely. When I came into the field as a young student, volunteering on summer digs with Honolulu's Bishop Museum, archaeology was dominated by the search for artifacts. The main goal of archaeological research was "culture history," the description of cultural change through sequences of artifact types. By the time I was a graduate student at Yale, the New Archaeology was in its heyday, advocating a "processual" approach to cultural evolution. Years later, a "post-processual" movement would raise fundamental questions about archaeological interpretation and epistemology. In recent years, archaeology has come to play a key role in multidisciplinary research focused on human "ecodynamics," the complex interactions between human populations and their ecosystems. Having lived through—and actively participated in—these debates about what archaeology is and should be, I want to show in this book how they have played out in the world of Pacific archaeology.

Because this is a memoir of my life in Polynesian and Pacific archaeology, I have written it chronologically. The ways in which my own knowledge and understanding of the islands and their ancient societies have grown and become more nuanced are best conveyed, I feel, in the sequence that I myself experienced them. Thus I begin at the beginning, as a *keiki o ka 'āina,* a "child of the land" in Hawai'i of the 1950s.

ACKNOWLEDGMENTS

Sadly, I can no longer directly thank my parents, Barbara and Harold William Kirch, for the opportunities they gave me, growing up in their adopted island home of Hawai'i; they have since departed this life. But as I have grown older I have come to appreciate just how much my life and career were the outgrowth of the love and devotion they showed their family. I am especially indebted to my father for encouraging the "precocious" predilections of his younger son by taking me on our "expeditions" to Lāna'i and Moloka'i in 1963 and 1964. I also want to acknowledge the aloha and support of my late brother, Michael, and of my sister, Pamela, and her family.

I was equally fortunate to fall under the influence of a series of mentors who guided my early efforts to become an archaeologist and scientist. Above all, Yoshio Kondo molded my initial foray into the world of science; becoming one of his malacology summer interns in 1963 was the most pivotal event of my youth. As I began to engage with Bishop Museum's archaeology program, Kenneth P. Emory, Lloyd Soehren, Peter Chapman, William (Pila) Kikuchi, and Yosihiko Sinoto all shared their time to help tutor a young student. Douglas Yen and Roger Green, in particular, recognized the spark in my youthful enthusiasm, giving me opportunities normally reserved for more advanced students. Later, Yen and Green would become two of my closest colleagues, with whom I shared research experiences and coauthored monographs and books.

At the University of Pennsylvania, George Dales and Ward Goodenough were inspiring teachers. It was gratifying to establish warm professional relationships with both of them later in my career. At Yale, my principal advisor Kwang-chih Chang graciously accepted my unexpected shift from Southeast Asian to Pacific archaeology, unhesitatingly supporting my research. Harold Conklin, Irving Rouse, Leopold Pospisil, and Harold Scheffler played strong supporting roles.

Most of my adult life has been shared, successively, with two marvelous women to whom I had the good fortune to be married; first to Debra Connelly during the years that I worked at the Bishop Museum and the University of Washington. Though our lives ultimately diverged along separate paths, I thank her for her support and continued friendship. Thérèse Babineau has been my muse and soul mate ever since I arrived in California. Together we have explored the jeep roads of Kahikinui, the ruins of Easter Island, and the deep valleys of Raʻiatea and the Marquesas. Without her loving support I would not have achieved half of what is recounted in the pages of this book.

The list of colleagues and students with whom I have collaborated or who have influenced my work and career is long, and it is with some fear that I will unintentionally leave some names unremarked that I list them here: Jim Allen, Melinda Allen, Emmett Aluli, Steve Athens, Alex Baer, David Burley, Virginia Butler, Alan Carpenter, Oliver Chadwick, Scarlett Chiu, Carl Christensen, Jeff Clark, Paul Cleghorn, James Coil, Sara Collins, Eric Conte, Ross Cordy, Claudio Cristino, Tom Dye, Tim Earle, Julie Field, John Flenley, James Flexner, Sam Gon III, Michael Graves, Jo Lynn Guinness, Toni Han, Jon Hather, Gil Hendren, Lisa Holm, John Holson, Terry Hunt, Sara Hotchkiss, Robert Hommon, Helen James, Jesse Jennings, Sharyn Jones, Elaine (Muffett) Jourdane, Adrienne Kaeppler, Jennifer Kahn, Kathy Kawelu, Charles Keau, Marion Kelly, Eric Komori, Thegn Ladefoged, Charlotte Lee, Dana Lepofsky, Kent Lightfoot, Sam Low, Mark McCoy, Patrick McCoy, Holly McEldowney, Sidsel Millerstrom, Peter Mills, Mo Moler, Guillaume Molle, Gail Murakami, Buddy Neller, Douglas Oliver, Richard Pearson, Nick Porch, Cedric Puleston, Storrs Olson, Tom Riley, Paul Rosendahl, Marshall Sahlins, Laura Schuster, Warren Sharp, David Sherrod, John Sinton, Aki Sinoto, Pilipo Solatorio, Matthew Spriggs, David Steadman, Elspeth Sterling, Leon Sterling, Robert Suggs, Catherine (Cappy) Summers, Jillian Swift, Julie (Endicott) Taomia, Cindy van Gilder, Jo Anne Van Tilburg, Kirsten Vacca, Patricia Vargas, Peter Vitousek, Marshall Weisler, and Alan Ziegler.

Several colleagues and friends helped in the preparation of these memoirs. Sam Low graciously read and critiqued much of the first draft, greatly improving the manuscript. Other chapters were read and commented on by Kent Lightfoot, Carl Christensen, Mark McCoy, Cordelia Nickelsen, and Jillian Swift. Thérèse Babineau critiqued many draft chapters; she also printed many of the black-and-white photos from my archival negatives. As usual, the book has also benefited from Masako Ikeda's editorial stewardship at the University of Hawaiʻi Press.

Finally—and most importantly—I want to acknowledge the people of the island communities who over so many years of field research have welcomed me into their villages, hosted and fed me in their homes, worked alongside me in my excavations, shared their knowledge of their traditional cultures, and graciously allowed me to explore their ancestral pasts. On the beaches of Anuta and Tikopia, in Mussau and Vanikoro, they welcomed and accepted me into their midst. In Futuna and Niuatoputapu, Manuʻa, Mangaia, Moʻorea, Maupiti, and Mangareva, and on Molokaʻi and Maui, they accepted me, my colleagues, and my students, facilitating our research through countless small acts of generosity. I cannot here thank each one of the literally hundreds of islanders who have befriended and aided me; the names of some of them are mentioned in the chapters of this book. But it is with great warmth and heartfelt gratitude that I dedicate this book to those descendants of "the Vikings of the sunrise." I can only hope that the accumulated fruits of my labors over all these decades, pulling back the veil of time from their collective history, in some small measure help repay my debt for their collective *aloha*.

Patrick Vinton Kirch
Quinta Pacifica
September 2014

CHAPTER ONE

Keiki o ka ʻĀina: *"Child of the Land"* (Oʻahu, 1950–1963)

My four-year-old hands gripped the thwart of Jack York's skiff as we cruised past the rocky headland of Makaliʻi Point, its seaweed- and limpet-encrusted boulders just a few yards away. My eyes were fixed on my father's taut grip on his trolling line. A silver streak flashed under our keel, my father yanked the line sharply, a *kākū* took the bait, and the hook set in its powerful jaw. A brief fight, then my father hauled the barracuda up to the gunwale, drove a marlin spike into its head, and tossed it into the bilge.

By now the skiff rode the inky blue-green waters of Kahana Bay; long swells rolled in through the wide gap in the reef. York eyed the combers warily, pointing the bow seaward to ride up and over them. To be caught sideway by a large wave could be disastrous. York then turned the skiff for another run at Makaliʻi Point.

My father and York—avid fishermen—loved to escape with their families each summer to two weathered board-and-batten beach houses up the windward Oʻahu coast at Punaluʻu. Fishing here since the late 1940s, they had coined their own name for Makaliʻi Point: "Kaku Corner." Sleek, silvery fish up to six feet long with firm white flesh, *kākū* can sever a finger with their vicious teeth. The *kākū* never failed to strike at my father's handmade trolling lures of fiberglass resin armed with steel hooks camouflaged by a skirt of red cloth.

The Johnson outboard spewed out its foamy wake as we made another run, this time heading toward Punaluʻu; again the strike, hook set, the fight between fisherman and fish, another *kākū* added to the bilge. These sorties might be repeated five or six times, but never more than necessary to satisfy the appetites of those waiting back at Punaluʻu. Up the coastline we then cruised, between beach and reef, with coral heads and the brilliant colors of *hīnālea* and *uhu* fish passing beneath us. Tying the boat up to its buoy we swam the remaining forty feet to the beach.

Evening fell as *kākū* fillets roasted over *kiawe* embers, and the sea breeze carried the relentless roar of surf on the outer reef. Our families feasted at a weathered picnic table under the spreading limbs of a *kamani* tree. After dinner, the adults talked of fishing or of the changing complexities of Hawaiian politics in the heady years after World War II. We kids ran around the periphery, playing hide-and-seek in the ironwood hedges.

A Kodak print in our family photo album shows me stark naked, six weeks old, on a mat next to my mother on Punaluʻu beach. The feel of those sands, the echoes of the surf, the warmth of subtropical sunlight filtered through coconut fronds must be deeply ingrained in my neurons. I am never more content than when lying semi-awake in some island home near the beach, the distant surf echoing in my ears.

Oʻahu in the early 1950s was not the congested megapolis it has become. Not a single building in Honolulu stood taller than the harbormaster's Aloha Tower. When my family left Honolulu for Punaluʻu each summer, we entered a different world. Beyond the sleepy village of Kāneʻohe lay a nineteenth-century landscape shaped by the rural economy of sugarcane plantations. In vestigial pockets, windward Oʻahu still preserved the traditional Hawaiian loʻi, irrigated taro fields.

My mother drove our big Buick loaded with suitcases and groceries, while my father rode his World War II army jeep. The narrow, winding road between Honolulu and Kailua, in places less than two vehicles abreast, traversed the Koʻolau Mountains and snaked its way down the precipitous Nuʻuanu Pali (the first tunnels through the Pali were not bored until 1959). The jeep's lack of doors added a certain thrill to the ride.

Kāneʻohe held little of interest outside of a quick stop at the Hygienic Store for a "shave ice." Past Heʻeia, we were in the country. At Kualoa, with picturesque Mokoliʻi islet offshore, we spotted the stone ruins of Judd's sugar mill in the tangle of koa haole bushes. On the reef flat at Kaʻaʻawa, a fisherman waded with a glass-bottomed viewing box, spear in hand, looking for tender heʻe. Then the furrowed hills and ridges of Kahana Valley came into view, cutting dark traces into the Koʻolau Mountains. As we rounded Makaliʻi Point, Punaluʻu beckoned.

In the early 1950s, the sugarcane fields of Kahuku Plantation stretched from the coastal road into Punaluʻu Valley. Narrow gauge engines of the Koʻolau Railway Company hauled loads of freshly harvested cane, with its sweet burnt aroma, up to Kahuku Mill. I can still recall the steam engine's whistle echoing off the mountain crests.

Some days we explored the inland recesses of Punaluʻu in my father's jeep, following the cane roads. But mostly we spent our summers swimming, hunting for leho shells at low tide or seeking the precious glass fishing floats that washed up on the beach after a storm, having floated all the way from Japan. My father and brother, and Jack York and his sons, set traps for eel and lobster, spear fished, and, of course, trolled for kākū off Makaliʻi Point.

Figure 1.1. The *S. S. Lurline* arriving at Honolulu harbor, with the Aloha Tower in the background. My parents arrived on this ship in 1940. (Source: U.S. National Park Service, via Wikimedia Commons [http://www.nps.gov/history/history/online_books/npswapa/gallery/albums/album100/WAPA_2505_012.htm].)

My parents, Barbara Ver and Harold William Kirch, were born and raised in Los Angeles. My father had a job there with the Armacost and Royston nursery firm, but his dream was to start his own orchid business. One day Mr. Armacost took my father aside; the firm needed a new agent, he said, to represent the company in far-off Honolulu. Wealthy *kamaʻāina* families grew orchids in greenhouses on their island estates; they competed over buying exotic new orchid species. Would my father be interested in a position in Honolulu with half-time salary plus commission? It would be a gutsy move for a young couple. Booking one-way passage on the *S.S. Lurline,* they arrived in Honolulu in early July 1940 (Fig. 1.1). With help from the wealthy heiress Wilhelmina Tenney, one of his first regular customers, my father purchased a property in Mānoa Valley where he could set up his greenhouses.[1] My parents hired a local Japanese contractor to build their modest house on Waipuna Rise in early 1941.

On December 7, 1941, the Empire of Japan attacked Pearl Harbor. Rumors of an imminent attack somewhere in the Pacific had been circulating for months, but the United States was caught completely off guard. Martial law was declared; the entire island went into blackout mode. Years later, my father would regale us with stories about the confusion and terror of those first few days when everyone feared a Japanese invasion. My mother, pregnant with my brother Michael, was tempted to leave the islands with other young married women. She opted to stay with my father, which turned out to be a smart decision because other wives who left their husbands then were unable to return until the war's end, four years later.

My father struggled to make ends meet during the war years, working for the University of Hawai'i's agricultural research station on papaya production and other war-related agricultural projects. Gas and food were rationed, but my parents raised rabbits and grew their own vegetables in Mānoa. My sister, Pamela, was born not long before war's end. With the war over, my father's orchid business started to burgeon (Fig. 1.2).

Figure 1.2. My father, Bill Kirch, with one of his orchid plants. This photo appeared in an article in *The Honolulu Advertiser* in February 1954, featuring my father and his orchid business.

I was born at Queen's Hospital in Honolulu, Territory of Hawaiʻi, in the summer of 1950. Some of my earliest memories are of playing amidst the greenhouses and potting sheds of my father's orchid nursery, surrounded by exotic *Vanda, Dendrobium,* and *Cattleya* orchids (Fig. 1.3). I grew up in Mānoa, running barefoot with my local Japanese American playmates as we explored the valley's hills and streams. In this fertile valley Hawaiians once farmed taro, bananas, sugarcane,

Figure 1.3. The author at age four, in the front garden of our house in Mānoa Valley. Like most children in Hawaiʻi, I went barefoot until the sixth grade.

and *'awa*. When I was young, ranks of taro patches still cloaked the valley floor, by then mostly taken over by Chinese truck farmers. Today the terraces are long gone, buried under houses and shopping centers.[2]

Across the street from our house, the Bartels family was one of our few neighbors. Peggy Bartels descended from a line of Maui chiefs, whereas Henry traced his ancestry to Kohala, Hawai'i. *Koa* calabashes, *kapa* beaters, and other artifacts filled their home, the floors covered with *lauhala* mats. Sitting on their wide *pūne'e* we listened to Henry Bartels tell tales of old Hawai'i. Their son Jimmy would later become the much-beloved curator of 'Iolani Palace, the last home of the Hawaiian monarchy.

We neighborhood kids explored the overgrown landscape behind our houses, climbing through the tangle of *koa haole* and guava to discover walls and enclosures of weathered stone, vestiges of ancient Hawaiian farmsteads. One day Jimmy Bartels found a stone poi pounder among the mossy walls. We had seen such artifacts on school excursions to the Bishop Museum in Kalihi, but here Jimmy held one in his hands. It amazed us that our own backyards could produce something we had previously thought was restricted to that darkly lit museum.

Like my brother and sister ahead of me, I attended the public Mānoa Elementary School. There were a few other *haole* (Caucasian) students, but most of my classmates were Japanese or Chinese Americans. Outside of school we spoke "pidgin" English, a dialect that to this day I can lapse back into within minutes. In my friends' homes I was exposed to the customs of their second-generation immigrant families. I saw how "Grandma" Matsunaga made sushi in her kitchen and puzzled at the Buddhist shrine in one corner of the Kohashi family's living room.

When I was in third grade, my parents decided that I should take the entrance exam for Punahou, a private school where most of the students were *haole*. My friends teased me for thinking about going to the school for white elites. "I don't want to go to the *haole* school!" I protested. But my parents insisted that I try Punahou for a year.

Punahou had been founded in 1841 by Protestant missionaries who, finding it onerous to send their children back to New England to be educated, started their own school. High Chief Boki gave them a choice piece of land in Mānoa, where a spring bubbled forth at the base of a rocky hill. Ka Punahou, "the New Spring," lent its name to the fledgling Congregationalist school, later to become one of the finest college preparatory schools in the United States.[3] With my newfound classmates I played during recess around the banks of the old lily pond, still fed by Ka Punahou. I now realize what a gift my parents bestowed upon me.

While my brother, Mike, loved the ocean and became a surfer, I was drawn to Mānoa's mountains. Not far from our house I would duck into the underbrush and climb up over boulders and cliffs, ascending the dry streambed up to Waʻahila Ridge. In the narrow ravine the understory opened up like a gallery under white-barked *kukui* trees, the ground covered with their hard-kerneled nuts. Reaching the ridge crest, a trail led *mauka* (inland) toward the crest of the Koʻolau Mountains, wending its way through endemic *koa* and *ʻōhiʻa* trees, entwined with *ʻieʻie* vines. I hiked this trail countless times. From those heights I gazed down on Diamond Head and Waikīkī; on clear days I could see as far as Mount Kaʻala in the distant Waiʻanae Mountains.

At night I was soothed by hearing Mānoa's sometimes crashing rains descending into the valley before the raindrops hit. Mānoa embodied *mauka,* muddy trails, valleys shaded by stately *kukui* trees, icy cold mountain streams. Punaluʻu evoked for me the sea and the windward sides of islands, salty air wafting down on trade winds, *hala* leaves rustling, the acrid smell of damp *kamani* groves. Mānoa and Punaluʻu, inland and coastal, mountain and sea, *mauka* and *makai:* These fundamental contrasts define island life. The balance between seaward and inland, windward and leeward, has sustained island peoples and cultures for millennia. I learned this first by living it.

In the summer of 1959 my father took our family to Molokaʻi. His friend Dave Nottage owned a cabin on the east end, near Waialua. We shipped my father's Willys-Overland Jeepster on the Young Brothers' barge over to Kaunakakai and a week later flew to Molokaʻi on an Aloha Airlines turboprop. I stared out the big square windows at the Hoʻolehua plain, dark green pineapple fields contrasting starkly with the famously red Molokaʻi dirt exposed in the symmetrical ruts worn down by the harvesting trucks.

There was not a single stoplight on the island. The one-story wooden facades of Kaunakakai's main street evoked a scene out of a John Ford Western. We bought fresh-baked Portuguese sweet bread at Kanemitsu's Bakery and other supplies at the Friendly Market. The Jeepster strained under the load as we headed out along the single paved road toward the east end.

Molokaʻi was then and remains the most rural and distinctly Hawaiian island. Only about six thousand people live there. The coastal plain fronts the archipelago's most extensive coral reef, which is up to a mile wide. Along this sheltered coast in ancient times the Hawaiians constructed nearly one hundred stone-walled fishponds. My father pointed out the arc-shaped fishpond walls as we drove leisurely toward Waialua.

Nestled between the road and a white sand beach, the rustic Nottage cabin enjoyed a stunning view across the channel to Maui and Lānaʻi. There were a couple of bedrooms with bunk beds and a simple kitchen; *lauhala* mats covered the living room floor while glass fishing floats hung in nets from the front porch rafters. A cluster of old coconut palms and *hala* trees in the yard offered shade. My father and brother immediately set out fishing poles and lines. My brother got a shock when—instead of the *ulua* fish he was expecting—his line hooked a stingray with a five-foot wing span!

One day we visited Hālawa Valley, an event that would influence my future. The unpaved road snaked its way up the mountainside in and out of little gulches, leveled off at Puʻu o Hoku Ranch, and then descended steeply into Hālawa, where it ended. Our first view of the twin waterfalls of Moaʻula and Hīpuapua at the back of the valley took our breath away. Hālawa had been all but abandoned after a devastating tsunami in 1946. We parked the Jeepster by the nineteenth-century Congregational Church, with its thick rock-and-coral lime-mortar walls, a large Hawaiian bible still sitting on the pulpit.

For a couple of hours we followed the muddy path inland toward the waterfalls, shaded by huge mango trees. Icy water swirled around our legs as we forded the boulder-strewn stream. Everywhere there were moss-covered stone walls. We climbed over low terraces and stone enclosures and hiked past imposing platforms. I had seen stone walls and cairns in the back ravines of Mānoa but nothing like these here in Hālawa. Had these stone-faced platforms been the foundations of ancient temples, *heiau?* My fertile imagination—fueled by visits to the Bishop Museum—conjured up images of white-bearded *kāhuna* or priests chanting in front of fierce wooden images. Memories of that day would haunt me for years to come.

During the winter of 1960 I began suffering massive migraines and then one morning passed dark-red blood in my urine. I had an acute kidney infection; for a few weeks the doctors were not sure I would live. They pumped me full of penicillin and confined me to bed for three months, a time when I developed a love of books and reading. When I recovered, my mother enrolled me in a summer art class at the YWCA across Richards Street from ʻIolani Palace. After the class I would walk over to the palace, built by King David Kalākaua from 1879 to 1882. Climbing the steep steps, walking under Corinthian columns and through glass doors etched with the royal coat of arms, it was a thrill to enter that central hallway with its grand staircase of glistening *koa* wood. In those days before the new State Capitol was built, the legislature met in ʻIolani Palace.

The curator of the throne room, open to the public when the legislature was not in session, was ʻIolani Luahine, a famed hula dancer. Born in 1915, Luahine was the *hānai* or adopted child of her great-aunt Julia Keahi Luahine, one of the last royal dancers in the courts of King Kalākaua and Queen Liliʻuokalani.[4] Often I was the only visitor in the throne room. ʻIolani Luahine, dressed invariably in a full-length *holokū,* would walk with me around the red carpeted room with its ornate ceiling and crystal chandeliers, pausing in front of portraits of the Kamehamehas, of William Lunalilo, David Kalākaua, and Princess Kaʻiulani— and of other high *aliʻi.* Standing in front of each portrait, Luahine would recount stories of the life of each person. I visited the throne room and Luahine almost every week. At summer's end my father gave me a potted orchid plant from his greenhouse to take to Luahine as a thank-you gift.

Aside from ʻIolani Palace, the other great repository of Hawaiian cultural traditions was the Bernice Pauahi Bishop Museum, known to Hawaiians as the "Treasure House of the Kamehamehas." Charles Reed Bishop founded the museum in 1889 in memory of his deceased wife Princess Pauahi, last descendant of the Kamehameha dynasty.[5] He intended it to be a home for the feathered cloaks and helmets, spears, and other artifacts passed down within her *aliʻi* line. Over the decades the museum had become a center for anthropological and natural history research in Polynesia (Fig. 1.4).

Visits to Bishop Museum, with its imposing chiseled basalt walls, were exciting occasions. Hawaiian Hall rose three stories surrounded by open galleries, its polished Victorian *koa* wood and glass cabinets containing endless wonders. The

Figure 1.4. The main façade of the Bernice Pauahi Bishop Museum. The basalt stones of Hawaiian Hall were quarried on site in the late nineteenth century.

skeleton of a sperm whale hung from the ceiling. In the center of Hawaiian Hall stood a scale model of the ancient *heiau* of Wahaʻula on the island of Hawaiʻi, complete with images and an offering platform. Near this was a thatched Hawaiian house or *hale* whose timbers had been recovered from remote Miloliʻi Valley on Kauaʻi. In cases and alcoves all around the ground level, dioramas with life-size mannequins of Hawaiian men and women captured ancient life. In one display, women beat *kapa* with wooden mallets. In another, a sorcerer bowed low in front of a carved image, frozen in the act of praying his victim to death.

I could not wait to climb the stairs to the second level of Hawaiian Hall, where a trove of artifacts gathered by the museum's scientists on expeditions to the far-flung islands of the Pacific awaited. There were coconut fiber armor and sharks' teeth weapons from the Gilbert Islands; drums from the Marquesas, beaten during tribal cannibal feasts; and a worm-eaten *rongorongo* tablet from mysterious Easter Island, incised with the intricate characters of Polynesia's only indigenous script.

The uppermost level—face to face with the giant sperm whale—was devoted to natural history. There were bottles of fishes pickled in alcohol with handwritten labels in India ink; bleached corals of every genus and species meticulously mounted on wooden blocks; and drawers filled with cowries, cones, whelks, and conchs from island reefs and lagoons.

Bishop Museum, as I experienced it through those childhood visits to the exhibition halls—and occasionally into the more mysterious storage rooms when they were opened once a year to public visitors on a Saturday—showed me that island life and cultures could be the subject of intellectual exploration. One could simultaneously live in the islands and make a life out of studying them. I cannot recall just when this realization came over me, but the islands had me in their grip.

Raised in Honolulu in the 1950s and 1960s, I was in the right place at the right time to be exposed to the rapidly developing field of Polynesian archaeology. Exciting discoveries were being made about the history of the seafaring Polynesians, whose migrations across the vast Pacific had puzzled generations of scholars. Most experts held that the Polynesians had originated in Asia, perhaps along the coasts of south China. Gradually they moved eastward in their outrigger canoes, from island to island, eventually discovering such remote outposts as Easter Island and Hawaiʻi.

Archaeology had a slow start in Polynesia.[6] In 1920, the Bishop Museum launched its famous Bayard Dominick Expeditions to solve "the problem of Polynesian origins." Field teams were sent to Tonga, Tahiti, the Marquesas, and the Austral Islands. But the pioneering archaeologists faced an insurmountable problem: There was no means to date the age of the monuments and artifacts they encountered. Hampered by its primitive methods, archaeology failed to yield much knowledge about the Polynesian past. Attempts to dig in Polynesian soils had also disappointed; despite the discovery of a few potsherds in a "kitchen midden" on Tongatapu, most Polynesian islands lacked pottery. Elsewhere in the world, archaeologists depended upon subtle stylistic changes in pottery over time to establish their chronologies. Without pottery, archaeologists had no clue as to when Polynesians first arrived in the islands.

In 1935 a Maori anthropologist from New Zealand—named Te Rangi Hiroa by his Maori mother and Peter H. Buck by his Scottish father—took charge of the Bishop Museum. Hiroa regarded archaeology as "a dry subject." His own specialty was the indigenous arts and crafts of the Polynesians. By making precise comparisons between the lashing patterns on hafted adzes and the weaving patterns of basketry, Hiroa believed he could trace the migrations and relationships of the Polynesian peoples.

In *Vikings of the Sunrise,* published in 1938, Hiroa told the story of a race of seafarers who "surpass[ed] the achievements of the Phoenicians in the Mediterranean and the Vikings of the north Atlantic."[7] Drawing upon Polynesian oral traditions and myths and using chiefly genealogies for his time scale, Hiroa traced the ultimate homeland of the Polynesians to Asia, charting their migrations through the tiny atolls of Micronesia. *Vikings of the Sunrise* appeared to answer age-old questions about "the problem of Polynesian origins." But archaeology—the science that studies the direct evidence of the ancient past—had yet to contribute to this endeavor.

In 1947, a Norwegian adventurer stunned the world with a brash 101-day voyage on a replicated Inca raft from Peru to the Tuamotuan atoll of Raroia. Contrary to accepted scientific opinion, Thor Heyerdahl was convinced that the Polynesians had originated in South America. Although he was not a trained anthropologist, after his *Kon-Tiki* voyage—highlighted in *Life* magazine and a best-selling book and documentary film—Heyerdahl became a household name.[8] His theory of the South American origins of the Polynesians challenged the accepted theories of Hiroa and other scholars at the Bishop Museum.

I was probably not yet ten years old when I first heard about the *Kon-Tiki* voyage. The story fascinated me. A precocious reader, I devoured Heyerdahl's book from cover to cover. I then sought out books about Easter Island, Tahiti, and other Polynesian islands, frequenting the Hawaiʻi and Pacific Reading Room at the Library of Hawaiʻi, pouring over musty tomes with depictions of Tahitian *marae* and Hawaiian *heiau.*

In the mid-1950s, Heyerdahl—whose *Kon-Tiki* book and movie royalties had made him wealthy—organized an expedition to mysterious Easter Island. His team of archaeologists dug around the enigmatic stone statues and in the stone foundations of ancient houses. While failing to prove Heyerdahl's theory of American origins (which most scholars quickly debunked), the team nonetheless showed that digging in island soils could yield new insights into the Polynesian past. I read Heyerdahl's account of the expedition, *Aku-Aku,* enthralled by his tales of the statue quarry, the "cave of the virgins," and the birdman petroglyphs at Orongo.[9] I was seized by an insatiable desire to become an archaeologist. My father—a pragmatic businessman—was skeptical but encouraged my reading. Probably he thought it was a phase I would grow out of.

Meanwhile, the Bishop Museum's scientists were struggling to defend their view of an Asiatic origin of the Polynesians against Thor Heyerdahl's popular theory of American Indian origins. In 1947—the same year that Heyerdahl was drifting across the east Pacific on the *Kon-Tiki*—Willard Libby, a University of Chicago chemist, invented a method for determining the age of ancient carbon-based materials such as bone or charcoal.[10] Libby's method of radiocarbon dating electrified the staid world of archaeology. At the Bishop Museum, Kenneth Emory had spent three decades studying stone temple ruins in Tahiti, the Tuamotus, Mangareva, and Hawai'i, struggling to put these temple foundations into a temporal framework. In 1950 (the year I was born) Emory began digging in a rockshelter overlooking Kuli'ou'ou Valley, not far from our home in Honolulu.[11] Finding fishhooks, stone adzes, tattooing needles, and other artifacts in the dry dust of the cave floor, Emory resolved to determine their age using Libby's new "carbon-14" method. Emory sent Libby a sample of charcoal from a hearth at the rockshelter's base.

In February 1951, Emory got the answer he was waiting for. Libby's Geiger counters in the Chicago lab had measured the decay rate of ^{14}C in the ancient Hawaiian charcoal, allowing the chemist to calculate an age of 946 years before the present, with an error range of 180 years. (This ± factor of 180 years was quite large, because the method was still in its infancy.) Emory now knew that Polynesian fishermen had camped at Kuli'ou'ou, carving their fishhooks out of bone and pearl shell with coral files, as long ago as AD 1004. "Boy, was I excited," Emory later recalled. "Immediately it opened a whole new vista of possibilities."[12] Emory launched a new program in Hawaiian archaeology, seeking out and digging sites on Kaua'i, O'ahu, Moloka'i, and Hawai'i. The Honolulu newspapers often ran stories about Emory's latest findings, whetting my appetite to follow in his footsteps.

Archaeology in the Pacific had entered a new era. While Emory was pursuing his Hawaiian excavations, Edward Gifford of the University of California at Berkeley launched expeditions to Fiji and New Caledonia in the western Pacific, uncovering deep sites with long sequences of pottery and artifacts. Radiocarbon dates from Gifford's digs dated back two or even three thousand years, supporting the idea that people had gradually migrated from west to east across the

Pacific.[13] Meanwhile, the *Aku-Aku* expedition's archaeologists dated samples of charcoal that suggested Easter Island might have been settled as early as AD 350.[14] With these exciting new results, Polynesia was becoming a hotbed of archaeological research.

In 1956, New York's American Museum of Natural History sent Robert Suggs, a Columbia University doctoral student, to Nuku Hiva in the Marquesas. Digging into a sand dune at Haʻatuatua, Suggs found not only stone adzes and shell fishhooks by the dozens but also scraps of earthenware pottery, establishing a link between the Marquesas and Samoa in Western Polynesia. I eagerly read Suggs's popular account of his year's fieldwork, *The Hidden Worlds of Polynesia*.[15] Turning the book's pages, I imagined myself exploring overgrown ceremonial *tohua* plazas in the recesses of Taipivai Valley or excavating in the mysterious "Cave of the Warrior Band." I remembered, once again, those moss-covered walls in Molokaʻi's Hālawa Valley. Perhaps—I thought precociously—I could make similar discoveries myself.

My early exposure to the archaeological discoveries of Emory in Hawaiʻi, the *Aku-Aku* expedition on Easter Island, Gifford's work in Fiji and New Caledonia, and Suggs's finds in the Marquesas fueled my desire to become an archaeologist. But fate was determined to take me on a circuitous path. Just before my thirteenth birthday, I encountered one of Bishop Museum's most eccentric scientists. Yoshio Kondo was a zoologist who studied the native land snails of the Pacific. Kondo, rather than archaeologist Emory, would become my first mentor, initiating me into an apprenticeship in science.

CHAPTER TWO

An Apprenticeship in Science
(1963–1968)

By the time I was twelve, I was hooked on Hawaiian and Polynesian history and culture. On a trip with my father to Hawai'i Island in 1962 I insisted that we visit *heiau* (temple) ruins in Kona and Ka'ū. The following year, during the winter of 1963, the Bishop Museum's newly appointed director, Dr. Roland Force, gave a lunchtime talk at my father's East Honolulu Rotary Club. After the talk, my father approached the new director to ask him whether the museum had any summer programs for someone like his "precocious" son, who was so absorbed by Hawaiian and Polynesian history. Force said he would look into it. "Have your son telephone me in a week or two," he said, no doubt expecting that would be the end of the matter.

I nervously telephoned Force, as instructed, only to be told that I should call back when summer was closer. A few months later I sent Force a letter and then telephoned again. It turned out that the museum's only educational program was the purview of the eccentric zoologist Yoshio Kondo. When Force eventually gave in to my persistence, a day was scheduled in June 1963 for Kondo to interview me.

Yoshio Kondo was the museum's malacologist or specialist in land snails (Fig. 2.1). Polynesian islands lack many kinds of plants and animals found on continents. But land snails had reached the islands long before people; millions of years of incremental evolutionary change had crafted a remarkable diversity of endemic species. These ranged from the brightly colored *Achatinella* tree snails I had often seen clinging to 'ōhi'a leaves on the ridges above Mānoa Valley, to minute snails only one or two millimeters across whose delicately sculptured shells have to be seen under a microscope to be appreciated. Since its beginnings the Bishop Museum had been collecting, classifying, and studying these invertebrate denizens of the islands.

Born in poverty to immigrant Japanese plantation workers in Hāna, Maui, Kondo graduated from Honolulu's Mid-Pacific High School with financial help from a sympathetic uncle. Having studied mechanics, Kondo was hired as the boat engineer on a fishing sampan chasing tuna in the northwestern Hawaiian Islands.

Figure 2.1. Yoshio Kondo in the Malacology Department at Bishop Museum around 1960. Kondo is examining a tray of marine shells from ancient Hawaiian house sites on Lānaʻi Island. In his right hand he holds a basalt hammerstone used to crack open the shells to extract the meat. (Photo courtesy Bishop Museum Photo Archives.)

In 1934 the museum chartered that sampan, the *Myojin Maru,* outfitted her with a laboratory, and rechristened her *Islander,* sending her off on the Mangarevan Expedition. For six months the *Islander* visited the remote islands of southeastern Polynesia. Along with scientists Te Rangi Hiroa, Kenneth P. Emory, Harold St. John, and Raymond Fosberg, boat engineer Kondo found himself in the company of expedition leader Charles Montague Cooke Jr. Wealthy scion of a *kamaʻāina* missionary family, Cooke had made the study of Polynesian land snails his life's passion.[1]

Cooke was then sixty years old and in fragile health; he had damaged his foot during a boat landing, making fieldwork even more difficult. Kondo soon became Cooke's assistant in the hunt for new land snail species. They were an odd-seeming team—the wealthy, Yale-educated scientist and the young plantation-born Japanese American. Kondo accepted Cooke's gifts of Player's cigarettes as compensation for arduous hikes up the island peaks and valleys in search of the diminutive snails. Kondo had a knack for finding the elusive prey; he was smart and a quick study. After the expedition's return to Honolulu, Cooke invited Kondo to assist him at Bishop Museum. In the depths of the Great Depression, the offer was a godsend.

Cooke sent Kondo to the University of Hawai'i to earn his bachelor's and master's degrees in zoology; they collaborated on research. Whereas Cooke had been trained in the classic methods of conchology—the comparative study of shells—Kondo picked up new methods of anatomical study of the snails' "soft parts." Together they authored a definitive study of the Achatinellid snails of the Pacific. When in 1948 Cooke suddenly passed away, Kondo was appointed to succeed him as the museum's malacologist.

In 1952, anthropologist Alex Spoehr took over the helm at the Bishop Museum, replacing Te Rangi Hiroa who had succumbed to a lingering bout with cancer. Spoehr breathed fresh life into the institution. Through connections with his former mentor George P. Murdock at Yale, Spoehr arranged for Kondo to receive a Guggenheim Fellowship to study for his doctorate at Harvard. In just two short years, Kondo completed his dissertation on the anatomy of the Partulidae family of land snails, returning to Honolulu with his PhD in 1955.

When at age thirteen my path crossed his, Kondo was fifty-three years old; his laboratory-office on the third floor of Konia Hall was a kind of shrine to the memory of Dr. Cooke. A framed glass case held Cooke's collection of pipes; it hung next to a portrait of the revered mentor. Kondo often said that he owed everything to Cooke, invoking the Japanese concept of *on*, the irreparable debt owed to one's patron.[2]

My initial interview with Kondo took place in this office, cluttered with mementos of the Mangarevan Expedition. The *Islander*'s brass bell hung prominently from a shelf. Kondo's work bench was the ship's black laboratory table, incised with the initials of the participating scientists. After perfunctory introductions, Kondo sat me down in front of a bulky 1960s reel-to-reel tape recorder. Placing a microphone in front of me, Kondo asked me why I wanted to join his group of summer interns. The reels slowly spun, my responses trapped on the magnetic tape. Kondo must have liked what he heard; the next I thing I knew I was a part of "Dr. Kondo's gang," numbering about twelve interns. I was the youngest at age thirteen.

The oldest was Hardy Spoehr (son of former museum director Alexander Spoehr), who had just started college.

Our assignment was to assist Kondo in curating the museum's vast mollusk collection. Glass-fronted cabinets held Mason jars full of land snail bodies; the preserving alcohol, having turned brown over the years, needed to be changed. The tiny shells were kept in pillboxes neatly clustered within cardboard trays labeled in India ink; these trays were arranged on wooden shelves in long rows. There were thousands of these trays, holding several million shells—the richest collection of Pacific land snails in any museum in the world. A backlog of specimens needed to be processed and cataloged. With a steel nib pen and India ink we carefully wrote out the details of collecting provenience in leather-bound catalogs. I was learning the ins and outs of a museum as well as the fundamentals of the Linnaean system of biological taxonomy.

Kondo's goal was to introduce science to young, impressionable minds. He showed us how to illustrate tiny land snail shells using a camera lucida attached to a stereoscopic microscope. On weekends Kondo took us hiking in the Koʻolau and Waiʻanae mountains to find the multicolored *Achatinella* tree snails adhering to the leaves of *ʻōhiʻa lehua* trees; sadly, these beautiful endemic species are now almost entirely extinct on Oʻahu.

When one intern asked Kondo how the preserving alcohol we used was made, he initiated an experiment in fermentation and distillation. Creating a mash of ripe pineapples, we purified the brew using a Bunsen burner and glassware still, dutifully recording the flow rate and alcohol content in a laboratory notebook (Fig. 2.2). Kondo devised a system to make sure that Director Force—who would have been appalled that teenagers were brewing alcohol on the museum's premises—did not get wind of our distilling. He hung a small red flag out of our lab window in Konia Hall when the still was operating; this was visible across the courtyard to librarian Margaret Titcomb from her window in Paki Hall. From her desk Titcomb also had a view of the doors to Director Force's office across the hallway. Being in on the secret, whenever Force left his office (not often), Titcomb would pick up her telephone and alert Kondo. We would quickly dismantle the still until the coast was clear. Nearly everyone in the museum knew what was going on up in the Malacology Department, except for Director Force.

Kondo applied a version of the Socratic method. When early on I asked if pineapples were native to Hawaiʻi, Kondo took a long drag on the powerful Player's cigarette he was addicted to and then turned to some other task. I had quickly gotten used to this quirky manner of his. But arriving in the malacology lab the next morning, I found on my work bench a neatly typed memo on blue museum stationary, which read as follows:

Figure 2.2. The glassware distilling apparatus in operation in the Malacology Department on the third floor of Bishop Museum's Konia Hall
in 1963. Museum director Roland Force never found out that Kondo
was teaching his summer interns how to make alcohol. (Photo by Yoshio Kondo, courtesy of Bishop Museum Photo Archives.)

TO: Patrick Kirch
FROM: Dr. Kondo
RE: Your assignment today

Go to the Museum's Library in Paki Hall and introduce yourself to
Miss Titcomb, the Librarian. Tell her you have been assigned the task of

researching whether pineapples are native to Hawai'i. When you have finished your research, write a report and put it on my desk.

It was a brilliant strategy. Learning about pineapples was not the point
(although to this day I can tell you about their origin in South America). What
mattered was introducing me to the treasure house of knowledge within the museum's venerable library. Once opened, I could not get back through the library
doors often enough. "Miss Titcomb"—as she preferred to be called—in spite of her
formidable appearance gave me free rein to browse among the stacks of musty
volumes. The library's two floors in Paki Hall, the museum's oldest research building, were connected by a wrought-iron circular staircase. I still recall the musty
odor of the thousands of old volumes, accumulated during the museum's founding years through "exchanges" with research libraries around the world. I discovered such treasures as the *Anthropological Papers* of the American Museum in
New York, with reports of excavations in South America and Baluchistan, and the
Bulletin of the École Française de l'Extrème Orient, in which the wonders of
Angkor Wat were described.

Recognizing that I was a serious student in spite of my young age, Miss Titcomb unlocked "Manuscript Case 3" in a special room on the third floor of Paki
Hall. This steel cabinet held treatises that—for one reason or another—had never
been published: William T. Brigham's account of the ancient Hawaiian religion;
Southwick Phelps' study of Moloka'i archaeology; Winslow Walker's manuscript
on Maui Island archaeology; and John F. G. Stokes' report on remote Rapa Island
from the 1920 Bayard Dominick Expedition. Here I discovered as well Stokes'
small notebooks with descriptions of Hālawa Valley *heiau* from his 1909 fieldwork
on Moloka'i. Remembering Hālawa from my family visit in 1959, suddenly I
wanted to return to that mysterious place. Miss Titcomb also introduced me to
Edward Craighill Handy, the senior ethnologist who was working up his notes
on traditional Hawaiian agriculture while on a visit to the museum. A grandfatherly figure with a formidable handlebar mustache, Handy kindly dug through
a box of his field notebooks to find the one with his notes of a visit to Hālawa in
the 1930s.

Other fascinating characters toiled away within the whitewashed walls of
Konia and Paki halls, the museum's research buildings. Botanist Harold St. John
had been a member of the 1934 Mangarevan Expedition. An expert on *Pandanus*,
the "screwpine" family, St. John was what taxonomists call a "splitter," naming
every slight variant of the plant as a new species. He knew his Pacific flora intimately; in later years he would help me identify botanical collections I made on
several islands. The Entomology Department was headed by J. Linsley Gressitt, a

lanky, balding man with a talent for getting large research grants. Under his leadership it was fast becoming the museum's largest research department; a new building, Pauahi Hall, was under construction to house the ever-growing insect collections. Almost as eccentric as Kondo was Edwin H. Bryan, who for many years held the catchall title of curator of collections. Bryan was a walking encyclopedia of the Pacific. Among his more bizarre habits were keeping two old cigar boxes on his desk, one marked "Pencils Too Short to Sharpen," the other "String Too Short to Tie."

In August 1963, Kondo decided to take Hardy Spoehr and me on a two-week field trip to Moloka'i (Map 1). We collected *Partulina* land snails in the 'ōhi'a forests overlooking Waikolu Valley and camped out on Moloka'i Ranch lands (owned by the Cooke family) on the arid west end where there were ancient Hawaiian adz quarries (Fig. 2.3). When we visited Hālawa Valley, I was again struck by the maze of stone walls, terraces, and now-dry irrigation ditches that evoked a time when the valley had teamed with people.

At the end of our Moloka'i trip I flew to Lāna'i Island to join my father and his fishing buddy Bill Hansen. Kondo had told me about the ancient village site of Kaunolū, nestled around a small bay on the island's southern coast. My father rented a rickety old Jeep in Lāna'i City, and the three of us spent a week camped out under a *kiawe* tree at Kaunolū. While my father and Bill Hansen fished from the rocky shores of the bay, I explored the dozens of rock-walled house sites, *heiau,* and petroglyphs of that fascinating ancient settlement, further whetting my appetite for archaeology.

The following June of 1964 I returned to join Dr. Kondo's "gang." Despite my budding passion for archaeology, I found Kondo's land snails fascinating. I was torn between aspirations to be an archaeologist or a zoologist. I now realize that my career as an interdisciplinary scientist owes everything to that early exposure to science that Yoshio Kondo gave me. But in 1964 what I yearned to do more than anything else was field archaeology. Kondo was sympathetic. He stopped in to see Kenneth Emory in the Anthropology Department one floor below in Konia Hall.

Emory was the leading guru of Polynesian archaeology. I suspect the Dartmouth-educated Emory may have harbored a mildly racist perception of the Japanese American former plantation boy who had become Cooke's protégé. Kondo had hoped that Emory would allow me to join the museum's archaeological project at Nu'alolo Kai on Kaua'i Island. But Emory would have none of it; he was not interested in having youngsters participate in his projects.

Politely but firmly rebuffed, Kondo—ever the iconoclast—had another idea. "Why don't you go to Hālawa Valley on your own?" he suggested one afternoon in his office. "Your father loves to go fishing. I'm sure he would help you organize

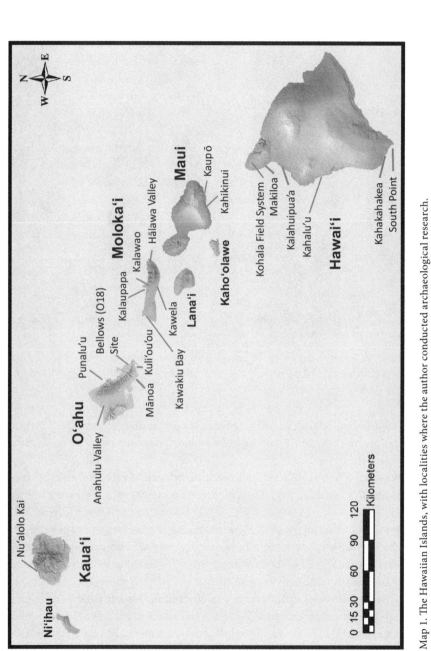

Map 1. The Hawaiian Islands, with localities where the author conducted archaeological research.

Figure 2.3. The author at Moʻomomi, Molokaʻi Island, in August 1963, examining flaked basalt cores from the nearby adz quarries. (Photo by Yoshio Kondo, courtesy of Bishop Museum Photo Archives.)

a trip to Molokaʻi. You can do your own archaeological study of the valley." I seized on the idea, checking out a stack of books on archaeological field methods from Miss Titcomb.

I began to develop a plan for archaeological fieldwork in Hālawa Valley. Proper permission was essential; my father contacted George Murphy, the owner of Puʻu o Hoku Ranch, which controlled Hālawa. When we met at Murphy's Honolulu car dealership, he seemed bemused by this teenage archaeologist but gave me the green light. I studied the books on archaeological methods, borrowed some equipment from Kondo, and worked weekends in my father's orchid nursery to earn money to buy a camera.

In August 1964 our little "expedition" arrived in Hālawa Valley—two aging amateur fishermen (my father and his friend Bill Hansen) and a precocious would-be archaeologist (Fig. 2.4). We cleared the guava bushes out of an abandoned taro pondfield not far from the rickety wooden bridge across Hālawa Stream, setting out our camp cots under a big tarpaulin. The first couple of nights were idyllic,

Figure 2.4. Bill Hansen and my father (with pipe) examining overgrown stone terraces in Hālawaiki during our field trip to Hālawa Valley, Molokaʻi, in 1964.

roasting fresh caught *pāpio* over our camp fireplace. The third night a rainstorm drenched us—it turned out that the irrigation ditch that had once watered the taro patch still worked! We were up to our calves in water. Nonetheless, I was thrilled to be doing archaeology. While my father and Hansen fished off the rocky headland, I explored the valley (Map 1).

After a devastating tsunami in 1946, most of the Native Hawaiian taro farmers had left Hālawa. In 1964 only one taro planter, Sam Enos, and his wife still cultivated a series of terraced fields on the north side of the stream. I walked over from our camp and introduced myself. Enos must have been amused by this young *haole* boy full of questions about how *kalo* was grown, but he indulged me, showing me his carefully tended *loʻi*. He let me take his picture holding his stone poi pounder, demonstrating how he pounded the taro corms on his aged *koa* board (Fig. 2.5).

I quickly discovered a promising site in the undulating sand dunes near the river mouth, where the Puʻu o Hoku Ranch cattle had dug a wallow in the sand, exposing a dark brown layer with bits of bone, shell, and charcoal flecks. I recognized it as a "midden deposit," containing the refuse of ancient meals, and carefully made a contour map of the low mound (Fig. 2.6). Hansen and my father reluctantly put down their fishing poles to help excavate a three-by-three-foot square into the sandy midden. I insisted that we meticulously follow Robert Heizer's *Manual*

Figure 2.5. Sam Enos, the last taro planter in Hālawa Valley in 1964,
demonstrating the use of his stone poi pounder and *koa* board.

of Archaeological Field Methods, digging by six-inch levels, screening the dirt
through wire mesh sieves, and bagging all of the *pipipi* and *hīhīwai* shells and
scraps of bone.

I returned from Molokaʻi with a box full of carefully labeled specimens. Kondo
let me use his Konia Hall laboratory on the weekends to sort and classify the ancient remains from my test pit in Hālawa's sand dune. After identifying the shells,
I counted and weighed each species. I painstakingly wrote up the results, typed
up my report illustrated by pen-and-ink drawings, and proudly put a carbon copy
in Emory's mailbox.[3]

However, Kondo had not informed Emory that I was going to Hālawa to excavate
on my own; when the museum's senior archaeologist saw my report he was incensed. A meeting was called in Director Force's office in Paki Hall, with Kondo

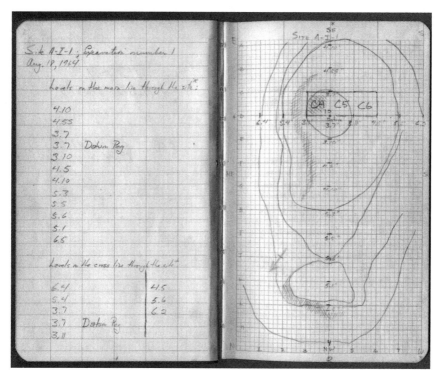

Figure 2.6. Facing pages of my 1964 field notebook in which I took elevations and drew a contour plan of the low mound with an exposed midden deposit near the beach in Hālawa Valley.

summoned to explain to Emory why he had encouraged such nonsense—an untrained teenager allowed to go off to Molokaʻi and carry out his own archaeological project.

Kondo later told me about the meeting, chuckling as he related what had transpired in the director's dimly lit office. Plantation-hardened Kondo stood his ground against the *haole* scientists from elite backgrounds. Facing the stern glares, Kondo asked Emory, "Was there anything wrong with the methods that Patrick employed?" Emory had to admit that I had followed the same field methods that he himself taught in his University of Hawaiʻi classes. Kondo continued, "Did Patrick take detailed field notes?" Well, yes, he had. "The landowner also gave his written permission?" Yes, that was true. "Was Patrick's report a full account of his findings?" Emory admitted that it was.

Seeing his opening, Kondo lunged for the kill: "Have *you* written up final reports on all of your excavations, Dr. Emory?" Emory knew he was defenseless against this charge. Kondo continued, "It was only after you refused to take Patrick on your Nuʻalolo dig that I suggested he go to Molokaʻi on his own." Emory knew what he had to do. It was agreed that the precocious teenage archaeologist would be enlisted as a member of the museum's archaeological team the following summer, which was headed for the Big Island to excavate sites in the remote Kaʻū district.

On June 22, 1965, a Tuesday, my father dropped me off at the inter-island terminal at the old Honolulu Airport along Keʻehi Lagoon Drive. Jimmy Bartels, my Mānoa neighbor, along with his friend Bud Norwood, were waiting at the terminal. Like me, they had volunteered to join the Bishop Museum's field team for the summer excavations on Hawaiʻi, under the direction of Lloyd Soehren. We made the low-altitude flight to Hilo on an Aloha Airlines turboprop Fairchild F-27, admiring views of Molokaʻi and Maui en route. Soehren met us in rainy Hilo. A tall man then in his early thirties, Soehren displayed his Scandinavian origins in his blond hair and blue eyes. Piling into the museum's Willys-Overland Jeepster, we made the long drive from Hilo to Nāʻālehu in Kaʻū.

On the drive Soehren told me about the museum's program in Hawaiian archaeology. After Emory had received that all-important first radiocarbon date from the Kuliʻouʻou rockshelter, he and his students sought out rockshelters and sand dunes on Molokaʻi, Oʻahu, Hawaiʻi, and Kauaʻi islands. Once used by ancient fishermen as camping places, these coastal sites were full of bone and shell fishhooks, along with abundant coral files and sea-urchin spine abraders used to make the hooks.

In 1954, Emory heard that a promising young Japanese archaeologist named Yosihiko Sinoto would be stopping in Honolulu, en route to Berkeley where he was going to study Paleolithic archaeology. When Sinoto's steamship docked in Honolulu harbor Emory went to meet him, insisting that Sinoto make a stopover to visit the museum's excavation in the Puʻu Aliʻi sand dune at South Point, Hawaiʻi. That amazing site was yielding hundreds of delicately carved bone fishhooks. At South Point, the older two-piece hooks mostly had notched bases, whereas those in the upper deposits were dominated by knobbed bases. There were differences as well in the shape of the head or lashing device to which the hook's line had been tied. Sinoto quickly realized that these subtle changes in fishhook morphology could be used to develop a chronology, in the same way that archaeologists elsewhere used changes in pottery forms. Sinoto decided to stay in Hawaiʻi, taking up Emory's offer to be his research collaborator at the Bishop Museum.

Throughout the 1950s Emory and Sinoto, along with University of Hawaiʻi student William Bonk, dug in every fishhook-rich site they could find. Sinoto cataloged the hooks, recording their variations in shape and their stratigraphic distributions. In 1959 the team published *Hawaiian Archaeology: Fishhooks,* based on the analysis of more than two thousand fishhooks excavated from sites throughout the islands.

Publication of the *Fishhooks* monograph marked a turning point for Emory. He had spent a decade searching out promising sites from Kaua'i to Hawai'i. Now sixty-eight years old, Emory longed to return to his first love, the islands of French Polynesia. His protégé Sinoto made a trip to the Marquesas Islands (following in the footsteps of Robert Suggs), finding sites rich with fishhooks and adzes. Emory and Sinoto turned their attention to Tahiti and the Marquesas. The continuing work in Hawai'i—supported for the first time by a grant from the National Science Foundation (NSF)—was handed over to Soehren, a graduate student at the University of Hawai'i. Soehren had trained with Emory in the Nu'alolo rockshelter site on Kaua'i, and he was now entrusted with the museum's Hawaiian archaeological field program for the summer of 1965.

After spending the night in the rustic home of "Uncle Willy" Meinecke in Wai'ōhinu, our team headed for a remote cove along the barren lava coast north of South Point. Kahakahakea, about two miles south of Pōhue Bay, could only be accessed by a torturous four-wheel drive track. We pitched our camp of surplus army pup tents on the sandy rubble just above the cove. Soehren broke out a kerosene camp stove and lanterns; we ate our dinner of canned pork-and-beans over rice while admiring the most brilliantly star-encrusted sky I had ever seen. In my notebook that evening I penned some comments about Soehren: "LJS is a good expedition leader. He knows how to handle people without being bossy. Has no respect for those who cannot help themselves. Likes *kim chee*."

Our objective was two lava tube shelters that Emory hoped would yield a rich trove of ancient fishhooks. We began digging at the larger shelter, site H65. Mindful that I was supposed to learn "proper field techniques," I dutifully wrote observations in my notebook on "Laying Datum and Rod Readings," on "Excavation Techniques," and on "Mapping." Seeing that I was keen to learn, Soehren taught me how to use the telescopic alidade and plane table to make site maps.

The plane table method of mapping is elegant in its simplicity. A wooden table about two feet square is mounted atop a tripod, which is fitted with a swivel head that allows the table to be precisely leveled. The alidade, beautifully machined of brass with glass optics, consists of a telescope (similar to that of a transit) mounted on a pedestal that is attached to a straight-edged blade. To construct a map, the surveyor attaches a sheet of heavy paper to the board and then takes sights on a stadia rod (with graduated intervals in meters or feet and inches) held by an assistant. The "rod man" holds the stadia rod on a point, such as the corner of an ancient temple enclosure, while the surveyor reads the interval between two stadia crosshairs in the telescope. The optics are calibrated with a 1:100 ratio between the crosshair interval and the distance on the ground. Thus a reading of 1 meter through the telescope equals a distance of 100 meters. The direction to the point being mapped (the azimuth) is given by the sighting direction of the straight-edged blade supporting the telescope. Calculating the distance, the surveyor plots the point on the map. As the points accumulate, one "connects the dots," drawing in architectural details and topography. Although optical transits have now been replaced by digital "total stations," a digital version of the plane table has never been invented. To this day, I prefer to map archaeological sites with the plane table and alidade, just as Soehren taught me to do fifty years ago.

The much smaller H66 rockshelter was just a blister in the *pāhoehoe* lava flow, with a floor area of only ten square meters; the ceiling was so low that one had to remain seated. But the cozy shelter had been a favored abode of fishermen who came to fish at Kahakahakea. We recovered 1,400 artifacts in just one cubic meter of earth. Among these finds were more than two hundred fishhooks, along with hundreds of worked bone pieces, coral and sea-urchin spine abraders, stone flakes, and other implements.[4] Never again in my career would I excavate so dense a concentration of artifacts!

By summer's end I had gained Lloyd Soehren's respect and friendship. Emory, too, had warmed up during a visit when we explored sites together within the Hawai'i Volcanoes National Park; he now realized that Kondo's student might have a promising career in archaeology. After flying back to Honolulu I dutifully reported to Kondo, filling him in on what I had learned. Kondo said little, but I could see that he was pleased.

As the summer of 1966 approached I was again eager to participate in the museum's archaeological program. This time there was no hesitation on Emory's part. His next objective was a "settlement pattern survey" of sites along the windswept coast of Kahikinui District, in southeastern Maui. The project was assigned to Peter S. Chapman, a doctoral student at Stanford University. Over two months, we surveyed hundreds of house enclosures, *heiau*, terrace walls, and other stone structures in the upland and coastal sectors of Kahikinui. Little did I suspect that decades later I would return to Kahikinui to complete and expand the research that our team began that summer (see Chapter Eighteen), as related in my book, *Kua'āina Kahiko*.[5]

Around 1967 I met two other Bishop Museum scientists who would play influential roles in my budding career: Roger Green and Douglas Yen. Roger C. Green, in his mid-thirties, was a rising star in Polynesian archaeology. He had gotten an early start in archaeology, joining Frank Hibben's famous New Mexico field school when he was just seventeen (Green probably recognized that I had the same youthful spark of enthusiasm). After graduating with degrees in anthropology and geology from the University of New Mexico, Green went to Harvard to study with Gordon Willey, the famous Mayan archaeologist. Green's plans to become a Mayanist were sidetracked when he took a course with anthropologist Douglas Oliver, who was studying Tahitian society. Oliver enticed Green to go to French Polynesia to apply Willey's "settlement pattern" approach, saying, "Every young man must go to Tahiti." Settlement pattern archaeology, as advocated by Willey, differed from Emory's emphasis on fishhook-rich sites.

For Green, archaeology was more than defining a sequence of artifact types. It was about reconstructing past lifeways, understanding how cultures changed through time. Using the settlement pattern approach, Green mapped the 'Ōpūnohu Valley on Mo'orea Island, recording everything from ordinary house sites and small family shrines up to the largest temples or *marae*. While teaching at the University of Auckland in New Zealand, Green organized a major archaeological project in Western Samoa. Recently arrived at the Bishop Museum, Green intended to bring the settlement pattern approach into Hawaiian archaeology.[6]

I shared the results of my fledgling research in Hālawa Valley with Green, who was willing to spare time for a promising young student. I had made additional trips to Hālawa in 1965 and 1967, gathering more data. Impressed with my work, Green introduced me to Douglas Yen. A decade older than Green, Yen was an agricultural scientist who had run a plant breeding research station in New Zealand. Yen had become intrigued by the old Maori varieties of sweet potato. With support from the Rockefeller Foundation he traced the origins of this enigmatic but important crop plant all over the Pacific,[7] research that brought him into contact with anthropologists. Bishop Museum had recently hired Yen as an ethnobotanist. I showed Yen my maps of Hālawa's taro fields and irrigation canals; we speculated about how these impressive works might have been created over centuries. Green and Yen became my second tier of mentors, encouraging my path toward a career in science.

By now I was a junior at Punahou School. In spite of my precocious love of archaeology, I had other interests of a normal teenager. I ran cross-country for Punahou in the fall semesters, gaining my "O" letter (for O'ahu College, Punahou's original name). In the spring I was a coxswain for the Punahou rowing team on Ala Wai Canal (a sport that has since disappeared from the island scene). I shyly pursued the object of my romantic desires, my classmate Barbara Ann.

In my academic work, I excelled in English, history, and biology and managed reasonably good grades in French. Unfortunately, a terrible teacher in algebra ruined my appetite for higher math. I managed a solid B in geometry (partly because I understood its relevance to surveying), but when it came time to enroll for my senior classes, I refused to take calculus. The class dean and I argued about this, the dean insisting that I would never get into a decent university without that course. My view was that it was better not to take the course than to have an F on my transcript! I had set my sights on getting into a university with a top anthropology program. Kondo urged me to try for Harvard or Yale; I was looking at Columbia and Penn.

As it turned out the lack of calculus did not stop me from being accepted into several top universities. In graduate school I taught myself how to understand the differential equations essential in scientific models and learned probability and statistics. Reflecting back, however, I realize now that I "think in prose," which is probably why I find the historical-narrative approach to scientific explanation (advocated so eloquently by the late Ernst Mayr) so compelling, rather than the mathematical approach favored by some.[8]

As the summer of 1967 approached, Soehren was busy writing up his Nuʻalolo excavation report, but he told me that Prof. Richard Pearson at the University of Hawaiʻi (UH) was going to excavate in a sand dune at Waimānalo on Oʻahu's windward shore, where interesting artifacts had turned up. Pearson invited me to join his team, which was organized as a UH field training class. Throughout August 1967, we dug into the sand hill next to the stream at Waimānalo, which had been designated site O18, the Bellows Beach site (Fig. 2.7). Each morning, our team assembled at the rickety old wooden shack on Maile Way that served as the UH archaeology laboratory, then rode to Waimānalo in the back of a motor pool pickup. Pearson was lively, talkative, and willing to share his enthusiasm for archaeology. He had recently completed his PhD at Yale under the direction of Prof. Kwang-chih Chang (with whom I too would later study). Pearson assigned Chang's recently published book, *Rethinking Archaeology*, to the field class. Chang argued that archaeology should be more than just recovering and classifying artifacts—its goal should be the reconstruction of ancient societies and cultures.[9] I found Chang's book stimulating and provocative.

Pearson put me in charge of making a contour map of the sand dune and taking the elevations of the different strata and features. There were two main occupation phases within the dune, each marked by a distinctive layer of charcoal-stained black sand. The higher and younger Layer II had postholes as well as several burials in pits. After Layer II had been peeled away, we dug through the clean sand separating it from the underlying and older Layer III. As we troweled into the darkened sand, postholes again appeared, marking where wooden timbers had once

Figure 2.7. Excavations in progress at the Bellows Beach Site (O18) at Waimānalo, Oʻahu, in the summer of 1967 (the author is in the checked shirt, kneeling on the left). The Bellows site is the earliest known Polynesian occupation in the islands.

supported pole-and-thatch structures. Our brushes uncovered a pavement of water-worn pebbles, the floor of a house. When the gravel was scraped away, the top of a pit, about one meter in diameter, appeared. It contained another burial, with the tightly flexed skeleton of an elderly woman. She had been buried beneath the floor of the gravel-paved house, a practice found in other Polynesian islands of the South Pacific but not one that was known for Hawaiʻi. Was this a clue that the site dated to an early period of Hawaiian history?

The artifacts we found while digging and sifting the sand—fishhooks of pearl shell and bone, adzes of basalt, coral files and abraders, pendants, and other objects—likewise suggested that the O18 site was old. The fishhooks lacked the

protruding lashing knob characteristic of later Hawaiian hooks, instead displaying a simple angled notch or, in one case, a double notch. Their shanks tended to
curve gracefully inward, giving the hook a "bent shank" appearance. These were
traits typical of fishhooks from early sites in the Marquesas Islands, found during the excavations of Robert Suggs and Yosihiko Sinoto. Several stone adzes were
also unlike the typical quadrangular Hawaiian form. One small adz had a "reversed triangular" cross-section and tapered toward the butt end. Another was
long and quite thin, well ground with an "incipient tang." These were forms that
were known from early sites in southeastern Polynesia.

A few years later, I helped Pearson analyze the artifacts and faunal remains
that we excavated at site O18, coauthoring an article on the site with him and
his UH colleague Mike Pietrusewsky.[10] The O18 site at Waimānalo turned out to
be one of the earliest in the Hawaiian archipelago, dating to the period when the
first Polynesians arrived from the southern homeland, around AD 1000–1200.[11]

On November 23, 1967, the museum held a gala bash in Hawaiian Hall to celebrate Kenneth Emory's seventieth birthday. "Code Project 70" had been kept a
secret: It was a volume of essays by Polynesian specialists published in Emory's
honor. Emory was speechless when the handsome bound copy of *Polynesian
Culture History* was presented to him.[12] I still treasure my copy with Emory's in-
scription to me on the half-title page, which he wrote out that evening: "To Pat
Kirch, who is showing every sign of making contributions such as these & already
has done his bit." It was high praise from the dean of Polynesian archaeology.

Graduation for the Punahou class of 1968 was fast approaching. That spring I
received offers of admission from Columbia and the University of Pennsylvania.
Knowing of Penn's world-famous University Museum of Anthropology and Archaeology, I accepted its offer. But there was one more summer before I would
matriculate at College Hall in Philadelphia. How to spend it? Kondo was planning a zoological expedition to the Loyalty Islands of the southwestern Pacific to
search for land snails of the family Partulidae, endemic to the Pacific. Over sashimi
in his Isenberg Street apartment one afternoon, Kondo posed the question: Would
I like to accompany him as his field assistant?

Kondo and I arrived in New Caledonia's capital of Noumea—a colonial backwater of quaint buildings with wrought-iron balustrades and French shuttered
doors—on June 10, 1968. The three islands of the Loyalty group paralleling New
Caledonia to the northeast—Lifou, Maré, and Ouvea—were a native reservation
regulated by the French. Although Kondo had contacted the French authorities
months earlier, they had failed to inform him that a special internal passport was

required for the Loyalties. It took five days of negotiating with snobbish bureau-crats, who did not hide their distaste for dealing with an eighteen-year old Amer-ican student who spoke schoolboy French (Kondo spoke no French at all).

With our internal travel documents finally stamped, we flew to Lifou Island on June 15. By this stage in his life Kondo was a serious alcoholic. To our zoo-logical collecting equipment and supplies, he added a case of Johnny Walker Red Label Scotch. When the Twin Otter prop plane landed on the crushed coral run-way at Lifou, we were met by the local gendarme (police officer). As our cargo came off the plane, the gendarme spotted the whiskey. "Who is bringing alcohol to Lifou?" he demanded. The authorities in Noumea had not bothered to mention that the importation of any kind of alcoholic beverage to the Loyalties was strictly prohibited. The offending case of booze was seized.

At the one-roomed gendarmerie (police station) the ruddy-faced policeman put the case of Scotch on his desk. "What have you to say about this?" he demanded. Poker-faced, Kondo ripped open the carton, pulling out a bottle and setting it in front of the gendarme. After a few seconds, the gendarme picked up the Scotch and put it in his desk drawer. Looking at me, he said sternly, "OK, but don't do it again." Kondo picked up the carton and we gladly left the premises. It was my first lesson in official corruption.

Kondo possessed peculiar working habits. He would rise after midnight, work-ing quietly on his field notes until dawn. When I arose we would have breakfast and then set out for a morning snail-collecting trip. After lunch Kondo would re-tire for a nap. With my afternoons unencumbered, I looked for a project to pass the time. I was not equipped to do archaeological excavations, but I was aware of a new approach called "ethnoarchaeology," in which archaeologists made ethno-graphic observations of living people as an aid to understanding ancient remains. In 1968 the Loyalty Islanders still lived in traditional thatched houses, organized in small hamlets. It occurred to me that a study of their houses and village orga-nization might contribute to the ethnoarchaeology of settlement patterns. I interviewed older people about how they constructed their houses, the terminol-ogy of house parts, and the different kinds of houses and their functions. I mapped the layout of a representative village. Later, I wrote up these results under the guidance of Prof. Ward Goodenough at Penn. "Houses of Lifou, Loyalty Islands" would become my first professional publication.[13]

After Lifou, Kondo and I returned to Noumea and then flew to Maré Island for a couple of weeks. Then we made a final trip to Ouvea, whose inhabitants are descended from Polynesian voyagers from 'Uvea Island in Western Polynesia. We made land snail collections on all three islands, although we failed to find the

Partulidae snails that Kondo was seeking. If he was disappointed, he did not show it. "Defining the limits of the Partulidae's distribution is just as important as finding it," he told me.

In early August, we flew from Noumea to Nadi on the island of Viti Levu, Fiji, where Kondo would continue with his collecting expedition. In Suva, Kondo handed me a reward for my hard work: a plane ticket to Tonga and then on to Samoa, before returning to Honolulu. I spent the next two weeks traveling on my own through those remarkable islands. It was my first exposure to "old Polynesia," where hereditary chiefs still ruled their villages of thatched houses. I explored Tongatapu and took the boat to 'Eua Island to collect rare *Eua globosa* snails for Kondo. Arriving in 'Apia, Western Samoa, I caught the ferry over to rural Savai'i Island. Carrying some bags of rice and tins of corned beef as gifts, I spent a wonderful week in the thatched *fale* of the Protestant minister of Sasina Village.

The return ferry from Savai'i to 'Upolu left before dawn. At sunrise when the ferry was in mid-channel, everyone was startled by the sun's peculiar orange-red color, as though it was obscured by some kind of unusual haze. When we docked at Mulifanua I asked Mary Judd (wife of Charlie Judd, a Honolulu doctor volunteering for a year in the 'Apia hospital) if she had also seen the unusual sunrise. "Oh, haven't you heard?" she replied. "The French military exploded an atomic bomb over Mururoa Atoll. They miscalculated the winds. The fallout has been blowing back to the west, right over Samoa." I might have been visiting the "old Polynesia," but there was no doubting that we were in a new era.

On August 18 I boarded an aging Polynesian Airlines DC-3 for the short flight from 'Apia to Pago Pago in American Samoa. The new Intercontinental Hotel was quite grand compared to the *fale* I had been sleeping in. The next evening a Pan American 707 jet whisked me through the night back home to Honolulu. A quick reunion with my parents in Mānoa, some fleeting, bittersweet hours with my girlfriend, and it was time to depart on a wholly different adventure five thousand miles away, in far-off Philadelphia at the University of Pennsylvania.

CHAPTER THREE

Moloka'i-Nui-a-Hina
(Hālawa Valley, 1969–1970)

Rounding the headlands of Ka'awila Ridge, I steered my salvaged 1942 Ford military jeep down the rutted dirt track leading into Hālawa Valley, the acrid scent of rotting Java plums filling my nostrils. On the ridge above me, the distinctive light green foliage of *kukui* trees marked the fabled grove that was once the abode of Lanikāula, priest and feared practitioner of the dark arts of *kahuna 'anā'anā*, sorcery. I had been driving this track every morning from our field camp next to an ancient stone-walled fishpond at Pūko'o on the southeast coast. Almost as a ritual, every morning I pulled the jeep over where the valley first comes into full view, three graceful arcs comprising her beaches and river mouth (Fig. 3.1).

Hālawa, at Moloka'i's eastern tip, greets both the dawn and the rising moon. Hina, the Polynesian moon goddess, has a special association with Moloka'i—the island was known as Moloka'i-Nui-a-Hina, "Great Moloka'i of Hina." At daybreak, the sun's horizontal rays sometimes peek under a lowering cloud bank to illuminate the twin waterfalls plunging down volcanic cliffs at the valley's head. Hīpuapua drops five hundred feet in a silver ribbon. According to tradition, Moa'ula—a succession of three shorter cascades—harbors Mo'o, the water lizard, who rises from the depths to seize unsuspecting swimmers. The waters of Hīpuapua and Moa'ula merge to become the source of Hālawa's ancient wealth and fame—her once vast fields of irrigated taro.

"Swell's up today," observed Kevin Alexander, my comrade in this summer's archaeological exploration of Hālawa, as we watched the heavy surf crash onto the boulder beach. "Too rough for Johnny Kainoa to fish with his throw net," I replied. We took in the stunning view for a few more moments, then climbed back into the jeep. I pulled back into the rutted track, rounded a blind curve, and nearly crashed headlong into Johnny Kainoa's jerry-rigged jeep/car contraption coming uphill. One advantage of a four-wheel track is that you cannot go very fast, so no damage was done. Kainoa was on his way to Kaunakakai for supplies, to visit friends, get the gossip, and exchange some taro for fish or *he'e*.

Once down in the valley, I pulled the jeep up next to a boulder beach where the bay meets the river. The salty sea spray hit us in the face. Offloading our

Figure 3.1. Hālawa Valley, Moloka'i. The sand dune site is located on the far side of the estuary and river mouth.

digging gear, we jumped a rusting barbed-wire fence and crossed the grassy floodplain to our excavation, all the while keeping a wary eye on the herd of Pu'u o Hoku Ranch bulls.

This was the same low sandy midden that I had discovered during my foray to Hālawa in 1964 (see Chapter Two). For a couple of weeks now, Alexander and I had been troweling our way down in a one-by-two-meter test pit. Slowly peeling off the sandy layers we painstakingly sieved the dirt, collecting the shells of 'opihi limpets and hīhīwai snails that once clung to rocks in the brackish estuary. Our screens also caught the bony jaws and spines of uhu and other fish that had nourished the valley's first inhabitants.

It was the summer of 1969; I had just finished my freshman year at the University of Pennsylvania. Earlier that spring, Bishop Museum's Roger Green had written to me about a National Science Foundation (NSF) training grant for an archaeological field school at Lapakahi on Hawai'i Island. Green proposed using a portion of that grant to fund a separate project in Hālawa. Would I be interested in returning to the valley along with two graduate students? I jumped at the opportunity.

Returning from Philadelphia to Honolulu, I met my future comrades in the newly proposed Hālawa Valley Project. Tom Riley was studying archaeology at the University of Hawai'i (UH), focusing on how the ancient Hawaiians had developed their famed irrigated agricultural systems. Gil Hendren, a student of Green's old professor Douglas Oliver at Harvard, wanted to do archaeological work on house sites. Green gambled that the three of us were advanced enough to do an independent project in Hālawa. He was giving us free rein to prove ourselves (or not!). Our budget was tiny, and mostly we would rely on our own hard work. Fortunately, a temporarily vacant Peace Corps training camp was available to use as our base.

While Riley and Hendren, aided by Moloka'i high-school seniors Steve Suyat and Major Rodrigues, slogged it out at sites in the rain-drenched upper valley, Alexander and I passed our days digging at the coastal dune. Our test pit descended steadily into the sandy midden. By now—crouched over on our knees troweling—we were below ground level, no longer fanned by the sea breeze. The earth gave off a musty smell with each scrape of the trowel.

Earlier that morning, near the bottom of the thick gray midden, I had uncovered a significant find: a stone adz about five inches long, made by percussion flaking followed by painstaking polishing of the dense basalt. I knew that this woodworking tool—thoroughly polished with rounded edges—differed from the typical Hawaiian adz. I had seen adzes like this before in the Bishop Museum's collection, adzes found by Kenneth Emory on Nihoa and Necker islands in the 1920s. Could there have been a link between whoever had settled those remote islets and the first Polynesians to step ashore at Hālawa?

The adz lay next to a small stone-lined hearth filled with black, greasy charcoal, which could be radiocarbon dated. I labeled a specimen bag with the site number, square, layer, depth, and date. With the point of my trowel I gently pried up the charcoal and placed it on a sheet of aluminum foil, wrapping the foil tightly around the charcoal and placing it in the bag. Was it possible that Hālawa Valley had been settled by Polynesians arriving in double-hulled canoes from the Marquesas? A radiocarbon date from the charcoal now securely in its sample bag might provide a clue.

Riley, Hendren, and I had agreed on a "research design" for our Hālawa Valley Project. The idea of a research design was something new in Hawaiian archaeology. Emory had not bothered with such scientific formality—his strategy of finding sites with lots of fishhooks or adzes did not require an elaborate statement of method. But in the late 1960s archaeology was struggling to become a serious social science. The "settlement pattern approach" advocated by Roger Green was one step in this direction. Green argued that, instead of just focusing on artifact-rich sites, we should be mapping sites over entire landscapes. This would enable us, he said, to reconstruct the spatial organization and community patterns of the ancient societies. An emerging interest in cultural ecology—the ways in which ancient and traditional peoples interacted with their environments—was also part of this new direction in archaeology.

We were caught up in the excitement of what was rapidly becoming known as the "New Archaeology." The New Archaeology sought to go beyond finding artifacts and placing them in temporal sequences; it was about studying human societies and cultures over the long term. New Archaeologists thought of themselves as social scientists, but they looked to the natural sciences for ideas about how to advance the practice of archaeology. Its proponents included Lewis and Sally Binford and Kent Flannery in the United States and David Clarke at Cambridge University in England. In our camp at Puko'o we read the Binfords' newly published *New Perspectives in Archaeology* as well as Clarke's *Analytical Archaeology*.[1] We argued long into the evenings about archaeological epistemology, our debates lubricated by the local Primo beer.

We agreed that our overarching goal in Hālawa was to understand how over the course of many centuries a group of colonizing Polynesians adapted their culture to the landscape of a windward Hawaiian valley. We began with the premise that the windward valleys—with their permanent streams and fertile alluvial soils—were likely to have been favored localities for the early Polynesian settlers, who arrived with tropical root and tuber crops and sought to establish the horticultural basis for their economy. How had people shaped the landscapes of these lush valleys, and in turn, how had their practices of land management helped transform their society? Hālawa would be a representative case study. The historical processes uncovered there would potentially apply to other valleys throughout the archipelago.

We laid out several objectives. First, to understand Hālawa's settlement patterns, we would intensively survey selected areas, each representing a different environmental zone. Second, Riley would investigate the elaborate taro irrigation systems, with nearly one thousand stone-faced pondfields and kilometers of stone-lined irrigation canals. He would map and dig into the terraces and canals in an effort to trace their construction sequences. Third, Hendren would study the inland house terraces and platforms situated on the slopes above the irrigated fields to learn how patterns of household life had changed over time. Finally, I would dig in the coastal sand dune, where the deep midden promised clues to the earliest periods in Hālawa's history as well as a rich faunal record of changing patterns of resource use.

A old oxcart track leading back into Hālawa is marked on nineteenth-century maps as the *ala nui,* the old government road. Along this track taro farmers once hauled their crop down to waiting schooners. Supplying the heavy demand from the whaling fleet anchored off Lahaina on Maui, Hālawa's taro farmers were famed throughout the islands. An American traveler publishing under the pseudonym "A Haole" in 1854 wrote this of Hālawa in the mid-nineteenth century:

> The cultivation of the *taro* is carried on here on a large scale. It is raised chiefly to supply the Lahaina market. I was informed by Mr. Dwight, at Kaluaaha, that the entire amount raised for sale and home consumption was valued at $15,000 to $20,000. The Valley of Halawa is the richest spot on the island.[2]

As the demand for taro slackened in the twentieth century, families began to leave Hālawa; the terraces fell into weedy fallow. In 1946, a massive tsunami slammed into the valley, with water rising to the very steps of the Congregational church, destroying the taro crop and salting the irrigated fields. Most people left; in 1964 only the families of Sam Enos and Johnny Kainoa remained. I had talked with Sam Enos in 1964 about his methods of taro growing (see Chapter Two), but by 1969 he had passed away, his house abandoned and overgrown with weeds. Now only Johnny Kainoa and his wife remained.

But other families had not totally severed their ties with Hālawa, maintaining ramshackle houses along the *ala nui,* which they periodically visited. Pilipo Solatorio, whose mother was from an old Hālawa clan, became interested in our project. On the weekends, we socialized with the Solatorio family in Kaunakakai; Pilipo's white-haired Hawaiian-speaking grandmother told us stories of Hālawa in the days before the tsunami. We had a "chicken skin" reaction when the old matriarch spoke of hearing the sounds of *pahu* drums coming from abandoned Mana *heiau* on moonless *pō kāne* nights, when the spirits were said to march along the old trails. Later, in the Bishop Museum, I found among the Bayard Dominick Expedition archives a glass plate photo of the valley's schoolchildren posed on the church steps. Solatorio recognized his mother, who had died when he was young.

By 1969, the taro fields below the *ala nui* were thickly overgrown with Java plum and *hau.* At the end of the *ala nui,* the route up into the valley became a muddy foot path, wending its way past the mossy rock walls of abandoned house enclosures. This area was known to old inhabitants as Kaio, one of twelve *'ili* or land segments into which the *ahupua'a* of Hālawa had been subdivided. In ancient Hawai'i, *ahupua'a* were the estates of the chiefs, *ali'i,* overseen by their *konohiki* or managers. At the time of the Great Mahele (land distribution) of 1848–1854, the *ahupua'a* of Hālawa was the estate of the young princess Victoria Kamāmalu, granddaughter of King Kamehameha I and the chiefess Kalakua.

Doug Yen had flown over from Honolulu to visit our team for a few days, seeing what we were up to and giving us advice (Fig. 3.2). The first day he nearly managed to set the valley on fire when he inadvertently dropped his pipe while climbing over a cattle fence on the dry lower slopes. Now Alexander and I were accompanying Yen inland to visit Hendren and Riley's excavations in Kaio. Diverging from the muddy trail, brushing aside kī plants, we made our way up a dry ravine between two rocky ridges. On the slopes above us Hendren and Suyat were excavating a small house terrace, nestled into a basalt boulder outcrop. The foundations of a former pole-and-thatch dwelling were marked by a rectangular curbing of basalt cobbles, about ten feet on a side. Hendren had chosen this site because of its position high up on the slopes, well above the larger house sites of the historic period. He reasoned that this unimposing structure belonged to an earlier period in the valley's history. Radiocarbon dating would later indicate that it had been built in the thirteenth century.

Hendren and Suyat had removed a thick layer of humus to expose the house outlines. Hendren had found, buried under rubble in a corner, a rare artifact: a tripping club carved of basalt used in hand-to-hand combat. Perhaps the occupant of this house had once seen battle in the famous wars between Kona and Koʻolau. The house floor was paved with river pebbles; light and warmth had been provided by a stone-outlined hearth.

Figure 3.2. Doug Yen and the author discussing archaeology in Hālawa, seated on boulders in the valley's stream bed, in 1969.

When Hendren excavated the hearth, he found that a shallow pit had been dug through the fireplace. In this pit a tightly bound human body had been placed, the bones now exposed by Hendren's trowel and brush. The acidic soil had weathered the bones to a chalky, fragile state. Not wanting to disturb this individual more than necessary, Hendren recorded the skeleton, then covered it back over; it lies there today. Because we could not study the fragile bones closely, we were uncertain of the person's exact age and sex, but it seemed to be an adult male, perhaps the owner of the tripping club. The symbolic burial of this person in the hearth probably marked the end of a household cycle, after which the house was abandoned.

What was so unusual about this Kaio house was that a deceased person had been buried *within* the structure. This was not a known Hawaiian burial practice. Typically, Hawaiians buried their dead in sand dunes along the coast or placed the bodies in lava tubes or burial caves high in the cliffs. Yet house burial was known to be a practice of other Polynesian societies of the South Pacific. Later, Hendren would find another subfloor burial in a terrace across the Kaio ravine. Clearly, at one time house burial had been practiced in the Hālawa Valley. We were uncovering a glimpse of an earlier time in Hālawa's history, a time before the development of the classic Hawaiian culture known to ethnographers.

Retracing our route from the house terrace, we descended back down the Kaio slopes to check up on Tom Riley's study of the valley's sculptured landscape of irrigation terraces. A few minutes later, we found Riley on his hands and knees inside the trench he had dug into a stone-faced earthen taro terrace. His clothes caked in mud, Riley was pondering what the buried soil layers deep within the terrace might reveal about the history of agriculture in Hālawa. Yen and I jumped down into the trench to look at what Riley was scrutinizing so intently.

Inside the trench, a dark, organically rich horizon marked the former pondfield soil in which taro had been grown. Beneath this, a discontinuous lens of gravel hinted at a major flood at some time in the valley's history. Under the flood layer there was brownish soil, with reddish-orange mottling and limonite tubes, iron-rich concretions that formed around the roots of taro plants. Flecks of charcoal in the mottled soil layer showed that this was not a natural stratum but one that had accumulated at a time when people had lit fires to clear the land for gardens. At the bottom of the trench was truly ancient colluvium, eroded thousands of years ago from the valley's cliffs, lacking charcoal flecks or other signs of human presence.

Riley thought that the mottled charcoal-rich layer represented an early phase in Hālawa's agricultural history when the people had practiced "shifting cultivation." This farming method is widely practiced throughout the tropics where land is relatively plentiful and population density is low. Vegetation is cut, left to dry, and then burned in place to inject a burst of nutrient-rich ash into the soil. After planting a garden and harvesting it for one or a few years, the plot is abandoned and left to return to forest, as weeds and young saplings gradually invade the plot. French ethnobotanist Jacques Barrau had proposed that Pacific peoples practiced "shifting cultivation" when they settled new islands.[3]

At some point in Hālawa's history—if Riley's interpretation of the sediment sequence was correct—shifting cultivations had covered the slopes of Kaio, filled with crops of yams and dryland taro, or with *wauke* or *'awa*. Year after year, as gardens were cut and burned, charcoal was introduced into the soil, gradually forming the charcoal-rich deposit Riley had carefully drawn in his notebook.

Then, the agricultural landscape of Kaio changed abruptly: The hillslope was artificially leveled into a stair-step series of terraces retained by well-built walls of basalt cobbles. Terracing the land had taken a lot of manpower, not to mention organizational and engineering skills to ensure that water flowed at just the right velocity through the stone-lined canal that tapped the dammed stream waters and then percolated down from field to field. What underlying social or political changes might have led Hālawa's farmers to change from shifting cultivation to irrigated pondfields, thereby transforming the valley's landscape?

One obvious hypothesis was that over time Hālawa's population had grown to the point where more intensive methods were required to feed the hungry mouths. When grown in irrigated terraces, taro yields up to twenty-five tons of tubers per hectare (roughly ten tons per acre), much more than the five to eight tons from a typical shifting cultivation plot. Moreover, the terraces produce multiple crops year after year and need only occasional periods of fallow to rest the fields and kill off pest infestations.

But the construction of massive irrigated terrace complexes reflected more than just a response to increased food pressures. Increased political complexity was also suggested by such major construction efforts. The terrace Riley had dug through was only one of 231 on the southern valley slope (with a total area of 9.8 hectares), all integrated into a functioning system watered by two separate canals with a combined length of 1,624 meters. Such an agricultural system involved many households; it crossed and integrated several *'ili* land segments. These included special *'ili kūpono,* sets of terraces whose harvest was reserved for the *ali'i,* the chiefs. When fully functioning, the system yielded as much as 245 tons of taro, enough to support a couple of hundred workers and still leave a surplus for the chiefs. In short, the construction of these massive irrigation works marked a late phase in the valley's history when the population was organized by chiefs and land managers who could mobilize labor on a substantial scale.

As we debated Riley's interpretation of the soil layers and their broader implications for the transformation of Hawaiian society, Hendren and Suyat suddenly came down the path. Clouds had been building over the East Moloka'i mountains. It was time to get out of the valley before pouring rain turned the dirt road into a slippery quagmire. By the time we reached the beach, rain was falling lightly. Winding our way up Ka'awila Ridge, the dank odors of the valley gave way to the fresh air of the tablelands. Then it was a bumpy trip downhill to our camp at Puko'o and another evening of talk around the camp kitchen.

Reflecting back—after half a lifetime has passed—that summer of 1969 seems a special time, a time when archaeology was undergoing an intellectual revolution. We were on the cutting edge of new methods, new ways of looking at the Polynesian past. Inspired by our mentors Roger Green and Doug Yen, our modest Hālawa Valley Project promised to rewrite aspects of Hawaiian prehistory. It was also a more naïve time, before the pace of "development" gripped the islands, before archaeology shifted from low-key academic research to fast-paced "contract archaeology." A time before convoluted academic arguments between "scientific" and "postmodern" ways of thinking about the past. A time before tense relations between archaeologists and indigenous peoples. These things would come, but in 1969 it was still a simpler time; I do not regret having lived it.

At summer's end we backfilled the excavations and said farewell to Suyat, Rodrigues, and the Solatorio clan. I shipped my jeep to Honolulu, spent a couple of weeks in Mānoa, and then made the long journey back to Philadelphia to continue my studies at the University of Pennsylvania. During my freshman year I had experienced culture shock. In the late 1960s the West Philadelphia ghetto, where Penn is situated, was suffering from a terrible period of urban decay. I had grown up in the multiethnic society of Honolulu and could speak Hawaiian pidgin fluently but struggled to understand the urban dialect of the Black folks on the West Philly streets.

Nonetheless, I loved the University Museum of Archaeology and Anthropology, which housed Penn's Anthropology Department and was one of the world's great centers for archaeological research. The imposing brick buildings of the University Museum, with its soaring central rotunda, housed a spectacular collection acquired on expeditions to Egypt, the Near East, Africa, and Mesoamerica. One gallery held an entire Egyptian palace, complete with granite sphinx, sculpted for the pharaoh Merenptah in the second millennium BC. Another gallery boasted gold and lapis-lazuli ornaments from the royal tombs of Ur, while in the Mesoamerican Hall imposing limestone stelae bore hieroglyphic inscriptions commemorating ancient Mayan kings.[4]

During my freshman year I had taken the obligatory introductory courses for the anthropology major. Introduction to Anthropology was taught by Prof. Ward Goodenough, a cultural anthropologist whose expertise was the indigenous cultures of Oceania. Goodenough's early morning lectures could put you to sleep, because he had a habit of reading verbatim from his notes. But in person Goodenough was accessible and charming. He liked to "hold court" in the museum's coffee shop. I became one of the many students who gathered round Goodenough, sipping coffee and listening to him talk about his fieldwork in the Truk Islands of Micronesia after World War II or his later research among the Nakanai of New Britain. One day Goodenough took a few of us down to the museum's basement storage rooms where, among other treasures, he showed us a Tahitian adz collected on Captain Cook's first voyage.

Back at Penn after my summer of fieldwork in Hālawa Valley, I signed up for a course on South Asian archaeology with Prof. George Dales. Dales had excavated at Mohenjo-daro, one of the centers of the Harappan civilization in Pakistan; he was also directing archaeological fieldwork in Thailand. Dales needed drawings made of pottery he had excavated at Chansen in Thailand. Having learned the art of pen-and-ink drafting from Yoshio Kondo, I soon found myself working in Dales' lab. Dales became my undergraduate advisor. I also learned a great deal from interactions with Dales' graduate students Ben Bronson and Louis Flam.

In addition to anthropology, geology held a particular attraction, and I took classes on geomorphology and paleontology. Prof. A. J. Boucout, a world expert on brachiopods, taught an upper level course on paleontology. Boucout's personal collection of fossil brachiopods filled dozens of cabinets in the basement of Hayden Hall. For each class he would pull out trays of specimens and lecture about the fine details of the fossils' morphology. Boucout told us about his ongoing synthesis of the Ordovician Period across North America, based on the brachiopod record. One day Boucout said to the class, "Never cling to an outdated hypothesis. I have seen more scientific careers ruined by those who refuse to accept that new evidence has overturned their pet theories." It was good advice and I never forgot it.

I read voraciously, often from volumes that I came across browsing in the stacks of Van Pelt Library. Edgar Anderson's *Plants, Man and Life* built on topics Doug Yen had discussed, such as how indigenous farmers created new crop varieties through manipulating plants' natural genetic variation. Ludwig Van Bertalanffy's *General System Theory* was hugely influential, with its ideas about how both the natural world and human societies are organized as systems, with positive and negative feedback loops. Robert MacArthur and E. O. Wilson's *Theory of Island Biogeography*, a book that I have turned to again and again in my career, sought to reduce the patterns of island life to elegant mathematical models. Ernst Mayr's *Systematics and the Origin of Species* revealed processes of evolution that the great biologist had deduced from his studies of island birds. And Carl Sauer's *Land and Life* reinforced the importance of putting human cultures within a larger landscape perspective.[5]

Tiring of the Philadelphia winters, I arranged to spend the spring semester of 1970 taking courses at the University of Hawai'i, having the credits transferred to Penn. I took Social Organization with the famous Pacific ethnographer Douglas Oliver, and Archaeology of Southeast Asia with Wilhelm G. Solheim II. Solheim, who sported an impressive mustache with meticulously waxed tips, told us about the exciting new discoveries he and his graduate students were making in Thailand, of early plant domestication and bronze smelting. Douglas Yen and Yoshihiko Sinoto offered an advanced graduate seminar on Problems in Pacific Prehistory, something they did only once. The seminar ranged from Sinoto's discussion of fishhook chronologies to Yen's hypotheses on the evolution of Pacific horticultural systems. For my research paper I analyzed faunal remains that Sinoto had excavated in the Marquesas, resulting in a published paper.[6]

That spring, Yen asked Riley, Paul Rosendahl (another UH grad student), and me if we would join him in a field study of an ancient irrigation system in O'ahu's Mākaha Valley. The four of us spent two days each week for several months mapping and excavating the stone-faced pondfield terraces in one of the first attempts to investigate a Hawaiian irrigation site. We were breaking ground methodologically, demonstrating that the site was stratified, with multiple episodes of cultivation.[7]

In late May 1970 Tom Riley and I met with Roger Green in his Bishop Museum office. Green was impressed by what we had accomplished during our first summer in Hālawa. His gamble had paid off. The question now was how to finance a second field season, with enough staff to expand our excavations beyond the modest scale of the first year's test pits. Green had a contact in the office of Hawai'i's governor John A. Burns; the contact thought some funds might be available for the work on Moloka'i.

Myron "Pinky" Thompson was a special assistant to Governor Burns, the island's Democratic strongman. Descended from Hawaiian *ali'i,* Thompson was deeply interested in his native culture, although I did not realize this at the time. Years later, after Thompson became a Bishop Estate Trustee, and after his son Nainoa rose to prominence as navigator of the replicated Hawaiian voyaging canoe *Hokule'a,* I came to appreciate his dedication to preserving Hawaiian language and culture. In 1970, I just knew that Thompson held the key to funds that might enable us to continue our research in Hālawa Valley.

We met in a conference room at the State Capitol. As Riley and I explained our Moloka'i research project Thompson listened for a bit and then cut us short. "The state is not in the business of giving out research grants," he explained. My heart sank. "But," Thompson continued, "the governor is concerned about the lack of jobs for young people on Moloka'i, especially for Native Hawaiians." Thompson said he might be able to tap some discretionary funds to hire Moloka'i high school students, giving them the opportunity to work with our team—doing work more meaningful than slugging it out day after day in the scorching hot pineapple plantations of Moloka'i's west end, the only summer jobs otherwise available to those kids.

A few days later Thompson called to say that the funds would be allocated to a local nonprofit group, Alu Like, to allow us to hire twenty high school students. Green had also squeezed some money out of Bishop Museum and the University of Hawai'i. We were soon back at the Peace Corps camp at Pūko'o. I was exhilarated at the prospect of expanding my dune site excavations. During the past year, we had received our first radiocarbon dates. The charcoal from the stone-lined hearth next to the polished stone adz had given a date of AD 610 ± 100. It seemed that Hālawa might have been one of the earlier settlements in the islands.

With our expanded team of Moloka'i students, I opened up a large area in the coastal sand dune, exposing the stone foundations of several round-ended houses (Fig. 3.3). This was an architectural form known elsewhere in Polynesia but not typical of the classic period of Hawaiian civilization.[8] Meanwhile, Riley and Hendren moved their digging from Kaio to Kapana, an 'ili farther inland. Here a side-valley stream, Maka'ele'ele, had delivered water to a series of irrigated fields lying higher than the main-stream irrigated fields. House sites and dryland agricultural terraces literally covered the Kapana hillsides. We mapped this interior landscape in loving detail with plane table and alidade, applying Green's settlement pattern approach. Hendren excavated several house terraces in Kapana, while Riley dug trenches into the old taro fields and irrigation ditches, continuing his quest to unravel the sequence of agricultural development. By the end of the summer, our modest Hālawa Valley Project had amassed a substantial body of data about the prehistory of this windward Hawaiian valley.

Research can be a painstakingly slow process, with fieldwork just the first step. Five years would pass before all the bags of specimens were analyzed in the Bishop Museum's laboratory and before our final reports were written.[9] In the fall of 1975—by which time I was already working on my doctoral dissertation at Yale—the Bishop Museum published *Prehistory and Ecology in a Windward Hawaiian Valley: Halawa Valley, Molokai,* a 203-page monograph, augmented with large foldout maps, tables, charts, and illustrations. This was my first major archaeological publication.

Figure 3.3. The completed excavation at the Hālawa sand dune site in 1970. My restored 1942 Ford military jeep sits atop the sand dune.

The Hālawa Valley Project, along with simultaneous research at Lapakahi and Mākaha Valley also organized by Roger Green, marked a turning point in Hawaiian archaeology. Green had shown us how the settlement pattern approach could help reconstruct social and economic changes over time. Doug Yen's periodic visits had inspired us to incorporate an ecological perspective. Being a part of this collective research endeavor, one felt a sense of excitement and discovery.

We were bringing the New Archaeology to Polynesia. Although we did not neglect changes in artifacts over time, we wanted to go beyond describing sequences of fishhook or adzes types, as Emory and Sinoto had done. In Hālawa, we were testing models of cultural evolution against the archaeological record, practicing an *anthropological* archaeology. Our story began with the arrival of Polynesians in what had been a pristine windward valley, one with ample resources to support a colonizing population. At first they had built their round-ended houses near the beach, fishing and farming the gentle slopes with shifting cultivations. Over the centuries, the population increased and expanded inland, where the settlers built rectangular houses with stone foundations, like the ones Hendren had excavated. But it was not just their artifact and house forms that changed over time. Their social and political organization gradually became more complex and hierarchical. By the final centuries prior to European contact the valley's settlement pattern had been transformed into an intensively managed landscape of irrigated, terraced fields whose surplus production supported a chiefly elite as well as hundreds of commoners. Looming over this landscape was the valley's impressive *luakini* temple of human sacrifice, Mana Heiau, dedicated to the war god Kū. In many ways, the history of Hālawa was the history of Hawaiian civilization.

In the spring of 1971, as I prepared to graduate from Penn, my future seemed up in the air. Yale had accepted me into its graduate program in anthropology for the coming academic year, but then a letter arrived from Doug Yen at the Bishop Museum. A four-month expedition to the eastern Solomon Islands was planned as part of a new NSF-funded project, co-organized with Roger Green, who thought that the eastern Solomons held important clues to the origins of the Polynesians. Would I defer my Yale graduate studies to join Yen in that expedition? How could I say no?

But there was one looming problem: the raging war in Vietnam and the draft. I had been part of the first national lottery, drawing a low number of fifty which virtually guaranteed that I would be drafted. My student deferment would expire when I graduated, and I did not fit the bill of a conscientious objector. The idea of fleeing to Canada did not appeal to me, but then neither did being a Viet Cong target wading through the rice paddies of Vietnam. What to do? I spent many sleepless nights pondering the question.

In the late spring I came down with what I thought was the flu, running a high fever. The Penn student health service nurse told me to take some aspirin and sleep it off, but the fever raged for five days. When I got back to Honolulu in late May I was weak and tired easily. When I finally saw a doctor he put his stethoscope to my chest, listened for a half-minute, and then asked me, "How long have you had this serious heart murmur?" Apparently, I had suffered a bout of undiagnosed rheumatic fever, which damaged one of my heart's valves. I am not sure the doctor, who was an older gentleman, understood why I instantly asked for a letter describing the murmur. I was familiar with the medical conditions that could trigger a 4F exemption from the draft, having researched them in light of my near-fatal bout with kidney disease when I was younger. I mailed the doctor's letter to the Honolulu Draft Board; to my intense relief the board sent my notice of 4F exemption by return mail. I would be free to join Yen in the Solomon Islands and then to take up graduate studies at Yale. My second adventure in the South Seas was about to begin. It would take me to Polynesia's smallest—and also one of its most remote and traditional—islands.

CHAPTER FOUR

The Smallest Polynesian Island
(Kolombangara and Anuta, 1971)

Honiara, the dusty capital of the British Solomon Islands Protectorate on the leeward coast of Guadalcanal, had been the infamous scene of bloody battles between the Imperial Japanese Army and the U.S. Marines in the early days of World War II. Henderson Field, the Japanese fighter airstrip taken at great cost by the American forces, was now the Solomon Islands' international airport. Paul Rosendahl and I arrived there on September 18, 1971, joining Doug Yen who had flown down a week earlier.

Roger Green had shown that the immediate homeland of the Polynesians was in Tonga and Samoa, and in nearby Fiji. But where had their ancestors come from? Answering this question was a major goal of the Bishop Museum's new Southeast Solomon Islands Culture History Project.[1] The obvious place to begin searching was in the cluster of small islands that make up the Santa Cruz Islands, at the juncture of the southeastern Solomons and northern Vanuatu, directly west of the Fiji-Tonga-Samoa triangle (Map 2). Green knew that some of the languages spoken by islanders in the region were closely related to Polynesian, implying a common ancestor. But almost nothing was known of the archaeology of the Santa Cruz group—it was *terra incognita*.

Clues to the earliest Polynesian migrations were thought to lie with sites containing a distinctive kind of pottery, called Lapita. On a hunch, Green had reconnoitered Nendö and the Reef Islands in the Santa Cruz group the previous year (1970). His discovery of several Lapita sites confirmed that he was indeed on the trail of the Polynesian ancestors. But the project that Green and Yen had designed was not just limited to seeking early sites with Lapita pottery. A second focus was on the ways in which island cultures had adapted to the varied environments of the Solomon Islands. Doug Yen was especially interested in the region's traditional agricultural systems. Because we had worked with him on Mākaha Valley's agricultural terraces, Yen was keen to have Rosendahl and me join him in a study of agricultural prehistory in the Solomons.

Our expedition would take us to two distant parts of the Solomon Islands. First, we would voyage to Kolombangara Island in the New Georgia group, in the

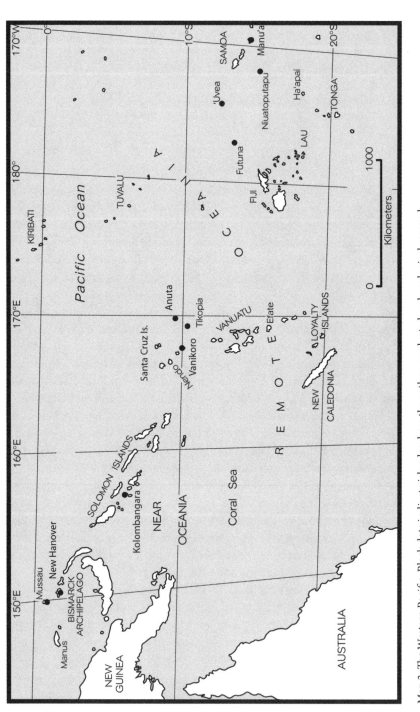

Map 2. The Western Pacific. Black dots indicate islands where the author conducted archaeological research.

Western Solomons, where ancient stone-faced irrigation terraces had been reported. Yen hoped these ruins might yield clues to the history of irrigated agriculture in the Pacific. Resupplying in Honiara, we would then sail on a much longer voyage to the remote Santa Cruz archipelago, where Green had made his Lapita finds. Our destination was the most isolated outpost in the entire Solomons: Anuta Island.

The night before our departure for Kolombangara, Yen took us to the Mendaña Hotel for a final "civilized" meal. From the hotel's terrace—where British planters and their wives came for dinner on the weekends—the peaks of Nggela were backlit by the sunset's multihued rays. Some said this view had inspired James Michener's fabled Bali Hai in his *Tales of the South Pacific*.[2] It was not hard for a young man to conjure up visions of Bloody Mary and her beautiful daughter Liat on that island across the sound.

The trip to New Georgia took two days by copra boat, slowly threading our way through the reefs and lagoons that make this part of the Western Solomons so distinctive. At Rendova Island we docked at a ramshackle wharf to drop off a load of seed coconuts. After twenty-four hours on deck we had accumulated a sticky, smelly veneer of sweat and salt spray, mingled with diesel exhaust. The boatswain told us that a small stream was just a short walk up the path. We eagerly headed inland, anticipating a refreshing bath. No sooner were we out of sight of the boat than a ruddy-faced, profusely sweating Englishman came striding toward us, his cane aimed at us like a shotgun barrel. Wearing shorts, shoes with knee socks, and a tattered and stained dress shirt, he was struggling to "maintain standards" on "his" island.

"Private property!" shouted the florid-faced planter. "Back to the boat! Private property!" I waited to see if Yen would challenge this aging holdout of the British Empire. Yen hesitated, then turned; we followed him back to the wharf. Colonial authority had won the day, even if the stakes were nothing more than preventing a handful of unwashed scientists from bathing in the planter's stream.

The boat deposited us at Gizo, administrative center of the New Georgia group of islands. From Gizo we hired a launch to take us to Kolombangara. As we approached the somber-looking island, its massive volcanic cone looming up into the clouds, I was struck by how different this landscape was from my home islands of Hawai'i. Ghatere Village proved to be a motley cluster of thatched huts elevated on poles, just inland of a mangrove swamp. Yen negotiated with the village headman to rent a one-room thatched hut with sago leaf walls. There was no running water; we would cook on a Primus camp stove. The village toilet was a slippery plank extending out into the mangroves.

As soon as we turned off the kerosene pressure lamp that first night, bedding down in our sleeping bags on the split bamboo floor, the thatch overhead came alive with the sound of scurrying feet. The beam of my flashlight caught not just one or two but literally a dozen or more large black rats peering down from the rafters. Soon they were gnawing at our bags of rice and other supplies. Yen—who has a passionate hatred of rats—grabbed a wooden stick and began chasing the fearless creatures around the hut. None of us got much sleep that night. In the morning, a small crowd assembled to gawk at the bodies of dead rats littering the ground outside the hut, victims of Yen's club.

The Ghatere people conversed among themselves in their indigenous Nduke language, but everyone also spoke the Solomon Islands dialect of pidgin English (also known as Neo-Melanesian). Although much pidgin vocabulary consists of English words, the grammatical structure is that of the Oceanic languages. I found pidgin expressions often amusing and easy to learn, rapidly gaining fluency in this lingua franca, which precariously unites a country with dozens of different languages into a single nation-state.

Kolombangara Island, an extinct strato-volcano, is a little less than ten miles across with a central peak majestically rising 5,810 feet above the sea. Ghatere Village lay at the mouth of the Ndughore Valley, alongside a deeply incised, branching stream whose headwaters descend along the southwestern slopes of Mt. Veve. Traditionally, the Ghatere people resided in fortified hamlets on ridgetops, cultivating taro in irrigated fields in the steep valleys. Prior to "pacification" by the famous Charles M. Woodford of the British Solomon Islands Protectorate in the late nineteenth century, the New Georgia islanders had participated in an elaborate system of raiding and head-hunting, shunning the coast where they risked being taken captive by raiding parties from Rendova or the Marovo Lagoon.[3]

With several Ghatere men as our guides, we followed the Ndughore Stream inland, leaving the coastal plain and gardens behind. In the dense jungle, Yen pointed out towering *Metroxylon* or sago palms whose starchy pith can be extracted to make a kind of flour. An hour after leaving Ghatere, we arrived at a place called Aghara. Here, on a narrow stream terrace were ranks of stone-faced terraces where the fathers and grandfathers of our guides had once cultivated their taro crops.

We made our bush camp at Aghara. While Rosendahl and I set up our canvas tent, the Ghatere men cut bamboo poles and sago leaves to construct a sturdy lean-to. (Yen returned every night to the village, braving the rats). Over the next several days as the rain fell incessantly, we watched the green mold creep higher and higher up the sodden canvas. After several days we abandoned the tent to its inevitable fate, joining our workers in the comfortable lean-to, with its warming fire and smoke that kept the malaria-ridden mosquitoes at bay.

With the help of the Ghatere men, Rosendahl and I mapped the Aghara ruins. Upstream, a more extensive complex called Ageglai displayed skillfully constructed terraces with stone-lined irrigation canals of which a Western engineer would have been proud. We trenched through the terraces, obtaining charcoal for radiocarbon dating. It was taxing work, because the tropical rains rarely let up. At day's end we would slog down to the camp, shedding mud-encrusted clothes to plunge into the icy stream for a bath. Dinner consisted of a few tins of bully beef or mackerel served over a pot of rice.

As we worked on the ancient irrigation terraces, our workmen told us about the fortified hamlets where their ancestors had once resided, high on the ridges overlooking the valley, in places with exotic names such as Patusugha, Nuskambu, Heriana, Ivivu, and Vavalondu. To understand the settlement pattern of Kolombangara prior to pacification, we would need to explore those sites. Finishing up our work at Aghara and Ageglai, we made plans to visit the ridgetop forts.

There were no trails up to these long abandoned hamlets, but a few of the older men knew how to find them. At Patusugha, on a ridge above Aghara, we found the stone outlines of former houses; test excavations turned up pig bones and shellfish, along with a few glass trade beads. A crypt-like mortuary shrine had been constructed of tabular rock slabs with a heavy capstone weighing perhaps 150 pounds. When the men managed to lift the capstone, the contents of the crypt were revealed: four pairs of human skulls and mandibles, accompanied by an assortment of shell artifacts. There were large rings of *Tridacna* shell, smaller cone shell rings, and elaborate filigree objects, part of a complex system of exchanges between people of the New Georgia Islands. After photographing the objects, we returned everything to the crypt and replaced the capstone.

The most remote site was Ivivu, an exhausting five-hour climb from Ghatere Village up steep, jungle-cloaked ridges. I still recall the spectacular early morning view from our camp on this ridgetop redoubt, swirling mist partially obscuring the Ndughore Valley below us. From Ivivu we were able to reach Hena, a ritual complex whose stone platforms were ornamented with striking anthropomorphic carvings (Fig. 4.1).

Our month-long sojourn on Kolombangara gave us a good idea of the traditional settlement pattern before European pacification. But the glass beads, scraps of iron, fragments of clay pipes, and other trade items told us that these sites dated only to the nineteenth and early twentieth centuries. These sites would not tell us the deeper history of Solomon Islands agriculture and settlement; they would not take us back to the period of the Lapita people. We hoped to have better luck on far-off Anuta.

On October 18 we said goodbye to our Ghatere Village friends, the launch returning us to Gizo. After a welcome hot shower and some cold beers in the little

Figure 4.1. A face motif carved into one of the stone blocks on the facade of a platform at the ritual site of Hena in the interior of Kolombangara Island.

Gizo motel, followed by a good night's sleep on a real bed, we flew by small plane back to Henderson Field the next morning. The *M. V. Belama* was scheduled to sail for the Eastern Outer Islands Province on October 22 and we had to be on board her then.

In the 1920s and 1930s, the *M. V. Belama* had served as the flagship of the High Commissioner for the Gilbert and Ellice Islands Colony. In 1971, she was the main vessel used by the British Protectorate to maintain contact with the far-flung islands of the Eastern Outer Islands Province. Every few months the *Belama* would make the long voyage from Honiara, southeastward past San Cristobal and tiny Santa Ana, reaching Santa Cruz Island (Nendö) after three days at sea. There she would pick up the district commissioner to proceed "on tour" to Utupua, Vanikoro, the Reef Islands, Taumako, Tikopia, and, finally, Anuta. Though showing her age, the white-hulled *Belama* was shipshape and run with impeccable discipline by her Kiribati captain.

We were fortunate to have secured a cabin with berths. Most of the Solomon Islanders slept on deck alongside trussed-up pigs and cackling chickens. At four bells (6:00 a.m.) a steward promptly woke us with steaming mugs of strong English tea. We took lunch and dinner in the officer's mess with the captain, district commissioner, and protectorate officials. Protocol was strict but not always obvious to a couple of American graduate students. One afternoon Rosendahl settled down with a book in a comfortable teak deck chair on the fantail. Nothing was said at the moment, but later Yen was reprimanded by the First Officer who informed him that it was a breach of protocol for anyone to sit in the district commissioner's special chair!

After stops at the Reef Islands (where we visited Green's newly found RL-2 Lapita site), Taumako, and Tikopia, the *Belama* dropped anchor off Anuta at dawn on October 30, 1971. Gathered at the rail, we gazed excitedly at the island that would be our home for the next several months. Although we knew that Anuta was small (the land area is 0.4 of a square kilometer, or roughly 0.15 of a square mile), the visual impact of seeing the tiny island in the tropical morning light was startling. To the north a low volcanic hill rose to a height of eighty meters, coconut palms dotting the summit. In the lee of this hill, the low-lying sandy plain was cloaked in vegetation. Smoke wafting up from cookhouses signaled the presence of a village behind the screen of trees.

Before leaving Honolulu, I had scoured the Bishop Museum Library for information about Anuta, one of eighteen "Polynesian Outliers" in the western Pacific, islands whose people speak Polynesian languages but are located outside of the main Polynesian triangle.[4] The Templeton Crocker Expedition had called at Anuta for a single day in 1933, and British anthropologist Raymond Firth had visited for a day in 1952, providing the sum total of knowledge about the island and its people.[5]

Anuta was rarely visited. The Melanesian Mission sent its ship, the *M. V. Southern Cross,* there once a year so the touring priest could baptize newborns, marry couples, and perform Holy Communion. The *Belama* called perhaps twice a year, weather permitting. Neither of these ships stayed more than a few hours. There was no priest, no government representative, no trader, or commercial operation of any kind on the island. Colonialism and capitalism had bypassed the place.

A few months prior to our arrival, the protectorate had placed a shortwave radio on Anuta, powered by a hand-cranked generator. When conditions were good one could contact the Eastern Outer Islands administration on Nendö Island. The Anutan people had been told that a party of scientists would be arriving. It would be the first time since World War II that any Westerners had spent more than a day on the island.

We descended the *Belama's* rope ladder into the launch. It was an unusually calm day so the boatswain easily negotiated the ridiculously narrow pass through the fringing reef. As the boat approached the beach I was surprised to see just two men. Each wore a tapa loincloth topped by a lava-lava of Western trade cloth; their bare torsos exhibited classic Polynesian tattoo designs. Speaking pidgin English, they introduced themselves as Pu Paone, a lineage elder, and Pu Tokerau, younger brother of the ranking chief. They told us that the island's chiefs awaited us inland. Pu Paone grasped my hand by the wrist, leading me up the steep beach.

Following a path shaded by towering *tamanu* trees, we emerged at a sandy plaza flanked by a cluster of thatched houses. Pu Paone led us to the base of a gnarled *Barringtonia* tree. To our left several old men, their bare chests intricately tattooed, sat cross-legged on *tapakau* mats. To the right sat a crowd of men, women, and children, all clad in barkcloth, the women bare-breasted with skirts, the men in loincloths. Everyone was silent; even the children were hushed.

Then, from behind one of the houses, a remarkable procession appeared. Two well-built, middle-aged men staggered forward, bearing on their shoulders a robust individual with a bushy head of wiry hair. All three wore fine mats over their loincloths, their chests and shoulders glistening with yellowish-red *renga,* turmeric dye, a sacred pigment in Polynesia. The two *maru* (as I later learned they were called) set the Ariki i Mua or first-ranked chief (also known as Tui Anuta) gently down on a *tapakau* mat directly across the plaza from us. Then a second set of *maru* appeared bearing a somewhat older man with a full chest tattoo, similarly anointed in turmeric. This was the Ariki i Muri, the "chief behind" or second ranked of the island's hereditary leaders (Fig. 4.2). I remember thinking to myself, "This is like a scene out of Captain Cook's voyages."

Pu Paone muttered that I should watch closely what he was going to do and then follow suit. Releasing his grasp on my wrist, Pu Paone got down on all fours and crawled across the sandy plaza toward the two chiefs, with the four *maru* standing guard behind them. Pu Paone kept his head low as he approached Tui Anuta. I recognized this as a gesture of respect, given Polynesian concepts about the sanctity of the head. I saw Tui Anuta grasp Pu Paone and pull him up, then pass him to the second chief. Seating himself a short distance from the chiefs, Pu Paone signaled that it was my turn.

Dropping to my knees, I did the same all-fours crawl across the sandy plaza to the waiting *ariki,* keeping my head bowed as I approached Tui Anuta. The burly chief grasped my shoulders, pulling me up; we pressed noses and gazed into each other's eyes. This was the classic Polynesian greeting of *ongi* (known as *honi* in Hawaiian). Tui Anuta then passed me to the Ariki i Muri, who likewise pressed

Figure 4.2. The two chiefs of Anuta in 1971. The Ariki i Mua, also known as the Tui Anuta, stands on the right, smoking his pipe. The Ariki i Muri, on the left, has a full chest tattoo.

his nose to mine. I then crawled over to Pu Paone who seemed pleased that I had correctly followed the protocol.

After everyone had gone through this ritual greeting, we were escorted into Tui Anuta's house. Built low to the ground, Anutan houses look like they have a thatched roof surmounting low walls of sago leaf. These "walls" are actually blinds, which can be propped open by sticks during the day to let in light and air. The roof is supported by four stout timber posts lashed with coconut sennit to an intricate framework of beams and rafters.

Speaking in pidgin, Yen described our project to the two *ariki*. Pu Tokerau, the younger brother of Tui Anuta, translated. Yen told them that we had brought our own food so as not to be a burden on the island. When this was translated, Tui Anuta broke out in a broad grin and shook his head. Pu Tokerau told us that when the chiefs had received the radio message that our group would be arriving, they had convened a council of elders. Polynesian hospitality dictated that the islanders would feed us. Every evening, it would be the responsibility of one of the *patongia* or households (there are nineteen of these) to host us. Yen protested, reiterating that we did not wish to be a drain on the island's food supplies. The *ariki* would have none of it.

As it turned out, this was a wonderful arrangement. Being guests of a different *patongia* every night meant that we got to know and socialize with everyone. Each evening we were escorted to a different house, taking bags of rice, packages of biscuits, and tins of beef or fish, giving these as gifts in exchange for the taro puddings, breadfruit, manioc, and fish prepared by our hosts. The Anutans were happy to indulge in the canned foods that for them were a special treat. After the meal we would all chew the mildly narcotic betel nut, chatting and socializing long into the evening.

Two small thatched houses not far from the plaza, normally occupied by a few bachelors, were cleared out for our use. By midday our gear and supplies had been offloaded from the *Belama* and carried up the beach by many willing hands. Long before the sun set we watched the *Belama* steam away. It began to sink in that we were isolated on one of the most remote islands of the South Pacific. The antiquated hand-cranked radio would be our only means of contact with the outside world. It was just the three of us and precisely 177 Anutans.

For a few days we explored our tiny island home, familiarizing ourselves with the layout of the two contiguous villages, Vatiana, where Tui Anuta resided, and Rotoapi (Map 3). With our hosts, we bathed at the spring (Te Vai), the island's only source of freshwater. Paths led inland to the cookhouses and then up the steep slope to the gardens cloaking the hill, Te Maunga (Polynesian for "mountain"). Standing on the highest point of Te Maunga, endless ocean extended to the horizon in every direction.

Yen was keen to begin studying the island's agricultural system, the most traditional he had ever witnessed. The leeward, sandy plain was cloaked in a random riot of coconut, breadfruit, sago palms, *Areca* (betel) palms, *Antiaris* trees that provided barkcloth, and an understory of *Cyrtosperma* swamp taro and yams. In contrast, the volcanic hill was precisely laid out in a reticulate grid of dryland taro and manioc gardens, interspersed with bananas and yams. This closely managed and highly productive system supported the tiny island's dense population.

Yen realized that Anuta presented a unique opportunity to observe the functioning of a traditional Polynesian agricultural system. Other islands had once had such systems, but virtually everywhere else they had succumbed to the inroads of colonialism, replaced by cash-cropping and commercial plantations. To properly record the Anutan agricultural system, Yen needed detailed spatial data on how much land was in tree crops and how much in short-fallow rotation of taro and manioc. But there was no map of the island, not even the most basic outline. Today

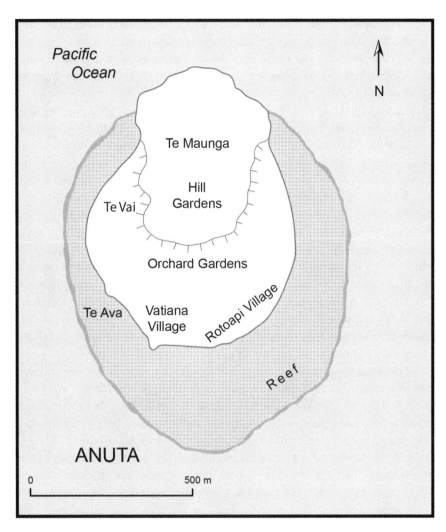

Map 3. Anuta Island, with localities mentioned in the text.

with GPS technology and Google Earth imagery, it would be a trivial task to construct such a map. In 1971, those technologies were decades in the future.

Aware of my surveying skills, Yen asked me to map the island. I had brought a plane table and alidade along, but I had never mapped an *entire* island before—even if it was a small one. Starting on the low-lying plain, I began mapping the villages. I numbered every house and cookhouse, along with the house names and the number of occupants, resulting in a census that would be useful for Yen's study. I also plotted in the canoes, *vaka*, pulled up between the houses and protected with woven coconut fronds. Each *vaka*, I discovered, had a proper name, as did the dwelling houses.

The Anutans were fascinated by the mapping. They were even more surprised when I let them look through the alidade's eyepiece, and they saw that the world was upside down! (The Gurley instrument I used was not "right reading.") There were always people standing around as I worked away at the plane table, eager to tell me the name of this or that house or canoe, how many people lived in that *patongia*, and so on. My notebook from those first weeks in November 1971 also contains long lists of Anutan words and phrases; I was rapidly acquiring an extensive Polynesian vocabulary.

Up on Te Maunga, I mapped every one of the 242 garden plots, recording which *patongia* owned each plot. Yen later added data on the crops. Yen spent a lot of time with Pu Notau and his wife Nau Notau[6] and their children, learning about the techniques of Anutan gardening. They showed him how they prepared their fields and planted taro and yams, weeding and tending the plants as they matured. Yen carefully recorded the hours that the Notau family spent in various kinds of agricultural activities.

Meanwhile, we were fitting into the rhythm of village life. Before long we knew almost everyone on the island by name. They called us "Mr. Heni," "Mr. Paul," and "Mr. Pat." We tried to get them to drop the honorific "Mr.," but they refused, probably because in their own language they insist on using the polite honorifics "Pu" and "Nau" before the proper names of married men and women.

Being so remote and isolated, Anuta was entirely self-sufficient. Although some people had a little Western cloth, mostly they still wore *mami* barkcloth beaten out by the women from *Antiaris* bark grown in the island's orchards (Fig. 4.3). The women spent much time weaving *Pandanus*, sleeping mats, and coconut frond floor mats. Men worked at carving wooden food bowls or repairing the canoes so essential for fishing. Everyday on Anuta we witnessed ancient Polynesian crafts and activities that had long since disappeared from most other Polynesian islands.

Some evenings, especially when there was a moon, everyone gathered in Rotoapi Village for communal dancing. There was excitement in the air when a dance was to be held. People plucked the fragment white blossoms of the *tiare* (*Gardenia taitensis*) growing near the houses, putting them into their pierced ear lobes and stringing them into garlands and headbands. They gave us flower garlands to wear as well. Anutan night dancing is performed in parallel rows of men and women (children join in as well), strutting back and forth while swinging one's

Figure 4.3. An Anutan woman and her daughter beating out strips of *mami* barkcloth, using wooden mallets against a hardwood anvil.

arms to the deep beat of wooden sticks striking an old canoe plank. Everyone chants the words to well-known songs, and the beat grows increasingly frenetic until the final crescendo is reached.

Sometimes, after we had returned from our evening meal or the dancing, the three of us would sit by the glow of our kerosene pressure lamp and talk. We were aware that we were experiencing one of the last truly traditional cultures in the Pacific. Of course, some Anutans such as Pu Paone and Pu Tokerau had spent time in the main Solomon Islands; they had learned pidgin English and experienced life outside of their little island. But on tiny Anuta daily life continued as it had for countless generations. It was as though we had entered a time machine, transported back to a lifestyle that had long since vanished from almost every other Polynesian island.

By mid-November I had completed the island map, leaving Rosendahl and me free to begin archaeological work. When had people first discovered and settled Anuta? Were those first settlers Polynesians, direct ancestors of the present population? Or had they been related to some other, possibly Melanesian, cultural group? Would we find evidence of Lapita pottery? We wanted to answer these and many other questions.

The Anutans have their own oral history, passed down from generation to generation. Several of the elders told us a tradition about the first people to inhabit the island, the Apukere or "Earthsprung" people.[7] The story goes like this:

> The Apukere were the original inhabitants of Anuta, with two chiefs, Ariki Apao and Ariki a Pakakana. Then Pu Ariki, a chief of nearby Tikopia Island, came to visit. The two chiefs of Anuta argued with Pu Ariki about who possessed the greatest *mana*, spiritual power. The Anuta chiefs boasted that they never suffered from cyclones or drought. Pu Ariki told them he would return to Tikopia, and they would then feel the strength of his *mana*. After he left a fearful cyclone lashed Anuta, uprooting the trees; storm surges broke over the lowlands. Then months of drought followed. Their crops destroyed, the Anutans were starving and dying of thirst.
>
> Pu Ariki sailed back to Anuta and found the Ariki Apao drawing his last breath. The land reeked with the stench of corpses. Pu Ariki buried the bodies, saying: "Sleep then in this land." He blocked the spring (Te Vai) with a stone. Pu Ariki planned to return later and give the island to one of his sons.
>
> Some time later Pu Ariki returned to Anuta. To his surprise he found people living there, people who had come from Tonga and from 'Uvea. When Pu Ariki confronted the newcomers, they claimed that they were the true people of the island, that their ancestors had always lived there. "If that is so, show me the water source," Pu Ariki challenged them. They showed him holes they had dug in the sand to get brackish water to drink. Pu Ariki then took them to Te Vai. Removing the stone, he showed them the true spring of sweet water. The newcomers from Tonga and 'Uvea were forced to acknowledge Pu Ariki's primacy in the land.

While fascinating, there was no way to tell if this tradition memorialized fragments of a "real" history or whether it was simply a kind of mythic charter. Nonetheless, the importance given to cyclones and drought—two disasters that the Anutans greatly fear—was noteworthy. The tradition also hinted that some of their ancestors had come from such Polynesian islands as Tonga, 'Uvea, and perhaps Samoa.

The elders showed us Pare Ariki ("Chiefly House"), near the eastern end of Rotoapi Village, which had been the island's principal *marae* or ritual center in pre-Christian times. The rectangular stone gravesites of nineteen deceased *ariki* lay just inland of an alignment of four god-stones where kava had been offered to the ancestors. The elders also took us to Tu Ariki, where a sacred house had been dedicated to the gods Rapu and Tukureo; to Te Pae, a former *marae*; to Paito

Karae, a *marae* where turtle and porpoise sacrifices were once made; and to Nuanga, a place near the spring where sacred turmeric dye had been extracted. These sites were fascinating, but none was likely to date back more than a couple of centuries.

The leeward, sandy plain was the most likely place to search for buried archaeological deposits. We started digging test pits, searching for traces of ancient occupation. After initial disappointments, we decided to test a location inland of Rotoapi Village, where we had found many *Tridacna* and *Cassis* shell adzes on the surface.

The first hint that we had hit an important site came in Test Pit 27, where about one meter below the surface we found the first reddish-brown earthenware sherds. Pottery was unknown to the Anutans, and our workers were surprised to see these potsherds. It seemed likely that we were into a layer with considerable antiquity. When we opened up the adjacent square to go deeper, a dark gray, charcoal-rich layer appeared a meter and a half below the surface. Many potsherds now turned up in the sifting screens as well as one-piece *Turbo*-shell fishhooks, coral and sea-urchin spine abraders that had been used to make the hooks, adzes and chisels of *Tridacna* shell, and ornaments of cone shell, *Spondylus* shell, and *Trochus* shell. We expanded the excavation, recovering more than one thousand artifacts from ten square meters.

The Anuta potsherds lacked the dentate-stamped decoration that Roger Green had found on the Lapita pottery in the Santa Cruz Islands. Mostly plain with a reddish-brown slip, only a few sherds had incised lines or other simple decoration. But the techniques of manufacture and the vessel forms showed undoubted similarities with Lapita. Clearly, the deeply buried pottery and other artifacts represented an ancient period in Anuta's past. Just how ancient we would discover when we later received radiocarbon dates from charcoal samples within the deeply buried midden. Three samples returned ages of $2,590 \pm 90$, $2,616 \pm 90$, and $2,830 \pm 90$ years before present (BP). The oldest of these indicated that the first people on Anuta arrived between about 1165 and 765 BC, not long after Lapita people had settled Roger Green's sites in the Reef Islands.

It turned out that some version of the Anutan origin story was correct. There had indeed been an original population—probably people descended from or related to Lapita pottery makers—who settled on the island in the early first millennium BC. After several centuries, a major cyclone devastated the island, resulting in a thick accumulation of beach sand, burying the original midden site. Anuta was then uninhabited for a long period, although it was perhaps periodically visited by people from Tikopia. Eventually, the island was resettled by Polynesian voyagers who came from several different islands to the east, especially Tonga and 'Uvea, at some time in the second millennium AD.[8]

Figure 4.4. The Tui Anuta with his outrigger canoe. The hull is carved from a single *tamanu* log with washstrakes added to increase the free board. These canoes are essential in allowing the Anutuans to fish the rich banks surrounding the island.

Living on Anuta was like stepping back in time. True, people used metal fishhooks, wore scraps of trade cloth, and lit their houses with kerosene wick lamps. But they still manufactured and mostly wore barkcloth, made their houses in the traditional way, fished on the reef with nets and spears, and went out to sea in sturdy canoes hewn from *tamanu* logs (Fig. 4.4). Their society was organized by rules of kinship, while their political leaders were hereditary chiefs. Although they had converted to Christianity about fifty years earlier, a few of the old men had participated in the pagan rites as young men. Rather than reading about Polynesian life in the musty stacks of the Bishop Museum's Library, on Anuta I was experiencing a vibrant Polynesian culture.

The tattoos gracing the bodies of the adult men and women fascinated me. Tattooing had once been widespread throughout Polynesia; indeed, the English word "tattoo" is borrowed from the Tahitian *tatau,* picked up by British sailors in the late eighteenth century. On most Polynesian islands, missionaries suppressed the practice. On Anuta, the Melanesian Mission priest forbade tattooing about two decades before we arrived. Thus none of the young people were tattooed, whereas all of the mature adults exhibited the blue-gray geometric patterns on their chests, backs, and arms. Only a few of the higher ranking men, such as the Ariki i Muri, had a full set of chest tattoos. I drew sketches of these designs in my notebook, recording the names of the motifs.

Toward the end of November Tui Anuta made a surprising proposition: Why didn't the three of us get tattooed? We replied that, it having been forbidden by the church, we thought the art was now lost. "No," replied the chief. "Pu Rangovaru and Pu Akonima are tattoo experts. They have their bone needles. They will tattoo you if you like." Yen, Rosendahl, and I decided that we would each be tattooed on our upper arms with traditional Anutan motifs.

On the appointed morning Pu Rangovaru arrived with a small, tattered coconut leaf basket holding four different needles, a few bamboo tubes containing black soot from burned *tamanu* (*Calophyllum inophyllum*) nuts, and a coconut half-shell in which the soot was mixed with water to prepare the ink. The needles, carved from frigate bird wing bones, had a comb-like business end with three or four sharp points, mounted perpendicularly to a wooden shaft and lashed with fine cord. Pu Rangovaru carved out two small mallets from green coconut fronds, each about six inches long. They would be used to drive the needles into the flesh, by sharply tapping on the wooden shaft.

After choosing the motifs that each of us would have indelibly inscribed into our flesh, Pu Rangovaru and Pu Akonima set to work (Fig. 4.5). To receive my tattoos, I lay on my side on the coconut-frond floor mats with my arm cocked and held tightly to my chest. Sitting cross-legged facing me, Pu Akonima drew out the design using a piece of coconut midrib dipped in the black ink. Holding the needle's shaft in his left hand, he positioned the teeth just above the mark then with a deft flick of his right wrist brought the mallet down crisply. Four sharp teeth, previously dipped into the ink, penetrated my skin, carrying the pigment down into the subcutaneous layer. The process was repeated, over and over, until the line became continuous and distinct. The pain of the needle was less than I had anticipated, probably because my endorphins quickly suppressed the nerve signals. Nonetheless, I began to feel a dull ache across my upper arm.

The entire process took several hours. While this was going on Tui Anuta and the other elders kept up a cheerful banter. When all was finished, we emerged out into the sunlight to admire our new body ornamentation. We had not anticipated that this would be just the first step in a two-day process of formally bringing us into Anutan society. Traditionally, young men and women were tattooed when they reached puberty, part of the "rites of passage" into adulthood. After receiving his first tattoos (which also took place at the time of circumcision) a young man could now sit on the *matapare* or seaward side of the house and go deep-sea fishing in the outrigger canoes.

Figure 4.5. Pu Rangovaru tattooing; he holds a small mallet in his right hand, which he is using to tap the tattooing comb held in his left hand. He wears a circlet of *Gardenia* flowers around his head.

Tui Anuta decided that we would be treated as young men would have been after their first tattooing. But first our wounds, oozing blood and lymph, had to be treated. Several women were waiting near the chief's house, having prepared large wooden bowls (*kumete*) of warm water scented with aromatic and medicinal leaves. While we sat on some coconut grater stools, the women dipped green *ti* (*Cordyline*) leaves into the warm water, then gently rubbed them over the newly tattooed flesh. This treatment finished, each of us was handed a fresh loincloth of *mami* bark and then given a fine mat woven from *Pandanus* leaves to wear around our waists. The women daubed sacred turmeric (*renga*) on our arms and chests,

Figure 4.6. Paul Rosendahl, Doug Yen, and the author on the day we were tattooed, after being dressed in barkcloth and fine mats and daubed with turmeric. The Tui Anuta stands between Rosendahl and Yen, and the Ariki i Muri stands between Yen and the author.

placing garlands of *tiare* flowers around our necks and heads. When we were properly decked out in feasting attire (Fig. 4.6), they led us to the plaza where the village population awaited for a feast of special puddings, washed down with green drinking coconuts. Large sprays of betel nuts had been harvested for chewing after the meal. I sat down with the *patongia* of Pu Akonima who was now my *tau soa*, or bond-friend. We had exchanged names, linking us and our families.

After the feast, the dancing began. First were the men's dances, performed with carved wooden paddles. Such dances are now virtually forgotten in Polynesia, but in the Bishop Museum I had seen grainy black-and-white movie footage from the Templeton Crocker Expedition taken on Bellona and Rennell Islands in the 1930s of harvest festival dances similar to these. Communal dancing continued long into the night.

The next morning Tui Anuta and Pu Tokerau woke us early. It was time to venture out in canoes for deep-sea fishing, again part of the puberty rites for a young man. Three outrigger canoes were being readied at Rotoapi. Anutan canoes have proper names, just like houses; these were named Puinga, Maratautemanga, and Vaovaomoana. About twenty feet long, each hull was carved from a single massive *tamanu* log; gunwales and washstrakes lashed on with sennit increased the freeboard. Five booms (*kiato*) joined the hull with its outrigger (*tautau ama*). The

heavy canoes were hauled from their storage places near the houses down the
beachfront using log rollers; they were then floated over to the beach in front of
the two tiny channels through the reef, Te Ava Rai and Te Ava Ti.

Tui Anuta assigned each of us to a canoe, along with four paddlers and a steersman. I was to sail in Vaovaomoana. In single file, the canoes negotiated the narrow pass, riding up and over the oncoming breakers and gliding out onto the deep
sea. For a couple of hours our little fleet paddled steadily away from the island,
until Anuta was a blip on the horizon. By mid-afternoon we arrived at a submerged
bank where the bottom was about twenty to forty fathoms deep. Letting down
baited lines, we soon pulled up enough groupers, squirrelfish, and emperors to
feed the entire island for a couple of days. The sun was getting low in the sky and
it was time to return.

With the wind in our favor, we hoisted sails for a speedy return (Fig. 4.7). During the day a sizable swell had come up, and coming near the island we watched
as six- to eight-foot breakers crashed down on the reef. The worried expressions
on the crew's faces signaled that getting the canoes back through the pass was

Figure 4.7. Anuta Island as seen from a canoe after returning from a fishing trip to the banks
surrounding the island.

going to be a challenge. The trick was to maneuver each canoe as close as possible to the reef edge without getting into the break. At the precise moment, the steersman has to call for his crew to paddle with all their strength to take the canoe in on the back of a wave, riding the high water. We watched as Puinga went first—a cheer arose as it successfully glided through Te Ava Rai. Then Maratautemanga made it through without mishap. Now it was Vaovaomoana's turn. We were so close to the reef that I could see the razor-sharp coral branches through the slack water behind the foaming break.

Pu Parekope aimed the bow at the narrow channel, shouting for his crew to dig in their paddles. Sitting near the stern, I watched four sinewy backs put all their strength into the task. But Pu Parekope was a couple of seconds too late. Rather than ride the back of the wave we hit the trough of low water between incoming breakers. I heard and felt the dull thud and shudder as Vaovaomoana's hull hit the coral and stuck fast in the narrow pass. Turning around, I watched an eight-foot wave crest directly over us.

Figure 4.8. Farewell scene on the beach at Anuta. The author is in the center with a *tiare* garland around his head, pressing noses with an Anutan woman.

I felt the rushing force of the wave and heard the sharp crack of five stout *kiato* booms snapping. No longer attached to its outrigger, the heavy timber hull began to roll over, pushed along by the wave's incredible force. I jumped to port as the hull rolled to starboard. Somehow—miraculously—no one was injured. We had managed to avoid getting caught between the rolling hull and the razor-sharp corals, a fate that would have meant mutilation, broken bones, and probable death. My only serious loss was my camera, still in my daypack tied to a thwart.

Vaovaomoana's scarred but not irreparably damaged hull was hauled up the beach. The *kiato* and outrigger would be repaired; it would sail again another day. The following day a special oven of food was made and shared by the canoe's *patongia*. Then the women gathered around Vaovaomoana, wailing for the injured canoe. They sang dirges and sobbed, tears and mucus flowing freely, just as they would have mourned for an injured kinsman. Had this accident not occurred, I would never have appreciated the way in which traditional Polynesians regard their canoes as embodying living spirits.

By now it was mid-December. Via the shortwave radio we received news that the *Belama* had engine problems. A much smaller ship, the *Coral Princess,* would divert to pick us up. Word came to be ready by December 16; we packed our gear and the boxes of archaeological specimens. That evening we had a farewell meal with Tui Anuta and his family. Everyone was in a melancholy mood, knowing that we would soon depart, most likely never to see each other again. Before dawn on the 16th we heard whoops and cries from Te Maunga; several young men had spent the night on the hill, keeping a watch on the horizon. The arrival of a ship was a major event, occurring only a few times a year. "*Te vaka! Te vaka!*" the cry went up. Within an hour the *Coral Princess* was offshore.

Every man, woman, and child on the island assembled at our hut—a couple of dozen packed inside and everyone else seated on the ground outside, looking in through the raised screens. Wailing dirges went up. "*Aue! Aue! Aue!*" Tears flowed and hands flipped streams of mucus from runny noses. After a half-hour of emotional wailing, everyone began to carry our gear down to the ship's launch. There were more tearful farewells on the beach and much pressing of noses (Fig. 4.8). Then we were into the launch, through the channel (thankfully calm that morning), and clambering up the ship's side. I lingered at the rail until Te Maunga's coconut palms sank below the horizon. I think all of us knew that never again in our lives would we experience another island society quite like that on Anuta.

CHAPTER FIVE

Lux et Veritas
(Yale University, 1972–1974)

I leaned into the stiff wind blowing down Hillhouse Avenue on the Yale University campus in mid-January 1972. Less than a month had passed since I watched Anuta's coconut palms slip below the horizon, but the tropical warmth of that island was a distant memory on this frigid New Haven morning. I had arrived the previous day, after a long journey from Honolulu via New York. Now I was on my way to meet the scholar who would be my mentor in Yale's anthropology graduate program.

Professor Kwang-chih Chang, just forty-one years old, was already the world's foremost authority on Chinese and East Asian archaeology.[1] Born in Beijing where his father had been a professor of Japanese literature, Chang fled the mainland with his family to Taiwan in 1946. He studied archaeology at Taiwan National University with the famous Li Chi, excavator of the ancient Shang capital of An-Yang. In 1954 Chang left Taiwan for the United States and Harvard University where he obtained his doctorate. Soon after he joined the Yale faculty.

Working with George Dales at Penn, I had become fascinated by the archaeology and prehistory of Southeast Asia. In spite of the raging Vietnam War—making archaeological work difficult—dramatic discoveries in Thailand had shown that this understudied region had huge potential for new research. During a semester at the University of Hawai'i in 1970, I listened to Prof. Wilhelm G. Solheim II lecture on the untapped archaeological potential of Southeast Asia. Solheim's graduate student, red-bearded Chet Gorman, told me about his own ground-breaking discoveries in Thailand. Digging in a small rockshelter called Spirit Cave, Gorman had uncovered evidence that plant domestication might have begun there much earlier than anyone had imagined. Doug Yen then identified the carbonized betel nut, peas, bottle gourd, and candlenut remains from Spirit Cave. With my growing interest in agricultural prehistory and human ecology, I had stated in my Yale application that I wanted to study the origins of agriculture in Southeast Asia. With Chang's interests extending to Southeast Asia, Yale had accepted me into the program.

Now I was preparing to tell my new mentor that I had changed my plans, even though I had not yet met him face to face! The four-month stint of fieldwork in the Solomon Islands had opened my eyes to research opportunities in the South Pacific. Most importantly, I realized that I loved working in the islands. I could still explore questions regarding ancient agriculture and human ecology, but I would pursue them in the Pacific. Regardless of the reasons for my change, I needed to inform Prof. Chang of my decision.

Climbing the steep stairs to Chang's second-floor office, my heart was pounding. Would Chang now refuse to be my advisor? Knocking on the door I heard a gentle voice bid me enter. Chang had a slighter build than I anticipated, his short-cropped hair showing a hint of graying at the temples. His penetrating eyes bulged slightly. I introduced myself; he gestured to a chair. "Just call me K. C.," he said in his disarming manner. Chang asked about my fieldwork in the Solomons. I described our discoveries in Kolombangara and Anuta while he listened patiently. Then I told him of my decision to focus on the archaeology of the Pacific Islands. His eyebrows may have twitched for an instant, but if he was disappointed he did not show it. "Well then," he said, "you'll have to teach *me*, because you know much more about the subject than I do."

I was taken aback, yet relieved. I assured Chang that I indeed had a great deal to learn from *him*, about settlement pattern archaeology for example, a topic that he had written on extensively. I also wanted to gain a thorough knowledge of East Asian archaeology, because Asia was the ultimate homeland of the Pacific islanders. Over the next two years I would take every seminar that Chang offered. Many years later, he would invite me to travel with him to Taiwan where I discovered how other Chinese scholars held him in immense esteem. But that lay in the future. For now, I was grateful that my new mentor had accepted my decision to focus on Pacific archaeology.

I soon met the rest of the 1971–1972 cohort of Yale anthropology graduate students, including Robert Dewar, David Joraleman, Carlos Arostegui, and Mike Raber. Over pints of beer in a student pub they plied me with gossip about the department's faculty, as only graduate students can do. On weekends we gathered at one or another's apartment to cook a meal and share inexpensive wine. Our research interests were diverse: Dewar in Chinese archaeology, Joraleman in Olmec iconography, Arostegui in Mixtec ethnohistory, and Raber in Mormon irrigation society. But we all shared a thirst for what anthropology could tell us about human cultures, societies, and long-term history.

In the early 1970s American anthropology was strongly committed to the "four fields" approach. The Yale faculty regarded anthropology as a social science, with an emphasis on *science*—on empirically based research. This was before the academic wars over "postmodernism," before the atomization of the discipline into subspecialties, before the very rejection of science by the American Anthropological Association. In the graduate program at Yale in the early 1970s, students were expected to gain competency not just in archaeology, or in cultural anthropology, or in linguistics, or in physical (biological) anthropology but in *all* of these branches of anthropology.

In addition to Prof. Chang, my advisory committee included Profs. Hal Conklin, Irving Rouse, and Harold Scheffler. During our first meeting I told them that along with Chang's seminar on East Asian prehistory I would be taking Prof. Floyd Lounsbury's course on kinship and Prof. Fredrick Barth's course on social structure (Barth was visiting from the University of Bergen). Then Conklin asked me, "What about linguistics? A Pacific archaeologist should know something about the linguistic history of the islanders. Mr. Isidore Dyen, in the Linguistics Department, is a world leader in Austronesian linguistics," he informed me. (Yale faculty referred to themselves as "Mr. or Mrs.," not "Prof.") "Go and introduce yourself and tell him you want to take his seminar." I dutifully followed Conklin's orders, gaining insights about language change that would serve me well in my later research.

There was no Polynesian specialist on the Yale faculty, but Harold Scheffler had studied the social organization of the Melanesians of Choiseul Island, and Leopold Pospisil had written an exhaustive ethnography of the Kapauku people in the highlands of New Guinea.[2] Pospisil was as eccentric as an academic could be. Descended from Czechoslovakian nobility, he had trained for the law at Charles University in Prague. After the Nazis invaded Czechoslovakia and confiscated his ancestral estate, Pospisil fled to the United States, receiving his doctorate in anthropology at Yale in 1956.

Pospisil was "old school" in his mannerisms and opinions. When Dewar, Raber, and I took his seminar on Oceanic cultures, Pospisil would stand at the podium in his three-piece suit, his left arm cocked behind his back while he turned the yellowing pages of his notes with his right hand. (He later explained that this was the way law students had been trained in Prague to argue before the court.) Pospisil's lectures inevitably reverted to his two favorite themes: the Kapauku of New Guinea and the horrors of the Nazi occupation of Czechoslovakia. Despite these eccentricities, Pospisil's meticulous studies of the Kapauku economy and sweet potato agriculture inspired me.

Harold Conklin taught cultural ecology, "primitive" agriculture, and ethnoscience (the study of indigenous systems of knowledge and classification). Increasingly interested in an ecological approach to archaeology, I took every seminar

Conklin offered. The field of cultural ecology was relatively new: Anthropologists and archaeologists were just beginning to integrate concepts such as the "ecosystem" into their thinking. Conklin's methods of studying indigenous agricultural systems and native use of the plant world excited me. He had done extensive fieldwork among the Ifugao irrigated rice cultivators of central Luzon. During his seminars, Conklin would pull out maps of irrigation systems and photographs of farmers building terraces.[3] I resolved to do a similar study in the Pacific.

Irving Benjamin Rouse and Michael Coe were the two other archaeologists on the Yale faculty. Out of earshot we graduate students referred to Rouse as "Gentle Ben" due to his patrician manners. Rouse's main interest was in the analysis of pottery styles. Like me, Rouse was an island archaeologist, although his area was the Caribbean. But Rouse was out of touch with the exciting new directions in archaeology, trapped in the old school of "culture history." Rouse maintained that the "ecosystem" and the "cultural system" were distinct entities, a proposition I found ridiculous. Coe, in contrast, had carried out a brilliant research project at San Lorenzo in Mesoamerica, integrating archaeology with a study of the region's cultural ecology. Regrettably, I never had the time to take any of Coe's seminars, although I read all his monographs with great interest.

There were no graduate courses taught at Yale during the summer months and the prospect of staying in New Haven—blighted with urban decay—was unappealing. I had kept in touch with my mentors at the Bishop Museum, which was increasingly engaged in what was then called "contract archaeology." After statehood in 1959 a huge influx of investment money began pouring into Hawai'i. The sugarcane and pineapple plantations that had dominated the islands' economy for more than a century were on their way out, unable to compete with cheap labor in the Third World. Tourism was rapidly replacing the plantations as the fiftieth state's principal source of revenue and employment. New hotels, resorts, and golf courses were being developed across the state.

Most of these developments were located in areas rich in archaeological remains. Federal and state historic preservation laws, as well as county ordinances, dictated that archaeological surveys be conducted prior to construction. Developers and state agencies turned to the Bishop Museum, with its expertise in Hawaiian archaeology, for this work. By the early 1970s the museum was struggling to find enough trained archaeologists to carry out its many projects.

Yoshiko Sinoto, now chair of the museum's Anthropology Department, assured me that there would be ample "contract archaeology" work if I wanted to come home during the summer. For a graduate student whose Woodrow Wilson Fellowship barely provided enough of a stipend to live on, the prospect was appealing. In June 1972 I met with Sinoto and Emory at the Bishop Museum. I would be assigned to Kahaluʻu on the Kona coast of Hawaiʻi Island where the Bishop Estate was developing a resort. The Bishop Estate was the legacy of Princess Bernice Pauahi Bishop, last of the Kamehameha dynasty, who had left her vast land holdings to support the Kamehameha Schools for Hawaiian children. Many of these lands had once been the estates of high-ranked *aliʻi,* chiefs. Kahaluʻu had been the royal seat of the seventeenth-century Hawaiʻi Island king Lonoikamakahiki.

Throughout June 1972 I directed excavations at Kahaluʻu, where Emory had identified the stacked stone walls of an unusually large structure as Lonoikamakahiki's house site. A nearby large stone structure had several adjoining rooms and platforms. Placing a series of trenches in and around the site, I defined six discrete construction phases, beginning about AD 1550 and continuing to the early postcontact period. I interpreted the structure as a *mua,* or men's house, associated with the nearby Lonoikamakahiki residence. I recommended that the men's house, along with the open space between it and Lonoikamakahiki's house site (which had been a *kahua* or plaza for royal games and entertainments), be set aside as an historic preserve.[4]

The Bishop Estate preserved the *mua* but ignored my broader recommendation. Forty years later I visited the site, appalled to find that even though the *mua* and royal house walls were intact, the plaza where Lonoikamakahiki and his warriors once practiced their martial arts is now a tennis court. Time-share condominium apartments—filled with tourists who know nothing of the history of Kahaluʻu and its once-famous king Lonoikamakahiki—press claustrophobically around the ruins. It was deeply disturbing to witness what the unbridled zeal for "development" had done to this fragment of Hawaiian history.

Returning to New Haven in September, I rented a cheap apartment on the ground floor of an old two-story house near Yale's Medical School, in what had once been a working-class Italian neighborhood but was now mostly an African American ghetto. My landlords, a quiet Italian couple, lived upstairs. The house adjoined what had been a small butcher shop, now boarded up, which shared a common wall with my kitchen. I was surprised to hear a phone ringing all day long on the other side of the wall. Every few weeks a black Cadillac sedan would pull up in front of the house, and a burly man in a pin-striped suit would get out and visit the couple who lived upstairs. I soon surmised that the boarded-up shop was a bookmaking operation under Mafia protection. This meant that I too, was under their "protection" as a tenant. Indeed, I was never hassled despite the fact that muggings were common in this part of New Haven.

The 1972–1973 academic year passed quickly as I took seminars with Conklin, Chang, and Rouse. Frank Hole arrived from Rice University as a visiting professor (he would later join the Yale faculty permanently). Hole had done cutting-edge work in the Near East on early plant domestication and the origins of agriculture; I enjoyed his seminar on problems in Near Eastern prehistory.

At Yale I got my first introduction to the use of computers in archaeology. This was a decade before the advent of the first primitive "personal" computers; the heart of the Yale computer center was an IBM System/360, the dominant mainframe then used at most universities. But Yale was on the cutting edge of distributed access, with remote terminals located at different locations around campus. Each terminal consisted of an IBM Selectric typewriter linked to the IBM System/360 by a dial-up telephone. There was no CRT screen; one interacted with the computer through the typewriter, using a programming language called APL.

I took the course, Statistics for Social Scientists, taught by Prof. Frank Anscombe, Yale's leading statistician. Anscombe taught us how to conduct statistical analyses using computer programs written in APL. I was struck by the power of computing for the analysis of archaeological data. With the help of Prof. Anscombe, I wrote my own program for "nearest neighbor analysis" of the spatial distribution of archaeological sites over a landscape. The program determined whether a mapped settlement pattern was random, clustered, or highly dispersed.

In May 1973 I made the long journey home from New York via Los Angeles to Honolulu once again. A Japanese consortium wanted to develop a resort with an eighteen-hole golf course, hotels, and condominiums along the South Kohala coast of Hawai'i Island. The developers had acquired the rights to an ancient 'ili or land division within the ahupua'a of Waikōloa, called Kalāhuipua'a, formerly the rustic retreat of kama'āina Francis 'Ī'ī Brown. The museum had a contract for archaeological survey of this property, and I would direct the work.

The parched, leeward coast of Hawai'i Island lies in the rain shadow of the great volcano of Mauna Kea; barren 'a'ā and pāhoehoe lava fields extend as far as the eye can see. However, at several places, small, protected bays afford canoe landings, while depressions in the lava flows inland of the shoreline hold brackish water in "anchialline ponds." These are ideal habitats for shrimp, edible shellfish, and, most importantly, for mullet and milkfish. The ancient Hawaiians had modified these natural ponds, adding walls and sluice gates to regulate the flow of tidal waters between the ocean and the natural influx of freshwater from the island's aquifer. Kalāhuipua'a boasted several acres of ponds, surrounded by groves of milo trees and coconut palms: an oasis within what otherwise was a wasteland of parched lava.

My team walked more than 3,800 acres centered around the "oasis" of Kalāhuipua'a, recording 179 archaeological sites, mostly concentrated near the rich fishponds. Hawaiian fishermen had camped in rockshelters while netting mullet in the ponds. There were fields of petroglyphs or "rock art" pecked into the *pāhoehoe* lava as well as small stone structures here and there. Inland of the main ponds we discovered a large burial cave with thirty skeletons, some laid out in wooden canoe hulls. In this arid climate, wooden artifacts did not deteriorate; other lava caves contained wooden bowls, a canoe paddle, and gourd containers.

Two years later I directed a season of "salvage excavations" at Kalāhuipuaʻa prior to the construction of the Mauna Lani Resort (as the area was fancifully re-named by the Japanese developers).[5] We dug into the rockshelters, finding bone fishhooks, coral files and abraders, and large quantities of fishbones and shellfish. While working in one of the rockshelters, we made a remarkable discovery. Holly McEldowney, a team member, noticed a low passageway at the back of the rock-shelter. Being very slender, she managed to shimmy her way through it. Soon I heard a voice calling me, "Pat, you've got to come back here and look at this!" I took my flashlight and got down on my stomach, shining the light back through the low tunnel. I reluctantly crawled through the eighteen-inch high passageway, rough lava catching at my shirt. After about ten feet I emerged into a larger cham-ber where I could sit up. McEldowney was sitting there with a big grin on her face. Laid out on the lava rock floor were sixteen large wooden fishhooks of the kind used to catch sharks, in various stages of manufacture (Fig.5.1). The cache must have been left there by an ancient expert at catching *mano*, sharks, which frequent the waters off Kalāhuipuaʻa.

In the fall of 1973 I returned to Yale, moving in with two fellow students who had secured a yearlong lease on a beach house in the quaint town of Guilford. It was the perfect place to spend my final semester studying for the dreaded oral examination that determined whether one would proceed to candidacy for the doctoral degree or politely be given a "terminal" MA degree and asked to leave Yale. I spent much of my time in a comfortable armchair next to the fireplace, surrounded by stacks of books from Yale's Sterling Library. I pored over ethnog-raphies of Polynesia, monographs on Polynesian archaeology, and treatises on Oceanic physical anthropology. For the oral exam, I would be expected to dem-onstrate competency in all of the "four fields" of anthropology for Oceania. After dinner, we went for long walks on the beach, enjoying the fall sky, looking across the sound at the flickering lights on Long Island.

At the same time I was fine-tuning plans for my dissertation fieldwork. Prof. Chang had suggested I apply for a National Science Foundation (NSF) "dis-sertation improvement grant" for $5,000 to help finance my project. This required writing a proposal spelling out the anthropological problem, the research area, and the methods to be applied. I wanted to do an "ethnoarchaeological" study of

Figure 5.1. Part of a cache of wooden shark hooks found in a deep recess of one of the lava tube rockshelters at Kalāhuipuaʻa, Hawaiʻi.

a traditional Polynesian island where irrigation agriculture was still practiced. Ethnoarchaeology was an exciting new approach within the discipline combining the ethnographic methods of cultural anthropology with archaeology. I proposed working on an island where the people still farmed using traditional irrigation and shifting cultivation and then applying the insights gained from those traditional practices to interpret the long-term history of agriculture, as revealed by digging in ancient irrigation terraces and other archaeological ruins.

My goals went beyond unraveling the history of agriculture or irrigation on one isolated island. I was seeking broader patterns of how the development of agriculture and irrigation had influenced the evolution of human societies. Some scholars had claimed that the invention of irrigation technology marked a critical phase in human social history. Historian Karl Wittfogel, in his book *Oriental Despotism,* argued that the rise of the political state and civilization was linked to irrigation, because the organization of labor to construct canals and terraces required an administrative elite. Wittfogel claimed that the management of water and the resulting agricultural surplus encouraged the growth of an incipient bureaucracy. He had even referred to ancient Hawaiʻi as a "crude, agrobureaucractic hydraulic state."[6] Anthropologist Marshall Sahlins likewise wrote that the degree of social stratification in Polynesian societies was linked to their level of economic development, especially their investment in irrigation.[7]

An ethnoarchaeological study of a Polynesian irrigation society could contribute to these intellectual debates. For instance, in a traditional society where irrigation formed the economic base, I could investigate the extent to which chiefs controlled labor to maintain the irrigation canals or regulated the distribution of water. I would also be able to gather quantitative data on the yields produced by irrigation and estimate the level of surplus above household needs. I could then use these kinds of data—which Polynesian ethnographers had not collected in the past—to interpret the archaeological record of irrigation development.

To carry out my project, I needed to find an island where the practice of irrigated agriculture was still alive. Although taro was still grown in Hawai'i, the farmers used tractors and commercial fertilizers in their fields. That would not do. I scoured the literature for possible field locations. Two islands were the obvious choices: Rapa in the Austral Islands of French Polynesia or Futuna in the Wallis Islands, a separate French colonial possession. John F. G. Stokes had gone to remote Rapa in 1920 on the Bishop Museum's Bayard Dominick Expedition. In his unpublished manuscript in the Bishop Museum library, he reported that the narrow valley bottoms were covered in irrigated pondfields; the people had formerly lived in fortified hilltop villages, much like the settlement pattern of Kolombangara.

Futuna, which lies midway between Fiji and Samoa, was the other possibility (see Map 2 in Chapter 4). Bishop Museum ethnographer Edwin G. Burrows had spent some months there in 1932, briefly describing the taro irrigation systems.[8] Doug Yen had visited Futuna as part of his sweet potato studies; he assured me that the island's irrigation systems were still intact, not influenced by Western agricultural technology as in Hawai'i. As with nearby Samoa and Tonga, it was also likely that Futuna had an archaeological record extending well back into the first millennium BC, with Lapita settlements. But no one had ever done any archaeological work on Futuna—the field was *terra incognita*.

I wrote up my proposal for an ethnoarchaeological study of irrigation and cultural adaptation in the islands of Futuna and 'Uvea (Wallis) and—with Chang's blessing and signature—sent it off to the National Science Foundation. Then I went back to cramming for my oral exam.

I will never forget the fateful day in late 1973 when my Yale committee convened in the Hillhouse Avenue seminar room for the examination. I was instructed to wait in the hallway while the committee reviewed my progress over the preceding two years. Then Harold Scheffler opened the door and said in his emotionless voice, "Enter, bleating lamb." For the next three hours Scheffler, Chang, Conklin, and Rouse grilled me relentlessly. The time passed excruciatingly slowly as they tested the boundaries of my knowledge. Suddenly, I was asked to leave the room and wait outside. A few minutes later they all emerged smiling, extending handshakes of congratulations. I was now officially a "candidate" for the doctoral degree in anthropology at Yale.

Soon after, I received word from the National Science Foundation that my research proposal had been favorably reviewed and would be funded. The realization began to sink in that I would soon be returning to the South Pacific. This time I would not be part of an expedition organized by others. I would be on my own, with the challenge of exploring and studying one of the last traditional irrigation societies of Polynesia.

CHAPTER SIX

Of Pigs and Pondfields
(Futuna and 'Uvea, 1974)

The rhythmic beat of *Capitaine Tasman*'s engine dropped to a hum, alerting me that the captain had signaled the engine room to slow our speed as we approached Futuna Island. I heaved myself out of my bunk, gingerly stepping over the slumbering bodies of Futunan passengers sprawled across the cabin floor; they preferred to stow their belongings on the bunks and sleep on woven mats. I walked forward to the flying bridge to catch my first glimpse of the islands that would be my home for the next six months. Futuna's mountains resembled the spine of a reptilian monster rising from the sea. To starboard lay Futuna's sister island Alofi, her stair-step terraces of upraised ancient reefs backlit by the dawn.

We had departed Noumea in New Caledonia four days earlier, sailing through the southern Vanuatu archipelago and then north of Vanua Levu in Fiji. The days at sea had passed leisurely; I spent one memorable night on the bridge drinking Scotch with the dejected French captain, whose Fijian mistress had locked him out of his cabin.

Having read everything that had been written about these islands, I felt I already knew them intimately, and yet I was ignorant of so much. Would the research design outlined in my National Science Foundation (NSF) proposal make sense once I was on the island? It was one thing to sit in the Yale library and design a research plan based on theory and assumptions; whether reality would cooperate remained to be seen.

Gazing at the fast approaching islands from the ship's rail, questions raced through my head. What kind of lodgings would be available? What was the local food supply like? The Maison Barrau store in Noumea had been unable to fill my order for rice, corned beef, tinned fish, coffee, and other staples before the ship sailed; I would have to depend on local sources until *Capitaine Tasman*'s return visit. How would I communicate with the Futunan people? My French was passable, but I was told that most adults spoke little or no French. If I were going to talk with the older people who would know the most about traditional taro farming, I would have to learn the Futunan language. A dictionary compiled by Catholic missionary Père Grézel in the 1870s would be my starting point.[1]

We were fast approaching Leava Bay, a narrow indentation in Futuna's south-western coastline, where in 1616 William Schouten and Jacob Le Maire had anchored the *Eendracht*, a century and a half before Captain Cook's more famous voyages.[2] There was little further contact until the French missionary Père Pierre Chanel arrived in 1837. Chanel's proselytizing landed him on the wrong side of the Futunan high chief Niuliki; his warrior Musumusu put an axe through the priest's skull in 1841. A mass conversion of the population followed, making Chanel a martyr (and recently a saint).[3] The twin towers of a huge stone church poking up above the crowns of coconut palms signaled the dominance of the Catholic Church in Futunan life.

As the *Capitaine Tasman* nosed into the bay, children ran along the black cobble beach toward the dock, excited by the prospect of greeting returning family members or perhaps seeing a new *papalagi* (foreign) visitor. More startling were the scores of pigs scurrying about among the children; I had never seen so many pigs in my life. As I would soon discover, Futuna is a land of pondfields and pigs.

There was no time for further musings. The captain shouted orders as the ship approached the tiny wharf; mooring lines were thrown out and deftly fastened. A uniformed gendarme marched up the gangway to begin arrival formalities. I showed him my research visa issued by the French consulate in New York, he stamped my passport, and my boxes and crates of equipment and supplies were winched out of the hold onto the rickety wharf. I gratefully took up an offer to lodge temporarily at the Catholic mission, next to the big church. Père Patrice's battered pickup truck—one of just a handful on the island—hauled my gear to the mission compound.

In the late afternoon from the mission's seawall, I watched the *Capitaine Tasman* back out of Leava Bay, turn, and make course for 'Uvea. I was exhilarated to be in the field, yet overwhelmed by the task I had set myself. In spite of the lulling sound of the surf on the fringing reef, I barely slept that night as I kept thinking, Where to begin?

The island was divided into two districts, rather grandly called *royaumes* ("kingdoms") by the French administration, each headed by a paramount chief or *sau* (styled *roi*, "kings," by the French). The *sau* of Sigave ruled over the western half of Futuna with the best irrigation land, whereas the *sau* of Alo's domain comprised eastern Futuna along with uninhabited Alofi Island (Map 4). A score of hereditary titled chiefs (*aliki*) were in charge of their respective villages. Sigave and Alo each had five principal villages, strung out along Futuna's leeward coast. The windward side, or Tu'a (literally "back"), was abandoned. An unpaved dirt track, used

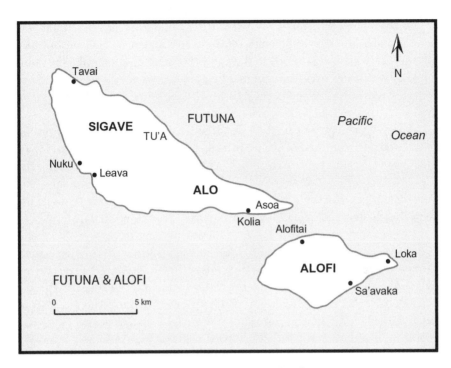

Map 4. Futuna and Alofi islands, with localities mentioned in the text.

by a few rickety pickup trucks, linked Sigave and Alo; Tu'a was accessible only by footpath.

Only a handful of the three thousand people on Futuna were Whites (the Résident or official representative of the French government, a French doctor, the gendarme, a trade store owner, and several Catholic nuns). Futuna was not so untouched by Western influence as Anuta, yet remained noticeably traditional. People mostly lived off of the productions of their irrigated taro fields and hillside gardens, raised seemingly endless numbers of pigs, and fished on the reef. Two small trade stores in Sigave sold rice, tinned fish and corned beef, biscuits, cloth, matches, and kerosene. But people still cooked in their earth ovens; Western foods were a luxury. Thatched *fale* with open sides and gravel floors covered with fine mats dominated in the villages. There was no electricity; water was piped by gravity from springs to village cisterns. Afternoon communal bathing—first the women and children, followed by the men—in the village cistern was a focal point of social activity and gossip as well as a great way for the newly arrived anthropologist to get introduced to the village.

I asked about renting a vacant *fale* where I could integrate myself into village life and begin my ethnographic research. Fortunately, a small *fale* in Nuku Village was available, attached to the *kaiga* (household) of Lalotilo, the main house of which was occupied by a middle-aged widow named Aloisia and her teenage children Nikola and Lucia. Aloisia belonged to the prominent Keletaona lineage; the *sau* of Sigave was her father's brother.

I borrowed a rough table from Aloisia to use as a desk, hung my lantern from the rafters, and set up a makeshift kitchen in one corner with my kerosene stove. My air mattress and sleeping bag were engulfed by a huge mosquito net purchased at the last minute in Noumea, a wise decision considering Futuna's hordes of mosquitoes. The sanitary facilities were more primitive; everyone simply relieved themselves on the cobble beach or reef flat at low tide, the pigs quickly cleaning up all traces.

The pigs were everywhere (Fig. 6.1), allowed to roam freely over the coastal plain. A continuous stone wall called the *a matua* (ancient wall) running behind the village kept the swine from roaming inland where they might devastate the irrigated gardens. The open-sided houses had low walls of coconut logs that people could step over but that prevented the pigs from entering. Wandering freely about between the houses, the pigs constituted the village garbage disposal force, also venturing onto the reef where they practiced a porcine form of fishing. It amused

Figure 6.1. Pigs are ubiquitous in Futunan villages. Here a sow and her litter feed on coconut meat that has just been provided for them, while the owner's children play.

me to watch the pigs use their agile snouts, overturning stones and searching out small fry, mollusks, and octopus.

After settling into my *fale* at Lalotilo I began to explore the terrain inland of the *a matua*. The order and symmetry of the hundreds of pondfields sculpted out of the gently sloping coastal plain, watered by an intricate network of canals and subsidiary ditches, impressed me. Some pondfields were near bursting with mature taro plants ready for harvesting, their heart-shaped leaves forming a rippling sea of blue green. Other fields had just been planted in neat rows of leafless slips (Fig. 6.2). In some fields sedges had been heaped up into large piles called *fakele*, then burned. I was eager to discover the cycle of planting, tending, and harvesting represented by these different fields. Hiking the muddy paths up into the Sausau Valley, I passed through shady breadfruit and banana orchards, skirted stands of tall *Metroxylon* palms, and climbed up steep slopes to examine shifting cultivations planted in a seeming riot of yams, dryland taro, elephant ear taro, sugarcane, kava, and bananas.

Futuna proved to be a living museum of Polynesian horticultural knowledge, passed down through countless generations. Such knowledge also once

Figure 6.2. Two young men of Nuku village working in the extensive *telenga* or irrigated taro fields. On the left, Talaku repairs the low earthen embankment, while on the right Apolosio sorts a pile of taro slips for planting.

existed in Hawai'i but was already dying out when Edward Craighill Handy conducted his studies of the Hawaiian planter in the 1930s. I was struck by a sense of urgency—this intact, traditional system of Polynesian subsistence gardening needed to be documented before it too succumbed to encroaching "globalization." The young people were less interested in learning to master the age-old gardening techniques than in going to New Caledonia or far-away France to seek their careers. The island's elders would be the last generation to command this traditional knowledge.[4]

As I meandered through this vegetal landscape, dozens of questions popped into my head. How did the village's social groups map onto different sections of the irrigation system? Who determined the flow of irrigation water? How was labor organized and work parties assigned to maintain and repair the canals and ditches? How frequently were the pondfields left to fallow? How long did it take a crop of irrigated taro to reach maturity? What was the average yield of a pondfield? How often did a household decide to cut a new swidden (slash-and-burn) garden? How did they choose which yam and banana varieties to plant? There was no end to the questions.

The best way to get a handle on an agricultural system is to map it. I had learned this on Anuta with Doug Yen, just as I had admired Harold Conklin's detailed maps of Ifugao terracing in the Philippines. I decided to map the Nuku *telega* or irrigation complex, the largest on the island. With the help of a Futunan assistant I began to survey the hundreds of pondfields along with the irrigation canals and ditches, simultaneously recording systematic data on each field—the stage of taro growth, whether in fallow, which household owned the field, and so forth.

Seeing me out in their fields day after day working at my plane table, some of the older farmers became curious. Occasionally one would wander over to see what I was up to; in a combination of French and broken Futunan I explained how the emerging map captured the spatial configuration of their *telega*. I began to talk to the farmers about their cultivation practices; the cycle of planting, tending, and harvesting; and their different varieties of taro. Sometimes, as we walked back to the village in the late afternoon, passing through Maumu, the zone of cookhouses, an elder would call out to me to join him as his earth oven was being opened, offering steaming hot breadfruit dipped in freshly squeezed coconut cream, or roasted Tahitian chestnuts.

Nuku Village is divided into two sectors, each under the authority of a hereditary chief: Tui Sa'avaka in the eastern half and Kaifakaulu in the western half. One evening as I was finishing my dinner of steamed rice and tinned sardines a young boy appeared to say that Tui Sa'avaka would like me to join in the evening kava drinking. I picked up my flashlight and followed him down the path to an open-sided *fale* with stout posts supporting a thatched roof, the gravel floor covered in woven mats. Futunans are great imbibers of kava, the psychoactive drink prepared from the dried roots of a pepper species, *Piper methysticum*. Formal kava drinking takes place during ceremonial feasts and is performed with great ritual and protocol. Informal kava drinking, known as the *tao'asu*, is done in the evenings in the house of a village chief or elder. The *tao'asu* is in effect a men's club, where gossip and information are shared and ancient traditions passed down.

Tui Sa'avaka, a squat, portly man then in middle age, motioned for me to join a circle of village men seated on *Pandanus* mats. A kerosene lamp softly illuminated intricate sennit lashings that bound the *fale*'s rafters and ridgepole to the stout posts. A basin-like wooden kava bowl about a yard wide sat on four stout legs in front of a tall, stern-faced man named Lino. The *mua* or "adjutant" of the Tui Sa'avaka, Lino prepared the kava for his chief. Lino poured fresh water from a bucket into the bowl, which held a mass of pounded kava root, then strained the infusion by sweeping shredded *Hibiscus* bark (*fau*) through the liquid. Lino raised the *fau* over the bowl, squeezing it as he wrung out the brownish liquid. He shook the *fau* out on a mat, then with a deft flick of his arm snapped the *fau* like a whip. This process, repeated many times, removed the grainy kava particles.

Between his thumb and forefinger, Lino grasped the rim of a coconut half-shell encrusted with a grayish patina from years of use; he gently submerged it into the kava, filling the cup to the brim. He called out the name of the cup's recipient, the first one going to Tui Sa'avaka. By custom, the recipient must drain the cup completely. After drinking, the recipient passes back the cup and then claps three times with cupped palms. The initial effect is a mild numbing of the lips and tongue, but soon a gentle euphoria settles in.

I became a regular attendee at Tui Sa'avaka's *tao'asu*. My efforts to learn Futunan were paying off; during the kava sessions I would try to speak in Futunan rather than French. Lino and the others laughed at my blunders, but I could tell from the way they gently corrected my errors that they appreciated my attempt to speak their language.

After mapping the Nuku *telega*, I turned to a survey of the shifting cultivations in Sausau Valley. To learn the varieties of yams, bananas, taro, and other cultivated plants, as well as the weeds and second-growth vegetation that surrounded the gardens, I started a systematic botanical collection, cutting branches with leaves and flowers or fruit and drying them in a plant press. My nearly two hundred carefully prepared specimens were later given to Bishop Museum botanist Harold St. John, who assigned scientific names to them.[5]

The irrigated fields and hillside shifting cultivations of Nuku and the Sausau Valley comprise an integrated agricultural system, patterned in space and time as well as intimately linked with the village's social and political organization. Central to this system was a fundamental dichotomy between the "wet" and the "dry." First, there was the spatial distinction between the intensive, irrigated taro gardens of the coastal plain and lower valley slopes (the wet) and the extensive shifting cultivations of the valley interiors and mountain slopes (the dry). Second, there was a temporal dimension to the wet/dry dichotomy. The dry season with reduced rainfall (and, in some years, drought) begins around May or June and extends into September or October, followed by the rainy months (and potentially devastating cyclones). Although the irrigated taro fields are cultivated year-round, the shifting cultivations must be planted according to this seasonal cycle. Yams, planted during the dry season, are the most important crop in these hillside gardens (two species are grown, *Dioscorea alata* and *D. esculenta,* with numerous varieties of each).

I was struck by the huge differences between these "wet" and "dry" forms of cultivation. The irrigated fields—which could be cropped almost continuously—had much higher yields and required relatively low levels of labor input. In contrast, the dryland shifting cultivations had to be cut anew each year from forest, produced lower yields per acre, and required significant labor inputs in weeding and tending. The greatest significance of this wet/dry dichotomy, however, lay in the geographic distribution of these two forms of agriculture. Western Futuna (Sigave) is volcanic, its mountainous terrain dissected by valleys whose streams carry the water essential to irrigate the taro fields. Much of eastern Futuna (Alo) and all of Alofi Island consist of ancient Miocene limestone, uplifted by the tectonic engine of the Pacific Plate slipping relentlessly under the Fiji Plate. This limestone karst soaks up water like a sponge. Consequently, irrigation is dominant in Sigave, whereas most of Alo and all of Alofi lack irrigated terraces. I wondered whether these differences might have influenced the frequent wars between Alo/Alofi and Sigave referred to in Futunan oral traditions.

Those long months of research in the wet and dry gardens of Futuna laid the seeds for my later understanding of large-scale ecological dynamics in Polynesia. Two decades later, in my book, *The Wet and the Dry: Irrigation and Agricultural Intensification in Polynesia* (1994), I would more fully develop a theory of the tensions between irrigation and dryland cultivation in Polynesia. Only after many more years of fieldwork on islands throughout Polynesia would I have the breadth of experience and knowledge to place the insights I was gaining in Futuna into a larger comparative context.

Since my arrival on Futuna I had kept my eyes open for archaeological sites. Up on the plateau of Mauga, overlooking Nuku, I found abandoned house terraces, confirming traditions that some elders told me about people formerly living on the mountain ridges. Farther inland there was a fortified ridge called A-fili, once defended by a ditch and palisade. On an eastern ridge of the Sausau Valley I came across another fortification, with telltale depressions of ancient ditch and bank earthworks. Clearly, people had once resided in defensive positions overlooking their irrigated fields and gardens. It seemed that warfare had been an important aspect of Futunan life.

I hired three young Futunan men to help me map the sites and dig test excavations. The acidic soils left little other than a few stone flakes and charcoal, more rarely a piece from a ground stone adz. I collected the charcoal for later radiocarbon dating. But since these sites were linked to oral traditions, I suspected that they went back in time only a few centuries, to the period just prior to European contact. I also dug trenches in the Nuku irrigation systems in abandoned and fallow fields, seeking a stratified sequence of pondfield layers. In a small pondfield system called Lotuma, I uncovered two successive layers of pondfield use and recovered charcoal for later dating.

I was concerned that my digging was only getting to the late stage of Futunan prehistory. For one thing, I had not found any pottery. I knew that elsewhere in Western Polynesia the earliest sites were characterized by abundant pottery. Why was I not finding sites with either Lapita or the later Polynesian plainware ceramics? This problem worried me. Then, a serendipitous event changed my perspective on the island's deep past.

My host family at Lalotilo kept pigs in the coconut groves at Tavai on the uninhabited Tu'a side of the island. One Sunday the family went out in Aloisia's cousin's battered truck for a picnic, inviting me to join them. When we arrived at Tavai the boys beat out a rhythm on an old gasoline drum, bringing an excited swarm of pigs out of the forest for their meat of dried coconut meat. Meanwhile, Aloisia set about preparing an *umu* (earth oven) for lunch. A couple of hours later, after watching Mikaele and Nikola unsuccessfully try to land some fish by surf-casting, we sat down to a feast of suckling pig and steamed tubers.

Appetites satisfied, everyone began to doze off on the mats spread out over the sandy beach ridge. Not being sleepy, I decided to search for seashells. As I strolled along the beach a flat reddish object caught my eye. At first I thought it was a stone, with edges rounded by the surf. Then I realized the reddish material had numerous small white inclusions in it. On an impulse I broke it in two, exposing the unweathered interior. There was no mistaking that this was a potsherd, with coral sand temper, much like those I had excavated on Anuta Island three years earlier.

Putting the sherd in my pocket, I walked farther up the beach, keeping a close watch out for other reddish "rocks." I soon found several more, including a rimsherd. By now I had reached the mouth of a little stream that cut through the Tavai coastal plain. I realized that the pottery must be coming out of this ravine.

Mikaele and Nikola had awakened from their nap, following me up the beach. I showed them the potsherds, explaining that these flat-sided, soft reddish "rocks" were actually pieces of ancient pottery. They looked at me a bit dubiously but were game to help explore the creek. Slashing at the tangle of *Hibiscus* choking the ravine we waded up the rivulet, knee deep in cool water. To either side the clayey banks rose over our heads. My bare feet felt something hard underfoot. Looking through the clear water, I saw that we were now on a platform of limestone reef, buried by the dozen feet of clay towering over us. My mind jumped to the unmistakable conclusion: The island's original shoreline had once been much closer to the base of the mountain slope that it is today.

Continuing up the ravine, we found larger pieces of pottery with unweathered edges. In the steep bank, I could make out a black layer partly inundated by the stream. Borrowing Mikaele's machete, I dug into the deposit, large potsherds tumbling into the water. A dark shiny object caught my eye. I pulled it out of the bank, washing it in the stream water, and saw it was a beautifully polished stone adz. The absence of a tang and the plano-convex cross-section told me that this was a "Type V" adz, characteristic of Samoan pottery sites dating to the late first millennium BC. A Sunday picnic and stroll up the Tavai beach had ended in the discovery of a site dating to Futuna's early period of Polynesian settlement. Months later, I would get a radiocarbon date on charcoal from this buried layer of $2,120 \pm 80$ years BP (calibrated to 210–40 BC).

The following week, I hired three workers to help me excavate a six-square-meter pit down through the nearly three meters of clay and gravel that buried the ancient pottery-bearing layer (Fig. 6.3). It took a good portion of my precious field funds to purchase a drum of gasoline so that the Keletaona family truck, barely running on three sputtering cylinders, could transport us to Tavai every day. After several exhausting days of digging through the overlying clay and then into the charcoal-rich layer, we recovered 7,305 pottery sherds, rims, and handles, along with several more stone adzes, chert cores and flakes, a grindstone, and two hammerstones.[6]

My discoveries at Tavai opened my eyes about Futuna's dynamic environment. I realized that part of this dynamism was natural and part was due to human actions. The buried reef sat at a level higher than the modern sea level, indicating that it had been uplifted by the same tectonic engine that had raised Alofi's stair-step terraces. But the thick clay that buried the old reef and the pottery-bearing layer was almost certainly a consequence of human land use.

Figure 6.3. The deep excavation at Tavai with Loselio holding the 3.6-meter-tall stadia rod. Loselio stands on the level of the ancient village site, dating to more than two thousand years ago, whose occupants had made and used pottery. The village site was later buried under 2.5 meters of clay eroded from the mountainside.

Hiking the interior ridges of western Futuna (Fig. 6.4), I saw large areas covered in degraded *Dicranopteris* fernland; remnant patches of climax forest were scattered here and there. The Futunans call this fernland *toafa;* it periodically burns off and nothing except the wiry fern grows on the nutrient-poor soil. It dawned on me that the *toafa* was a result of centuries of shifting cultivation on the interior mountain ridges. After the climax forest had been felled, the thin soil was exposed to the heavy tropical rains and periodic cyclones. Once this soil was stripped off, only the tough *Dicranopteris* fern would grow on the oxidized laterite.

At Tavai, the clay that washed off the mountain ridges had buried the old village site dating to the late first millennium BC. Had this happened elsewhere on

Figure 6.4. I took this self-portrait during a hike in the hills above Nuku. I am smoking a French *Gauloises* cigarette and had placed a cluster of wild *Dendrobium* orchid flowers behind my ear, in island fashion.

the island? I took a closer look at the area behind Nuku Village, suspecting that the broad coastal plain on which the Nuku irrigation system had been constructed was—like Tavai—an accumulation of alluvial sediments. My suspicions were confirmed when I found the badly disturbed remnants of a pottery site at the base of a small hill. The irrigated fields had encroached onto the ancient village (about 200 meters inland of the present village); centuries of digging and planting had smashed the pottery into fragments so small they looked like little pebbles.

These discoveries made it clear that the extensive irrigation system at Nuku—as well as all of the other coastal irrigation complexes around eastern Futuna—had been relatively late developments in the island's history. They could not have been constructed until centuries of shifting cultivation inland—followed by erosion and deposition of the coastal plains—had created sufficient alluvial land. Thus, an earlier emphasis on shifting cultivation had gradually led to the creation of alluvial plains suitable to large-scale irrigation works. It was not that the earliest

Polynesian settlers had *planned* it that way but rather that the gradual interaction of natural and cultural processes had channeled the island's agricultural history along a particular pathway. These insights were to guide much of my later research in other Polynesian islands.

In the pre-Christian era, the Futunan chiefs exercised control through a ritual cycle marked by periodic feasts.[7] After the conversion to Christianity, these feasts or *katoaga* became linked to Catholic saints' holy days. Every year, each village hosts a *katoaga* in honor of its patron saint. *Katoaga* promote community solidarity but are also an arena of political action through the formal kava ceremony in which the calling out of chiefly titles reaffirms the political status quo.

I was not anticipating the spectacle that I would witness when Aloisia invited me to join the Keletaona clan on Sunday, April 28, for an island-wide *katoaga* at Kolia Village in Alo. As we bumped along the dirt road in the old Keletaona pickup, Aloisia explained that Kolia—home of the infamous Musumusu who had murdered Père Chanel—had never been allowed to have a chapel of its own. Recently, this injunction had been lifted and a new chapel constructed, which was now to be consecrated. The entire island had been invited, including both kings and all the hereditary chiefs.

The day began with a lengthy consecration mass in the newly constructed chapel, after which we emerged into the morning sunlight to be greeted by the most impressive feasting display I have ever witnessed in my decades of Polynesian fieldwork. The gravel-paved Kolia Village plaza or *malae* had been laid out with row after row of food presentations, or *kalauniu*. I counted about three hundred of these *kalauniu,* each consisting of a woven coconut frond basket containing uncooked yams, dryland taro, and other tubers and bundles of cooked *faikai* puddings, topped with a small to medium-sized cooked pig. As if this were not enough, the seaward edge of the *malae* was lined with ten piles of stacked yam tubers about four feet high, each topped with three huge roasted hogs. Lying across the backs of the hogs were rolls of barkcloth and woven mats, while long stalks of sugarcane festively decorated each giant heap. On the inland side of the *malae* was a row of huge kava plants, dug up whole with roots and stalks intact.

I was astounded by this display of traditional wealth, estimating that the *kalauniu* and other offerings included something like four thousand yam tubers, three hundred smaller pigs, at least thirty full-grown hogs, and many rolls of barkcloth and mats. All of this had been produced in the gardens and work sheds of the Kolia Village people, now to be shared among the entire island population.

In an open-sided pole-and-thatch structure fronting the *malae,* the hereditary chiefs arranged themselves in the distinctive semi-circle known as the *alofi.*

At the center of the *alofi* were the two *sau;* the chiefs closest to them on either side were of higher rank, whereas those of the least rank occupied the extremities of the semi-circle.

The preparation of a royal kava requires great solemnity.[8] At the seaward edge of the *malae,* in front of the great heaps of yams and hogs, sat the kava mixer (*palu kava*), the pounder (*tuki kava*) and announcer, and the *mua* or adjutant (Fig. 6.5). The *tuki kava* and the *mua* alternately called out in loud, sonorous voices:

> *Tuki kava:* "*Kava kua oki le tuki!*" (Finished is the kava pounding!)
>
> *Mua:* "*Malo le tuki ku matuʻa. Tuku ki lalo kae palu!*" (Praise be to the pounding. It is ready. Sit and mix.)
>
> *Tuki kava:* "*Kua siu.*" (It is poured.)
>
> *Tuki kava:* "*Maʻa le kava!*" (The kava is clean [strained]!)
>
> *Mua:* "*Amanaki kae fakatau!*" (Await that it be served!)

Figure 6.5. Preparing kava at a *katoaga* in Vaisei Village. The shirtless man is the *palu kava* or kava mixer, straining the liquid through *fau* bast. To his right sits the *tuki kava,* who announces each cup.

The cup bearer, a young man adorned with banana leaves, rose to receive a full coconut cup of the liquid, then turned to face the *alofi* with the cup held high in his two hands. The *mua* now let out a long-drawn out cry of "*Oheka!*" (It is served!).

Mua: "Tuki mai a ia ma Keletaona!" (Offer it to Keletaona!)

The young man strode across the *malae* between the long rows of *kalauniu* and bowed low in front of the *sau* of Sigave, offering the cup to the seated king. A cry of "*Oheka!*" went up again as the second cup was offered to the *sau* of Alo. Then, in rapid succession, the servers carried cups to the respective chiefs as the *mua* called out their hereditary titles.

Tui Sa'akafu now rose to begin the food distribution, his hereditary privilege. The largest hogs went to the two kings and the village chiefs. But the food distribution continued until every household had received a share. Imagine my surprise when a *kalauniu* basket topped by a suckling pig was suddenly set at my own feet!

Archaeologists debate the significance of feasting in ancient societies. But on that Sunday morning in Kolia Village I had the privilege of seeing a great island-wide feast and kava ceremony unfold before my eyes, witnessing the visual power and political significance of such a communal event. It was one of a number of fieldwork experiences in the traditional societies of the South Seas that have greatly enhanced my understanding of what I have excavated from the ground.

In early June the opportunity arose to spend five days on Alofi Island, in the company of Sosefo Sekemei of Vele Village. Then in his sixties and a lineage elder, Sekemei was an expert in Futunan oral traditions. With Sekemei and a few other Vele men, I crossed the channel over to Alofitai in an outrigger canoe. Hiking over the island's upraised coral escarpments and central plateau, I saw low walls of stacked boulders running off into the forest. At one point we entered a garden clearing where the Vele folks had planted yams. Here the low walls formed a reticulate grid, presumably defining ancient garden plots, along with the low oval foundation of a house site. I recalled how the Dutch explorers in 1616 had been visited by the "king" of Alofi along with about three hundred of his warriors. I surmised that these limestone walls were part of an extensive system of dryland gardens that supported this once sizable population.

By late afternoon we reached Loka, near Alofi's eastern tip. Sekemei took us to the entrance to a subterranean cavern, eroded over the eons out of ancient marine limestone. In the semi-darkness I could see stalagmite pillars and stalactites hanging from the cave's ceiling. Seated on a boulder Sekemei began to chant, in a deep voice, "*Le matagi e fuga Alofi, si'i motu mataga lelei . . .*" (The wind blows from Alofi, little island beautiful to behold). I still recall his words echoing off the damp walls.

Loka had been the seat of the Mauifa chiefs, independent rulers of Alofi. Sekemei led me to an alignment of cut-and-dressed limestone slabs, obscured by the dense undergrowth. These slabs had defined one edge of the *malae* or ceremonial plaza at Loka. With the huge *katoaga* at Vele still vivid in my mind, it was not hard to imagine similar feasts having taken place here, the king of Alofi and his warrior chiefs seated in front of the great line of limestone slabs, the *malae* laid out with scores of *kalauniu* baskets.

After spending the night at Loka, we continued around to Alofi's windward coast. Camped at Sa'avaka, the men went night hunting for coconut crabs. Returning with a basket full of the giant crustaceans waving their fierce claws, they roasted them along with ripe breadfruit on an open fire. It was my first taste of the exquisite flesh of this terrestrial crab, which unfortunately is now close to extinction on most Polynesian islands.

In late July I heard that the Vele men would be returning to Alofi to do more dryland gardening; I offered to pay them to clear off the ancient *malae* at Loka. After the site was cleared of vegetation, I would then follow and map the complex. They agreed to the deal, and on July 25 I headed back to Alofi. I could only afford to pay one assistant to join me. For three days we camped out at Loka. With my plane table and alidade I mapped the backrest stones (Fig. 6.6), the foundation of the chief's house, his coral slab tomb, and a number of other house foundations and smaller burial sites.

Excavations at Loka would have to wait for a return expedition. But I had established that Alofi had been heavily populated and that its paramount chief occupied the most impressive monumental site known on either island. All of this was grist for my nascent theory that the dryland regions of Alofi and Alo had been the centers of political power in late Futunan prehistory, not the irrigated chiefdom of Sigave. This ran counter to the theory of Karl Wittfogel who correlated the rise of political centralization with irrigation. Perhaps the orthodox theories were wrong. Maybe it was the stresses of life in the drylands that provided the impetus to competition and warfare between political entities. Certainly the oral traditions of the Futunan people supported this argument, encapsulating a repeated history of aggression from Alofi and Alo against the irrigated chiefdom of Sigave. Perhaps, just perhaps, I had the evidence to turn accepted theory on its head.

Five months had passed since I arrived on the *Capitaine Tasman*. It had not been easy going, given my tight budget; food, kerosene, and petrol were expensive on

Figure 6.6. This line of quarried beachrock slabs once formed the edge of the *malae* at Loka, seat of the ancient chiefs of Alofi Island. The largest slab was the backrest of the Alofi *sau* or paramount chief when he presided at kava ceremonies.

the island. My food supplies eventually arrived from Noumea, but I was weary of my diet of rice, tinned fish, and corned beef. The occasional gifts of taro, breadfruit, and pork from Aloisia had been godsends. I was now reasonably conversational in Futunan and had filled a dozen notebooks with ethnographic data. The archaeological results, however, were less robust than I would have liked, mostly because I could not afford to hire enough helpers to open big excavations. Nonetheless, my test pits at Nuku and the deep excavation at Tavai had given me key evidence on which to base an outline of Futunan cultural history. I thought I had enough data for a credible PhD thesis. Delving more deeply into the Futunan past would have to wait for another expedition. In my journal I sketched out plans to return, as soon as I could complete my doctorate and secure a position, I hoped, at the Bishop Museum.

My original research plan proposed investigating not just Futuna but also ʻUvea, the other island making up the Territory of Wallis and Futuna. I now knew that this plan had been overly ambitious—just trying to tackle Futuna and Alofi had been a daunting challenge. But I wanted to have a quick look at ʻUvea, mostly to get comparative ethnographic data on that island's agricultural system. A six-seater aircraft occasionally flew between the two islands, carrying French administrators and landing on a crushed coral runway at Vele. With the last of my field funds I booked a seat on the plane to 'Uvea.

My hosts, Sosefo Taufana and his wife Fano in Vailoaloa Village, graciously took me into their thatched *fale* as a guest. With the background I had acquired in Futuna, I gathered enough information from Taufana and his relatives to summarize the main aspects of 'Uvean agriculture, allowing a comparison between the two islands. 'Uvea lacks pondfield irrigation, but taro is grown in drained raised-bed systems along the swampy coastlines. Taufana also took me to several archaeological sites, covered in dense bush. At one location there was an immense walled fortification, nearly smothered in old-growth jungle, along with monumental pigeon-snaring mounds similar to those recorded by Bishop Museum archaeologist McKern in Tonga. I made crude sketch maps of the sites, but any serious study of these ruins was beyond my means.[9]

After a couple of stimulating weeks on 'Uvea the *Capitaine Tasman* steamed through the pass and docked at Mata-utu. I sailed with her back to Futuna where I had left my collections, loaded those into the hold, and then made the round of goodbyes to my friends in Nuku Village (Fig. 6.7). I told everyone that I would

Figure 6.7. My host family at Lalotilo in Nuku Village, standing under a spreading *futu* (*Barringtonia asiatica*) tree. On my left is Aloisia, the widowed head of the *kaiga*, while to my right are her children Lusia, Nikola, and Mikaele. This picture was taken near the end of my stay in Futuna.

return as soon as I completed my Yale thesis and could secure more research funding. Tui Sa'avaka and Kaifakaulu gave me their assurance that the chiefs would welcome me back.

Standing on the fantail as the *Capitaine Tasman* headed out to sea, I watched Futuna's reptilian spine sink below the horizon. Little did I suspect that, despite my best efforts, I would never return. The next morning we docked at Lautoka on the island of Viti Levu. I cleared Fijian customs and arranged to have everything put on the next Quantas flight to Honolulu. Booking a room at the airport hotel, I luxuriated in my first hot shower in six months. A day later, I was home in Honolulu.

Yosihiko Sinoto greeted me in his office in Bishop Museum's Konia Hall, surprised to see how much weight I had lost but pleased to hear that I had found an early pottery site. The museum had an old two-story house on the grounds. Although invaded by termites, Brigham House had a certain charm. The Anthropology Department had taken over some rooms on the second floor, including an office for Doug Yen. A spacious room with windows looking out toward Waikīkī and Diamond Head was vacant; Sinoto told me I could set up shop there. For the next few months I cataloged and classified the pottery from Tavai while organizing my voluminous ethnographic data. I began to write my dissertation, mailing draft chapters to Prof. Chang at Yale for his critique.

Toward the end of 1974, Sinoto took me aside. The museum's contract archaeology program was rapidly expanding. With Doug Yen's urging, Sinoto had proposed to museum director Roland Force that I be appointed assistant anthropologist. It would be a one-year position, at an annual salary of $10,000. Was I interested?

Aside from the fact that I had virtually grown up in the museum—since meeting Yoshio Kondo in 1963—to be part of the institution's staff had always been my dream. But there were other compelling reasons to accept the job offer. The country was in recession, and academic jobs were scarce. Although I would be concentrating on contract archaeology, rather than "pure" research, I hoped that this would be a foot in the door.

The museum's burgeoning archaeology program, with new projects on O'ahu, Hawai'i, and Moloka'i, occupied my days. In the evenings, I consumed endless cups of coffee and worked on my dissertation, developing my theory that the tensions between "wet" and "dry" agricultural systems had played a key role in the evolution of Futunan society and political systems. I took a month's leave from the museum to be "in residence" at Yale in the spring, summarizing my thesis in an oral presentation attended by the faculty, a requirement for graduation.

I finished the 461-page dissertation in the fall. In December 1975 I was informed that the external examiners had approved my dissertation; I would be awarded the degree of Doctor of Philosophy.[10] The museum acknowledged the change in my status with reappointment for a second year, changing my title to associate anthropologist.

Although I had been hired to do contract archaeology, my goal was to continue my Polynesian research. With Doug Yen's urging, I prepared a proposal to the NSF requesting funds to continue the Futunan project. For a few weeks the proposal sat on Director Force's desk. I worried that he would not sign it, because it committed the museum to pay my salary for a year—but in the end the proposal went off to Washington, DC. Six months later an official-looking envelope arrived from the NSF—six peer reviewers had judged my project worthy of funding. I would be able to return to Futuna for eight months and even pay a trained assistant to accompany me. Overjoyed by this good news, I began to plan for my next expedition to Futuna in early 1976.

CHAPTER SEVEN

The Isle of Sacred Coconuts (Niuatoputapu, 1976)

I never intended to go to the "Isle of Sacred Coconuts." My plan was to return to Futuna. News of my Futunan archaeological discoveries—especially the pottery site at Tavai—had created a stir among French archaeologists. Daniel Frimigacci of the Office de la Recherche Scientifique et Technique de l'Outre-Mer, or OR-STOM (the ponderous name of the French overseas research agency), contacted me at the Bishop Museum about my plans for further work in Wallis and Futuna. Frimigacci agreed to a loose collaboration in which I would concentrate on Futuna while he and a French colleague, Jean-Pierre Maître, would work on 'Uvea. They assured me that the Noumea office of ORSTOM would coordinate all necessary research permits.

On May 5, 1976, after weeks of hectic preparations I boarded a Pan American Airlines flight to Nandi, Fiji, and then connected with an Air Pacific flight to Noumea. Accompanying me as a research assistant was Tom Dye, a young photographer with archaeological experience in Hawai'i. Jean-Pierre Maître greeted us as we stepped off the plane at Tontouta Airport. The frown on his face signaled that something was amiss.

"Qu'est-ce qui se passe, Jean-Pierre," I asked. "What's up?"

"The l'Administrateur Superieur has telegraphed that our project has been denied permission."

I could not believe what I was hearing: "That's not possible—you and Daniel told me you had all the permits arranged."

Unfortunately, it was true. The reasons given by the "l'Ad Sup" (as the administrator was known) were vague but stemmed from problems caused by an ORSTOM oceanographic team that had recently visited the island. The next ten days passed in a succession of futile efforts to get the "l'Ad Sup" to reverse his decision.

Soon after our arrival, I began to set an alternative plan in motion. I had contacts at the South Pacific Commission dating to my first visit to Noumea with Kondo in 1968. The administrative officer, Sione Kite, was a Tongan sympathetic to my research. Kite thought the Kingdom of Tonga might grant me a research permit and urged me to send a letter of inquiry to Dr. Langi Kavaliku, Tonga's minister of education.

The National Science Foundation (NSF) had approved my research for Futuna, not Tonga. But I was aware that a small island in the far north of the Tongan archipelago, Niuatoputapu, offered conditions suiting my research objectives. Garth Rogers, a cultural anthropologist from the University of Auckland, had reported pottery sites and stone monuments on the island.[1] I dashed off a telegram (this being well before the age of email) to the NSF's Anthropology Program, requesting permission to change research localities. Within a week the NSF program officer telegraphed back her approval.

After ten days of hopelessly fighting the French bureaucracy, Dye and I returned to Fiji. My request to the Tongan government had been hand-carried to Nuku'alofa. Now we would sit out the next week or so in Fiji waiting to hear whether His Tongan Majesty's government would be amenable to my proposal.

We explored Viti Levu's southern coast including the famous dune site of Sigatoka, where Lawrence and Helen Birks had excavated Lapita pottery in the 1960s. After several days we arrived in Fiji's capital of Suva. I nervously telephoned the Tongan prime minister's office. The voice at the other end of the line identified himself in impeccable British English as Tofa Tuita, chief secretary to the prime minister. My research application was still on Dr. Kavaliku's desk, but Tuita thought that it would be favorably received, and he suggested that we proceed to Tongatapu.

Not much had changed since I had visited the Tongan capital in 1968 on my way back from my land snail collecting expedition with Yoshio Kondo. The dusty port town's most interesting building was the palace, a Victorian gingerbread structure topped with a cupola and surrounded by a low coral-lime mortar wall that kept the royal family's famous pet—a 100-plus-year-old Galapagos tortoise—from roaming outside the palace grounds. Dye and I took up rooms in the venerable old Beach House—the perfect setting for a Somerset Maugham short story—on the waterfront past Queen Salote Wharf. High tea was set every afternoon punctually at 3:00 o'clock on the veranda while dinner was served *en famille* around a huge old table in the Victorian parlor.

Soon after our arrival, Tofa Tuita informed me that the cabinet had formally approved my research; we could now proceed to Niuatoputapu with the full support of His Majesty's government. The challenge was how to get there.

Niuatoputapu lies at the northern extremity of the Tongan Kingdom. In 1976 there was no airfield; a small ship named the *Pakeina* voyaged back and forth between Niuatoputapu and Vava'u roughly every two to three weeks. But Vava'u itself is nearly 180 miles north of Tongatapu. We could fly to Vava'u in a small plane, but that would mean leaving all of our surveying and digging equipment behind. I canvassed the waterfront docks, inquiring about any boats that might be heading north. After several days I was told that a steel-hulled fishing boat, the *Ata,* would sail for Vava'u via Ha'apai. With our essential cargo we boarded the *Ata* on Monday, June 14.

Arriving in the quaint town of Neiafu in Vava'u after two nights and a day at sea, I tried to get information on the whereabouts of the elusive *Pakeina.* Some told me that the ship had mechanical problems and would have to return to Nuku'alofa for repairs; others indicated that it might be coming down from Niuatoputapu in a few days. In the meantime we found lodging in a little *"motele"* run by a Tongan family struggling to make a business out of the occasional tourists who found their way to Vava'u.

Determined not to waste our time in Vava'u, we spent the days surveying some large stone-faced burial mounds.[2] More importantly, we intensively studied the Tongan language using an excellent textbook that had been prepared for the Peace Corps. My prior efforts at learning Futunan were paying off, as I now had a large base vocabulary of Polynesian words; about 70 percent of Tongan words are shared with Futunan. I was already speaking in simple Tongan phrases, and my comprehension increased daily.

It would be another three weeks before the *Pakeina* finally appeared and we could make the last 200-mile leg of what seemed like an interminable odyssey to get to the "Isle of Sacred Coconuts." ("Niua" signifies a place with *niu,* coconuts, whereas *toputapu* is the reduplicated form of *tapu,* "sacred.") Walking down to the wharf to have a look at the ship I was appalled. Seventy-three feet from stem to stern, its white hull streaked with rust, the *Pakeina* was one of the filthiest ships I had ever seen. The one lifeboat had a sizable hole in the bottom, and there were no life preservers. Worse still, I was told that the radio was out of commission. The sole navigational instrument was the ancient compass binnacle in the wheelhouse.

Despite the risks, there was no choice if we were ever going to get to Niuatoputapu. I purchased two tickets, consigning our freight (now consisting of twenty-one crates and boxes of food and supplies, plus kerosene drums for months of anticipated fieldwork) to the supercargo. Dye and I commandeered a bit of space on the afterdeck where we would not be swamped by waves in a heavy sea, lashing our packs to the rails. I had not counted on the thick black smoke that came belching out of *Pakeina's* smokestack, engulfing us as we got underway.

The overnight voyage to Niuatoputapu was largely uneventful, although the *Pakeina* rolled heavily in the long swell, causing the Tongan girl next to me to throw up all night. The captain, Tolati, consulted the ship's compass from time to time, but in the old tradition of Polynesian navigators relied more upon his knowledge of the stars, the winds, and the ocean swells to guide his little ship from island to island.

The Tongans had once been famed seafarers and navigators, sailing in impressive double-hulled canoes carrying cargoes of whale's teeth to Fiji, bringing back precious red parrot feathers, then trading the feathers to Samoa, and returning with fine mats to Tonga. They had been masters of what has been called the "Tongan Maritime Empire," ruling from the royal seat of the Tu'i Tonga or sacred kings at Mu'a on Tongatapu.[3] Niuatoputapu and 'Uvea had once been a part of this far-flung "empire."

Dawn broke clear and bright, but there was no sign of an island. Finally, around 11 a.m. we sighted Tafahi, a cone-shaped volcano a few miles west of Niuatoputapu. Four hours later Tolati steered the *Pakeina* through the narrow pass, and we dropped anchor near the village of Falehau. A whaleboat came out to take us ashore. Climbing up the slippery steps of the stone jetty, filthy with diesel smoke and salt spray, I was greeted by an aristocratic Tongan in his early sixties, dressed impeccably in a black shirt and black cotton kilt, topped off by a finely woven *tao'vala* mat skirt. Two Tongan women, likewise in black, stood at his side. Nikolasi Fonua introduced himself as the *fakafofonga pule'anga* (mouthpiece) of the government. He had received Tuita's cable regarding the two *toketa fakatotolo* (literally, "crawling along slowly doctors," what Tongans call researchers). Fonua bid us sit on two chairs while the women held umbrellas over our heads to shade us from the sun. Green coconuts were offered for us to drink. I felt like a colonial "booh-bah," but I knew that we were being shown a great deal of respect.

Nikolasi Fonua, the nephew of Fakafonua, one of Tonga's highest ranking nobles, had a long and distinguished career as a magistrate and was knowledgeable in Tongan history and traditions. He was serving a six-month term as the island's administrator (his word was basically law on the island), living in the government house attended to by the middle-aged women who cooked for him. With his wife remaining in Nuku'alofa, Fonua was lonely. Over the ensuing months I spent many hours conversing with him, gleaning much about Tongan culture and traditions. Before departing at the end of his tour of duty, Fonua bestowed on me the kava name of one of his ancestors, Kinikinilau. It was a great honor from this Tongan aristocrat.

Dye and I moved into a comfortable thatched *fale* with an adjacent cookhouse in Hihifo Village, where most of the island's 1,300 occupants lived. The modest rent I paid for the *fale* hardly made up for the endless gifts of food from our host

Taniele Loholoho and his family. We reciprocated with corned beef and rice from our supplies.

Unlike Futuna, where many aspects of my daily life had been a struggle, everything on Niuatoputapu was beautifully organized for us. Tonga, along with Hawai'i, was one of the most highly stratified of Polynesian societies.[4] At the apex was the king (*tu'i*), followed by the great nobles (*nōpele*), then the ranks of village chiefs (*hou'eiki*), and finally the commoners (*tu'a*). Soon after our arrival Fonua invited me to the weekly *fono* or meeting attended by the heads of households in the island's villages. I explained our project, with Fonua translating. He made it clear to everyone that they should assist us and then dismissed the *fono*. I was getting an inkling of how a stratified chiefdom really worked.

I reconnoitered the island, thinking out a plan of action for our archaeological investigations. In Futuna I had struggled to find pottery-bearing sites; even late-period monumental sites were not common. In contrast, on Niuatoputapu there seemed to be potsherds everywhere; several stone and *Tridacna* shell adzes turned up as I walked along the paths. Large earthen mounds and stone-faced monuments were numerous. The problem here was not finding sites; it was deciding which ones to focus on.

A mere 6.8 kilometers long with a total land area of 15.2 square kilometers, Niuatoputapu is much smaller than Futuna. Dye and I hiked to Fungamuihelu, the rocky summit of the island's central volcanic ridge, from which we had an unobstructed view (Fig. 7.1). To the northwest lay the island's leeward side with the barrier reef protecting a broad lagoon (and the little *motu* of Hakautu'utu'u); in the distance Tafahi stood sentinel. Turning to the southeast we gazed over the windward or *liku* side. Here a broad, flat expanse of low-lying sandy terrain took up about the same area as the leeward lagoon.

Niuatoputapu sits atop the western edge of the Tonga Trench, a deep submarine chasm running all the way from New Zealand, marking the edge of the Pacific Plate. Along this highly active tectonic boundary, the Pacific Plate is "subducting" or plunging down under the adjacent Fiji Plate. This gigantic tectonic engine is gradually pushing Niuatoputapu upward, on a slight northwest to southeast tilt. Thus the island's broad apron of sandy terrain extending from the volcanic ridge out to the *liku* coast is actually the bed of a former lagoon—which a few thousand years ago looked just like the island's present leeward side—that has been raised a few meters above sea level.

Reconnaissance confirmed that pottery sherds were concentrated in a continuous zone encircling the island's central volcanic ridge. This zone coincided with

Figure 7.1. View of the leeward side and lagoon of Niuatoputapu, with Tafahi Island in the distance, taken from Fungamuihelu, the island's highest point.

a slightly elevated terrace of calcareous sands. I recognized it as a former beach ridge, surmising that at the time the first Polynesians settled the island the shoreline had been situated at the base of the ridge. The sandy apron to the southeast would still have been a lagoon. Thus, the island's land area when people first arrived would only have been about five square kilometers, a third of its modern land area. At the same time, this smaller island would have been surrounded on all sides by lagoons full of fish and shellfish.

This pottery zone, which evidently contained the early period of Niuatoputapu's history, ranged in width from about 60 to 150 meters but had a total circumference of 8.4 kilometers, a formidable area to investigate. In the mid-1970s considerable debate raged among archaeologists about how best to design sampling strategies. Earlier generations of fieldworkers, such as Emory and Sinoto, had simply dug where they happened to find lots of artifacts. That kind of "shotgun" approach often missed important deposits and did not lead to representative coverage of the archaeological record. A scientific approach to archaeology, to which I was committed, called for the use of explicit sampling designs.

I decided that the best way to sample the concentric zone of potsherds would be to dig along "transects" that cut perpendicularly across the zone, with test pits spaced out at ten-meter intervals. After clearing the vegetation along a transect line I would take a series of elevations with my telescopic level. The resulting profiles revealed patterns of undulating old ridges and swales, geomorphological features that developed as the island was pushed upward by tectonic forces and the shoreline steadily shifted seaward. Test pits along the transect revealed stratigraphic variations across the pottery-bearing zone.

To help with the digging I employed a crew of Tongan workmen, starting with four and gradually adding more until our group included ten well-trained assistants. Only my foreman, 'Ofa Halapua, spoke English fluently, giving Dye and me further impetus to improve our Tongan language skills. The crew members became expert diggers, competing with each other to see who could cut the straightest side walls on their test pits. They were fascinated by what we were finding, not only the ubiquitous potsherds but also shell fishhooks and ornaments, abraders of coral and sea-urchin spine, and adzes of stone and *Tridacna* clam shell. They were amazed to learn that their distant ancestors had once made pottery, something that they had thought was a strictly European trait.

Because most of our digging took place some distance from Hihifo Village, I hired our neighbor, Sione "Heke" Hoa, to cook lunch for the crew. The workers arrived in the morning with yams or taro tubers while I provided tinned beef, fish, or sometimes salt mutton. During the morning Heke made an earth oven, baking the tubers and banana-leaf wrapped packets of meat with taro leaves (*lū pulu*). Around noon he saddled up his horse and rode out to wherever we were working, the still-hot meal in saddlebags of coconut leaf baskets. Coconut fronds were laid out as a sort of table, and someone would climb a nearby coconut tree to pick a bunch of green drinking nuts. Following a prayer by one of the men (several were lay ministers of the Free Church of Tonga), we all sat down to a delicious noonday repast. Suitably refreshed, we continued digging until the lengthening shadows of the coconut palms signaled that it was time to head back to the village.

At most of the transects the potsherds consisted of "plainware;" that is, they were from undecorated earthenware vessels, including bowls, jars (some with handles), and cups. But one location, a place called Lolokoka, was special. It was the only place with classic dentate-stamped sherds typical of Lapita pottery. The Lapita people, dating to between about 1300 and 500 BC, had been the first to discover and settle Remote Oceania, the islands and archipelagoes east of the Solomons. I knew it would be important to spend some time carefully investigating the Lolokoka site.

Instead of using a transect, at Lolokoka I laid out a grid over an area of 2,400 square meters, subdividing it into blocks of 100 square meters each. Using a table of random numbers, I then chose a test pit within each sample block. This "stratified random" method assured a representative sample across the entire area. Once I had finished the random sample pits, I plotted out the density of potsherds on a map of the site. A narrow band through the site had a much higher frequency of sherds and other artifacts. This allowed me to implement the second stage of my strategy, laying out several one-by-two-meter trenches in this band. In these trenches we recovered more sherds with the dentate-stamped decorations characteristic of Lapita. Then, in the third and final sampling stage, we homed in on the area of greatest artifact concentration and opened up a twenty-four-square-meter excavation (Fig. 7.2). It exposed a number of intact features such as earth ovens and trash pits.

Our excavations produced a large collection of pottery sherds (more than 43,000), artifacts, and faunal materials that would allow me to reconstruct the early history of Polynesian occupation on Niuatoputapu. After returning to the Bishop Museum I obtained radiocarbon dates from charcoal and shell samples recovered in association with the pottery. Lolokoka, with its Lapita style pottery, was indeed the island's first settlement; a date on a giant clamshell indicated that people might have arrived as early as 1255 to 1085 BC. Other areas such as Pomeʻe

Figure 7.2. Excavation in progress at the Lolokoka site on Niuatoputapu. Lolokoka is the only location on the island where Early Eastern Lapita pottery was found; it was probably the island's initial settlement, early in the first millennium BC.

and Lotoaʻa that yielded only plainware ceramics dated to later in the first millennium BC or to the early centuries of the Christian era.

As in Futuna, I wanted to complement the archaeological work in Niuatoputapu with ethnoarchaeological studies focused on the island's agriculture and ecology. Because Niuatoputapu lacks flowing streams, all of the cultivation was of the dryland variety. I took time out from our digging to explore and map the island's gardens and record the traditional cultivation methods. Several of our workers were noted gardeners; at times I would accompany them when they cleared, planted, and harvested their fields. The most important crop was the *ʻufi* or greater yam (*Dioscorea alata*), although other kinds of yams, dry taro, elephant ear taro, bananas, and other crops were also raised. The Niua people kept pigs in pens, but these animals were not nearly so abundant as in Futuna.

What Niuatoputapu lacked in agricultural system diversity it made up for in the realm of fishing. A diversity of rays, sharks, fishes, mollusks, crustaceans, and turtles teemed in Niuatoputapu's sheltered lagoon, surrounded by fringing and barrier reefs equally rich in marine life. Men, women, and children gathered and caught these marine foods using a wide range of techniques. In our excavations we were finding not only fishhooks and net weights but also a large quantity of shellfish and fishbones. I decided to include marine resource exploitation in our ethnoarchaeological studies. By studying the range of traditional methods that people used to obtain fish and shellfish, I thought we could improve our interpretations of the role of marine resources in the past.

Tom Dye wanted to tackle this part of the ethnographic work. So, while I concentrated on agriculture and plant use, Dye spent time with the island's fishermen (and fisherwomen). Some of our workers took Dye along on their fishing sorties. One lanky bachelor in his forties, Vili Talikihaʻapai, was renowned for catching large parrotfish that sleep at night in the crevasses of the windward reef crest. This kind of fishing—done only by men—not only requires great skill but also is very dangerous, because the swells surging over the *liku* reef can catch a man unawares and sweep him out to sea. On nights when he judged the sea not to be too rough, Talikihaʻapai would venture out to the windward reef carrying a kerosene lantern in his left hand, a three-pronged spear in his right hand. A small sack tied to his waist held dried coconut meat that Talikihaʻapai chewed and mixed with his saliva. Approaching a crevasse in the reef, he would spit out a wad of the oily mass, quickly calming a little "window" into the dark water, which allowed the light of his lantern to illuminate the fish below. Taking careful aim he lanced the spear at the two- or three-foot *menenga,* the most prized kind of parrotfish. More often than not the spear found its mark.

Other fishing methods were less dramatic. Women waded in the shallows of the leeward lagoon swishing about small sacks containing the pounded roots of the *futu* tree (*Barringtonia asiatica*); a toxin within the root stupefied the fish, which then floated to the surface and could simply be picked up and placed in their baskets. Other times they used small scoop nets called *kukusi* to catch small fry among the coral heads. Many other fishing methods involved nets, both smaller hand nets and larger seine nets (*kupenga*), primarily in and around the lagoon. To our surprise, fishing with hook and line proved to be less common than netting. Even rarer was trolling for larger game fish such as *'aku* or *'ahi* (tunas) beyond the reef.

The data we collected on Niuatoputapu fishing changed my ideas about how the ancient Polynesians had exploited the sea. It made me realize that the shell and bone fishhooks often found in Polynesian archaeological sites gave a skewed picture of the importance of hook-and-line fishing. Being made of perishable fiber cordage, nets rarely preserve in the archaeological record (except occasionally in dry rockshelter sites), although we do at times find net weights of shell or stone. But the data from Niuatoputapu showed us that netting, spearing, and fish poisoning were responsible for a greater proportion of the island's total catch than was angling with hooks. In fact, many fish species (such as parrotfish and wrasses) rarely if ever take a hook and must be captured by spearing or netting. The fact that we were finding hundreds of bones of these fishes in our excavations meant that spearing and netting techniques must have been part of the Lapita and early Polynesian fishing repertoire. After we returned to Honolulu, Dye and I coauthored an article in the *Journal of the Polynesian Society* on our findings; it was the first major contribution to an ethnoarchaeology of fishing in the Pacific.[5]

For a third time, I found myself deeply immersed in the daily life of a traditional Polynesian society. Anuta was a tiny society in which the two chiefs mingled freely with the rest of the population, and there were few overt signs of hierarchy. Futuna had two ranks of chiefs (the *sau* and the *aliki* such as Tu'i Sa'avaka), and social stratification and rank were more pronounced, as expressed in the elaborate kava ceremonies. But even though Niuatoputapu was a small and isolated outpost of the Tongan kingdom, it was evident that hierarchy had reached its Western Polynesian apogee in Tonga. The chiefs or *hou'eiki* were accorded considerable status and prestige. Telai, a leading *'eiki* of Hihifo Village, even had the aristocratic habit of speaking about himself in the third person.

Niuatoputapu had once been ruled over by a lineage of high chiefs bearing the title Ma'atu. Eleven generations earlier the founding ancestor, Latumailangi, a collateral relative of the Tu'i Tonga or sacred king of Tongatapu, had arrived on the island, marrying into an older indigenous chiefly line. Under Latumailangi and successive generations of Maʻatu, Niuatoputapu became part of the far-flung Tongan "maritime empire." Each year the Maʻatu sent canoes south to the capital at Muʻa carrying tribute for the great ʻinasi ceremony held on the malae fronting the burial mounds of the Tongan kings. When the eleventh title-holder passed away in 1935 without leaving an heir, the title and the Maʻatu estate passed into the hands of the king.

In the highly stratified Tongan kingdom, a class of great chiefs known as nōpele (a word borrowed from the English "noble") sits between the king and the lesser village chiefs (such as Telai). Each nōpele controls a hereditary estate (tofiʻa); the households residing on these estates are essentially vassals of their lord, with obligations to provide tribute such as food and pigs for feasts (katoanga). After arriving on Niuatoputapu I was told that a nōpele, bearing the title Tangipa, resided in the central village of Vaipoa whose surrounding lands constituted his tofiʻa. Tangipa was reclusive, however, and after several months on the small island I had never met him.

Late one afternoon I was returning to Hihifo along the shady inland trail that skirts the mountain slope, accompanied by Mosese Falala, one of my workmen then in his late forties. At Vaipoa we came across a middle-aged man seated on a log, opening coconuts with his machete and feeding the meat to an excited swarm of pigs. Barefoot, wearing an old pair of trousers and a stained and tattered shirt, he looked like any other island man in old work clothes tending to his chores.

"Mālō e lelei," I called out as we approached the seated figure, using the common Tongan greeting. He did not reply, nor did he rise from his seat on the log. Almost immediately it dawned on me that this individual—despite his dress and the fact that he was feeding a herd of pigs—must be none other than the reclusive nōpele Tangipa. I was embarrassed because I should have greeted him with the expression Mālō e laumalie, which one uses for persons of rank.

Turning to Falala, the nōpele quietly said in Tongan, "You there, go and climb one of those coconut trees and fetch some good drinking nuts for our friend." Climbing a coconut palm is strenuous, a task normally left to teenage boys and young men. Falala had probably not climbed a tree in fifteen years. But the nōpele had given his command and Falala had no choice. Returning flushed and sweating a few minutes later with a large bunch of green nuts, Falala put them down in front of Tangipa, who opened one for me with his machete. Tangipa then uttered another command: "Husk those nuts and lash them to a carrying pole and take them back to the house of our friend so he will have something to drink later." Falala did as ordered. Shortly we were on our way down the path, my companion bearing a heavy load of husked coconuts over his shoulder. It was a fascinating lesson in Tongan noblesse oblige.

As in Futuna, there were periodic feasts or *katoanga* on the island, each associated with a religious holiday, either of the Catholic Church in Vaipoa (Fig. 7.3) or of one of the Methodist churches such as the Siasi Tonga Tauataina (Free Church of Tonga), which Dye and I attended on Sundays. Formal kava ceremonies accompanied these feasts, with the protocol of the *alofi* semi-circle and formal calling of chiefly titles, much as in Futuna. After the kava and feasting, the afternoons passed in long dance performances.

Informal kava drinking on Niuatoputapu was done in the church parish halls, taking a different form than on Futuna. On Friday and Saturday evenings, Dye and I attended the kava drinking at Hihifo's Methodist church, where most of our workers assembled to imbibe and socialize. Inside the large room with its coral stone walls and tin roof, groups of six to twelve men each sat cross-legged in a circle on woven mats. Each group was attended to by an unmarried young woman (the *tou'a*) whose task it was to prepare and serve the kava in a wooden *tano'a* bowl. Each man paid a small fee, the money going into the church coffers. Sometimes, especially on Friday nights, a large *pola* or platter heaped with cooked yams and taro, baked fish or lobsters, and a suckling pig and topped with two or three cakes

Figure 7.3. Women performing an impromptu *tau'olunga* dance during a *katoanga* at the Catholic Church in Vaipoa Village, Niuatoputapu.

was set up on a low dais at one end of the room. Throughout the night each drinking group would bid money toward the prize; the group that ended up contributing the most stumbled away carrying the *pola*. On more than one occasion our group won, hauling our prize to Heke's cookhouse where we gorged ourselves on pork, yams, and cake before going off to bed just before dawn.

By October, hundreds of sample bags full of potsherds, faunal remains, and other artifacts had piled up in our cookshed. Judging that I now had ample materials with which to reconstruct the earlier period of Polynesian life on Niuatoputapu, I decided to turn my attention to the island's earthen and stone monuments. They would be the most likely source of information on the later time periods, especially after Niuatoputapu became integrated into the Tongan maritime empire.

During our surveys of the island we had recorded ninety-five structures that could be loosely classified as "mound" sites, consisting of artificially heaped-up earth or sand, often surrounded by moats or borrow pits from where the earth to build the mound had been dug. These mounds could be divided into those whose sides were faced with quarried limestone slabs in a rectangular configuration and mounds without facings, usually circular and flat topped. Earlier work by pioneering Bishop Museum archaeologist W. C. McKern in the more southerly Tongan islands had shown that the faced mounds were most likely sepulchers, the burial places of chiefs; in some cases they were where certain lineages had interred their dead.[6] Such burial mounds were known as *fa'itoka* or, in the case of a few mounds with especially impressive, large dressed stone facades, *langi*.

The unfaced mounds could likewise be subdivided into two types. One set had their flat tops paved with fine gravel; informants called these *'esi* and told us that they were sitting platforms for persons of high rank. The other category lacked paving, but often there was a shallow depression, sometimes outlined with stones, in the center of the mound's flat top. Many of the flat-topped unfaced mounds were impressive, ranging from ten to forty meters in diameter and standing three or even four meters above the surrounding ground. The largest mounds incorporated more than two thousand cubic meters of earth, requiring a great deal of labor from people who lacked mechanical digging implements.

The mounds with the central depressions were called *sia heu lupe*, literally "mound for snaring pigeons." *Lupe,* the Pacific pigeon (*Ducula pacifica*), flourishes in areas with *Eugenia* plum trees, whose fruit they consume. McKern described how in pre-European times the Tongan chiefs practiced the sport of pigeon snaring:

The sportsmen occupied the structure, some on the mound surface where they manipulated the heu [net] poles, and some in the pit to take the pigeons from the snare. Captive pigeons attached to long cords, were allowed to fly among the tree tops above the mound where they served as decoys to attract their wild kin. When the wild pigeons came, the heu manipulators dropped the net over them and brought them down into the pit, where they were caught and disposed of by the men assigned to that task.

I mapped several of these *sia heu lupe* and excavated trenches across a particularly large example at Funga'ana, hoping to find charcoal to radiocarbon date. Unfortunately, the trenches revealed only sandy fill.

It was important, I felt, to get some evidence for the age of mound construction. Excavation of a stone-faced burial mound was the obvious choice but posed ethical issues. Most of the larger *fa'itoka* and *langi* were associated with family lineages or with oral traditions linking them to notable chiefs. We could hardly go about digging up the ancestors of the island's population. However, on the island's *liku* coast at a place called Houmafakalele, I had seen a group with one large and three mid-sized mounds, all faced with cut-and-dressed coral limestone blocks. No one seemed to have any knowledge of who might be interred in these structures; there were no traditions related to the Houmafakalele mound complex.

I asked Telai, the chief of Hihifo, whether it would be permissible for our team to open up an excavation in the main mound at Houmafakalele to see if it did indeed contain burials and, if so, to take a small sample of bone for radiocarbon dating. After consulting with other village elders, Telai agreed to this plan. The work began with a prayer service conducted by one of our workers who was a minister of the Methodist church, asking that we be watched over and that no harm should come to any of us. In a two-by-three-meter excavation in the center of the mound we uncovered three adult skeletons, all lying in extended, supine positions. Dark black stains in the white sand surrounding the skeletons may have derived from the black pigment used to dye barkcloth in which the bodies were wrapped for burial. There were no grave goods or artifacts.

We carefully photographed and mapped the skeletons, making all of our observations without removing the bones from their original position. We took one small sample of bone from one skeleton for radiocarbon dating, which later gave an age of AD 1420–1815, confirming that these formal burial mounds were a late aspect of the island's history. We then respectfully re-covered the skeletons with sand, restoring the mound surface to its original condition.

The work at Houmafakalele took until the middle of November. We had been gone from Honolulu for more than six months; my field funds were starting to run low.

Doug Yen had written from Hawai'i to tell me that the NSF was going to fund a second phase of the Solomon Islands Culture History project. The time had come to close up the Niuatoputapu research. I wanted to have at least a few months' rest in Honolulu before going out on another long expedition to the eastern Solomons.

We packed up the artifacts, pressed plants, and other natural history specimens, along with rolls of mats and barkcloth that I had obtained for the Bishop Museum's ethnology collections. Our friends and workers held a big *kai mavae* or farewell feast and kava drinking on November 22. Two days later the *Pakeina* maneuvered out through the narrow passage with Tolati at the helm, headed for Vava'u. Luck was with me on the return trip; after only four days' wait in Nei'afu the *Olovaha* ferry departed for Nuku'alofa. I spent the first week of December making official rounds in the capital and also visiting Nikolasi Fonua. Returning via Fiji, I arrived home in Honolulu on December 9, 1976.

It would take me twelve years to complete the analysis of all of the materials we excavated in the rich sites of Niuatoptapu. Eventually, in 1988, I published my scientific account of the island's archaeology in a thick monograph titled *Niuatoputapu: The Prehistory of a Polynesian Chiefdom*. With fifty tables of data and illustrated with more than one hundred maps, plans, charts, and photographs, the volume records for posterity the findings of our 1976 expedition.[7]

In *Niuatoputapu* I outlined a sequence of cultural change beginning with Lapita voyagers around 1000 BC and ending with the arrival of the Wesleyan missionaries around AD 1830. In spite of being one of the smallest of the Western Polynesian islands, Niuatoputapu's unbroken cultural sequence encapsulates the emergence of an Ancestral Polynesian culture from earlier Lapita origins. Niuatoputapu and other islands of Western Polynesia such as Futuna, 'Uvea, Samoa, and Tongaputapu were the original *Hawaiki,* the homeland in which early Polynesian language and culture developed. Our months of digging into the middens of Niuatoputapu provided a cornerstone for our understanding of that critical time in the history of the Polynesian peoples.

CHAPTER EIGHT

Matou, Nga Tikopia
(Tikopia, 1977)

A couple of days after returning from Tonga in December 1976 I knocked on the frosted glass doors of Doug Yen's office at the Bishop Museum. Hearing Yen's distinctive Kiwi-accented voice within, I entered the spacious oval room filled with the scent of Dunhill pipe tobacco. Makeshift work tables were piled high with notebooks and specimens of *Canarium* almond whose variation across the Pacific Yen was studying. "Doug, I hear we are heading back to the eastern Solomons." Setting down his pipe, Yen motioned to a chair opposite his desk. "Yeah, NSF has funded the new grant. We'll be one of several field teams going to the Solomons early next year." Yikes, I thought to myself, I would barely have time to sort out my Niuatoputapu collections before heading off on another lengthy field season.

The first phase of Bishop Museum's Southeast Solomon Islands Culture History Program in 1970–1971 had succeeded beyond Yen's and Roger Green's expectations. The new, second phase of the project would encompass the entire Santa Cruz group of islands, including the large island of Nendö, as well as Utupua and Vanikoro to the south and the Polynesian Outliers of Anuta, Taumako, and Tikopia (see Map 2). The logistics would be complicated. Several teams would alternate over two years, sharing a common pool of equipment based out of Mbanwa Village on Nendö. Yen and I would make our first six-month trip beginning in March 1977; a second trip was planned for 1978. Meanwhile other teams would work on Nendö, the Reef Islands, and Taumako.

The project's first phase had established the primacy of Lapita as the founding culture in these islands, a key steppingstone to Fiji and the Ancestral Polynesian homeland in Tonga and Samoa. Roger Green's excavations in the Reef Islands had already filled in gaps in our understanding of the Lapita culture at the end of the second millennium BC. But there were lots of unanswered questions. The cultural sequences of the larger islands needed to be fleshed out, especially the transition from early Lapita to later time periods. Had the diverse mix of indigenous cultures and languages in the Santa Cruz Islands derived from a common Lapita ancestor? Our 1971 excavations on Anuta had shown that the island had been settled almost as early as the Reef Islands with their Lapita sites, yet the Anuta pottery had its own distinctive characteristics. Did these two kinds of pottery indicate the presence of two distinct cultures in the eastern Solomons three thousand years ago? What was the relationship between Green's Lapita sites and the early settlement on Anuta? To address these questions I planned to reopen our 1971 excavations on Anuta. In addition, Yen and I would spend several months investigating Tikopia, another Polynesian Outlier a day's sail from Anuta.

No Polynesian island is more famed among anthropologists than Tikopia, thanks to Sir Raymond Firth who studied the island's people and culture intensely. In the 1920s Firth was mentored by the famed Polish scholar Bronislaw Malinowski, the "father of ethnography." Malinowski urged anthropologists to immerse themselves in indigenous cultures, learning the language and engaging in "participant observation." Malinowski himself had shown the way with his multiyear study of the Trobriand Islands.[1]

Firth found his opportunity for deeply engaged ethnography on Tikopia in 1928–1929, an island so isolated and small (it has a land area of 4.6 square kilometers) that the modern world had bypassed it. The Tikopia speak a distinct Polynesian language, govern themselves through a system of four hereditary chiefs, and provide their own food through intensive farming and fishing using age-old methods. There are no trade stores, no resident missionaries or government officials, not even a doctor. As it had been on Anuta in 1971, living on Tikopia in the late 1970s was like stepping back in time—most people wore barkcloth garments (Fig. 8.1) and practiced material arts and crafts that had long disappeared from other Polynesian societies (Fig. 8.2). They occupied thatched houses grouped into small clusters (*noforanga*) strung out along the sandy beach ridges, fronted by the graceful outrigger canoes with hulls hewn of *tamanu* wood hauled up on the sand.

Firth had meticulously documented every aspect of Tikopia society and culture. In 1928, half of the islanders still practiced their traditional religion with its annual cult cycle; Firth became witness to what the Tikopia call "the work of the gods." *We, the Tikopia*, published in 1936, described the island's kinship system and social organization.[2] The title is a translation of the expression "*Matou, Nga Tikopia*," a phrase often on the lips of the Tikopia. For decades *We, the Tikopia* was required reading in introductory anthropology courses around the world; I had absorbed it while taking Prof. Douglas Oliver's class at the University of Hawai'i in 1970. Now, I was about to experience Tikopia culture firsthand.

As dawn broke on May 6, 1977, I stood on the heaving bridge of the *M. V. Bilikiki*, peering into the mist, searching for a speck of land, any land. The previous night we had ridden out a gale that brought waves crashing over the forecastle of the 120-foot former long-line fishing boat. Water sloshed over the cabin floor. Every

Figure 8.1. Tikopia women, wearing barkcloth skirts bound with sennit belts. The two women on the left have old loincloths of a deceased relative around their necks, a sign that they are in mourning. The woman on the right is carrying a bundle of freshly made barkcloth on her back.

time the ship plunged into a trough between the towering swells, her stern rose up, thrusting the propeller out of the water and causing the drive shaft to send gut-wrenching vibrations down the length of the keel. The ship was not in the best condition to begin with, and I feared that the *Bilikiki* might break apart.

The captain, flanked by the first mate and helmsman, scanned the horizon with his binoculars. *"You me stop long way?"* (Where are we?) I asked the captain in Solomon's pidgin. His reply was not reassuring: *"You me no savvy."* (I've got no idea.) Like all of the small ships that made these Eastern Outer Islands runs, the *Bilikiki*'s captain navigated by dead reckoning. GPS was still years in the future and the captain was not trained in celestial navigation. The storm had thrown us way off our intended course. All we could do was to sail in big, overlapping circles, endlessly searching.

As the hours passed, I recalled the events of the past month and a half. I had left Honolulu forty-five days earlier, meeting Yen in Honiara. Accompanied by

Figure 8.2. A Tikopia man carving a canoe hull from a *tamanu* log. He uses an adz, much as his ancestors would have, except that its blade is of iron rather than *Tridacna* clam shell.

Lawrence Foanaota, curator of the newly founded Solomon Islands Museum, Yen and I flew on the weekly small plane to Nendö, then sailed on the *M. V. Bona* for Vanikoro. At Puma Village on Vanikoro's Tevai islet we set up camp in a thatched hut elevated on wooden posts a few feet from the beach. Our goal was to quickly reconnoiter Vanikoro to assess the unexplored island's archaeological potential.

For eleven days Yen, Foanaota, and I surveyed parts of Tevai islet and Vanikoro's eastern coast, ringed with crocodile-infested mangrove swamps. Only a few hundred people live in scattered hamlets on this densely forested island. There being few roads or even trails, our survey was done by dugout canoe, propelled by an ill-maintained tiny Seagull outboard engine. On a long trip up the east coast the Seagull refused to start, forcing us to paddle for hours back to Puma. Another day we had climbed a steep watercourse on Tevai, fruitlessly searching for a rumored site. Yen slipped on the mossy rocks and cut his shin, an injury that would later plague him on Tikopia. Despite these challenges, on a deserted beach called Emo on Tevai, I found *Tridacna* shell adzes and pottery sherds scattered over the surface of a large sand dune. The site looked promising for excavations the following year.

In mid-April the *Bona* returned to Puma and we sailed through the night to Tikopia. The plan was to drop Yen on Tikopia, while Foanaota and I would return to Nendö. There I would await another ship, the *M. V. Bilikiki,* which would take me to Anuta where I would reopen excavations in the early pottery-bearing site that we had dug in 1971.

Yen off-loaded his supplies and equipment, while I had a quick look around Tikopia. If all went according to schedule, I would be back here in about six weeks, joining Yen who would have started his investigation of Tikopia horticulture. That afternoon, leaving Yen settled in a thatched *fare* made available by the island's second-ranked chief, Foanaota and I said our farewells and reboarded the *Bona* for the return to Nendö.

The night after we left Tikopia, the *Bona* nearly ran aground on Pileni Island. Relying on dead reckoning again, the captain had miscalculated our position. Because he thought we had ended up east of Taumako, he then decided to run through the night to the Reef Islands. In fact, we were far west of Taumako and quite close to the Reef Islands, a dangerous cluster of atolls. Fortunately, the sea was calm, and in the moonlight the helmsman spotted the thin white line of breakers crashing on Pileni's reef just in time to avoid running the *Bona* onto the coral rampart.

For eleven days I waited in Mbanwa Village for the *Bilikiki* to arrive. We finally sailed from Graciosa Bay on May 2, stopping first at the Reef Islands and then proceeding the next day to Taumako. The weather had been perfect; I was optimistic about making a safe landing on Anuta. As we steamed from Taumako toward remote Anuta, however, the weather changed for the worse. Thursday morning, May 5—the day of our intended landfall on Anuta—I awoke to a gray sky with hanging misty clouds. The sea was running a big swell with lots of chop; Anuta was nowhere to be seen. At 9:30 a.m. the mist abruptly parted, revealing a volcanic spire rising sheer from the ocean, two or three miles dead ahead. This was Fatutaka, an uninhabited bird island thirty-five miles southeast of Anuta. Unknowingly, we had run past Anuta in the early morning, the thick mist hiding the little island. Our error revealed, the captain turned course.

By the time we approached Anuta in the early afternoon the island was engulfed by a wall of crashing foam. One canoe braved the surf and came out through the narrow pass. Watching it brought back memories of Vaovaomoana being sundered on the reef in 1971. The lone canoe picked up Pu Paone and his wife with their few bundles of possessions from the *Bilikiki*. As the canoe left the ship's side Pu Paone shouted that they would try to return and get me, but I had a sinking feeling that would not happen. They were lucky to make it back through the pass. I watched through binoculars as the canoe was hauled up the beach. As waves broke over *Bilikiki*'s bow, we turned and headed for Tikopia.

Now, after that dreadful night at sea, we were searching for Tikopia. Around noon a shout went up as someone's sharp eyes picked up the island's 380-meter peak poking above the waves. The *Bilikiki* dropped anchor off the reef at Matautu a couple of hours later; I waded ashore across the same reef flat I had left eighteen days earlier. Yen greeted me on the beach: "What the hell are you doing here? You're supposed to be on Anuta."

"It's a long story, Doug. Let's go boil up a pot of tea in your hut and I'll tell you the whole saga."

Of all the islands that I have spent time on, Tikopia is without doubt the most stunningly beautiful (Fig. 8.3). Firth described his first impression, from the deck of a heaving ship, "of a solitary peak, wild and stormy, upthrust in a waste of waters." Looking down on the island from the peak of Reani, one sees "a hollow bowl, old, battered, and moss-grown, with a broken irregular rim, one side of which is very much gapped and the interior partially full of water." The circular mountain crest is the remnant of an andesitic volcano that blew up about eighty thousand years ago, leaving the deep crater—Lake Te Roto—which was breached by the sea. To the west of the volcanic hills, a low-lying plain of calcareous sand has accreted on the island's leeward side.

About 1,200 people lived on Tikopia in 1977. The island is divided into Faea District on the northwest and Ravenga District on the south, fronting the lake. The inner shore of the lake, Uta, was in Firth's day the sacred district where each lineage had its own temple (*fare tapu*); today Uta lies abandoned, but the district is still regarded as a *tapu* place (Map 5). Here and there among the betel nut groves of Uta one comes across moss-covered upright stones marking the former sites of sacred kava ceremonies.

Everyone belongs to one of four primary clans (*kainanga*), each headed by a hereditary chief (*ariki*) whose title bears the clan name. Ariki Kafika ranks first among the four, followed by Ariki Tafua, Ariki Taumako, and Ariki Fangarere. Ariki Tafua resides in Faea; the other three *ariki* live in Ravenga. Because his

Figure 8.3. Te Roto, the crater lake of Tikopia, as seen from Reani, the island's highest peak. The larger volcanic pinnacle on the left is Fongotekoro, the "fortress hill" famed in Tikopia traditions. The smaller pinnacle on the right is Fongoanuku; the house where I lived in Ravenga lies at its base, on the lakeshore.

noforanga or hamlet is at Matautu, near the main anchorage and landing spot, Ariki Tafua by custom greets visitors to Tikopia. In his late fifties, Ariki Tafua was a generous and well-regarded chief. He spoke no English and little pidgin, although his sons Edward and Patterson both spoke reasonably good English. Ariki Tafua ordered that a bachelor hut (bearing the house name Taraula) be cleared out for our use. Following Polynesian customs of adoption, Ariki Tafua insisted that Yen and I address him as "Daddy" and his wife as "Mommy," words he had been told were the proper English form of address to one's parents!

My prior efforts to learn Tongan on Niuatoputapu now paid off handsomely, as I quickly learned to make the necessary phonetic and grammatical shifts from Tongan to Tikopian. The Tikopia laughingly corrected my mistakes, but it made a huge impression that I was talking to them in their own language. It also meant that I was able to obtain ethnographic data on fishing, gardening, and other topics.

We had plenty of canned food, rice, and kerosene for the lanterns and stove. But our Tikopia neighbors continually brought us taro and manioc puddings,

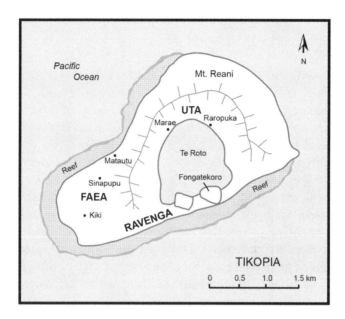

Map 5. Tikopia Island, with localities mentioned in the text.

baked breadfruit, and fish. We reciprocated with tinned fish and corned beef, a rare treat on an island without a trade store. The young Tafua men often went night spearing for parrotfish or groupers. Often, after returning past midnight, they would shake the thatch of our hut to wake us, tossing a couple of lobsters or some fish onto the mat-covered floor. Lacking refrigeration, we would rise and light the Primus stove, boiling the crustaceans for an early breakfast. Sometimes, they brought us flying fish, whose firm flesh is delicious when pan-fried. One of the most entrancing sights I have ever witnessed was that of scores of canoes dancing on the waters just beyond the reef, each illuminated by the light of sputtering co-conut frond torches on a moonless night, netting flying fish.

Other aspects of our life were more primitive. Like everyone else we used the beach as our toilet. Water for bathing and cooking had to be carried in buckets from the single tap near the chief's house. Shared by the whole village, the water flowed from a small spring inland through a one-inch metal pipe (in Firth's time the water flowed through bamboo tubes). Our hut had no furniture, only woven coconut mats covering the sandy floor. We got used to doing all of our chores on our hands and knees, sitting cross-legged to eat or write up notes. The most annoying thing was the presence of countless flies during the day (they would descend in droves on a plate of food), matched by the ceaseless mosquitoes at night.

Comfortably settled in Taraula, we began the archaeological work. In the first few days of walking around the island, I noticed stone walls and alignments—the foundations of former *noforanga*—in the Faea lowlands. Ariki Tafua told me that some ruins at a place called Takaritoa were the abandoned houses of Nga Faea, one of the ancient clans that had been driven off the island in a war with Nga Ariki. I had read about this war in Firth's *History and Traditions of Tikopia*.[3] Based on the genealogy of Ariki Tafua's ancestors, this fight took place during the seventeenth century AD. Takaritoa had obviously been an important place, because between two house foundations stood a row of upright basalt slabs, the backrest stones of the ancient Nga Faea chiefs when they held their kava ceremonies to honor Feke, the eel god. The largest slab—which reminded me of the *marae* at Loka on Alofi—had been that of Pu Perurua, a famed Nga Faea warrior.

Walking the muddy paths through the orchard gardens of Faea, searching the ground between the thickly planted taro and yams, I began to find artifacts, especially *Tridacna* shell adzes. I surmised that this area inland of the present hamlets had once been a main habitation zone. Then, in a manioc garden at Kiki, I found the first potsherds, dislodged from the ground by a planter's digging stick. The reddish-brown sherds tempered with calcareous sand looked much like the pottery we had recovered on Anuta.

My experience in Niuatoputapu had convinced me that my transect method was the best way to sample these sites, along lines running from the coast inland, extending if need be to the base of the volcanic hills. Several of Tafua's sons and nephews helped with the digging as we opened test pits throughout the Faea coastal flat. These pits revealed deep stratigraphic sequences, going down two meters or more before hitting ancient beach sand. A few of the pits turned up potsherds unlike those from the Kiki garden; they had lithic temper and were decorated with incised lines. We also recovered adzes made from giant *Tridacna* clam shell, along with shell ornaments and armband fragments. It looked like the archaeological record of Tikopia was going to be rich.

After digging the first five transects a pattern began to emerge. The deeper layers containing pottery were concentrated in the inland test pits, with only recent or historic period artifacts in the seaward pits. This confirmed my suspicion that the island's shoreline had moved progressively seaward over time. In the past, the old shoreline had been closer to the volcanic hillside; the area now in orchard gardens had then been the main village zone. As the shoreline moved seaward the older habitation areas were abandoned, and new houses were constructed closer to the beach. The soil around the abandoned house sites, enriched with charcoal raked out from countless cookhouse fires, provided fertile ground for new gardens.

I turned my attention to the stone house foundations that Ariki Tafua had pointed out as the ancient village of the Nga Faea. These structures sat atop a sandy ridge that I suspected marked the original shoreline. A short distance from the old *marae* at Takaritoa, in a garden called Sinapupu, I found a well-preserved rectangular structure, about twelve and a half by nine meters, whose basalt curbstones had once been the foundation for a thatched house. Ariki Tafua told me that this was Tarengu, the *kafika* or temple of the banished Nga Faea clan.

I laid out a trench one by six meters long, bisecting the curbstones and extending into the middle of the floor of the Tarengu enclosure. Almost immediately we hit two burials. I was worried that the Tikopia workers might object to exposing these skeletons, but they were unperturbed, explaining that these were the remains of the ancient Nga Faea chiefs; hence, they were unrelated to the modern Tikopia. After recording the skeletons I placed the bones in a basket until they could be reburied.

Below the burials we encountered successive layers of grayish-brown sandy midden full of fire-cracked oven stones, shellfish and fishbones, and artifacts. More lithic-tempered pottery with incised designs appeared; some of the larger sherds exhibited reddish pigment between the hachured lines. Unlike the pottery I had found in the Kiki garden site, these sherds resembled Mangaasi pottery from the Vanuatu Archipelago, excavated in the 1960s by French archaeologist José Garanger.[4] Did this mean that the Tikopia people had once been in regular contact with islands to the south? Only more digging would tell.

The trench in Tarengu kept going deeper. Two meters down, I had to confine the digging to a single square meter for fear that a longer trench might collapse. The men kept troweling down, reaching a depth of three and a half meters. I was not sure we were at the bottom of the cultural deposits, but lacking any materials with which to reinforce the sidewalls, I could not risk going any deeper. I was amazed at the thickness of the layers that underlay the Tarengu structure. Nga Faea's temple had only been the final phase of a long sequence of human occupation at Sinapupu.

By now I was eager to test the garden site at Kiki, where I had found the sandy tempered sherds that resembled Anuta ceramics. Here I used the same stratified random sampling method that I had developed at Lolokoka on Niuatoputapu. The cultural deposits at Kiki were shallow, situated at the inland edge of the ancient beach ridge. We found lots of pottery, along with chert and obsidian flakes and other artifacts. The *Tridacna* adzes at Kiki were made from the massive hinge section of the giant clam shell, an early adz type associated with Lapita. One day we found a trolling lure made of *Trochus* shell, a rare artifact type. I was beginning to suspect that the Kiki site was the island's oldest occupation, followed by a later period with the incised pottery similar to that of Vanuatu. Eventually, the Tikopia people had lost the art of ceramics altogether, and pottery was unknown to the Tikopia in historic times.

Yen, who had been helping me with the excavations, was having a rough time. The daily grind of life in Tikopia, without Western comforts, was taxing for me, let alone for a man in his late fifties. For Yen this difficulty was compounded by the cut he had sustained on his leg at Vanikoro. The ugly, ulcerated wound was now the size of a silver dollar, exposing the shin bone. Yen changed the dressing every day, but the ulcer was not responding to antibiotics. He began to tire easily, leaving the dig to go back and rest in Taraula. One afternoon I returned to find Yen shaking uncontrollably in a high fever. There was no way off Tikopia except on one of the government ships; both the *Bona* and *Bilikiki* were in Honiara for repairs. I was seriously worried.

Ariki Tafua and his sons were concerned as well. The *ariki* told me that he wanted to treat Yen using traditional Tikopia medicine; its key element was the *mana*, the spiritual power, that would flow through the chief's hands into Yen's body, helping him heal. It was worth a try. Yen feebly walked up to Ariki Tafua's house, lying down on the soft mats. Taking a container of coconut oil infused with medicinal herbs, the chief poured some of the liquid onto Yen's chest, then began to massage him. Yen said it felt good, warming. I could see the tension go out of his face. Ariki Tafua repeated the treatment over several days. Gradually, Yen's fever disappeared; he regained his appetite. The ulcer did not heal, but it stopped expanding. Yen would not fully recover until we left the island, but Ariki Tafua's treatment prevented a much worse fate.

By late June I was ready to turn to the Ravenga and Uta districts. Walking through Uta, the former center of Tikopia ritual life, I had seen that the narrow plain underfoot consisted of an extensive midden. The black, charcoal-enriched soil contained abundant shellfish remains. I wanted to excavate those deposits to find out if they held the same kinds of pottery and artifacts as in Faea or something different.

Father Luke, the Tikopian Anglican priest, offered the use of his ancestral *noforanga* at Nuku in Ravenga, near the lake at the base of a volcanic pinnacle called Fonganuku. The house was situated in a grove of betel nut palms, with a moss-covered stone terrace that evoked a Japanese garden. The Nuku *fare* was an old and revered dwelling, with stout posts of *tamanu* wood supporting the roof framework of carved rafters held together with sennit lashings. The spacious interior was a miniature museum of Tikopia material culture, filled with canoe paddles, bows and arrows, *tiri* fishing nets, and dance paddles; bundles of sacred turmeric wrapped in white barkcloth hung from the main rafters. Stone uprights edged the *matapaito* side of the house, facing the lake; in front were the *tapakau* grave mats of the ancestors. Father Luke told me that a dozen of his predecessors were interred beneath the woven mats. He admonished us to sleep with our heads to the *matapaito* side, as the Tikopia themselves do, thus "cradling yourselves on the ancestors' heads." It took awhile to get used to the idea of sleeping in a graveyard.

After settling in, I laid out a plan for the Ravenga and Uta excavations. We would begin with a series of transects across the narrow sand spit that separates the lake from the sea, where most of the Ravenga people live. Then I would move systematically through Uta District in a counterclockwise fashion, testing key localities.

The Ravenga excavations progressed quickly, exposing shallow cultural deposits lacking pottery. In fact, many pits contained artifacts of Western origin, dating back only to the past several centuries. The narrow sand spit that separates the lake from the sea was obviously a geologically recent feature that had formed on the old reef flat, probably at the same time that the Faea shoreline prograded seaward. I realized that the brackish water lake, Te Roto, must have originally been an embayment open to the sea. No wonder that the Uta middens I had walked across were filled with the shells of marine mollusks—the shores of Uta had once been productive reef flats. It was becoming clear that Tikopia had undergone dramatic ecological changes in the not-too-distant past.

I enjoyed living in the beautiful old *fare* at Nuku. My Tikopian language skills had reached a level of conversational fluency. I visited with Ariki Kafika, the island's first-ranked chief, a shy man in his early thirties who seemed uneasy about the weighty role he had inherited. But I was forming a closer bond with the fourth-ranked chief, Ariki Fangarere, whose *noforanga* was a short walk from Nuku. A true Polynesian aristocrat, Ariki Fangarere had an erect bearing and confident, soft-spoken manners. He wore his long hair in the traditional style, falling down his back; he was extensively tattooed. Not long after we settled in Nuku, Ariki Fangarere invited me to take meals with him. Conversing over our dinners of baked fish and taro, I tried to explain, in my best Tikopian, the nature of our work, one day showing him a copy of our Anuta monograph. He looked at the drawings and photographs with great interest.

Yen, however, was not happy in Ravenga. Unable to converse in Tikopian, he did not share the same intimate social relationships that I was enjoying. Worse, he was constantly heckled by the kids who followed him along the paths chanting

"*Tsiaina, tsiaina, e!*" *Tsiaina* is Tikopian for "Chinaman." There was much prejudice throughout the Solomon Islands against the Chinese, who controlled most of the trade stores. Hearing these taunts, Yen told me, reminded him of the tough times he had faced as a young man growing up in White-dominated New Zealand. By the end of the first week of August Yen had had enough of Ravenga, returning to Matautu where he felt at home in the company of Ariki Tafua and his family.

The Uta test excavations began at Somosomo where tradition held that the first rites of turmeric extraction had been held; an upright stone slab marked the event. Another stone was dedicated to the Atua Fafine, the Female Deity. Our test pits revealed a stratified midden containing potsherds with the same incised and red-painted pottery that I had found at Sinapupu.

We then moved to Raropuka, ancestral seat of the lineage bearing the same name, a high-ranking group within the Kafika clan. This too, had been the scene of sacred kava ceremonies. Here, as at Somosomo, we uncovered a layer containing the characteristic incised and painted pottery.

Arriving at Raropuka one morning, I noticed a black *Emoia* lizard, about a foot long, hopping about in the bottom of the pit, unable to climb out. The Tikopia workers were afraid of it, explaining that these lizards were known as Atua i Raropuka, the deity of Raropuka. Since this was the ancestral temple site of Raropuka, they firmly believed that the lizard was a manifestation of the deity. I jumped down into the excavation, chasing the beast around for a few seconds until I could get a hold of it. The men leapt backward in fright as I tossed the lizard out of the hole.

Perhaps the appearance of the Raropuka lizard-god was an omen of things to come. On Friday, July 22, I was sipping my breakfast coffee when one of my workers arrived with the news that Ariki Taumako, the third-ranked chief, had forbidden any further work at Uta. The oldest of the chiefs, Ariki Taumako lived alone in his seaside *fare atua* or temple, which despite his conversion to Christianity he had refused to destroy. Most of Uta District belonged to the Taumako clan; without the *ariki*'s permission it would not be possible to complete the excavation program.

Taking the day off to think things over, I recalled that one strip of land within Uta, Vaisakiri, belonged to Ariki Fangarere. That evening I walked down to Ariki Fangarere's *fare*, entering as always on all fours through the low entryway. We passed some pleasantries and then I broached the subject of Uta. "I suppose you know, my chief, that Ariki Taumako has put a *tapu* on any further digging at Uta." He raised his eyebrows in the classic Tikopian manner (as we would nod our heads). "But what of the place called Vaisakiri? That is your land, not the land of Ariki Taumako. Will you give your permission for me to work there?"

Ariki Fangarere said nothing for a few minutes. Then, looking straight at me he said, "Come here tomorrow morning. Then we two shall talk and I will decide."

It was hard to sleep that night. The *raki* season—hot and humid—was upon us. The light of a full moon peeked through the thatched roof. I got up, walked down the stone-lined path to the lakeshore, stripped off my clothes, and plunged into the cool water. The peak of Reani and the ring of hills, illuminated by moonlight, were reflected in the placid lake.

I woke before dawn to make my coffee, then walked to Ariki Fangarere's house as the sun broke the horizon. The chief too had been up early, hauling in the seine net he had set on the lake the previous evening. Dozens of small tilapia were roasting on hot coals. Sitting cross-legged across from each other on the coconut frond mats, we shared a breakfast of fresh fish and *susua* pudding. Our meal finished, Ariki Fangarere said, "Come. We two will go to Uta. I will show you something."

I followed the *ariki* down the short path to his canoe landing. Gesturing for me to get in, he paddled us across the lake, beaching the canoe at Marae. There is no more sacred place in all of Tikopia.[5] During Firth's visit in 1928–1929, the four clans gathered annually at Marae to perform the *Taomatangi* (the dance to quell the wind) and the *Urangafi* (dance of the flaming fire.) As a young man, Ariki Fangarere had taken part in these rituals, before they were abolished after the final conversion of the Ravenga chiefs to Christianity in 1956.

Grasping my wrist, the chief walked me through the grove of betel palms to what remained of Marae. The wood-and-thatch temple houses had long ago decayed, but the upright stones honoring various deities remained, partly obscured by weeds. The *ariki* showed me in turn the twin stones of Pu Ma, ancestral brothers who were first in the land; the stones of the gods of Kafika, Taumako, and Tafua; the stone of the Female Deity; and others. Periodically he paused, asking in a hushed voice, "*E laue, soa?*" (Is it good, friend?) "*E laue,*" I assured him.

Ariki Fangarere pointed to the low mound called Tae Kava, where the sacred fire burned through the night as the dancers circled it. We walked around the mound, the *ariki* softly chanting the verses of the *Taomatangi*, remembered still from his youth:

Te ata ne tafa i te tonga E!	The dawn broke in the east, O!
Kau ono mai—o	To me appeared
Ko Reani ra E!	Reani then, O!
Turi oke i te toi.	Risen in the sea.
A uru o a maungo	The crests of the mountains

| *ka nokotanumia* | Which were formerly buried [hidden] |
| *E te tai roroto.* | By the swollen tide [empty ocean]. |

I was incredibly moved. Ariki Fangarere was sharing with me the sacred rituals of his island's pagan past. He pointed out the place where the *tapakau* mat marking the burial of the first Ariki Fangarere had once been laid out, on the landward side of the Rarofiroki temple. "Is it good, friend?" He wanted to know that I too, respected the rites that had transpired here, year after year, for centuries. "*E laue, toku ariki*," I reassured him.

After touring Marae we returned to the canoe, paddling the short distance to Vaisakiri. We walked up a little path; the *ariki* pointed out where his *fare tapu* or clan temple had stood. A single rotting post marked the spot. He asked me where I would like to dig. "Not where the temple stood," I replied. It was not necessary to disturb the sanctity of that spot. I merely wished to put down some test pits in the dark midden underfoot. He smiled broadly and raised his eyebrows in consent.

The next day my workers and I dug two test pits at Vaisakiri. We did not encounter pottery, but there was a rich midden with several shell artifacts. I had accomplished my goal of at least sampling Uta. Some day another archaeologist may have the opportunity to continue where I left off, for surely there is much more to discover under the betel orchards of Uta, Tikopia's sacred district.

Our field season was rapidly coming to a close. Word came over the radio that the mission ship *M. V. Southern Cross* would arrive at Tikopia on August 2. We had a *kai faka mavae* or farewell feast with the Tafua clan at Matautu; I assured them I would return the following year to continue the work. It took almost a month after the *Southern Cross* picked us up before I returned to Hawai'i. After touching at Utupua, the ship dropped me at Nendö where I had to wait for the *Bona* to transport my crates of specimens and me back to Honiara. Yen flew back on the small plane to get his ulcer treated. Meanwhile I passed the time in Mbanwa Village cataloging the rich artifact collections. After 160 days in the field I arrived back at Honolulu's international airport on August 28, 1977.

CHAPTER NINE

The Ghost of Sinapupu
(Tikopia and Vanikoro, 1978)

"The tomb of Pu Lasi [Great Ancestor] lies just above us," Father Luke whispered hoarsely below the summit of Fongotekoro, a volcanic pinnacle sandwiched between the lake and the ocean in Ravenga. For a half-hour we had worked our way up the knife-edged ridge that is the only route to the top, clinging to banyan tree roots and lianas. Sweat poured out of us in the tropical morning heat. To my right a sheer cliff plunged two hundred feet to the surf crashing at the pinnacle's base.

Fongotekoro translates as "fortress hill." Father Luke, the island's first Tikopian priest, had offered to guide me to the top of Fongotekoro to see the tomb of Pu Lasi, famed ancestor of his Taumako clan. Thirteen generations before Raymond Firth's fieldwork—according to the genealogy of the Taumako chiefs—a voyager from Tonga named Te Atafu arrived in Tikopia. Claiming to be the son of the Tu'i Tonga or sacred ruler of Tongatapu, Te Atafu asserted his status in this new island. The war club that he brought with him from Tonga, representing the eel god Tuna, is still in the possession of Te Atafu's descendant, Ariki Taumako.

Te Atafu married Matapona, a daughter of Ariki Kafia Veka, who bore him a son, Pu Lasi.[1] Uniting the Tongan blood of his father and the *afukere* or "earth-sprung" blood of the ancient Kafika lineage, Pu Lasi became the founding ancestor of the Taumako clan. When he was old, Pu Lasi withdrew from the daily affairs of the chiefship, taking up residence atop the fortress pinnacle of Fongotekoro. Upon his death he was buried there. It is the duty of every Taumako clan member, Father Luke told me, to climb Fongotekoro at least once in his lifetime, carrying a small basket of sand to place upon the tomb of Great Ancestor.

Cresting the ridge we stood on the few square yards of level ground atop the pinnacle. In the center of a small clearing was Pu Lasi's resting place, a simple mound faced with volcanic slabs. The tips of two femurs protruded above the sand. Father Luke pulled a small sack from his pocket, pouring clean white sand over the exposed bones. We sat for a long while on Fongotekoro's summit, admiring the superb view. Long swells crashed relentlessly on the windward reef, curls of salty mist rising into the air, while red-footed boobies and white-tailed tropic birds glided effortlessly on the air currents.

It was mid-August 1978; I had arrived back on Tikopia on July 20. As usual, the trip out via Nendö had been complicated. Arriving in the Solomons, I had purchased supplies in Honiara and then flew on the small Solair plane to Graciosa Bay, settling in to the thatched hut in Mbanwa Village that served once again as our base camp. Yen, who had preceded me, was on Utupua, waiting for the *Bona* to take him back to Nendö.

The Solomon Islands were in the throes of a transition; the British Solomon Islands Protectorate would become an independent nation on July 7. The frenzy of preparations for the Independence Day celebrations had thrown everything into chaos. The Eastern Outer Islands' shipping schedule, never completely trustworthy, seemed to change every day. I passed several rainy days reading and doing odd chores in the one-roomed, sago-leaf hut. On July 2 the *Bona* entered Graciosa Bay, and I walked the two miles from Mbanwa to the wharf to greet Yen.

Over warm beers in the Mbanwa hut we hashed out plans for the coming months. As soon as the Independence Day celebrations were concluded, we would sail again on the *Bona*. Yen would go to Vanikoro, accompanied by Jocelyn Powell, a New Zealand palynologist, and her husband, John. Yen planned to core Vanikoro's swamps to extract pollen that Powell would use to reconstruct the long-term history of vegetation changes. I would continue on to Tikopia to excavate two key sites for about six weeks. Then, boat schedules and weather permitting, I would make another try at landing on Anuta. Toward the end of the field season, if everything worked out, I would join Yen on Vanikoro for several months of combined archaeological and ethnobotanical work.

The Powells flew in to Nendö a few days later. John Powell, it seemed, was quite a drinker. Most of his baggage consisted of cartons of Australian wine-in-the-box. On the night of July 6, the eve of Solomon Islands independence, he downed glass after glass of cheap red wine. An Englishman, Powell was maudlin about the end of the British Empire. Just before midnight he stumbled into the circular stone-curbed dance plaza in the middle of Mbanwa, singing at the top of his voice, "Rule, Britannia! Britannia rules the waves; Britons never, never, never will be slaves." Heaven knows what our Mbanwa neighbors thought of this.

Independence Day passed with no sign that the ships would be sailing any time soon. The shack at Graciosa Bay that passed as a store had laid in countless crates of Four-X Castlemain beer for the celebrations; *Bona's* crew seemed determined to drink every last bottle. They were grumbling that they had not received their wages from the new government and might go on strike. The *Bilikiki* finally arrived on July 14 with my cargo; she tied up next to the *Bona* where the two crews proceeded to get drunk together. A few days later the local council clerk agreed to advance the crew's wages and we finally sailed on the night of July 18. The next day we dropped Yen and the Powells at Puma Village on Vanikoro, the *Bona* departing for Tikopia at sunset.

The following day I was greeted by "Daddy" and "Mommy" Tafua and their family, sharing a welcome meal of fish and *susua* pudding while seated on the woven *tapakau* mats in the chief's spacious house at Matautu. We moved my supplies and gear into Taraula, the same hut I had shared with Yen the previous year. The following day I made the rounds to visit the three chiefs in Ravenga. Ariki Fangarere in particular seemed pleased that I had returned, insisting that I come and eat with him sometimes.

If the *Bona* kept to her schedule she would be back in about six weeks, giving me just enough time for some concentrated excavations in Faea, where I had found the best archaeological deposits in 1977. My first goal was to expand the excavations at Kiki (site TK-4). After studying the Kiki pottery in the Bishop Museum laboratory I had become convinced that Kiki had been the island's first settlement. The pottery, which I now called Kiki Ware, was a variant of Lapita, made by the first people to settle this region. Second, I wanted to dig a transect of test pits across the old beach ridge at Sinapupu. I felt that this locality with its deep layers underlying the Tarengu temple held the key to Tikopia's long history. I needed to work out the full stratigraphic sequence and to sample the deposits with the interesting incised and painted pottery, what I now tentatively called Sinapupu Ware. Coming after the Lapita-related Kiki Ware in the stratigraphic sequence, I thought that the Sinapupu Ware might represent a period when the island had contacts with islands to the south, in northern Vanuatu. But more work was needed to confirm this hypothesis.

With my crew of Tikopia workers we started at Kiki, opening test pits along four transects, allowing me to define the extent of the layers containing the Kiki Ware pottery. I estimated the size of the island's founding settlement to have been about 1,500 square meters (a little less than a half-acre), just big enough for a cluster of thatched huts that might have sheltered three or four families. The test pits revealed that the thickest deposits were in the site's western corner. Laying out two larger excavation blocks, we recovered lots of potsherds (some with simple dentate stamped designs proving that Kiki Ware was a variant of Lapita pottery) along with shell adzes, fishhooks, and ornaments.

I was especially excited when we found several flakes of obsidian, which I knew did not naturally occur on Tikopia. Later geological analysis traced these flakes to sources in the Bismarck Archipelago, more than 1,300 miles to the west. We also recovered flakes of chert and chalcedony from the main Solomon Islands, some 700 miles distant. These discoveries showed that the island's founding population had been linked into the long-distance Lapita trade network. Ancestors of the later Polynesians, the Lapita voyagers maintained contacts between the islands they settled, sailing in outrigger canoes propelled by woven mat sails. A charcoal sample pried out of an earth oven at Kiki later yielded a radiocarbon date between 981 to 801 BC, overlapping in time with Lapita settlements that Green had excavated in nearby Nendö and the Reef Islands.

More mundane objects filled our sifting screens as well, including thousands of bones of fish and other animals, the garbage from countless ancient meals. After I returned to Honolulu, Bishop Museum zoologist Alan Ziegler would identify the bones of pigs, dogs, and chickens among my specimens, showing that these domestic animals had been introduced to Tikopia by the first colonizers.

Tikopia had abounded in bird life when people first arrived. The deepest deposits contained bones of extinct megapodes and flightless rails as well as abundant bones of frigates, boobies, tropic birds, terns, and other seabirds. There were more than one thousand bones of sea turtles, indicating that when humans first stepped ashore, Tikopia's sand beaches had been a turtle nesting ground. The thousands of gastropod and bivalve mollusks included many whose shells were among the largest I had ever seen. Having never previously been exploited by humans, Tikopia's reefs, beaches, and forested hills were a natural larder for the island's first colonists.

After these successes at Kiki, I turned my attention to Sinapupu. Starting at the Tarengu temple of Nga Faea, we cut a transect through the bush up and over the former beach ridge until the ground leveled out ninety meters inland. We dug test pits at ten-meter intervals; the pits near the top of the old beach ridge exhibited the deepest and most complex stratigraphy, similar to that beneath the Tarengu temple. The deeper layers contained the hard-fired, incised pottery that I called Sinapupu Ware, whereas the uppermost layers lacked pottery entirely.

About halfway along the transect there was a stratigraphic transition where the incised Sinapupu Ware petered out, with the deeper layers now yielding sand-tempered Kiki Ware pottery; the upper layers continued to lack pottery. When the transect test pits were completed I plotted these data, confirming that at Sinapupu I had a nearly complete sequence of the island's history. When first settled early in the first millennium BC, Tikopia's shoreline had been much closer to the volcanic hill. Some centuries later (which my radiocarbon dates would show to have been around 100 BC), the Faea shoreline started to shift seaward, the result of a Pacific-wide drop in sea level of about one meter. As the shoreline moved, the people shifted their houses seaward as well, keeping them on top of the beach ridge, which was slowly creeping seaward. Around this time people stopped making the sand-tempered Kiki Ware pottery. Instead, they imported pots decorated with incised lines and reddish pigment (the Sinapupu Ware). Later analysis of the pottery temper showed that it had been made somewhere in the Vanuatu Archipelago to the south, possibly on the large island of Espiritu Santo or on one of the smaller Banks Islands. These contacts with Vanuatu continued over many centuries.

There were other differences in the artifacts and faunal remains recovered from the middle layers containing the Sinapupu Ware. The *Tridacna* shell adzes of this period, made from the shell's outer valve, were ground so that the butt end came to a sharp point. Adzes like this were common in Vanuatu, again demonstrating that Tikopia once had close links with those southerly islands. The people who imported this incised pottery continued to fish and gather shellfish from the island's reefs, but they also raised pigs in large numbers. This was fascinating, because the Tikopia historically did not keep pigs. Firth had been told that a former Ariki Kafika had ordered all of the island's pigs to be killed because they were devastating the gardens. My archaeological evidence confirmed the veracity of that tradition.

Around AD 1200, according to our radiocarbon dates, the contacts with Vanuatu ceased. Although obsidian from the Banks Islands continued to be imported, the uppermost layers in the Sinapupu sequence contain no potsherds. This last period I called the Tuakamali phase. It represents the time when people speaking Polynesian languages arrived in canoes—some of them probably drift voyagers— from islands in Western Polynesia. The oral traditions of the Tikopia, recorded in detail by Firth, speak to the origins of various lineages from Rotuma, Samoa, 'Uvea, and Tonga. Te Atafu—the founder of the Taumako clan—was just such an immigrant.

It was during this final period in Tikopia's long history that the three groups referred to in the oral traditions—Nga Ravenga, Nga Faea, and Nga Ariki— struggled for control of the island's lands. The ruins of Nga Faea's houses and temples at Sinapupu connected the archaeological record with the realm of oral history as passed down from the ancestors of the Tikopia with whom I was living and working.[2]

I had now accomplished the objectives I laid out for myself. If the shipping schedule would cooperate, I was ready to pack up and make another attempt to get to Anuta. Each evening I tuned in to Radio Honiara on my shortwave radio to listen to the shipping news. The *Bona* had gone back to Honiara for repairs; the *Bilikiki* was at Graciosa Bay but would not continue on to the outer islands. It seemed that I was not going to get off Tikopia right away. Wanting to make the most of my time, I decided to open up a larger excavation at Sinapupu (Fig. 9.1). I gridded out a nine-square-meter block where I knew that the deposits containing Sinapupu Ware pottery were the thickest.

About one meter down into the nine-square-meter pit at Sinapupu (site TK-35) we encountered a burial. The skeleton of a young adult lay on its back with hands

Figure 9.1. The block excavation at Sinapupu in Faea, Tikopia. The well-stratified deposits here span nearly three thousand years of Tikopia history.

over the abdomen. As with burials we had uncovered the previous year under the Tarengu temple foundations, my Tikopia workers were not concerned: These were the bones of a Nga Faea person they said, not one of their own ancestors. After recording the skeleton I removed the bones so that we could dig beneath them. Placing the bones in a basket, I set it at the base of a coconut tree; when the excavation was completed I would rebury them.

Several days passed as we dug deeper into the dark gray sediments containing fire-cracked oven stones along with numerous potsherds of the incised Sinapupu Ware. Late one afternoon while returning from my bath at the village water tap, I passed Ariki Tafua. Greeting me, the *ariki* asked, "When are you going to put that dead man back into the ground?" I was taken aback, because I had not thought that the chief was concerned by the bones lying in the basket under the coconut tree. "They are Nga Faea bones," I started to reply. "I know," he cut me short. "But when I walked past the coconut tree this afternoon, the *tanetane* bushes shook. It was that man's spirit. He is not happy being out of the ground." I assured

Ariki Tafua that we were nearly finished digging, that I would soon return the bones to their resting place. "*E laue,*" he replied, "It is good."

I was sure that the rustling of the *tanetane* bushes as the chief walked past had simply been the wind. Nonetheless, the idea of a discontented spirit on the loose must have subtly been working on my subconscious. The next evening, after eating my dinner at Taraula, I decided to walk over to the house of Pa Somosomo. I enjoyed visiting with his family, sitting on the soft *Pandanus* mats by their hearth, sharing stories.

There had been rain squalls earlier in the day; the moon and stars were blacked out by clouds. Puddles of water covered the ground. I took a shortcut leading behind the main village, following the long narrow dart pitch called Te Marae Lasi. Longer than a football field but only twenty feet wide, this artificial groove in the landscape is where the Tikopia assemble to play the competitive sport of dart pitching. Dense vegetation crowded in on either side; the wind whistled through the breadfruit branches overhead. Alone with just the light of my flashlight to guide me I hurried along. Te Marae Lasi passes close to Takaritoa, the abandoned village of Nga Faea, where the bones lay in their basket. I suddenly remembered Ariki Tafua's words about the restless spirit.

Peering into the darkness, something caught my eye. I stopped dead in my tracks. At the end of the dark tunnel of vegetation, perhaps seventy yards away, a ghostly apparition slowly danced back and forth. It had no clear shape that I could discern, just a whitish cloud about the size of a man, slowly weaving back and forth. My heart throbbed. Not knowing whether to turn and run or advance and confront the Nga Faea spirit, I just stood and watched. Then, I noticed that the movements of the ghostly light coincided with the slight trembling of my hand, holding the flashlight. I shifted my hand to the right; the ghost moved to the right. I shifted it back to the left, the ghost following suit.

I threw my head back and began laughing in sheer relief. The ghost was the faint reflection of my flashlight's weak beam off a puddle of rainwater on the whitish sand of the dart pitch. Greatly relieved but not wanting to tarry any longer in that spooky place I hurried on to Pa Somosomo's house. Later I returned to Taraula via the main village path. The following day, reaching the bottom of the TK-35 excavation, we backfilled the deep pit, returning the Nga Faea bones to where they had lain for centuries.

I had become increasingly fascinated by the Tikopia historical traditions. The previous year, Ariki Fangarere and other elders had told me some of these stories. After returning to Honolulu, I reread Raymond Firth's *History and Traditions of Tikopia*, absorbing the details of lineage origins, accounts of ancient wars, and other events as only someone who has spent time on the tiny island could truly appreciate. Now back on Tikopia, I thought about how my archaeological findings might relate to the Tikopia's own accounts of their history.

Nineteenth-century scholars such as Abraham Fornander and Percy Smith had accepted Polynesian oral traditions as real history. Te Rangi Hiroa, too, relied on these traditions in his synthesis of Polynesian migrations. But later anthropologists preferred to see them as mythologies lacking a real historical basis. Firth was not one of those; he thought that the Tikopia traditions were founded on real history. He recognized, however, that in a society where history is passed down orally from generation to generation, embellishments, errors, and lapses of memory occur. Thus Firth called the Tikopia traditions a "quasi-history."

Firth's book on Tikopia traditions had been savagely attacked by Edmund Leach, a prominent English academic who was fiercely promoting a new "structuralist" school of anthropology.[3] Structuralism was the brainchild of the French sociologist Claude Lévi-Strauss. To Lévi-Strauss and his disciple Leach, the traditions of "primitive" people such as the Tikopia were timeless, ahistorical myths, invented after the fact to make sense of their marriage rules, clan organization, and other aspects of their culture. Structuralists love symmetry. For Lévi-Strauss, the "savage mind" was organized around basic dichotomies such as "the raw and the cooked." Invoking these structuralist principles, Leach argued that the Tikopian origin account of their four clans had to do with four being a symmetrical number, a reduplication of the fundamental dualism of the human mind. To Leach (who had never set foot on Tikopia) the Tikopia had *invented* an elaborate mythical history of their four clans.

I was not opposed to structuralism; it has analytical strengths when judiciously applied by scholars such as A. M. Hocart in his study of Fijian culture or by Marshall Sahlins in his brilliant decoding of the fateful encounter between Captain Cook and the Hawaiians.[4] But I was bothered by Leach's rejection of Polynesian oral tradition as mere myth without historical basis. On Niuatoputapu, I had spent long evenings listening to Nikolasi Fonua recount stories of the Tongan kings and their maritime empire. My archaeological results confirmed that Niuatoputapu had come under the sway of an expanding Tongan regime in the sixteenth or seventeenth centuries, just as the traditions suggested. Why, I wondered, were anthropologists so reticent to accept that Polynesian oral traditions were, at least in the main, accounts of real events that had been passed down over the generations?

One day I walked over to Ravenga to visit the aging Ariki Taumako. Although he had opposed my excavations in the sacred district of Uta the previous year, the chief was by no means unfriendly. Blind and infirm, the *ariki* had taken to living in his seaward temple (*fare atua*), the only pagan structure that had not been destroyed after the chiefs' conversion to Christianity in 1956. From the outside, the low thatched house looked like any other Tikopia dwelling, but as my eyes adjusted to the dim light within, I could see that I had entered a special place. The heavy wooden posts, glistening with the body oil of countless elderly backs that had leaned against them during long ceremonies, were carved with representations of 'ahi, the "fire fish" (yellowfin tuna). The sooty rafters—decorated with rows of nubbins called *fakataratara*—were lashed to the ridgepole with sennit fiber in intricate chevron patterns. In a corner stood the chief's sacred kava bowl. In Tikopia, kava was drunk only on ritual occasions when it was offered to the clan gods.

The chief sat alone, cross-legged on the *matapaito* or sacred side of his house. John, a nephew of Ariki Tafua who had come with me, broke the silence. "*Toku ariki,*" he began, "my chief, our friend would like to see the club brought by your ancestor from Tonga." Firth had written of this club, a representation of the eel god Tuna. For a while the chief said nothing. Then he cleared his voice asking, "Does our friend know the *tara tupua* [sacred history] of Taumako?" I now spoke for the first time: "*Toku mana* [My father, a polite way of addressing a chief], I have read of it in Raymond's book." The old chief smiled; in his youth he had known Firth and greatly respected him.

Ariki Taumako began to recount the story of Te Atafu, the ancestor who had come from Tonga fourteen generations before him. Just as Firth had written, the chief told me that Te Atafu was a son of the Tu'i Tonga, the sacred Tongan king. But then, unexpectedly, the Ariki Taumako added a small detail that I had not read in Firth's monograph. Te Atafu, he said, left behind two brothers. I asked the chief if he knew the names of those brothers who had remained in Tonga. Oh yes, he replied, they were called Tu'i Sa'apai and Tu'i Peresa.

I could not believe what I had just heard. Only because I was familiar with Tongan oral traditions—having recently worked in Niuatoputapu and carefully read the unpublished field notes of Edward Gifford from 1920 in the Bishop Museum's archives—did I know that Tu'i Ha'apai (Lord of Ha'apai) was a Tongan chiefly title that existed in the eighteenth century but was long since defunct. The Tongan *h* sound is rendered in Tikopian as *s*, so Tu'i Ha'apai was the same Tu'i Sa'apai whom the chief claimed as one of his ancestor's brothers. But what of the other name, Tu'i Peresa? Most likely it was a rendering of Tu'i Pelehake, another prominent Tongan noble title (Tongan *l* goes to *r* in Tikopian, *h* goes to *s*, and the dropping of the final syllable is not unusual). There was no way that the *ariki* or any of his predecessors had simply "invented" these names as part of a neat origin myth, as Leach's structuralist theory would have it. No, I was listening to a fragment of real history, passed down over fourteen generations of Taumako chiefs.

The Ariki Taumako instructed John, "Go and take Tuna down from its place there." John crawled across the floor to the end of the temple where the *ariki* was seated. An adzed timber held in place with sennit lashings served as a shelf on which there were a number of objects. Raising himself up on his knees John grasped the yard-long, worm-eaten, wooden club brought by Te Atafu from Tonga fourteen generations earlier. I was allowed to look at it for a few minutes, ascertaining that its form and carved ornamentation were consistent with eighteenth-century Tongan war clubs held in European museums. Any remaining doubts that the *tara tupua* or sacred history of Taumako was "mere myth" were dispelled.

When I wrote up my synthesis of Tikopia prehistory after returning to the Bishop Museum, I integrated the archaeological evidence for the Tuakamali or late phase of the island's sequence with the indigenous oral traditions.[5] It was clear that the traditions regarding struggles for control of land and resources between the island's three original social groups—Nga Ravenga, Nga Faea, and Nga Ariki—had a real basis in environmental changes that my field research had demonstrated. According to the Tikopian account, Nga Ravenga and Nga Faea were *afukere,* earth-sprung or autochthonous inhabitants; probably they descended from the original colonizers who settled at Kiki thousands of years earlier. Nga Ariki (literally, "the Chiefs") were more recent arrivals, including the Kafika, Tafua, and Taumako chiefly lineages that traced their origins to islands in Western Polynesia. As relative newcomers, Nga Ariki were confined to the lands around the inner shore of Te Roto, the district known as Uta. Isolated from the sea, this was the least desirable part of the island. Nga Ravenga occupied the island's windward coast, whereas Nga Faea held the leeward coast and flat sandy plain, the island's best garden land.

Firth recounts how, according to the traditions, Nga Ariki intensely felt the pressure of inadequate food supplies:

> Time and again, I was told how day by day they and their households saw the scrapings of giant yam from the cooking houses of their Nga Ravenga neighbors float past them on the waters of the lake. Feeling the pinch of hunger, they collected these scrapings, and baked them for food in their own ovens.

What the traditions did *not* say, but my archaeological excavations around Ravenga and Uta had shown, was that around the end of the sixteenth century (the period that the chiefly genealogies refer to) a dramatic change occurred in the island's environment. Up until this time Te Roto (the caldera created by a volcanic explosion about eighty thousand years ago) had been a marine embayment, open to the sea. The shores of Uta were fringed with coral reefs, providing rich shellfish beds and net fishing grounds. Then, possibly due to a tectonic shift, this bay rapidly closed off and a sand spit formed along the Ravenga coastline. With the marine bay becoming a brackish water lake, the rich shellfish beds died off; only a few species of fish such as *kiokio* (*Chanos chanos*) could survive in the new conditions. Little wonder that Nga Ariki felt the pinch of hunger!

Provoked by a dispute over garden boundaries, Nga Ariki rose against Nga Ravenga, slaughtering the latter in a surprise attack. Only an infant son of Nga Ravenga's chief survived, to become the founding ancestor of the Fangarere clan. Nga Ariki moved their dwellings onto the newly formed sand spit along the Ravenga coastline. Their former houses in Uta remained, however, to become their clan temples, such as that at Vaisakiri, where the Ariki Fangarere had permitted me to dig in 1977.

For a time there was peace between Nga Ariki and Nga Faea, but the pressures of population on such a small island inevitably mounted. The Tafua clan saw how the Taumako people had greatly enriched their holdings after the slaughter of Nga Ravenga. They coveted the rich garden lands of Faea. This time, Nga Faea were forewarned of the impending attack. Realizing that they were outnumbered, Nga Faea put up only token resistance, fleeing to their canoes and putting out to sea, abandoning their ancient homeland. As he headed out through the pass, the Nga Faea chief Tiako called out to the victors that they should honor and take care of Feke, the Octopus God whose stone they had left behind at Takaritoa. Feke assured the fertility of the Faea reef. Ariki Tafua, now lord of Faea, heeded this parting advice: The rites of the Octopus God continued to be performed annually well into the twentieth century.

Regrettably, the round stone representing Feke—which Firth had been shown in 1928–1929—had been buried by a zealous Christian convert a few years before my fieldwork. But there was no reason for me to doubt the veracity of the traditions regarding Nga Faea. I had mapped Nga Faea's house foundations at Takaritoa and seen their *marae* with Pu Pererua's backrest slab; I had dug into the floor of Tarengu, the Nga Faea temple. My radiocarbon dates for the construction of Tarengu agreed well with the chronology provided by the Tikopian chiefly genealogies.

Our archaeological findings provided too many direct links to the oral traditions for me to doubt their historical reality. The Tikopian traditions were not "mere myths" as the structural anthropologists would have it; they recounted real historical events. To be sure, these traditions extended back in time only two to three centuries. They did not go back to the earlier periods of Tikopia prehistory, to what I called the Sinapupu and the even earlier Kiki phases. Human memory has its limits. But in showing that the main corpus of Tikopian traditions was—as Raymond Firth had claimed—based on history, our research opened new possibilities of relating archaeology to traditional history. It is an avenue I would follow in subsequent work in Polynesia, including Hawai'i.

The Sinapupu excavation completed, boxes full of specimen bags lined one side of my hut. In the expectation that the *Bona* would soon arrive, I packed up the digging gear, spending my days working on a reference collection of fish skeletons. To identify all of the fishbones I had been excavating, I needed a comparative collection of reference fish skeletons. Each time someone brought me a different fish I would photograph it, key the species with a taxonomic manual, and then boil it down and clean the bones. One night the Tafua men pulled in two *Ruvettus,* a large, oily fleshed fish caught in deep water by lowering a big iron hook baited with live flying fish. It took the chief's largest pot to boil down the head and teeth for my collection.

On September 3 I woke early, scanning the horizon for the *Bona.* I had been on Tikopia since mid-July with no contact with the outside world. Soon I saw her masthead; an hour later she was anchored off Matautu. Coming ashore in the ship's boat was Doug Yen. Yen handed me a parcel of mail, including twenty-one letters from Debra Connelly, to whom I had become engaged before leaving Honolulu. The letters had piled up in the Nendö post office with no way for them to get to me.

Yen and I walked down the path to Ariki Tafua's house for a meal of *masi,* fermented breadfruit cooked with fresh coconut cream. Yen's Vanikoro work, he said, had gone well. Unfortunately, however, the *Bona* was not going on to Anuta but directly to Utupua where Yen would begin ethnobotanical work. I would need to stay on Tikopia, in the hopes that the mission ship *M. V. Fauabe-Towmey* would arrive in a few days and could take me to Anuta. Fortunately, the *Bona* had brought new supplies of food and kerosene. After saying goodbye to Yen, I tarried on the beach to watch the *Bona* make course for Utupua.

For the next few evenings I tuned in to Radio Honiara for the whereabouts of the *Fauabe-Towmey.* On September 7 she was at Taumako, and the next day at Vanikoro. That news did not bode well. By the following day I knew that the *Fauabe-Towmey* was returning to Honiara without bothering to call at Tikopia or Anuta. There was only one thing to do: unpack the excavation gear and continue to dig into the artifact-rich sands of Tikopia.

For the next six weeks I expanded the Tikopia excavations, first returning to Kiki, where we dug a twelve-square-meter block in the most intact part of the site, finding many more shell fishhooks, ornaments, and, of course, the Kiki Ware pottery. Then we returned to Sinapupu, opening up a twelve-square-meter excavation at the inland end of our long transect. Here the deposits contained materials similar to those at Kiki. In this last excavation (site TK-36), we came upon a thin, gravelly house pavement. In it we found no less than 125 fishhooks of *Turbo* shell, in all stages of manufacture (Fig. 9.2), along with the coral and sea-urchin spine files used to make the hooks, greatly expanding our knowledge of early Tikopian fishing technology.

The additional weeks spent on Tikopia gave me time to expand my reference collection of fishbones, which now numbered more than one hundred different species. The collection would prove invaluable when I later went to identify the thousands of archaeological fishbones that I had excavated. I also compiled a card file with more than 250 Tikopian fish names, including information on which kinds of fishing techniques were used to catch each species. Meanwhile, I enjoyed my daily interactions with the Tikopia people, learning to make string figures with the youngsters or joining in their dance festivals (Fig. 9.3).

One fascinating observation came out of my ethnographic inquiries about fishing: the Tikopia are deathly afraid of moray eels. When I showed some Tikopia fishermen pictures of moray eels in my fish reference manual, they recoiled in horror at the sight of the multicolored moray eel heads. They hissed, "*Atua kovi! Atua kovi!*" (Evil gods!). This reaction surprised me, because most Polynesians enjoy eating eels and also because we had found many eel jaws and bones in the Kiki and Sinapupu excavations. Later, when I analyzed the fishbones in my lab, I discovered that eel bones were absent from the uppermost layers of the Tuakamali period. At some point the Tikopia had abruptly stopped eating eels. Delving into the scientific literature, I found that eels are noted concentrators of ciguatera toxin. An outbreak of ciguatera on the island may have caused the death of people who ate eel. Such an experience could have changed the Tikopian view of eels, from desirable food to "evil gods."

On October 25, Radio Honiara announced that the *Bilikiki* would arrive at Tikopia in two days. But she was going to stop first at Anuta! There was no way now that I would get to Anuta this field season. The *Bilikiki* finally arrived three days later. I had been on Tikopia for 101 days, much longer than the six weeks originally planned, and I had dug far more than intended. But my understanding of the island's past was all the richer for it.

The *Bilikiki* steamed for Nendö via Vanikoro and the Reef Islands, landing me at Graciosa Bay on October 31. I dropped my Tikopia collections off at the Mbanwa hut for safekeeping, then sailed the next day on the *Bilikiki* for Utupua. In the ship's hold was a large consignment of food, kerosene, and other supplies that had been intended for both Yen and me but had been delayed due to the changes in shipping schedules. I would be well supplied in Vanikoro.

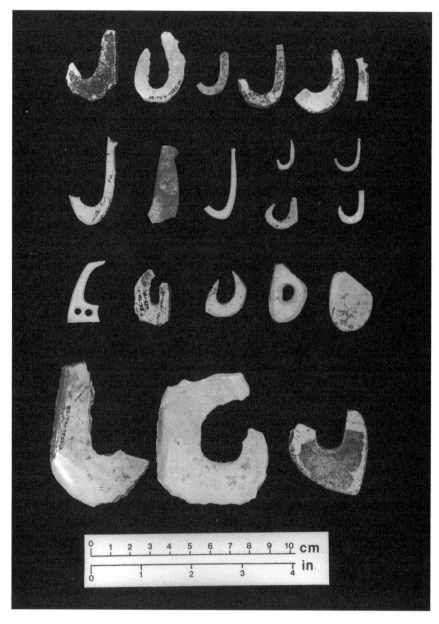

Figure 9.2. The Tikopia excavations yielded a wide array of fishhooks made from *Turbo* and pearl shell. The sample shown in this photo includes finished hooks as well as those in earlier stages of manufacture.

Yen greeted me on Utupua's rickety wharf. Stuck in the small village on that somber, jungle-clad island since early September, he was more than ready to head for home. We drank most of a bottle of Johnny Walker Scotch that night sitting on *Bilikiki*'s stern in the calm bay, swapping yarns of our respective adventures over the past few months.

The next morning the *Bilikiki* sailed for Vanikoro, the passage from Utupua taking only a few hours. By early afternoon we were off Puma Village, sending my crates of cargo and equipment ashore in the ship's boat. I would again stay in the one-room pole-and-thatch hut that we had occupied in 1977, near the water's edge. This time I knew that I had to avoid the sand fleas that had given me such awful bites on the last trip. I said goodbye to Yen, then watched the *Bilikiki* steam away toward Nendö. The captain told me that the ship would not return again until the new year. With the *Bona* in dry dock in Honiara, this meant that the mission ship *Fauabe-Towmey* was my only lifeline to civilization.

I settled into my stilt house next to the beach. The Melanesian Vanikoro culture was different from that of Polynesian Tikopia; I could not speak their language. There was no ethnography such as Firth's to guide me regarding their traditions and customs. But nearly everyone spoke pidgin English so communication was not a problem. I had so much rice and tinned food that I gave much of it away to the Puma people, a gesture that made me welcome in their village. After a

Figure 9.3. Men's paddle dance on a feast day in Ravenga, Tikopia. The three seated men are beating out the rhythm with wooden mallets on a piece of old canoe hull.

couple of days of rest I hired several of the Puma men. We set out for Emo, the site on Tevai Island where I had found shell adzes and other artifacts on the surface in 1977.

After hiking several hours through coastal forest and wading through mangrove flats, we arrived at Emo, a high beach ridge with an intermittent stream at its southern end. Ducking under the tangle of *Hibiscus* shrubs that covered the dune, I saw that the surface was extensively pockmarked with large land crab burrows. Finding many shell adzes and a few pieces of pottery scattered about, I realized that the artifacts had been brought to the surface by the busy crustaceans. I was worried that the dune's stratigraphy would be compromised by all this crab disturbance but decided to test the site anyway. We began digging two pits of four square meters each.

The first fifty centimeters of the Emo sands yielded almost nothing; this was the depth to which the crab burrows penetrated. The creatures had "mined" the deposit of all its artifacts, carrying them up to the surface with their claws and dumping them on the tips at their burrow entrances. Below that depth, however, the deposit was intact; we started finding potsherds, pieces of *Trochus* shell armbands, *Spondylus* shell beads, and other artifacts. There were lots of shell and bone midden. The pottery was essentially the same as the Sinapupu Ware on Tikopia—hard fired, lithic tempered, with incised designs. Later analysis would show that it too derived from the south, from Vanuatu.[6] These finds were important in showing that both Tikopia and Vanikoro had once been part of a more extensive trade network linking the Santa Cruz Islands with northern Vanuatu.

The cultural layer at Emo went down almost two meters before we hit the old beach surface. A charcoal sample near the bottom was later radiocarbon dated to 1750 ± 85 years BP. It was disappointing not to have had time to explore Vanikoro more thoroughly. I was certain that given the time and resources I would have found Lapita settlements, but Vanikoro's archaeological secrets would remain hidden until another day.

I listened every night to Radio Honiara for the whereabouts of the *Fauabe-Towmey*. On November 20 the radio announced that the ship had arrived at Graciosa Bay. I hurriedly packed up my gear and specimens. The *Fauabe-Towmey* showed up off Puma the next day, packed to the gunwales with schoolchildren from the mission's boarding school on Nendö; the ship was taking them back to their home islands for the Christmas holidays. It was all I could do to squeeze into a cramped space on the cargo hatch where I lay down on my mat and sleeping bag. Departing for Tikopia at dusk, we promptly ran into high seas. The *Fauabe-Towmey*'s ferro-concrete, round-bottomed hull rolled horribly. Several dozen kids upwind of me were seasick, their vomit blowing back and hitting me in the face.

All of us had to hold on tight to rope lines to avoid being tossed overboard. Unable to get up, the children started to relieve themselves where they lay; throughout the night I felt the trickle of warm urine under me. I have never in all my travels spent a more miserable night at sea.

At Tikopia I went ashore for a long bath and then a final meal with Ariki Tafua and "Mommy" at Matautu. That evening we sailed for Anuta, arriving at dawn. The irony was poignant. For two years I had tried to get to Anuta, thwarted by bad weather or the unavailability of ships. Now, on my way home and with no time left, here I was at Anuta with perfect weather for landing. I went ashore with Bishop Ellison in the first boat, taking gifts of kerosene, rice, and other items for the Akonima and Notau families. Pu Akonima, my bond-friend who had tattooed me in 1971, walked me inland to "our" gardens where he plucked fresh betel nut for us to chew. The Anutans knew that I had been trying to get to the island; they were terribly disappointed that now I could not stay. Nau Notau daubed me with turmeric pigment, and Nau Akonima gave me a fine mat to wear. Bishop Ellison was in a hurry to leave, so our visit was truncated. After tearful farewells the ship's boat slipped through the tiny pass; we were en route to Taumako before noon. I deeply regret not having been able to spend another season on that lovely, smallest of Polynesian islands.

Another week passed as the *Fauabe-Towmey* made her way from Taumako through the Reef Islands, to Nukapu, and then to Nendö, followed by the long passage to Honiara with stops at Kirakira, Paumua, and Uki. I spent the entire voyage on deck, although conditions improved after the last schoolchildren were dropped off at Nukapu. By the time we docked at Honiara I was unspeakably filthy and achingly exhausted. It took all my strength to clamber down into the steaming hot hold, reeking of rancid copra, to recover my boxes of specimens and baggage. Hiring a truck I asked the driver to stop at a store where I bought a case of cold beer and then checked in to the Hibiscus Hotel. I stood in the hot shower for more than an hour, reaching out periodically only to grab another beer.

After a week in Honiara, I flew home to Honolulu on December 9, having been gone for 171 days. I was eager to return to my fiancé and to a life with normal creature comforts. I was warned that I might get stranded in Nauru due to an outbreak of cholera, but fortunately, the Solomon Islands Health Service nurse gave me a quick vaccine and stamped my international health card, allowing me to pass through Nauru without the usual two-week quarantine. Despite the disappointment of not working on Anuta, as well as the shorter than planned stay on Vanikoro, the trip had been a great success. The material I had collected on Tikopia was extraordinarily rich. I was excited to start working it up at the Bishop Museum.

CHAPTER TEN

Aloha ʻĀina
(Hawaiʻi, 1979–1984)

Over the previous five years, I had spent nearly half of my time on remote islands in the South Seas, accumulating a mountain of data and collections. Now I needed to analyze and work up the results and publish my discoveries. I was also ready for a more "normal" existence, to enjoy life in Honolulu.

Debra Connelly and I had met between my Tikopia field trips. A graduate student studying social anthropology at the University of Hawaiʻi (UH), Debra was researching the impact of tourism on Tongan society. She had a fellowship at the East-West Center, where we both got to know Dr. Langi Kavaliku (who as Tonga's minister of education had approved my research permit in 1976), director of the center's Pacific Islands Development Program. On March 3, 1979, Debra and I were married at my parent's home in Mānoa. Tom Dye was my best man. Kavaliku and his wife Fuiva attended the ceremony, bringing a huge roll of Tongan barkcloth as their wedding gift.

The pace of "development" in Hawaiʻi continued to heat up; new resorts, golf courses, and condominium projects were going up everywhere. The demand for contract archaeology was high. Although Bishop Museum provided much of the work, several private consulting firms had set up shop as well. No longer an ivory tower research endeavor, archaeology in the islands was increasingly intertwined with land development.

The Bishop Museum, too, was in the throes of change. In 1976 the museum's trustees dismissed director Roland Force. In a scheme to raise much-needed revenue, Force had purchased a derelict four-masted schooner, the *Falls of Clyde*. The ship cost a fortune to refit and never recouped its costs from tourist visits. We called it "Force's Folly." Force had also unwisely accepted an offer from developer Chris Hemmeter to operate a hula theater at King's Alley in Waikīkī; a fleet of double-decker London buses ferried tourists between Waikīkī and the museum. The old buses repeatedly broke down, and the tiny theater did not have enough seats to cover the high overhead. At the annual staff Christmas party in 1975 the museum's comptroller—after drinking one too many glasses of spiked punch—

started telling anyone who would listen about how the museum was on the verge of bankruptcy. Force ordered the security guards to haul him away.

In 1977 the trustees appointed Ed Creutz as the museum's new director. A grandfatherly sort with a PhD in physics, Creutz had been deputy director at the National Science Foundation (NSF). It was soon evident that Creutz was in over his head. He had no background in Pacific anthropology or biology and no intuitive vision for the institution. Worse, as a federal administrator he had been used to disbursing funds, not raising them—he had no idea of how to go about private fundraising and no connections in the tight-knit Honolulu community of business people and wealthy *kama'āina* families.

In spite of these problems, the museum's Anthropology Department was an exciting place to work. Kenneth Emory, getting on in years but still sharp, had been promoted to the Ledyard Chair of Pacific Culture History, a kind of sinecure. Force originally intended that Roger Green would take over from Emory, but Green had gotten on Force's bad side by critiquing the money-losing ventures, the *Falls of Clyde* and King's Alley. When Green took up a prestigious Captain James Cook Fellowship in New Zealand, Force promoted Yosihiko Sinoto to be department chair. Green soon accepted a senior professorship at the University of Auckland; it was a big loss for the museum.

Emory, nervous and high-strung, possessed a huge ego. He thought that pretty much everything worth doing in Polynesian archaeology had already been accomplished—by him! One day in the archaeology lab where the staff ate lunch together, I listened aghast as Emory chastised Patrick McCoy for "wasting" his time at the Mauna Kea adz quarry. McCoy had secured a big NSF grant to study that amazing high-altitude quarry and was doing cutting-edge research. But in Emory's opinion the best adz specimens had already been collected by himself back in 1947. He shouted at McCoy, "Go find a site with some fishhooks and dig it!" and stomped out of the room.[1]

In spite of his oversized ego, Emory could be charming. He loved to recount tales of his fieldwork on remote Napuka Atoll in the Tuamotus or on the Polynesian Outlier of Kapingamarangi. On a number of occasions Emory demonstrated his mastery of complicated Tuamotu string figures ("cat's cradle"), the different stages of which are accompanied by chants. Emory also had a reputation of being something of a lady's man. Whenever an attractive new female volunteer showed up at the museum, Emory would bestow her with a lei made of *pua kenikeni* flowers from a tree he cultivated in his Nu'uanu garden.

One day in the late 1970s Emory had a visit from Margaret Mead, probably the most famous anthropologist of the twentieth century. They had met in the

1920s when Mead had done her famous study of Samoa, partly under the auspices of the Bishop Museum. In her later years Mead had taken to wearing a dark cloak and carrying a wooden staff. I can still picture her stomping formidably down Konia Hall to Emory's office, the thumping of her staff echoing off the specimen cabinets lining the hallway.

Later, a reception was held in the courtyard in Mead's honor. Someone had set up the folding chairs in a broad semicircle, probably unaware that this configuration mimicked a Western Polynesian *alofi* circle at which kava is presented to the high chiefs. Entering the courtyard and spying the chairs, Mead without hesitation proceeded to occupy the chair at the center of the semicircle, signifying that she was the highest-ranking person present! For several minutes Mead sat there alone. Then Doug Yen poked me in the ribs and said, "Come on, let's go talk to the old girl." We sat to either side of Mead and in spite of her formidable demeanor found her to be very congenial.

Sinoto was fiercely loyal to his mentor Emory with whom he had worked closely since 1954, actively promoting what Doug Yen called "the cult of Emory." Emory and Sinoto enjoyed spacious offices facing each other on the ground floor of Konia Hall. Sinoto was firmly set in the old, artifact-centered paradigm of archaeology, spending his time refining the details of the fishhook chronology he and Emory had developed in the 1950s and 1960s. Sinoto never adopted Roger Green's settlement pattern approach, nor was he interested in applying the new methods of ethnoarchaeology or ecological archaeology. Nonetheless, Sinoto was a meticulous excavator who discovered a number of important sites. Among these were Hane in the Marquesas and Vaito'otia in Huahine, the latter remarkable for the waterlogged preservation of wooden artifacts including part of a canoe hull. Unfortunately, Sinoto never published full accounts of his excavations. Among archaeologists, the complete description and publication of one's excavations and finds are considered essential, because once dug, like Humpty Dumpty, a site can never be put back together again. That Sinoto left most of his important sites unpublished has deprived Polynesian archaeology of a great deal of potential knowledge.

Marion Kelly served as Emory's and Sinoto's primary assistant. Kelly's father had been captain of the *Islander*, the sampan chartered for the 1934 Mangarevan Expedition (see Chapter Two). More or less raised around the museum, Kelly studied for her MA at the University of Hawai'i. Kelly was married to John Kelly Jr., the "Save Our Surf" activist and son of the famous island painter John Kelly. A stunning beauty in her youth (and still attractive in middle age) Marion had modeled for many of her father-in-law's paintings. She had also acquired expertise in Hawaiian history and land tenure matters, often collaborating on contract archaeology projects.

The other two younger PhD archaeologists at the museum were Patrick Mc-Coy and Paul Rosendahl. McCoy had conducted a settlement pattern study on Easter Island for his doctoral research. His special interest was the production of adzes and other stone tools. He had organized a cutting-edge project to study the massive Mauna Kea adz quarry but as noted earlier, this venture did not receive the respect it deserved from Emory. Sinoto invited McCoy to collaborate in the first season of fieldwork at Vaitoʻotia on Huahine but then inexplicably cut him out of the project. I thought that these slights—which were undeserved—undermined McCoy's confidence.

Rosendahl had studied for his PhD at the University of Hawaiʻi, working on the Lapakahi Project in Kohala, Hawaiʻi Island, where he conducted an impressive analysis of upland residential and agricultural sites. We had bonded during the 1971 expedition to Kolombangara and Anuta (see Chapter Four). Unlike McCoy, Rosendahl had a thick skin and a high opinion of his own work. He and Sinoto quickly began to butt heads. In 1978, Sinoto recommended to the director that Rosendahl's contract not be renewed. Rosendahl then formed his own consulting firm and, with a good nose for business, soon became one of the most prominent cultural resource management (CRM) consultants in Hawaiʻi. Unfortunately, Rosendahl let the profit motive run rampant over his better judgment as an archaeologist. Consequently, in later years Native Hawaiian activists vilified Rosendahl as a "developer's man."

In the ethnology division on Konia Hall's second floor, Adrienne Kaeppler concentrated on material culture, curating the museum's collection of Hawaiian and Polynesian artifacts. She organized a stunning exhibit of artifacts collected on Captain Cook's voyages, "Artificial Curiosities."[2] A protégé of Roland Force, Kaeppler soon left the museum for the Smithsonian Institution where she has had a distinguished career.

Patience (Pat) Bacon served as the Anthropology Department's secretary, although in many ways she was overqualified for that position. The *hānai* (adopted) daughter of famed Hawaiian scholar Mary Kawena Pukui, Bacon spoke fluent Hawaiian and was an expert hula dancer. I would often chat with her about Hawaiian culture and history. It was typical of her aloha spirit that she offered to type the manuscript of my first book in her "spare time."

Doug Yen would soon leave Bishop Museum to become a professorial fellow at the Australian National University in Canberra. Disappointed when Roger Green did not succeed Emory as Anthropology chair, Yen disdained the "cult of Emory." He felt that the museum's younger scientists were not being adequately recognized. Yen also did not like the emphasis that Sinoto was putting on contract archaeology. Over beers at our favorite Korean bar near the museum, Yen would grumble, "We're *better* than this. We should do *research*," accenting the second syllable of "research" in his Kiwi accent. His departure from Bishop Museum at the end of 1980 was a big loss. Both Yen and Roger Green were later elected to the National Academy of Sciences—the nation's highest scientific honor.

I had kept up my connections with my old mentor Yoshio Kondo in the Malacology Department on Konia Hall's third floor. Kondo officially retired in 1980, becoming "Malacologist Emeritus," but like many museum scientists this change made no difference in his daily routine. He still drove his old Buick from his apartment to the museum around 2 a.m., working on his land snail dissections and drawings of Partulidae anatomy until dawn. Once every week or two my office phone would ring around 9 a.m., the familiar voice asking, "Patrick, are you free to come up for a cup of coffee?" It was always a pleasure to climb the stairs up to Kondo's lab, where he served up cups of fresh Kona coffee brewed on his Bunsen burner. I would tell Kondo what was happening downstairs in Anthropology, and he would offer sage advice.

On other occasions Kondo would invite me to stop by his home for cocktails after work. Arriving at his modest Isenberg Street apartment, I would find Kondo preparing a slab of fresh 'ahi sashimi that he had procured at the Tomashiro Fish Market, laying the thin slices over a bed of grated daikon. We would partake of the delicious raw fish, our conversation lubricated by glasses of whiskey.

After returning from the Solomon Islands at the end of 1978, I devoted as much time as I could to analyzing the rich Tikopia collections in the archaeology lab. There was so much that needed to be accomplished before Yen and I could publish a coherent account of the island's 3,000-year history. Laypeople often do not realize that for every day spent digging, at least another two or three days are necessary to study the material, tabulate statistics, and write up the results.

First, to provide a chronological framework for our history I selected charcoal samples from different sites for radiocarbon dating. A few months later the results from the Isotopes Lab came back indicating that the oldest settlement at Kiki had been established around 900 BC. Sand-tempered Kiki pottery continued to be made on the island until around 100 BC. I called this first period the Kiki Phase. Then, from 100 BC until around AD 1200, Tikopia was linked into a regional interaction sphere that included islands in the northern Vanuatu Archipelago. During this long period Sinapupu Ware pots with their incised and painted designs were imported through these trade networks. I called this the Sinapupu Phase. After AD 1200 the southern trade network was broken; the archaeological deposits of this late time period—the Tuakamali Period—lacked pottery altogether. It was then that the ancestors of the present Polynesian-speaking people arrived in Tikopia; they were known known collectively as Nga Ariki, "the Chiefs." After defeating Nga Ravenga and Nga Faea (descendants of the island's older populations), Nga Ariki became masters of the island.

The chronological sequence established by the radiocarbon-dated pottery types merely provided a framework for the bigger picture of Tikopia's history. Doug Yen and I had set out to trace the evolution of the island's human ecology over three thousand years. For this it was essential to turn to the thousands of fish, bird, and other animal bones that I had excavated, along with more than a ton of mollusk and invertebrate remains. The reference collection of fishbones that I had assembled while on Tikopia now found its value. For several months we sorted the fishbones, bag by bag—identifying the dentaries, pharyngeal grinders, and distinctive spines and tangs—and then comparing the ancient bones with their modern counterparts. From this painstaking work, changing patterns of fishing and marine resource use emerged.

Other bones required specialist attention. Zoologist Alan Ziegler, whose office was just down the hallway from mine, offered to examine the nonfish bones. With a PhD from Berkeley, Ziegler spoke with a Southern drawl and had a droll sense of humor. His specialty was the fauna of the New Guinea region, so he had the expertise to identify the bones of fruit bats, lizards, megapodes and other birds, as well as turtles, from the Tikopia middens. When tabulated, these bones revealed that initial human arrival on the island had resulted in some extinctions of local fauna, such as megapode birds. There had also originally been large numbers of nesting turtles that were taken for food.

Ziegler loved a practical joke. One day he convinced Tom Dye that a fruit bat specimen I had brought back from the Solomons was a new flightless species. When I had gotten the bat from some boys in Mbanwa who had shot it with an arrow, I had cut away and salted the furry pelt before sending it to Ziegler. I then boiled down the bones, including the wings, for reference material. When Ziegler stitched the pelt back together at the museum, the poor specimen, lacking wings, looked rather like a large rat with just its two hind legs hanging down. Ziegler went on and on pulling Dye's leg, telling him that the specimen was a "marvelous example of adaptive radiation on islands," evolving flightlessness as its ancestors had pursued fallen fruits on the forest floor!

Doug Yen, for his part, was busy working up the results of the trenches he had dug in an area called Rakisu, where the Tikopia practiced intensive farming. Yen's evidence showed that the distinctive Tikopia system of orchard gardening had developed in the later periods; earlier in the island's history the people had practiced shifting cultivation. Sometimes on Friday afternoons, over beers in the lab or in the nearby Korean bar, we held informal seminars hashing out what our results meant—both for the long-term history of Tikopia and for the role and impact of humans in island ecosystems.

After Yen left the museum for Canberra in 1980, we continued to send draft chapters of our joint monograph back and forth for each of us to review and critique. In 1982 the Bishop Museum Press published *Tikopia: The Prehistory and Ecology of a Polynesian Outlier.*[3] Almost immediately it received a favorable review in the prestigious journal *Science.* But more than anything I was deeply touched by the letter I received from Sir Raymond Firth after he received the inscribed copy we sent him. Here is part of what he wrote me:

> I am gratified to find that your discoveries and analysis fit so closely into my own ethnographic results, particularly as regards my interpretation of Tikopia oral tradition. . . . Your demonstration of the linkage between archaeological and ethnographic interpretation should provide a classic case for study of the general problem. Little did I think when I argued for the importance of archaeological investigation to reveal Pacific history . . . that the results would be so spectacular.[4]

Bishop Museum's rapidly expanding contract archaeology program was mostly focused on Hawai'i. But in early 1978 we were asked to carry out archaeological reconnaissance surveys in the western Micronesian islands of Palau and Yap. The airfields on these islands were World War II legacies, constructed by the Japanese and later expanded by the U.S. Army. Now the Federal Aviation Administration wanted to modernize the airfields to accommodate increasing air traffic and larger jet planes. I was excited by the opportunity to experience firsthand the archaeological landscapes of these Micronesian islands.

In mid-January 1978, I took the Air Micronesia flight from Honolulu to Guam, accompanied by Tom Dye as my assistant. After a quick visit to Saipan we flew on to Palau, settling into a little motel in the capital town of Koror. For the next week we traversed the area surrounding the airfield on the southern part of Babeldaub Island. Walking through thick *Miscanthus* grass, we had to be careful to avoid pit-traps—some with rows of upright rusting bayonets in the bottom—dug by the Japanese troops around the old fighter strip. The area surrounding the airfield, however, consisted of an extensive array of artificial terraces cut into the old volcanic ridges and swales. Babeldaub was famous for these terraces, which had transformed much of the island's landscape. The age and function of the massive terraces were unknown. Dye and I found lots of potsherds on the terrace surfaces, suggesting that they might have been residential features, although others were probably used for agriculture. These sites cried out for a major research program, not just a quick reconnaissance.

After a week in Palau, we flew on to Yap, one of the most beautiful islands in Micronesia. Renowned for their huge stone "money" disks, the Yapese are also heavily addicted to chewing betel nuts. Set in vast groves of betel nut palms, their hamlets are connected by intricately laid stone pathways. Walking through these shady groves past moss-covered stone platforms and through plazas lined with rows of the giant limestone disks, I fancied myself in some kind of Oriental garden. Surveying the area around the airfield, Dye and I again encountered numerous relics of World War II, including rusting old Japanese antiaircraft cannon.

These brief visits to Palau and Yap whetted my appetite, and for a number of years afterward I contemplated organizing a major research project in one or both of these islands, whose archaeology was so little known. Unfortunately, other opportunities always took me elsewhere, and I never did return to investigate the deeper histories of those fascinating landscapes. I did, however, enjoy one more Micronesian fieldwork interlude, in 1980 when I spent a few weeks with Tom Dye on Arno atoll in the Marshall Islands. This time Dye was in charge of his own project; he did an admirable job of applying the kind of geomorphologically informed research design that I had pioneered on Niuatoputapu and Tikopia. Doing archaeology on a coral atoll such as Arno—where the terrain is never more than about six feet above sea level—was quite a different experience from the high volcanic islands I had always worked on.

What really shocked me, however, was the acculturated and impoverished state of Arno society. In contrast with the vibrant, traditional cultures of Anuta and Tikopia, the Arno islanders lived in squalid tin shacks and had become dependent on the largess of the U.S. Trust Territory administration. It was a depressing experience.

In early 1980, Sinoto put me in charge of the Archaeology Division, responsible for the museum's contract archaeology program. One August morning, I got a phone call from Harry Otsuji, an attorney representing Hawaiʻi state senator Wadsworth Yee. Cleary agitated, Otsuji said he urgently needed the services of an archaeologist on Molokaʻi. Senator Yee was developing a tract of land to the east of Kaunakakai where there were ancient Hawaiian sites. "Can you fly to Molokaʻi tomorrow morning?" Otsuji demanded. "The contractor is already at work and this delay is costing us a lot of money." I had heard nothing about a major development project on Molokaʻi and wondered what was going on. I assured Otsuji that I would be on the morning flight to Hoʻolehua.

The next morning I pulled my rental car up to the freshly bulldozed entry road to what a sign called "Kawela Plantation Estates" on Moloka'i's leeward shore. Several large D9 bulldozers and other earth-moving equipment were idled by the roadside. An earthen mound next to the road had been sliced clean through by the D9, exposing a deep midden full of shell and bone. Kawela, as the area was called, was a well-known burial ground. I wondered whether the developers had cut through Hawaiian burials as well.

Otsuji greeted me, explaining that no sooner had the Hood Construction team started to doze the new roadways than they encountered rock walls. The local Moloka'i residents were upset. No one had informed them that this project was imminent, and there had been no public hearing. When a barge loaded with heavy equipment arrived at the island's wharf, their worst suspicions were confirmed. Someone lit a brush fire the night after the dozing started, burning off the tall, dry grass that had obscured the many stone walls on the rocky hillsides. These walls were now glaringly visible from the main road. Otsuji had gotten threatening calls from angry locals demanding to know what they were doing about the sites. The Moloka'i people have a well-deserved reputation for fiercely defending their island's low-key lifestyle.

"Didn't the Maui County Planning Commission require you guys to do an archaeological survey before they OK'd the project?" I asked. Otsuji looked sheepish. "Well, we didn't go through the Commission," he said. I stared at him in disbelief. "How'd you get the grading permit then?" He said that the area was already zoned for two-acre agricultural plots, so the county had just given them the OK.

"But isn't this going to be a residential subdivision?" I pressed him. Otsuji did not answer; he knew Senator Yee's under-the-table plans were now out in the open. Under the guise of opening up two-acre plots for some "gentlemen farmers," they had gotten away with approval for a major subdivision covering more than five hundred acres. There had been no archaeological survey or environmental impact assessment. That was the way things often worked in the good-old-boy networks of Hawai'i, where the state's legislators and government officials were often silent investors in *hui,* or development schemes.[5]

Walking up the bulldozed road cut, I saw where the D9 operator had sliced through several rock walls, shell midden and bones scattered over the bulldozed ground. At this point the Hawaiian bulldozer operator had gotten spooked, telling his boss he would not go any farther. I could see more stone structures ahead.

"How long will it take you guys to do an archaeological survey? Two, three days?" Otsuji asked when we came back down to the car. I looked at him in disbelief. "Are you kidding? The place is *covered* in sites. We'll need at least two or three weeks to do an initial reconnaissance survey and make some recommendations.

Then we'll take it from there." Otsuji's jaw dropped. You could see the dollar signs going round in his head. But with the Molokaʻi community up in arms, he had little choice.

In the end the museum's archaeological survey and excavations at Kawela and adjacent Makakupaʻia would take a full year of fieldwork. I hired Marshall Weisler, a young Californian archaeologist who had shown up in my University of Hawaiʻi class on Hawaiian archaeology, to be the field director. I flew over periodically to supervise the work (Fig. 10.1); it was always a pleasure to get out of my museum office and into the field.

The Kawela project provided an opportunity to study the settlement pattern of a large leeward *ahupuaʻa,* one that contrasted dramatically with what I had studied a decade earlier in Hālawa. This arid part of Molokaʻi receives only around twelve inches of rain each year, too little to support Polynesian crops. However, Kawela Gulch tapped headwaters in the east Molokaʻi mountains where rainfall is higher; the stream probably had perennial flow in precontact times. We discovered small sets of formerly irrigated *loʻi* terraces in the mid-reaches of Kawela Gulch. Nearer to the coast, there were the remains of *ʻauwai* or ditches that carried water from the stream to the floodplain, where the Kawela farmers had cultivated sweet potato, relying on heightened streamflow during the winter

Figure 10.1. Bishop Museum staff making a site visit to Kawela, Molokaʻi. From left to right: Patrick McCoy, Douglas Yen, Carl Christensen, Yosihiko Sinoto, and the author.

months. Their other major food resource consisted of several large fishponds for raising mullet and milkfish, arc-shaped stone-walled enclosures constructed out onto the broad reef flat that skirts southern Molokaʻi.

In our year of fieldwork we surveyed nearly eight square kilometers of that hot, parched landscape, recording 499 archaeological features including *heiau* and shrines, residential complexes, agricultural complexes, and petroglyphs.[6] A noteworthy discovery was the *puʻuhonua,* or place of refuge, which straddles the steep ridge between the two forks of Kawela Gulch. Samuel Kamakau had written about how Kawela had been the scene of several important battles, but no one had found the actual *puʻuhonua* structure before. Under my direction, Weisler also excavated several of the habitation complexes, recovering a great deal of new information about how space and activities were organized in these *kauhale.*

After completing the survey, we convinced Senator Yee to rearrange the subdivision roadways and house lots to protect the most important sites, including the *heiau,* two chiefly residential complexes, and several petroglyph sites. It was a great disappointment, however, when Yee failed to follow through on his promise to fund the analysis and publication of our results. His investment *hui* ended up in bankruptcy.

While the Kawela project was proceeding on Molokaʻi, I got to know some of the local activists, including Emmett Aluli, Colette Machado, Walter Ritte, and Karen Holt. They shared their concerns that the Hawaiian cultural heritage was being bulldozed under for the sake of development. They pressed me to use archaeology as a lever to shut down Senator Yee's project. I was sympathetic but explained that I had to follow my professional standards. I would do the best I could to protect significant sites, but if I claimed that every rock mound was "significant" I would lose credibility.

Aluli, whom I respected a lot, grasped the fine line that archaeologists were walking. An MD practicing in the island's only clinic, Aluli was a founder of the Protect Kahoʻolawe ʻOhana (PKO). With several others, he had occupied Kahoʻolawe Island in protest, hiding out from the U.S. military for days. In 1976 Aluli filed suit in federal court to stop the military's use of Kahoʻolawe as a bombing range, citing damage to archaeological sites. While the Kawela survey was in progress, the PKO was granted legal access to the island to make cultural visits under a consent decree by the court.[7]

In 1980 Aluli invited me to join him on Kahoʻolawe on the second cultural access visit. With us were my good friend from Maui, Charles Pili Keau, and "Uncle Harry" Mitchell, both respected *kūpuna,* along with a group of Hawaiian students from Kamehameha Schools. We landed at Hakioʻawa Bay where there are *heiau* and other sites. For three days we hiked the barren landscape, a team of U.S. Army explosive ordnance disposal experts in front to keep us from stepping on one of the countless unexploded bombs that littered the island. At night we sat around the campfire at Hakioʻawa, "talking story." The students danced hula. The last day we made a grueling hike to Ahupū to see a magnificent petroglyph panel, then swam out to the boat, which took us back to Lahaina.

The experience made me appreciate all the more the growing *Aloha ʻĀina* movement. "Love of the land" was PKO's watchword. *Malama ka ʻĀina*—"Take care of the land." Don't bomb it, bulldoze it, scrape it, or pave it over. Not only the PKO and Native Hawaiians but also many island people were getting fed up with the rampant development that was sweeping Hawaiʻi, driven by profit-seeking corporate boards in Tokyo, Chicago, and New York. Lots of people wondered where it was all leading.

With all the changes in Hawaiian archaeology there was much talk about setting up a professional organization to promote archaeology in the state. In September 1980 many of Hawaiʻi's archaeologists gathered for a meeting at the Bishop Museum organized by Tom Riley. The discussions droned on throughout the humid afternoon about the new Society for Hawaiian Archaeology's mission and its proposed bylaws. Then, discussion turned to whom the fledgling society's officers would be. Having my hands full, I did not want to put my name forward, and I stepped outside. Doug Yen, sitting under the shady mango tree, had breached the cooler of beers awaiting the meeting's end. He handed me a bottle. While we were chatting, Riley emerged from the meeting, extending his hand and telling me, "Congratulations, Pat. You've just been unanimously elected president of the Society for Hawaiian Archaeology." A lesson learned the hard way—always stay in a meeting if there is a possibility you might be nominated.

Despite my initial reticence I took the charge seriously. The society's board of directors set up committees to address the challenges facing archaeology in the islands. One committee, chaired by Rose Schilt, was Standards and Ethics. With the increasing number of for-profit archaeology consulting firms, it was not clear that everyone was adhering to the same professional standards. Some outfits operated at the margins, cutting costs to turn a profit. The consultants knew that an archaeologist who took a hard line about site preservation was unlikely to get hired for the next contract. Developers talked to each other; word got around.

Early one morning in 1981—it was still pre-dawn—the phone rang in our apartment. Half asleep I picked up the receiver to hear Emmett Aluli's voice: "Aloha Pat. Hope we aren't waking you up [he was]." Then I heard Colette Machado, Karen Holt, and Alan Murakami all chime in. I was on the receiving end of a conference call from the Kaunakakai office of the Legal Aid Society, a non-profit group helping Native Hawaiians. The four of them had been up all night plotting strategy.

"We understand that the Society for Hawaiian Archaeology [SHA] has set up a Standards and Ethics Committee" Aluli said. "Yes, that's right," I replied, wondering what was coming next. "Do you know about the proposed project at Kawākiu Bay, on the West End? A development *hui* wants to put in a condominium along with a golf course."

Murakami chimed in: "An archaeological consultant has issued a report saying that there are no significant sites at Kawākiu. But we've been out there. We think important sites have been overlooked. Will SHA help us? Will you guys do an independent review to see whether the consultant did a proper job?"

I told them I would talk with my colleagues and call back later that afternoon. I knew it was a critical moment for archaeology in Hawai'i. Did archaeologists really care about the Hawaiian past, about preserving the island's cultural and historical legacy? Or were we just there to make money from the developers?

I talked with the other members of SHA's board of directors. There were mixed feelings. Taking this on could tear the newly founded society apart. The consulting firm being challenged by the Moloka'i activists included several people with prominent political connections. On the other hand, to ignore the request would be to turn our backs on the Native Hawaiians. I felt we at least owed it to them to have a look at Kawākiu. My colleagues agreed.

A few days later I flew to Moloka'i with Standards and Ethics Committee chair Rose Schilt and Paul Cleghorn, a committee member. Aluli, Machado, and Holt met us at Ho'olehua. We jumped into the back of a pickup truck and started down the long dirt road to Kawākiu. The property was private land, belonging to Moloka'i Ranch, but Aluli and the others had won a lawsuit giving them access to the West End beaches. However, they could only do so via this long, unpaved dirt track.

Kawākiu is a beautiful bay framed by two lava rock promontories. The most important site was, without question, a stone enclosure on the southern headland. It had unusual architecture, with an exterior facing of large upright basalt slabs. Emory had recorded the site back in 1952, calling it a *heiau*. I thought it was probably a *ko'a* or fishing shrine. The consultants had dug out about half of the interior, finding more than fifty bone fishhooks. I was shocked that they had recommended that this unique site—a religious shrine to the fish god Kū'ula—simply be bulldozed away.

More surprises were to come. The fishing shrine was surrounded by an extensive midden that the consultants claimed was "deflated," destroyed by wind erosion. But the consultants' unfilled test pits clearly showed intact stratigraphy.

So, the remains of an extensive fishing village that had once surrounded the *koʻa* would also be destroyed to make way for condominium units to be purchased by wealthy *haole* from the Mainland.

We began walking around the bay, finding nearly a dozen sites that the consultants had missed. We sat down on some boulders near the beach. "What do you think, Pat?" Holt asked me. "Karen, there is no way that this report meets the standards that SHA's members expect." Schilt and Cleghorn nodded in agreement. "We'll write a report and provide testimony if the project is contested."

The Kawākiu controversy dragged on for months. SHA produced our promised report, which the Legal Aid Society used to challenge the proposed development. Holt called to tell me that the Land Use Commission would hold an on-site visit at Kawākiu. Would I come over to Molokaʻi to be present at the site visit?

Roger Green was in the islands, teaching for a year at the University of Hawaiʻi. I called Green to say that I would be flying over to Molokaʻi for the Kawākiu hearing. Would he join me? Always an advocate for site preservation, Green did not hesitate.

On a Saturday morning, Green and I took the early morning Air Molokaʻi DC-3 flight to Hoʻolehua. Aluli, Machado, and Holt met us, delighted that two prominent archaeologists were joining them to protest the potential destruction of sites at Kawākiu. Once again we piled into the back of a pickup for the long, dusty ride down to the bay. Meanwhile the commissioners were riding in air-conditioned vans via the paved road to Kaluakoʻi Resort, a much shorter route but one denied to the Hawaiian activists.

Arriving at Kawākiu we found the commissioners and the developers' attorneys, as well as reporters and cameramen from the Honolulu TV stations. The controversy over Kawākiu had hit the news media. Each side spoke their piece. I pointed out the *koʻa,* the midden, and sites that had been missed in the consultant's survey. The commissioners did not say much or ask questions; one got the feeling that the commissioners' site visit was merely a token formality, that the decision had already been made. Toward the end of the visit, a group of Hawaiian *kūpuna* who had come down on pickup trucks with us formed a circle near the *koʻa.* Instinctively, Aluli and I joined the linked circle. A strong voice began singing:

E Hawaiʻi e kuʻu one hanau e	O Hawaiʻi, o sands of my birth
Kuʻu home kulaiwi nei	My native home
ʻOli no au i na pono lani ou	I rejoice in the blessings of heaven
E Hawaiʻi, aloha e.	O Hawaiʻi, aloha.
E hauʻoli na ʻopio o Hawaiʻi nei	Happy youth of Hawaiʻi
ʻOli e! ʻOli e!	Rejoice! Rejoice!

Mai na aheahe makani e pa mai nei   Gentle breezes blow my way
Mau ke aloha, no Hawai'i   Love always, for Hawai'i

"Hawai'i Aloha" is one of the most powerful songs of old Hawai'i. Composed in the nineteenth century by Reverend Lorenzo Lyons of Waimea, Hawai'i, the song had became part of the repertoire of the emerging protest movement. Holding hands in a circle, we joined in as the commissioners watched silently and the TV cameras whirred.

The following Monday morning I got a call from museum director Creutz's secretary. "Dr. Creutz would like you to come to his office immediately," she informed me. I had a pretty good idea that Cruetz had seen the Sunday TV news, including me standing in the circle at Kawakiu, singing "Hawai'i Aloha."

Sitting down opposite Ed Creutz, the director looked me in the eye and said, "I've just got one question, Pat. When you testified over the weekend on Moloka'i, did you do so in the name of Bishop Museum?"

"No, Ed," I replied. "You know that I'm president of SHA. I testified in that capacity. And I explicitly disclaimed that I was representing the museum."

"That's what I thought, but I wanted to know for certain. You did the ethical thing. I'll support you." Earlier that morning one of the museum's trustees, a powerful business leader and member of an old *kama'āina* family, had called to demand that I be fired. The trustee was also an investor in the *hui* that wanted to build the condominium at Kawākiu. Creutz may not have been the most effective director of the Bishop Museum, but he had integrity. I remain in his debt for protecting me when I stood up for scientific ethics.[8]

The whole affair made me think hard. Bishop Museum scientists did not have tenure. We were on year-to-year contracts. Although we liked to think that we had academic freedom, the next time I might pay a steep price for speaking up too prominently. Maybe it was time to think about leaving the museum for a university position.

In fact, I had already begun teaching part-time at the University of Hawai'i. After I finished my Yale dissertation at the end of 1975, the UH's Anthropology department asked if I would teach a course on data processing in archaeology. Back then the use of computers to analyze archaeological data was still in its infancy. Computing was done on giant mainframes such as the university's IBM-360, which took up an entire floor. The data had to be fed in on stacks of punch cards; then you waited hours for the printout to be delivered. I had learned statistical computing at Yale and was using computers in my own research to analyze the pottery and adzes from Niuatoputapu and Tikopia. I happily agreed to teach the course, not the least because it would augment my museum salary.

The use of computers both in research and in daily life was changing rapidly. During the early 1980s "personal" computers first began to appear on the market. Given my experience using university mainframes to analyze archaeological data, I could see the potential value in having one's own desktop computer. In 1984 I took the plunge and purchased a Kaypro-4/84, coughing up the equivalent of two months' salary for it. Housed in a sturdy aluminum box, the machine (which I still have stashed in my closet) is a primitive fossil in the evolution of computers. It had just 64K of active memory and a green monochrome CRT screen nine inches wide, and it read a single 5 ¼-inch "floppy" disk on which data had to be stored. Yet it seemed a marvel at the time, a crucial step toward our contemporary world in which computers dominate every aspect of our lives.

I continued to teach courses at UH's Manoa campus. I even took a leave from the museum during the 1979–1980 academic year to teach full time at the university. At the end of that year the UH department offered me a position as assistant professor. I was tempted, but the position was offered to me without tenure. Ed Creutz matched UH's salary offer, and I decided to remain at the Bishop Museum.

In the fall of 1981 a filmmaker named Sam Low contacted me. Raised on the Mainland, Low was descended from a Hawaiian *paniolo* (cowboy) family; his cousin was the *Hokuleʻa*'s young navigator, Nainoa Thompson. Low had gotten his PhD in cultural anthropology from Harvard and then began making anthropological films. He had become fascinated with Polynesian migrations and voyaging after hearing about the path-breaking voyage of the *Hokuleʻa* from Hawaiʻi to Tahiti in 1976, guided by the Micronesian way-finder Mau Piailug. Low wanted to make a PBS documentary featuring Piailug, weaving in discoveries in Polynesian archaeology. As we bounced around ideas in my museum office, I got more excited about the potential for a major documentary film. When Low asked if I would be his consultant on the project I did not hesitate to accept.

Much of 1982 was spent in developing the film's script as well as shooting on location in Hawaiʻi, Fiji, Huahine, and on Piailug's home island of Satawal in the Caroline Islands. Low hired Boyd Estus, an Academy Award-winning cinematographer. His gorgeous scenes of Piailug sailing his outrigger canoe and of teaching star paths to the young men of Satawal in the men's house are ethnographic classics.

Roger Green and I traveled to Fiji to film the famous Sigatoka sand dunes with their Lapita pottery. Green was nervous in front of a camera and kept blowing his lines; he finally managed to get out a coherent explanation of the pottery sherds eroding out of the dune. In one of Sigatoka's villages we also filmed two of the last women potters, inheritors of the Lapita pottery-making tradition. On Molokaʻi Island, the team filmed me at the Hālawa dune site that I had excavated a few years earlier.

The Navigators: Pathfinders of the Pacific was released in 1983 and shown nationally on PBS. In 2013 it was digitally remastered and re-released as a DVD. The film was featured at the Hawaiʻi Book and Music Festival in May 2013; watching it there three decades after it was produced, I was still impressed at how well it tells the story of the Polynesian seafarers. (I was also impressed at the size of the bushy black beard I wore in those days!)

By the end of the 1970s, the museum's Hawaiian contract archaeology program was busier than ever. Sinoto wanted to bring in as many contracts as possible. In contrast, I thought that we should be more selective, only taking on projects that could produce new insights into the Hawaiian past. Such an opportunity arose in late 1979 when the state's Department of Transportation (DOT) approached the museum about a proposed new highway between the town of Waimea and the port of Kawaihae on Hawaiʻi Island.

Surveying a thirty-two-kilometer road corridor did not at first glance seem like an exciting prospect. But I realized that the Waimea-Kawaihae highway project provided an opportunity for an innovative research design. The road corridor was in essence a transect, running from the lush uplands of Waimea down through the intermediate zones to the arid coastal region around Kawaihae. It would give us an excellent sample of the settlement patterns across a range of environmental zones.

Meeting with the planners and engineers from the DOT, I told them that, in addition to the standard archaeological survey and test excavations, I wanted to include an interdisciplinary collaboration with natural scientists to help us reconstruct the ancient environment along the transect. This collaboration would be based on charcoal, pollen, land snails, and other materials that we expected to recover in the excavations. The DOT administrators gave me the OK to include it in our budget.

The fieldwork, conducted from 1980–1981, took more than a year to accomplish. A PhD student from the University of Illinois, Jeffrey Clark, directed the day-to-day work; I flew over to Waimea as often as I could to check up on the progress. I enlisted Gail Murakami, a lab assistant to UH botanist Charles H. Lamoureux, to identify the charcoal that we dug out of the many hearths and earth ovens. Deborah Pearsall came over from the Mainland to work on opal phytoliths (microscopic silica "skeletons" within plants) from the site sediments; they gave hints about changing grasslands over time. Palynologist Thecla

Bennett from the UH extracted pollen grains for additional clues to ancient forest conditions, while malacologist Carl Christensen at the museum worked up land snail shells. Meanwhile a team of archaeologists analyzed the artifacts and faunal materials from the many sites we tested.

In 1983 the results of our Waimea-Kawaihae project were published by the museum in a 532-page volume edited by Clark and me. Pulling together varied strands of evidence, we demonstrated how centuries of Hawaiian land use transformed this leeward landscape from pristine dryland forest to open grasslands and—in the wetter uplands—intensively farmed dryland fields. The Waimea-Kawaihae project took Hawaiian settlement pattern archaeology to a new level, placing sites into the context of dynamic landscape change. The project demonstrated that contract archaeology could be combined with cutting-edge research.[9] I still feel that it represents the best of what the Bishop Museum accomplished during the heyday of its Hawaiian archaeology program.

CHAPTER ELEVEN

The Anahulu Valley
(Kawailoa, Oʻahu, 1982)

In the early 1970s Marshall Sahlins, a rising star in American anthropology, began to work on the historical anthropology of the Hawaiian Kingdom. Sahlins
had written an influential study of Polynesian social stratification,[1] and after working with the famous Claude Lévi-Strauss in Paris, published his widely read
Stone Age Economics.[2] In his book Sahlins argued that Hawaiian society at the time
of Captain Cook had pushed what anthropologists call the "chiefdom" mode of
political organization to its limits. A deeper investigation of traditional Hawaiian society would surely be rewarding.

The problem was that you could not just do an ethnography of Hawaiian society the way you could do one on Anuta or Tikopia. After Cook's arrival in 1778–
1779, a succession of fur traders, merchants, missionaries, ranchers, and sugar
planters descended on the islands. The Native Hawaiian population plummeted;
people adopted new ideas and new technologies, abandoned their old religion, and
converted to Christianity. The old chiefship morphed into a kingdom incorporating European concepts of monarchy and American legal codes. Then, in 1893,
Queen Liliʻuokalani was deposed; in 1900 Hawaiʻi became a territory of the United
States. By the time anthropologists such as Edward Craighill Handy began to study
"traditional" Hawaiian culture in the 1920s and 1930s, Hawaiian society had been
through a century and a half of wracking changes.

Sahlins decided to turn to the rich documentary record of Hawaiʻi from the
late eighteenth and early nineteenth centuries, stashed away in the Hawaiʻi State
Archives and other libraries. They contained the journals of early explorers and
traders, missionary letters and church ledgers, archives of the fledgling kingdom
after literacy was introduced in the early 1820s, and, most importantly, the claims,
testimony, and surveys from the Great Mahele of 1846–1854 when the kingdom's
lands were divided among the king, high chiefs, and the common people. These
sources constituted a treasure trove largely untapped by anthropologists.[3] Sahlins
realized he would need the expertise of scholars familiar with Hawaiian documents, who could read Hawaiian-language texts; he enlisted the aid of Marion
Kelly and Dorothy Barrère of the Bishop Museum. Kelly studied Hawaiian

land tenure, whereas Barrère—who had edited the works of the famous Samuel Kamakau—was familiar with nineteenth-century Hawaiian language.

With support from the National Science Foundation (NSF), from 1971–1974 Sahlins and his team delved into the archives, mostly focusing on Kaua'i. But they also uncovered a mass of documents relating to the Anahulu Valley, a deep, narrow gash cutting through layered lava beds of O'ahu's Ko'olau Mountains. Anahulu Stream issues into Waialua Bay, setting for the historical plantation town of Haleiwa. Anahulu Valley formed the core of Kawailoa, the central *ahupua'a* of Waialua District. After the death of King Kamehameha I in 1819, Waialua became the most important estate of the high chiefess Ka'ahumanu, the late king's favorite wife and regent over the young King Liholiho. Irrigated taro fields and abundant fish harvested from the Loko'ia and 'Uko'a fishponds supplied Ka'ahumanu's establishment in Honolulu. After her death these estates passed to her heir Kīna'u and then to Kīna'u's daughter Victoria Kamāmalu. Because of Waialua's importance to these high *ali'i*, there were reams of documents relating to land tenure, social organization, and the local economy. In addition, the Rev. John S. Emerson had established a mission station at Anahulu in 1832; his extensive records were preserved in the Hawaiian Mission Children's Society.

After I returned from Futuna in 1974, Sahlins asked me one day at the Bishop Museum if I would like to collaborate on a combined archaeological and historical study of the Anahulu Valley. Although both archaeology and social anthropology were in principle integrated into the holistic discipline of anthropology in American universities (as at Penn and Yale where I had studied), in practice the two subfields almost never collaborated. Sahlins' idea of using archaeology to uncover physical traces of the social and political system revealed through his "historical ethnography" was truly innovative.

Taking Sahlins up on his offer, I reconnoitered Anahulu in the spring of 1975, locating stone house platforms and taro terraces that were mentioned in the archival records. My team also dug into a rockshelter that took the valley's past back into the precontact era (Fig. 11.1) There was clearly overwhelming potential to link the valley's archaeological landscape with the rich documentary record of the nineteenth century.[4]

In 1980 Sahlins took a year's leave from the University of Chicago, coming to Honolulu to teach at the University of Hawai'i. Meeting often at the Bishop Museum, we drafted an NSF proposal implementing our vision of a dual archaeological and historical ethnographic project. We pointed out that archaeologists and social anthropologists working in Polynesia had rarely collaborated. Archaeologists focused on the precontact era, whereas social anthropologists were interested either in reconstructing an idealized "ethnographic present" at the time of

Figure 11.1. Completed excavation in a rockshelter in the Anahulu Valley, Oʻahu Island.

first contact, or in studying contemporary Polynesian societies. We wanted to break down these academic silos, to pursue an integrated *anthropology of history,* a synthetic collaboration between the two subdisciplines. While Sahlins would use archival research to uncover the cultural structures and trends of Hawaiian history, I would seek to discover how they were materially manifested in the archaeological sites of the Anahulu Valley.

But our goals went beyond the innovative collaboration of archival-based historical ethnography and field archaeology. Rather than concentrate on the period before European contact—and on the reconstruction of an idealized late precontact Hawaiian society—we wanted to unravel in fine-grained detail the changes that swept through Hawaiʻi in the decades following the fateful arrival of Captain James Cook in 1778–1779. Once again, we were pushing the envelope, moving into a time period that had largely been ignored by previous scholars, at least in Hawaiʻi and Polynesia.

The National Science Foundation funded our project, and I organized a team to carry out the fieldwork during the summer of 1982. The months of June through August are usually the driest time of the year on Oʻahu, but in 1982 they turned out to be one of the wettest on record. The trails descending from the sugarcane fields of Waialua Plantation into the valley turned into slippery, muddy slides; Anahulu Stream repeatedly rose to flood stage. At one ford we had to string up a rope line to keep the crew from getting washed away while crossing. The clay soils in the house sites stuck to our trowels and would not pass through the mesh sieves; we carried buckets of water-logged dirt to the stream to wet-sieve it so that we could find the fragments of iron nails, glass beads, and crockery in these early postcontact sites. It was taxing work, but I was fortunate to have a young and enthusiastic team, many of whom later went on to careers in Pacific archaeology (Fig. 11.2).

Braving rain, floods, and mud, we excavated in a dozen house sites dispersed over the upper valley, between 'Ili Keae and 'Ili Mikiai.[5] The stone-faced house terraces were situated on low bluffs overlooking the formerly irrigated fields. Stone walls, *pā hale,* surrounded many of the house terraces dating to the time of the Mahele. Constructing enclosures around houses was a missionary idea, reflecting Yankee concepts of private property. The large house platform once occupied by Kamakea in 'Ili Kapuahilua was fronted by a *lānai* or patio paved with smooth stream cobbles. Kamakea, a prominent member of Rev. Emerson's

Figure 11.2. The 1982 Anahulu team at the end of a long day of fieldwork. From left to right: Matthew Spriggs, June Cleghorn, Sara Collins, the author, Marshall Weisler, Laura Carter Schuster, Melinda Allen, and Jim Landrum.

church and a kind of leader or "big man" of the upper valley, had been visited by the missionary in June 1837. After feeding the reverend "a chicken and some sweet potatoes cooked in the native stile [sic]," Kamakea "blew his horn of shell and in a few moments abut 50 people assembled" to hear a short sermon.[6]

While the house site excavations continued, I dug into three rockshelters in 'Ili Ke'eke'e. The upper layers produced gun flints and trade beads, early postcontact trade items, whereas the deeper deposits contained basalt flakes, bone awls, fragments of bone and shell fishhooks, and, in one shelter, a bone tattooing needle. The largest rockshelter, Ke'eke'e Nui, had been occupied since the fourteenth century. In that earlier time before European contact, the upper valley was cultivated with shifting cultivations. The irrigation systems on the alluvial flats came later, after Kamehameha conquered O'ahu in 1795, redistributing the lands to his warriors.[7]

While we dug in the house sites and rockshelters, Sahlins pored over the archives in Honolulu. He discerned that the early postcontact history of Waialua could be divided into three phases. The first—the Conquest Period—spanned the time from Kamehameha's 1795 conquest (followed by his reoccupation of O'ahu in 1804) until the great warrior king returned to Hawai'i Island in 1812. During this Conquest Period Kamehameha and his followers intensively exploited the best agricultural lands of O'ahu, greatly expanding the irrigation works in Waialua and elsewhere.

The next phase in the valley's nineteenth-century history was the Sandalwood Period, from 1812 until 1830. Sandalwood was one of the few items that China was interested in obtaining from Western traders; after the discovery that the Hawaiian forests contained abundant sandalwood trees there was a frenzy to log the fragrant wood. The commoners worked long days in O'ahu's mountains, cutting and hauling the logs at the direction of the chiefs, who in turn sold the wood to American and British traders. In 1829 the sandalwood trade abruptly collapsed; the forests had been stripped of all the large trees, while a new, cheaper source had been discovered in Vanuatu. This marked the beginning of the Whaling Period, which ran through the 1830s and 1840s. The rapidly expanding Pacific whaling fleet offered the chiefs a new economic opportunity: supplying and refitting the vessels. This in turn spurred a renewed phase of agricultural intensification in Anahulu, where the commoners' farms supplied the food, pigs, barkcloth, cordage, and materials that the chiefs traded to the whalers.

Occasionally Sahlins would leave the archives and come out to Anahulu to see what we were up to. On one such visit when, uncharacteristically, it was not raining, Sahlins and I decided to hike upstream. We wanted to find 'Ili Mikiai, the inlandmost named land section, where a man named Mailou had once lived. Mailou was a true *kama'āina* of 'Ili Mikiai, noting in his 1848 Mahele claim, "My parents lived and died there, and at this time I am there." Mailou was a noted cultivator, listing in his claim not only irrigated *loʻi* but also many *ʻokipū* in the *kuahiwi* or forests, places where he had gardens, probably planted with such crops as *ʻawa*, bananas, and *ʻolonā*.

As Sahlins and I headed up the valley we heard the buzzing of helicopters echoing off the canyon walls ahead. The upper reaches of Anahulu had, since the time of the Vietnam War, been used as a jungle warfare training area by the U.S. Army. We crossed the stream, following an indistinct footpath used by pig hunters. Walking under some huge old mango trees, a Huey gunship suddenly appeared, just above the tree canopy. The roar of the big chopper's rotor was deafening. A couple of minutes later the gunship passed overhead again; this pattern was repeated several times. I realized that the pilots must be using an infrared sensor, picking up our body heat, as they did with Viet Cong soldiers during the war. They were tracking us.

After a few minutes we came to another stream crossing. Suddenly, the dark green chopper came roaring down the valley, no more than a hundred feet off the ground. We could see the pilot and co-pilot looking at us through their plexiglass windshield. Sahlins, an early opponent of the Vietnam War, harbored a visceral dislike of the military; he had organized one of the first antiwar teach-ins at the University of Michigan in 1965. As the Huey thundered overhead Sahlins showed the pilots his middle finger.

I never imagined that a big Huey could be maneuvered so deftly. The pilot whipped the chopper around, banking it to give us a broadside of rotor wash. The blast ripped pebbles from the stream bank, hitting us like birdshot. I could see the gunner in the side door, aiming his machine gun at us with a sinister grin on his face. For a split second I thought he might pull the trigger. Having answered Sahlins' gesture, the Huey turned and flew back up valley.

We found the traces of Mailou's house site on the slopes at ʻIli Mikiai, marked by two ancient, towering coconut palms; Mailou himself had most likely planted them. Retracing our route, we returned to join the diggers. When he heard of our encounter with the gunship, one of the crew members became incensed. He vowed to call his father, a high-ranking officer at Schofield Barracks, to report that a prominent professor from the University of Chicago had been harassed by a U.S. Army helicopter.

The next morning I stopped by the museum to get some equipment before heading out to Anahulu. When I entered the Anthropology Department office, Pat Bacon handed me a couple of slips with telephone messages. "This colonel has already called several times," she told me. "He seems pretty agitated." After I got the youngish-sounding colonel on the phone and identified myself, he demanded to know, "What are your coordinates, Sir!" Word had come down the chain of command after the crew member told his father what had happened. The colonel in charge of helicopter operations was going to make sure that they knew our field position and that nobody got rotor-washed again!

During the Great Mahele of 1848–1854 the people of Waialua—Mailou, Kamakea, Kainiki, and others—entered their claims for their house lots, loʻi fields, and other lands before the Board of Commissioners to Quiet Land Titles. Their parcels were later surveyed by the Rev. Emerson. Using these sources, it was possible to reconstruct the valley's hierarchical system of land tenure. Extended family groups, often centered around a local "big man" such as Kamakea, inhabited the many ʻili segments into which the ahupuaʻa was subdivided. Eight such ʻili in the upper valley occupied alluvial flats sandwiched between the steep cliffs and the meandering stream (Fig. 11.3). The amount of taro land awarded by the commissioners reflected the relative rank of the households. Older, kamaʻāina households who traced their tenure back to the time of Kamehameha I received more irrigated loʻi, whereas newcomers known as hoaʻāina (literally "friends of the land") worked smaller plots under the supervision of the konohiki. These hoaʻāina either received very small landholdings or nothing at all. The idea that all makaʻāinana in traditional Hawaiʻi had been equal was clearly false.

The archives contained a remarkable record of the demands made by the high-ranking aliʻi such as Kaʻahumanu, Kīnaʻu, and Kamāmalu upon the common people of Waialua. A series of letters written by Paulo Kanoa, secretary to the premier (Kuhina Nui) Kīnaʻu in the mid-1830s, and addressed to Gidiona Laʻanui, the valley's konohiki, detail the constant demands for taro, pigs, fish, and other products. A minor aliʻi, Laʻanui had married Kaʻahumanu's sister Piʻia. Kanoa always began his letters to Laʻanui with the saluation, "Aloha to you, Gidiona."[8] One such letter, written on July 17, 1837, contained this demand:

> Aloha to you, G. Laanui and your wife and children:
>   Here is an order to you. The ship has come [to Waialua] for the sweet potatoes and also the annual 20 pigs for the aliʻi, also fish, also a little taro, whatever is available. But don't be slow, because we are starving . . .

Another letter in September 1838 began by complaining that the last load of fish had been short; then Kanoa continued:

> You are to send over the taro from there. You are to count it and the fish correctly and then write. . . . You are to load twenty pigs . . . good ones, for the king on his arrival with the man-of-war.

Figure 11.3. A view of the middle sector of the Anahulu Valley, Oʻahu Island.

The "Aloha Gidiona" letters reveal the constant strain that the *makaʻāinana* of Anahulu were under to ensure that Paulo Kanoa's demands were met.

Up in the valley, I had located and mapped the archaeological remains of nine irrigation systems. The largest, in ʻIli Kaloaloa, covered about 1.7 hectares; the smallest consisted of a handful of small plots. Sahlins was fascinated when I showed him how the branching pattern of the irrigation canals mirrored the kinship relationships between farmers.

I invited Matthew Spriggs, a newly arrived assistant professor at the University of Hawaiʻi, to collaborate on my study of Anahulu irrigation. An enthusiastic blond Englishman, Spriggs brought new energy to the university's archaeology program. For his thesis at the Australian National University, Spriggs had done ethnoarchaeological work on traditional taro farming on Aneityum Island in Vanuatu. Drawing upon his Vanuatu data, Spriggs estimated labor inputs and yields of the Anahulu irrigation systems. The results amazed me. When they were in full production, the Anahulu taro fields had likely produced a surplus of 50 percent more than what was required to feed the workforce; the surplus might even have been as high as 70 percent. No wonder Kamehameha I had coveted the Oʻahu lands with their rich pondfields—they could fuel the political ambitions of a chief who wanted to become a king.

Before European contact, the Hawaiian political economy had been largely supported by an agricultural "staple economy," as my colleague Timothy Earle called it. But a parallel "wealth economy" based upon the manufacture and distribution of durable, prestige goods—especially featherwork such as capes, cloaks, and helmets, and also high-quality stone adzes, barkcloth, and other items—had also emerged in the centuries before Cook's arrival. The *ali'i* differentiated themselves from the common people in part through their consumption and display of these prestige items.

After European contact, a vast new range of Western goods began to be imported to Hawai'i by the sandalwood traders and merchants. The chiefs, no longer content with their feathered garments, purchased large quantities of sumptuary items, ranging from swords, uniforms, and silk stockings to porcelain and silver table settings, paying for them with shiploads of sandalwood. The old wealth economy based upon feathers gave way to what Sahlins called a "political economy of grandeur" as the *ali'i* vied to outdo each other with the newly acquired Western goods.[9]

The Hawaiian political economy became increasingly entangled with the tentacles of a predatory Western capitalism; the extravagant expenditures of the chiefs had to be paid for, at some point, in cash. Racking up huge debts in the sandalwood trade, the *ali'i* turned in the 1830s and 1840s to new ways of producing income. In Honolulu, there was a booming business in provisioning the growing whaling fleet with taro, yams, and sweet potatoes. Ships and rigging were refitted using barkcloth for caulking and *'olonā* for cord and line. All of these materials were part of the surplus generated by the *maka'āinana* farmers in Anahulu and in O'ahu's other valleys.

The original Hawaiian system of *ho'okupu* (tribute) owed by the commoners to their *konohiki* and *ali'i* landlords, collected annually in the name of Lono during the Makahiki circuit, had morphed under the influence of capitalism into an increasingly oppressive form of surplus extraction. Rev. Emerson, observing the effect on his flock in Waialua, wrote to his brethren in Honolulu bemoaning this oppression of the common people. His wife Ursula noted in her diary that when King Kamehameha III toured Waialua in 1833 with an entourage of two hundred or more retainers and lesser chiefs, the commoners were obliged to slaughter "pigs, dogs, fish, and fowl . . . in large numbers" and to provide "ever so many calabashes of poi." Upon the king's departure Rev. Emerson commented, "They go now like a company of locusts, eat all before them & leave the land behind them *pilau loa* [hugely stinking]."[10]

A schoolteacher named Kai'aikawaha, when asked by Emerson about the chiefs' demands upon the *maka'āinana,* responded with a parable. There was, he said, a man of Paʻalaʻa who had been beaten and thrown into a deep pit where the people went to dispose of their excrement. After a time the man was heard to talk; passersby would call out to him, "*Kanaka ʻai kūkae*" (man who eats shit). The Paʻalaʻa man would answer, "*Kiʻo mai, kiʻo mai,*" (shit on me, shit on me). Just so, explained Kaiʻaikawaha to Emerson, the people of Waialua have nothing left but to say "*kiʻo mai, kiʻo mai.*"[11]

Yet it was not just the high *aliʻi* in Honolulu who exploited the common people of Waialua. The *haole* newcomers coveted the lands and water rights of the *makaʻāinana*. Cattle ranching had begun in Waialua before the Mahele—the herds descending into the valley, wreaking devastation on the gardens and irrigated fields. To little avail, the *makaʻāinana* built stone walls to keep the foreigners' beasts at bay. In the aftermath of the Mahele, with land now available for purchase in fee simple, sugar plantations sprang up all over the islands. The tablelands surrounding Anahulu were ideal for planting sugar, but they needed to be irrigated. The Waialua Agricultural Company started buying up the *kuleana* or small plots of the commoners scattered throughout the valley so as to control the water rights that went with the *loʻi* fields. By the 1870s the last *makaʻāinana* gave up and moved out, selling their water rights. The company dammed the stream, diverting its water into flumes to irrigate the thirsty sugarcane.

The Anahulu Project was a different kind of archaeology from what I had done in Futuna, Tikopia, or Niuatoputapu. Instead of thousands of years of prehistory, in the Anahulu Valley I was concentrating on a mere five or six decades. Nonetheless, those fifty years had witnessed enormous changes, a complete transformation of Hawaiian society and culture. We were innovating a "micro-historical" archaeology, focusing on the material record of the abandoned *kuleana* holdings of just a few *makaʻāinana* households. Yet in this landscape one could trace the broader historical patterns of the Hawaiian Kingdom during the wrenching changes of the early nineteenth century.

This micro-history of radically changing economic and social life following European contact was especially evident in the three contiguous *ʻili* of Koilau, Pulepule, and Kaloaloa, which had been occupied and farmed by the *makaʻāinana* families of Kainiki and Kaneiaulu. We excavated their house sites and mapped the formerly irrigated terraces; also digging into the pondfield soils, we uncovered the sequence of rebuilding of the irrigation works.

The three *ʻili* had been occupied immediately after Kamehameha's conquest of Oʻahu. Three houses were built, the most prominent by Koaliʻi, the father of Kainiki. Koaliʻi had received this land from Kamehameha's warrior chief Keʻeaumoku. Koaliʻi then built extensive *loʻi* fields at Kaloaloa. This intensified landscape, created soon after the conquest of Oʻahu, did not last more than a couple of decades. By 1830, two of the three original houses were abandoned, leaving only Koaliʻi and his son Kainiki in residence. Probably the pressures of the sandalwood era, combined with the continuing effects of Western diseases, were responsible for two of the three founding households dying off.

In the 1830s, newcomers arrived to take the place of those who had abandoned their houses and farms, having been given plots of *loʻi* land to farm as *hoaʻāina*, tenants under the *konohiki* and chiefs. Kaneiaulu was such a *hoaʻāina;* he built a house with a stone *lānai* at Kaloaloa, on a rise overlooking the pondfields originally constructed by Koaliʻi. Kaneiaulu, along with three other *hoaʻāina* (Koleaka, Kahue, and Moi) who resided farther downvalley, now took over half of the Kaloaloa taro fields.

Digging into the irrigation canal at Kaloaloa with students from the university, Spriggs found that it had been rebuilt after the new *hoaʻāina* cultivators arrived. Originally, there had been just one long, central canal bringing water to Koaliʻi's fields. When Kaneiaulu erected his new house overlooking the fields, he dug a secondary *ʻauwai* or canal, diverting a portion of the water directly to his fields and then down into the successive plots of the newcomer *hoaʻāina* Koleaka, Kahue, and Moi. Thus, even though Koaliʻi and Kainiki had precedence on the land, they were obliged to share the water with the newly arrived *hoaʻāina.*

Koaliʻi passed away before the Mahele, leaving Kainiki in possession of the ancestral house and fields of his father. As an old *kamaʻāina,* Kainiki was granted his claim of his house site and pondfields by the Land Commission. Kaneiaulu, though a *hoaʻāina,* had been put on the land at Kaloaloa directly by *konohiki* Gidiona Laʻanui in 1845; his claim for a house and some *loʻi* was only partially awarded (with an area of just 0.57 acre), but some parcels asserted by him in his Mahele claim were denied. Kahue, another *hoaʻāina,* received an even smaller award of 0.37 acre of taro land. The other two, Koleaka and Moi, had their claims for their taro plots in Kaloaloa denied by the commissioners. As with so many other *hoaʻāina* throughout Anahulu and elsewhere, these farmers were regarded as being merely "tenants," cultivating their plots at the whim of the chief. In theory, the Mahele was supposed to protect the rights of such tenants. In practice, people like Koleaka and Moi now found themselves landless.

Kaneiaulu and the other *hoaʻāina* left not long after the Mahele. Kainiki held on until the end; he died in April 1881, still living in the house his father had built. A month before he died, Kainiki made a will; witnesses stated that he was then about sixty years old. He left the *kuleana* to his second wife, Wahinehune, who sold it to the sugar plantation in 1885. No longer would their neighbor Kamakea blow his conch shell to assemble the people of the upper valley.

Writing up the Anahulu study posed a challenge. Sahlins and I were dealing with different kinds of data, his archival and documentary, mine in the form of sites and artifacts. We had no template to follow for this new kind of historical anthropology that combined archaeology with historical ethnography. Yet as Sahlins put it, our "modest aim" was no less than "to bring the history of the world down into the Anahulu River valley, . . . [to] show how Hawaii's entrance into this world history . . . was realized in the cultural forms of Anahulu history."[12] We struggled with different outlines before deciding to each write one volume of a two-volume work. We called it *Anahulu: The Anthropology of History in the Kingdom of Hawai'i.*

Anahulu, published by the University of Chicago Press in 1992, attracted considerable attention. In his volume on *Historical Ethnography,* Sahlins asserted that "Hawaiians too were authors of their history and not merely its victims." Without downplaying the greed and commercial exploitation of the *haole* capitalists, Sahlins argued that preexisting Hawaiian cultural structures (such as the deeply ingrained competition among *ali'i*) "gave capitalism powers and effects unparalleled even in other Pacific societies."[13] It was a message some did not want to hear.[14] For the most part, however, the scholarly world recognized *Anahulu* as a path-breaking study, integrating ethnography and archaeology to achieve new insights about a crucial time of wrenching cultural changes in the Hawaiian Kingdom. In 1998 the School of American Research in Santa Fe awarded its prestigious J. I. Staley Prize for the best book in anthropology to Sahlins and me for *Anahulu.* The beautifully hand-lettered citation that hangs in my study reads, "A truly unique book of prestigious scholarship, written with incredible power and enriched by a critical understanding of history."

CHAPTER TWELVE

"Looking for the Lion"
(Seattle and the Burke Museum, 1984–1988)

In January 1984, Bill Morris, president of Bishop Museum's Board of Trustees, invited me to lunch at the Pacific Club, an exclusive establishment frequented by Honolulu's business elite. I was pretty sure I knew what he wanted to talk about. The trustees had finally awakened to the fact that Ed Creutz was not the man to lead a troubled institution. The museum was hemorrhaging financially; it would soon be bankrupt if something were not done. Creutz had been quietly asked to resign, and the search for his replacement was nearing its end.

The search for a new director had come down to two finalists. The first was well known to me: Roger Green, the respected Pacific archaeologist and now a distinguished professor at the University of Auckland. Green had never run a museum, but he was smart and energetic; he had vision. The other finalist—Donald Duckworth—had come out of the blue, strongly promoted by Acting Director Frank Radovsky, head of the museum's Entomology Department. An entomologist, Duckworth held a mid-level administrative post at the Smithsonian Institution. Leafing through his résumé, I was unimpressed. He had no experience in Polynesia or the Pacific. Duckworth's supposed claim to fame had been to oversee the construction of a collections storage facility in Maryland, all funded with federal dollars, none of which he had personally raised. Radovsky pushed the trustees to appoint Duckworth, thinking that an entomologist as director would favor Radovsky's own Entomology Department.

Sitting down to lunch, Morris asked how my research was going. Then, he got to the point. "Pat, the trustees have chosen the new director. I know you strongly support Roger Green, but we believe that Don Duckworth is the man for the job." My heart sank. I knew that Green would do everything he could to strengthen the museum's proud tradition of Polynesian research. In choosing Duckworth the trustees would again be bringing someone from the Mainland, with no background in Pacific science and no proven record of fundraising. But there was no point arguing; it was a done deal.

Driving back to the museum along Vineyard Boulevard, I mused about my future. The museum provided a great deal of freedom to do research, but there was no long-term job security; the research staff were all on one-year contracts, with no tenure. I recalled what Duckworth had told us when we interviewed him: "The Bishop has always just been a research institute not a real museum." Duckworth intended to make the Bishop a "real museum," whatever that was. I did not like the sound of that. Fortunately, I had another option, as I had recently been offered a position as director of the University of Washington's Burke Museum, in Seattle. Maybe it was time to leave the Bishop with its troubles and become the head of my own institution.

Just then a song came on KCCN, the all-Hawaiian music radio station that I was fond of listening to. Olomana, the popular local duo of Jerry Santos and Robert Beaumont, often played at gatherings supporting Protect Kahoʻolawe ʻOhana; their songs helped promote the growing *aloha ʻāina* movement. The song coming from the speakers of my battered Datsun was Santos' adaptation of "The Lion Sleeps Tonight" (also known as "Wimba Way"), first made famous by the Tokens in 1961. Santos' rearrangement of the verses went like this:

All my thoughts like water flow to the lion
Looking for the lion
And we sail, and we sail way up to San Francisco
Looking for the lion
In the village, the peaceful village, the lion sleeps tonight
Looking for the lion.

And we sail, and we sail way up to Portland
Looking for the lion . . .

Looking in me, looking in you for the lion
Looking for the lion,
And we sail, and we sail, looking for a brand-new start
And we sail, and we sail . . .

For those of us raised in the islands the message in Santos' lyrics is clear enough. A lot of young people end up leaving Hawaiʻi, seeking their careers and fortunes on the Mainland. They sail "way up to San Francisco" or to Portland, "looking for a brand-new start." Of course, it is always a bittersweet journey. Years later we find ourselves like the subject of another Olomana favorite, "Kuʻu Home o Kahaluʻu," remembering "the days when we were younger . . . catching ʻopuʻu in the mountain streams . . . riding horseback round the Koʻolau hills."

That day I knew that I too would make the journey, "looking for the lion." It would take me not to San Francisco or Portland but to Seattle.

The United Airlines 747 touched down on the Sea-Tac Airport tarmac on a gray Seattle morning in mid-June 1984. With me were my wife Debra and our cat Pilo.

After dropping our bags off at the brick house I had rented in the Ravenna district, I made my way over to the University of Washington (UW). On Memorial Way just inside the Forty-Fifth Street entrance to campus stood the Thomas Burke Memorial Washington State Museum, a handsome two-story glass-and-concrete structure (I would soon shorten its imposing name to the Burke Museum). I had been selected by a university search committee to be the museum's new director, a position that came with a tenured appointment as associate professor in the UW Anthropology Department.

The Burke Museum, founded in 1885, was the University of Washington's and the state's natural history museum. Its greatest collections were from the Northwest Coast tribes, such as the Tlingit, Kwakiutl, and Haida. But the Burke also encompassed archaeology, paleontology, ornithology, and mammalogy.

My predecessor in the director's office for the previous seventeen years had been Prof. George Quimby, a colorful archaeologist who had cut his teeth on Work Projects Administration excavations in the Deep South during the Great Depression.[1] Now retired, Quimby still came into the museum where he retained an office. Stroking his handlebar mustache while we chatted in the Boiserie, the museum's elegant wood-paneled coffee shop, Quimby offered advice about how to manage the museum. "Don't bother the administration," he said, "and they won't bother you."

It was soon apparent just how faithfully Quimby had followed his own advice over the years: The UW administration barely paid any attention to the museum. While the Boiserie provided a steady but limited flow of discretionary income, the university's core contribution to the museum's budget was pitiful. The deans regarded the Burke as neither a teaching department nor a research unit; it was listed as an "ancillary facility." In reality, thousands of students used the museum's collections each year, while the curators carried out important research. But none of this was credited to the museum, because the faculty curators' research grants were run through their academic departments. I had a lot of work ahead of me to change these perceptions.

After settling into the high-ceilinged director's office I was shocked to discover that the museum was on the cusp of its centennial, yet there were no plans to celebrate this milestone. I assembled a small team including the museum's development officer Ellen Ferguson and registrar Roxanna Augustiny, who were delighted that the Quimby era of "don't bother us" had come to an end. In addition to an exhibit to showcase the Burke's one hundred years, we cooked up the idea of a book to highlight its outstanding Northwest Coast collections. One hundred of the most significant and beautiful objects would be showcased with stunning color photos, the objects to be described by Bill Holm, the museum's respected authority on Northwest Coast art.

Publishing a large-format book with full color plates is expensive; the funds trickling in from the Boiserie's coffee sales were not going to be enough to pay for it. Ferguson suggested that I approach Seattle businessman John Hauberg, who had made a fortune in the timber business. Hauberg collected Northwest Coast art; as a young man he had been tutored in connoisseurship by Erna Gunther, a previous Burke Museum director. As we walked into Hauberg's office in the old part of Seattle one morning, Ferguson warned me, "Quimby rebuffed Hauberg a few years back. I think he still holds a grudge."

Hauberg proved to be a gruff, no-nonsense businessman. I told him about the book project, that I needed seed money for the high-quality photography. Hauberg lectured me for ten minutes about how Quimby had brushed him off when Hauberg first suggested donating his impressive personal collection to the Burke (it would later become a core collection of the Seattle Art Museum). "Well," I replied, "I deeply regret Quimby's actions. But I'm trying to put the Burke Museum on a new footing. Erna Gunther helped you when you were a young man. I'm asking you to honor her memory." Hauberg looked at me long and hard. Then he asked, "How much do you need?"

With Hauberg's gift in hand we moved rapidly. Bill Holm selected the one hundred artifacts and wrote the text. I hired noted photographer Eduardo Calderón to take the large-format color photos. With Holm's manuscript and Calderón's plates ready, I went to meet the director of the University of Washington Press. Printing and distributing a big coffee-table book was going to cost tens of thousands of dollars, more than Hauberg had given us. But the UW Press director knew that Holm was a respected author and that the new book would be sure to sell out. *Spirit and Ancestor: A Century of Northwest Coast Indian Art at the Burke Museum* was co-published by the UW Press and the Burke Museum in time for the museum's centennial celebration.[2]

On October 5, 1985, a crowd of six hundred Burke Museum supporters gathered on the front steps for the opening of the celebration. Over the preceding months Bill Holm had carved an exquisite replica of the Howkan Killer Whale sculpture (the surviving original dorsal fin is part of the museum's collection), which was now installed on the front steps; it was to be dedicated that morning. The whale became the museum's new logo; I thought it was a fitting symbol of the revitalized energy now surging through the institution.

A few months after arriving in Seattle I received a message from Chilean archaeologists Claudio Cristino and Patricia Vargas who had worked for a number of years on Easter Island. They were organizing the first International Congress on Easter Island and the Pacific, to be held on the island in September 1984. The U.S.

Embassy in Santiago had funds to take me to the Congress; would I attend? I could hardly pass up this offer to visit the most enigmatic and famous of all Polynesian islands.

Stepping off the plane in Santiago, I heard my name paged over the loudspeaker in the Immigration area. An impeccably dressed man in a dark gray overcoat greeted me. "Prof. Kirch, the government of President Pinochet is pleased to welcome you to Chile," he said in perfect English. "Where are your bags?" Picking up my suitcase he whisked me through Immigration and then into a dark limousine heading toward the city center.

I was vaguely aware of the tense political situation in Chile, but as we pulled into the main plaza, I was not prepared for the sight of a phalanx of police in full riot gear. As my host (who I by now realized was one of Pinochet's secret police) walked me past the formidable array he calmly remarked, "There have been a few demonstrations lately. Nothing to worry about. But, as the hotel is very comfortable, my advice is to stay inside. A car will take you to the airport tomorrow for your Lan Chile flight to Easter Island." Stay inside I did, hearing sporadic gunfire in the streets outside during the night.

On the morning flight to Easter Island—which took five hours in an aging Boeing 707 over the endless deep blue South Pacific Ocean—was none other than Thor Heyerdahl, making his first return visit to the island since 1956. When we descended to the tarmac, greeting "Señior Kon-Tiki" was s special delegation headed by the island's first Rapa Nui governor, Sergio Rapu. I knew Rapu a little, because he had been an archaeology student at the University of Hawai'i. Heyerdahl was presented with a large bunch of ripe bananas and a couple of white chickens, special gifts in traditional Rapa Nui culture.

The Congress brought together many of the famous archaeologists and ethnographers of Polynesia, along with younger scholars. The days passed in stimulating symposia while in the evenings *cervesa* and *pisco* flowed in the little hotel bar as we argued and debated, often past midnight. One day an impromptu "exchange" was organized between Roger Green and Thor Heyerdahl. The room was packed. Heyerdahl was Old Worldly and poised. Green was the consummate scientist, trying to get Heyerdahl to admit that all the evidence went against his theory of a South American origin of the Polynesians. But Heyerdahl did not care; he was world famous and rich. He shrugged and smiled as Green got increasingly flustered, muttering, "But Thor, can't you see that . . ." Indeed, Heyerdahl did not give up his theory until the day he died.

As the Congress neared its conclusion, Cristino and Vargas asked if I would stay on an extra week or two. They were keen to discuss a possible collaboration, offering to take me around the island to show me sites they had discovered. I rebooked my return flight for a later date and telegrammed Debra that I would be delayed.

Cristino, Vargas, and I spent several days walking over the island, looking at sites, and developing a plan for joint research (Fig. 12.1). One day Thor Heyerdahl joined us; at every site we visited he would proclaim that it was "just like" the Inca ruins of Peru! Christino and Vargas had mapped much of the island's landscape, recording thousands of sites. What was needed now was an intensive program of excavations, radiocarbon dating, and detailed analyses of floral and faunal remains to reconstruct what had transpired on the island during a millennium of Polynesian occupation. I was excited about the possibilities.

Figure 12.1. The author standing next to one of the *moai* or statues on the slopes of the Rano Raraku quarry on Easter Island, in 1984.

Throughout my stay on the island I had been fighting off a nasty respiratory infection. Now it was flaring up badly. I was coughing constantly, feeling tired and run-down. But as I would be flying home in two days I shrugged it off.

That night I went with Cristino, Vargas' sister Marie Te, and a few Rapa Nui friends to the island's little nightclub, "Toroko," on the outskirts of Hangaroa town. It was just a shack situated within a rock-walled enclosure where you could buy *pisco* sours. The only customers there, we had a few drinks and then got up to leave. Walking out the front door I got a shock. About twenty-five of Pinochet's *carabineros* (paramilitary police) stood in the grassy yard, armed with AK-47s. A few were mounted on big horses. There was a paddy wagon parked by the gate. I had not a clue what was happening.

Cristino said nothing but just walked to the Land Cruiser, motioning for us to get in. Putting the key in the ignition he said, "We have to make a run for it." Before I could as much as say "are you nuts?" the police captain yanked open the driver's door, grabbed Cristino by the arm, and pulled him out. They pushed him into the paddy wagon and the whole entourage departed. Obviously, they were not interested in us.

Cristino's sister-in-law was hysterical; she knew what it meant to be arrested by Pinochet's police. One was likely to be tortured, then "disappeared." In the dark we made our way on foot across the village to the governor's house. The chain-link fence was locked, but we climbed over it. Knowing Governor Rapu a little, I thought perhaps he would intercede. It was around midnight when I knocked on his door. Rapu was shocked to see me standing there. "Cristino's been arrested," I said breathlessly. The lack of expression on Rapu's face suggested that he might be in on the game. "OK, I'll call the captain," he told me. "You go on to the police station."

It took an hour to get to the station where they were holding Cristino; it was situated on the other side of the airstrip from town. Again, the gates were locked. Marie-Te and I climbed the chain-link fence. "What the hell am I doing?" I thought to myself as the adrenaline raced through my system. I was climbing into a compound of Pinochet thugs.

Fortunately, Cristino was not tortured; the presence of an American professor demanding to see his colleague probably helped forestall that fate. They released him around dawn; we all went to Cristino's house and poured some drinks. "Why are they after you, Claudio?" I demanded. It was a long story, but essentially he had gotten on the wrong side of the police captain by refusing to allow an overt "police presence" during the Congress. The captain had trumped up charges of driving an official vehicle after dark without a special permit; that was all it took in Pinochet's Chile to get you arrested.

Later that day we drove out to have a final look at the Rano Raraku statue quarry. While Cristino and Edmundo Edwards recorded a site on the crater's inner slopes, I hiked up to see a unique "kneeling statue" that the Heyerdahl expedition had unearthed in 1955–1956. My breath was short; I felt a stabbing pain in my chest. Suddenly I collapsed on the grass a few feet from one of the giant statues. Looking up into that emotionless stone face, I thought to myself, "You're going to die on Easter Island."

Cristino and Edwards found me an hour later, semi-conscious and in great pain. The traumatic events of the previous day had turned my respiratory ailment into a case of pneumonia. They half-carried me down the path and drove me to Hangaroa where a burly Chilean nurse stuck a hypodermic full of penicillin into my buttocks.

On the flight back to Santiago that night, I relapsed. By the time we landed I was feverish and the pain had returned. Fortunately, Marie-Te Vargas was on the same flight. Taking one look at me she said, "You are coming with me." I was more than happy to acquiesce, spending the next ten days at the Vargas compound outside of Santiago being treated by the family doctor and recuperating.

We never did get to implement the research program on Easter Island. Soon after Cristino's arrest, he and Vargas fled the island, taking their two children and the few possessions they could fit into their suitcases. They flew not to Chile but on the once-a-week flight to Tahiti, where they could be free from Pinochet's clutches. A Chilean friend, Maeva Navarro, was in charge of the French Polynesian archaeology department; she hired Cristino and Vargas for a few years until they could safely return to Chile.

My academic reputation received a boost in 1984 when Cambridge University Press published *The Evolution of the Polynesian Chiefdoms,* in which I explored how the varied Polynesian cultures had diverged from their common ancestor, the Lapita culture.[3] I had started writing the book in the early 1980s after being contacted by the anthropology editor of Cambridge University Press. He had read an article of mine in the *American Scientist* outlining some of the major trends in Polynesian cultural evolution and thought that it provided a good outline for a book. I signed a contract with Cambridge and throughout 1982 and 1983 worked away on the manuscript in the evenings, downing endless cups of coffee in our little apartment in Honolulu.

The Evolution of the Polynesian Chiefdoms sought to explain how some thirty distinctive Polynesian cultures had all evolved from a common ancestor. I began by arguing that after Lapita voyagers had discovered and settled the Tonga and Samoa Islands—along with nearby Futuna and 'Uvea—an Ancestral Polynesian culture gradually emerged in this Western Polynesian homeland region. Then, in the first millennium AD some of the Polynesian descendants of the Lapita people began voyaging eastward again, discovering the islands of Eastern Polynesia, including Tahiti, the Marquesas, the Tuamotus, Mangareva, the Australs, Easter Island, New Zealand, and Hawai'i. But it was not just the gradual process of discovering new islands that led to the different forms of Polynesian culture witnessed by European explorers in the seventeenth and eighteenth centuries. Other processes of cultural evolution were at work: adaptation to different environmental conditions posed by large and small, high and low islands; population growth and the rise of high-density populations straining island resources; the intensification of agricultural systems through irrigation and dryland field systems; and the rise of conflict and warfare as chiefs sought control over resources and surplus production. Drawing upon what I had learned in my expeditions to Tikopia, Tonga, and Futuna, as well as in Hawai'i, *The Evolution of the Polynesian Chiefdoms* explored each of these topics. The book was well received and indeed remains in print today: It is my most-cited work.

A second book, *Feathered Gods and Fishhooks: An Introduction to Hawaiian Archaeology and Prehistory,* was published in 1985, based on lectures I had given in courses at the University of Hawai'i.[4] In this first book-length synthesis of Hawaiian archaeology, I pulled together the earlier work of Emory, Sinoto, Soehren, and others, along with more recent developments in Hawaiian settlement pattern research, presenting a four-phase sequence of how Hawaiian civilization had developed over more than one thousand years. Finally, in 1986, Cambridge University Press brought out my edited volume, *Island Societies: Archaeological Approaches to Evolution and Transformation,* based on a conference I had organized.[5] With three books appearing in as many years, the University of Washington promoted me to full professor in 1986.

The other archaeologists in UW's Anthropology Department were Robert Dunnell (the department chair), Donald Grayson, Julie Stein, Robert Wenke, and Bob Greengo. Dunnell, who had received his PhD from Yale a few years before me, dominated the archaeology program. Dunnell was convinced that his particular theoretical approach was *the* sole path to truth and enlightenment. His mission was to create a "strictly Darwinian" archaeology, explaining the evolution of human cultures in terms of natural selection. I appreciated Dunnell's arguments (he was definitely smart), but I felt he wore intellectual blinders.[6] Some colleagues jokingly referred to this as "Dunnell-vision." I read Dunnell's writings but simultaneously tried to broaden my own horizons to include Marxist perspectives and that of the *Annales* school of long-term history deriving from the work of such French scholars as Marc Bloch, Fernand Braudel, and Le Roy Ladurie.[7]

Dunnell was definitely an odd duck. He had two modes of dress: On days that he played the role of department chairman he wore a dark three-piece suit and necktie. It was his "going to see the deans" attire. (Unlike Quimby, Dunnell did give me some sound advice about dealing with administrators. "Get every promise in writing," he told me.) On other days, when he worked in his lab, Dunnell wore faded blue jeans with flannel shirts and went barefoot. I never saw him in other than those two costumes. Debra and I sometimes socialized with Dunnell and his Southern-belle wife Mary at their home near campus. Dunnell had an old, droopy-eared hound with whom he shared a ubiquitous mug of cheap jug wine; Dunnell would take a sip and then put the mug down for the hound to lap out of.

Julie Stein was a rising young star in the emerging field of geoarchaeology. I visited her excavations on San Juan Island, learning quite a lot about her methods of micro-stratigraphic recording and sedimentary analysis. Don Grayson focused on zooarchaeology, developing a strongly quantitative and statistical approach. As Grayson's lab was in the Burke Museum basement, I saw quite a lot of him and we had a good rapport.

There was a tradition for the archaeology faculty to have lunch together on Tuesdays at a small restaurant a couple of blocks off campus. Dunnell dominated the discussions, making it clear that he saw himself as the acknowledged leader. I was not particularly happy with the way that my colleagues always seemed to defer to Dunnell, but I had my hands full with the museum and did not see any point in rocking the boat.

My administrative appointment relieved me of teaching, but I held a graduate seminar on the Lapita culture. Several UW grad students were studying Pacific archaeology. Terry Hunt and Melinda Allen were Dunnell students, whereas Virginia Butler was working with Don Grayson. I took on two grad students: Dana Lepofsky, who was interested in paleoethnobotany, and Marshall Weisler, who after working with me in Hawai'i had decided to pursue his doctorate. I pushed the students to critically examine the literature on Lapita sites. Their research papers were so good that I edited and published them in a small volume through the Burke Museum.[8]

In the fall of 1987 I got a phone call from the public relations manager of the *Seattle Post-Intelligencer.* Virgil Fasio, the paper's publisher, had returned from Chongqing in Sichuan, China, where a museum wanted to loan dinosaur skeletons for exhibition in the United States. Would the Burke Museum be interested?

I met with Fasio in his office at the *Post-Intelligencer.* He wanted to sponsor the exhibit but told me that the paper could only contribute $50,000. However, United Airlines was also willing to be a corporate sponsor. United would fly the two tons of dinosaur bones from Shanghai on their nonstop service to Seattle, and they would make twenty round-trip tickets from Shanghai to Seattle available for our use.

In November I flew to Hong Kong and then on to Chongqing, accompanied by Ellen Ferguson and Fasio's hard-nosed comptroller. The CAAC flight from Hong Kong was delayed (an aging Russian-built Ilyushin Il-62 whose cabin swarmed with cockroaches), so we did not touch down in Chongqing until dusk. Looking out the window, I could barely make out the runway lights through the heavy smog. The Chongqing airport terminal had been constructed by General "Vinegar Joe" Stilwell during World War II, when the city had been Chiang Kai-shek's redoubt against the Japanese Imperial Army. The building's walls still bore pockmarks from aerial strafing!

We began negotiations with the city cultural affairs chief and staff of the Chongqing Dinosaur Museum, drinking endless cups of tea. The Chinese wanted more cash than Fasio had authorized. The negotiations were not going well.

Our hosts invited us on a three-day excursion into the countryside. Jammed into a rickety van, we toured ancient Buddhist temples and stood in awe of the spectacular Three Gorges (before the massive dams were constructed). We stayed at little country inns, unheated but with wonderful food. One feast was a Sichuan "hot pot" in which diners select morsels of different raw foods, plunging them into a pot of fiery broth with their chopsticks to briefly cook them. There were baby eels and other delicacies, but one plate of tube-like organs mystified me. It turned out to be the vas deferens of water buffalo; when this was announced I thought the comptroller was going to lose his cookies.

Back at the negotiating table, the Chinese insisted they wanted a rental fee of $100,000. I said, "Look. I only have $50,000. But I will make it possible for twenty of your staff to fly to Seattle to help with the exhibit. It's your chance to experience America." After the translator conveyed this, there was much heated discussion in Chinese. After a few minutes the translator spoke: "We accept your proposal."

One point remained to be decided: the exhibition's name. I had come up with the name *Chinasaurs*. Our team thought it was brilliant from a public relations standpoint, but it was not clear that the Chinese would go for it. "We want to call the exhibition *Chinasaurs*," I told them. The translator rendered this in Chinese as "Middle Kingdom Thunder Lizards." There was a second of hesitation, then they broke out in smiles. The project was a go.

In March 1988, two tons of Chinese dinosaur bones arrived at the Burke Museum (the real thing, not casts). The towering skeletons of *Yangchuanosaurus shangyuensis, Omeisaurus fuxiensis,* and *Huayangosaurus taibaii* were installed in the main gallery. True to our word, we housed a rotating group of Chongqing museum staff in Seattle over the next few months. Ferguson had her hands full keeping them supplied with Chinese groceries in the apartment we had rented for them near the Burke.

Chinasaurs was a smashing success. The *Seattle Post-Intelligencer* gave us great publicity, including a special section in the Sunday newspaper with learning exercises for kids that could be used in the city's schools. My staff designed supplementary exhibits, including one on the skull of a *Triceratops* that had been excavated by the Burke's curator of paleontology. Over six months, more than a quarter-million visitors passed through the Burke's front doors. The University of Washington's president spoke at the opening reception; it was no longer a matter of "don't bother them and they won't bother you." With the help of my dedicated and tireless staff, we had put the Burke Museum back on the map.[9]

CHAPTER THIRTEEN

The Search for the Lapita Homeland (Mussau Islands, 1985)

In February 1983 the Fifteenth Pacific Science Congress convened in the sleepy town of Dunedin, on New Zealand's South Island. Jim Allen, a research fellow at the Australian National University, had written to several Pacific archaeologists in advance of the Dunedin meeting; he wanted to discuss an idea for a new multi-institutional research program focused on Lapita. I had met Allen, a big gregarious Australian with a scruffy beard and a deep knowledge of Australian wines, during a previous visit to Canberra. He struck me as direct and someone who brooked no nonsense. Allen had been impressed by Green and Yen's Southeast Solomon Islands Culture History project. The strategy of putting several field teams to work simultaneously in a key geographic region was clearly more effective than waiting decades for individual researchers to tackle archaeological problems piecemeal.

One evening a dozen of us assembled in Cook's Bar not far from the University of Otago, a favorite "watering hole" of New Zealand archaeologists. Roger Green was there, along with Jack Golson, Wal Ambrose, and Jim Specht, all of whom had done important research on Lapita sites. Sitting around a table well supplied with large jugs of New Zealand bitters, Jim Allen sketched out his proposal.

"Roger's work in the Southeast Solomons has shown that Lapita was the founding culture in that region," Allen began. "But what was the homeland of the Lapita people themselves? The obsidian in Roger's sites has been traced back to New Britain. This suggests that we ought to be looking at the Bismarck Archipelago."

Green chimed in: "That's where the German priest, Father Otto Meyer, first found Lapita pottery when he dug the foundations for his church on Watom Island." Meyer had reported his finds in the German journal *Anthropos* in 1909.[1] But its significance had gone unnoticed until Berkeley's Edward Gifford made the link in 1952 between the pottery from Watom, his own finds from the site of Lapita in New Caledonia, and potsherds that W. C. McKern had found in Tonga in 1920. Gifford recognized that the designs on the potsherds at all three localities were closely related.[2] A few years later, Jack Golson described Lapita as a "community of cultures" that had once spanned the southwestern Pacific.[3] In the 1970s Green had shown that the "Lapita cultural complex" in the eastern Solomon Islands dated to ca. 1200 BC. One branch of Lapita, which Green called "Early Eastern Lapita," had been the founding culture in Tonga and Samoa at the beginning of the first millennium BC.[4]

Allen continued with his pitch: "Some of us think that the Bismarck Archipelago was the original Lapita homeland. The culture probably developed there over thousands of years, given that people have been in New Guinea since the late Pleistocene."[5] He was referring to sites on the large island of New Guinea, dating back to 27,000 years BP.

"I'm not so sure about that, Jim," Green interrupted. "My research with Andy Pawley on the history of Oceanic languages indicates that the Lapita people spoke Proto Oceanic. Oceanic is a branch of the Austronesian language family. It traces back to Taiwan. So the Lapita homeland may lie farther to the west, in island Southeast Asia."

Green, along with his linguist colleague Pawley, had published a couple of articles arguing that the people who had made Lapita pottery spoke a dialect of the widespread Austronesian language family.[6] If they were right, it was doubtful that the Bismarck Archipelago was the original Lapita homeland but rather was a midpoint along a trail of Austronesian migrations that stretched all the way to the coast of the South China Sea. But not everyone accepted Green's and Pawley's arguments. Allen and his colleague, Peter White, narrowly trained as archaeologists, were skeptical of linguistic arguments.

The beer flowed as we argued back and forth. Then Allen leaned forward and half-shouted in his booming Australian accent, so as to be clearly heard over the din in the bar, "The only way we're going to prove which side is right is by going and digging in the Bismarcks." To that, no one could disagree.

Allen would take the lead in organizing the international Lapita Homeland Project. The Australian National University put up some funds, and Allen got additional support from the National Geographic Society. Because travel to the remote islands of the Bismarck Archipelago is haphazard at best, Allen would charter a research vessel to transport our field teams throughout the Bismarcks during the summer of 1985.

Allen asked if I would take on the Mussau or St. Matthias Islands, on the northern rim of the Bismarck Archipelago, as my assignment (see Map 2). In 1978, Brian Egloff of the Papua New Guinea National Museum had briefly tested a large Lapita site on Eloaua Island. A radiocarbon date of 1900 BC obtained from

Egloff's test pit was the oldest from any known Lapita site. If we were going to find the Lapita "homeland" then Eloaua was a good bet.[7]

In August 1985, I stepped off a Quantas jet in Port Moresby, the dusty capital of Papua New Guinea, en route to Kavieng, in New Ireland Province, several hundred miles to the north. There, I would meet up with the *Dick Smith Explorer,* which would take me to my final destination, Eloaua Island. Before continuing on to Kavieng, I spent a few days taking care of research formalities and visiting Papua New Guinea's National Museum. In the museum, I had a look at the potsherds that Egloff had excavated from his Eloaua test pits a few years earlier. Many of the sherds were covered with the fine-toothed "dentate-stamped" designs made by impressing a comb-like tool with rows of tiny "teeth" into the damp clay. These designs are a hallmark of Lapita.

As I turned the small, dusty potsherds from Eloaua Island over in my hands, I pondered how little was still known about the earliest phases of the Lapita culture. We needed to know more not only about the origins of Lapita—whether from Southeast Asia or in the Bismarck Archipelago itself—but also about the culture of the people who had made this finely decorated pottery. Were they, as some had suggested, "strandloopers" who subsisted solely by exploiting the bounty of the region's tropical reefs and seas, or did they possess a fully developed horticultural economy? Were they highly mobile, or did they occupy large permanent villages? What was the nature of their social organization? Was theirs an egalitarian society, or did they have some form of inherited rank and status? These and many other questions begged to be answered.

A few days later, I boarded an Air New Guinea plane bound for Kavieng, the capital of New Ireland Province. Jim Allen greeted me as I stepped off the plane. "The *Dick Smith Explorer* is a couple of days behind schedule, Pat," Allen informed me. "But this will give us time to go down to Panakiwuk where you can have a firsthand look at our recent finds." Allen was referring to a limestone rockshelter about a four-hour drive south of Kavieng, where he was excavating with Rhys Jones and Chris Gosden. Tossing my gear into the Land Rover, we headed down the dirt track that serves as New Ireland's main highway.

The next morning, Allen and I climbed a slippery trail leading into the island's central limestone spine. Panakiwuk proved to be a smallish overhang on one face of a great sinkhole, a place where more than 20,000 years ago people took refuge from the elements while hunting marsupials and foraging for wild tubers or edible fruit. Allen's excavations were opening a window into the truly deep past of the Bismarcks, showing that humans had occupied these islands thousands of years before the Austronesian speakers arrived. That evening we sat around a crude table in Allen's field house as he showed me the chert and obsidian stone flakes recovered from the excavations. Allen did not yet know the age of these artifacts but guessed that they went back to the late Pleistocene. His hunch was later confirmed by radiocarbon dates. It was all exciting and fascinating.[8]

The following day we drove back to Kavieng, where the *Dick Smith Explorer* now lay at anchor in the harbor. On the wharf I met Pru Gaffey and Sally Brockwell, two Australian archaeology students who would assist me in Mussau. Gaffey took me aside to say that the supplies of cheap canned spaghetti, pork-and-beans, and such that had been purchased in Sydney for the expedition were pretty disgusting. Eating well is one of my tenets for successful fieldwork; we quickly rounded up additional supplies in the Chinese trade stores in Kavieng and loaded them into the ship's hold.

The Mussau Islands bake under a near equatorial sun on the northern arc of the Bismarck Archipelago. Unfortunately, the *Dick Smith Explorer*'s steel hull and deck were designed for Antarctic exploration rather than tropical cruising. It was unbearably hot below decks, so I opted to pass the night curled up on a hatch cover. The passage was wet and squally as the ship plugged along at six knots. I spent several hours watching a heavy lightning storm off of New Hanover Island to the southwest.

Just after dawn we sighted the 650-meter-high peak of Taleanuane on the main island of "Big Mussau." Aware that the World War II vintage hydrographic charts of this region were notoriously inaccurate, Captain Taffy Rowlands posted a lookout in the masthead to watch for coral heads. We were now close to Eloaua Island (Map 6); I could see the stair-step succession of limestone terraces that revealed it to be a classic *makatea* island, each terrace marking a distinct stage of tectonically uplifted reef.

We dropped anchor off the main village, waiting for several dugout canoes to come out. Johnny Saulo, who worked at the National Museum, had alerted his uncle Ave Male by radio that our team would be arriving. I jumped into one of the canoes and went ashore to meet Male, a traditional leader of the Eanaiyu clan that owned the land where the Lapita site was situated. A slender man in his late fifties, with a cheerful grin and stubbly beard, Male welcomed me warmly, offering to put one of his two houses at our disposal.

Returning to the ship, we off-loaded a fourteen-foot aluminum launch—appropriately named the *Lapita*—powered by a 25 hp Johnson outboard. The *Lapita* would give us the flexibility to reconnoiter other small islets in the Mussau group as well as to get to the little administrative center of Palakau on the main island. Waving goodbye to Captain Rowlands, I took the *Lapita* in through the narrow pass off of Male's house, our base for the next six weeks.

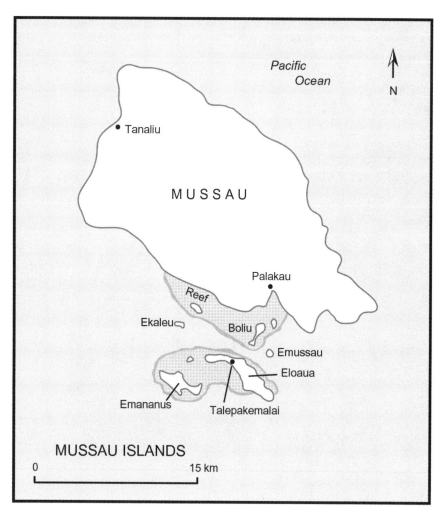

Map 6. Map of the Mussau Islands.

Male made us feel at home in his tidy compound nestled behind the coral sand beach, shaded by fruit trees. We settled into a house elevated on stilts, with three rooms. It was a hybrid construction with wooden walls and floor. Of course, it had no plumbing or electricity. We used kerosene lanterns for light and a couple of Primus stoves to cook on. Male thoughtfully cobbled together a small bath house with thatched panels where we could wash in private using well water carried in pails.

Our first task was to relocate Egloff's original site, situated in a yam garden to one side of the crushed coral runway, which was used once a week by the small Talair plane. Lapita pottery had first been turned up during the clearing of the small plane landing strip in 1973. Male took us to where Egloff had excavated in 1978. Opening up a new test excavation, we found pottery in the dark black soil overlying coral beach sand. The sherds were disappointingly small, broken up by centuries of gardening with digging sticks. Additional test pits paralleling the runway revealed the same shallow, disturbed cultural deposit. In every pit, the potsherds were small and worn. After several days of digging, it began to look like we might not get much further than Egloff had in answering our questions about the Lapita people.

In spite of these disappointments, I was enjoying my time on Eloaua. Several friends of Ave's in their fifties had taken to coming to our house in the evenings to tell stories. Bauwa Sagila, Aimalu Lavatea, and Pastor Ororea, along with Male, became what I called the "Giaman Club" (Fig. 13.1). In pidgin English, *giaman* means "nonsense, to tell tales;" in general, "to bullshit." They thought this name

Figure 13.1. Members of the "Giaman Club" of Eloaua, Mussau. From left to right, Bauwa Sagila, Aimalu Lavatea, the pastor Ororea, and Ave Male.

was hilarious. I made them weak tea with lots of sugar, which they sipped while regaling me with stories of their youth in the islands.

These men had all been young boys or teenagers at the time that World War II descended with a fury upon the western Pacific. The U.S. military constructed an airfield on nearby Emirau Island, from which the B-17 "Flying Fortress" bombers relentlessly attacked the Japanese stronghold at Rabaul, on New Britain. Although Eloaua itself never saw action, ships and planes were constantly on the seas and in the air around the island. Sagila and Male had attached themselves as camp hangers-on to the Americans on Emirau, doing odd chores in exchange for gifts of clothes and food. They were utterly in awe at the material wealth of the Americans. Four decades later they had not forgotten this feeling. Indeed, many island cultures in this part of the Pacific were radically transformed by similar encounters with the U.S. troops and their "cargo." After the war, a number of charismatic leaders promulgated "cargo cults," seeking to bring the wealth of America to their islands.

One day a village boy brought me a large coconut crab trussed up with lianas. I consider these crabs to be one of the South Pacific's greatest delicacies. The Mussau islanders, who were converted to the Seventh Day Adventist faith in the 1930s, follow the dietary restrictions in the Book of Leviticus, which forbids eating creatures such as crabs. On most Pacific islands coconut crabs are now rare or extinct, but in Mussau they were everywhere, because no one was eating them. When I told Male I wanted to eat the creature for dinner, he brought out his largest cooking pot. The huge aluminum pot had been a parting gift from a U.S. Army camp cook. As I lowered the big crab into the boiling water it hooked one of its powerful claws onto the pot's rim. Before succumbing to its fate, the crab put a deep dent into the 1/8 inch thick aluminum; I shuddered to think what it might have done to my finger! Male was none too happy with his bent pot.

Although they had given up eating shellfish and pigs, the Eloaua villagers caught abundant fish from the extensive reefs surrounding their island; they were not protein deprived as were the Kolombangara Island people I had seen in the Solomons in 1971. On the uplifted limestone plateau the Eloaua people grew taro, yams, and manioc in swidden gardens. A diversity of fruit and nut-bearing trees shaded the village houses. I traded tins of the Australian spaghetti for fish and vegetables. Gaffey, a good cook, improvised delicious curry dishes with the spices and relishes we had bought in Kavieng.

The young Australian women were not, however, used to my work regimen. Pacific islanders like to rise early, with the sun. They prefer to work in their gardens while it is cool, returning to their homes by early afternoon when the tropical sun becomes nearly unbearable. I had learned from prior expeditions to organize my excavation teams the same way, starting early and then quitting work by mid-afternoon. The men I hired from Eloaua Village showed up right after first light. I had already made a pot of coffee, putting out crackers, butter, and tinned cheese for breakfast. "Pru, Sally, coffee's on!" I cheerily announced. Not a peep from their room. I banged around in the makeshift kitchen, hoping the noise would rouse them. Nothing. I could see the men outside were ready to go to work. "OK, we're leaving for the site. I'll see you out there," I yelled, slamming the door as I left just to make sure they were awake.

About an hour or two later, Gaffey and Brockwell showed up at the excavation, a pattern to be repeated throughout our stay. If they had been my students, I would have read them the riot act. But because they were from the Australian National University, I just shrugged and let it pass. I never once protested to them about not starting the workday with the rest of the crew. But later, after we had all returned home, I heard from Jim Allen that the women had complained mightily about me when they got back to Canberra. Apparently they thought I was a slave driver. As one of them put it, "I thought we had signed up to go to the Bismarck, not the Gulag, Archipelago."

Reconnoitering the island, I realized that the crushed-coral airstrip lay on a slightly elevated natural terrace a meter or two higher than the modern coastal plain. I discerned a faint dropoff in the topography to the north of the airfield. When sea level had been slightly higher about three to four thousand years ago, I reasoned, the Lapita settlements might have been situated at the top of what was then the active beach. When sea level fell to its modern level, this would have left the former beach ridge slightly elevated, to be claimed later by the jungle as the shoreline advanced. The slight dropoff, just about a one-meter difference in elevation, presumably marked the old shoreline.

I decided to test this hypothesis by laying out test excavations along a transect extending across the old beach ridge and then down onto the lower coral sand flat. Male told me that this locale was called Talepakemalai. I expected to find Lapita pottery distributed across the higher terrace, which represented the old beach ridge. As our test pits crossed the slope marking the old shoreline, these finds should cease because we would now be digging on what had been the original reef flat.

The first few test pits met my expectations. Lapita pottery, shellfish and fish bones, and obsidian flakes caught in our sifting screens all indicated that Lapita people had lived on the higher, ancient beach ridge. Unfortunately, pit after pit showed the same shallow cultural layer, disturbed by centuries of gardening. Moving along our transect line, I laid out a new test pit on the lower sandy flat. Expecting to find only a "sterile" deposit of beach sand, I was startled when Gaffey called out for me to come have a look at what she was encountering at a depth of about fifty centimeters.

Peering down into the neat meter-square pit, I watched as Gaffey's trowel deftly exposed several large pieces of Lapita pottery. One sherd had a distinctive human face motif, whose almond-shaped eyes stared back at me. Unlike the small, worn sherds we had been finding, these were well preserved. A smooth, shiny circular object proved to be a complete ring, exquisitely carved from the shell of a giant clam. Several large pieces of razor-sharp obsidian turned up next, followed by more potsherds and then an entire pig's tusk drilled for use as a pendant.

The sand in the test pit was soggy; we were approaching the lens of brackish water that lies not far below the ground surface on coral islands. Yet pottery and other objects continued to appear. I took over digging from Gaffey, periodically bailing the water that was now rapidly seeping into the pit. A curious dark organic stain, mushy at first, became firmer as I worked my trowel around the object to expose it. I soon discerned that this was a shaft of wood, extending downward into the sand, preserved for thousands of years in the waterlogged, oxygen-deprived sediment. It suddenly hit me: This was the base of a stout post, which had once supported a wooden structure of some kind. When the post was later removed we saw that its end had been sharpened to a point with a stone adz.

Over the following weeks, we expanded the initial Test Pit 14 into a twelve-square-meter excavation. It revealed not just one but numerous wooden post bases, set in an alignment that had formed one side of a stilt or pole house, which had stood over the shallow lagoon flat adjacent to the beach ridge. Radiocarbon dates later revealed that the house had been occupied around 1300 BC.

My hypothesis about the location of the old shoreline was correct. What I had not anticipated was finding the remains of a stilt-house village that had once extended out over the lagoon. This discovery radically changed our ideas about Lapita settlement patterns as well as where to look for Lapita sites. Not that this find should have been wholly unanticipated: Other Austronesian societies in Southeast Asia, along with some skirting the New Guinea coasts and as far east as the Solomon Islands, built stilt houses over coastal waters. They just had never been found in a Lapita context.

We took time out from the digging at Talepakemalai to do additional reconnaissance. Farther to the northwest on Eloaua was another, smaller Lapita site called Etakosarai, which we tested. But this site lacked a waterlogged component like that found at Talepakemalai; the cultural deposits were thin and had been highly disturbed. Over on Emananus Island, across the lagoon, was a third Lapita site, Etapakengaroasa. We tested this site as well, finding sherds with delicate dentate-stamped designs. It was apparent that we had just uncovered the tip of the iceberg in terms of Lapita archaeology in Mussau.[9] I would have to come back and expand the excavations at Talepakemalai. In fact, I would return twice more to Eloaua, in 1986 and 1988 (see Chapter Fourteen).

After six weeks, we were ready to return to Kavieng. A message arrived saying that the *Dick Smith Explorer* was delayed off New Britain. I needed to get back to my duties at the Burke Museum, and the new school semester was starting soon for the Australian women in Canberra. We left several crates full of Lapita pottery and other samples in Male's care, along with the *Lapita* launch. The *Dick Smith Explorer* would pick these materials up a few weeks later. Meanwhile the three of us flew out of Eloaua on the once-a-week, six-seater Talair flight to Kavieng.

One more adventure awaited me before I left the Bismarcks. Standing on the tarmac at Kavieng airport as I stepped out of the Talair plane was archaeologist Paul Gorecki, who had been digging a Lapita site at Lamau, on New Ireland. A Belgian who had emigrated to Australia, Gorecki excitedly asked, in his French accent, whether I would go with him on a reconnaissance trip to New Hanover Island.

After six weeks on Eloaua I was looking forward to a hot shower and some cold beers in the Kavieng Hotel. "Pat, we can't wait. I have organized zee boat. It eez at zee wharf. We need to leave now." What the hell, I thought. A few extra days will not make a difference. I might as well have a look at New Hanover, a big, high volcanic island that no one had ever explored archaeologically. Maybe we would find more Lapita sites. "OK, Paul. What do I need to bring?" "Nothing, I have all zee supplies in zee boat."

Dropping my bags off at the Kavieng Hotel, we proceeded to the harbor where a twenty-foot launch was loaded with two five-gallon fuel tanks and one case of Four-X Castlemain beer. The latter constituted the "supplies" that Gorecki had prepared. I briefly thought about backing out, but John Aini, a young man who worked for the New Ireland Fisheries Service and would be our guide, had already untied the boat and started the engine. A few seconds later, we were headed for New Hanover.

During the four-hour trip across the deep lagoon, passing small coral islets that lie between the tip of New Ireland and New Hanover, Aini filled us in about our destination. Lavongai Village was the home of the Johnson Cult, a cargo cult that got its name in 1964 when the Lavongai people insisted on voting for U.S. president Lyndon B. Johnson during the first national elections in the newly independent country of Papua New Guinea. They thought that if Johnson represented them, he would send the "cargo" that the Americans had been famous for since World War II. Aini told us that the cultists called America "Dead Land

Fifty," because they believed that when they died their spirits went to dwell in the fifty states. To put it bluntly, Americans were Lavongai ghosts.

Arriving at dusk at Lavongai, we walked up the path to Aini's parents' house where, fortunately, a hot meal awaited us. As Catholics, the Aini family was not part of the Johnson Cult. But word quickly spread through the village that two White men had arrived, one of them an American. Several curious cult leaders showed up. Gorecki began peppering them with questions. "*Yu pela kisim sumting bilong 'ol tumbuna?*" Gorecki asked. ("Do you have any old artifacts?") The leaders nodded. "*Me pela kisim samting bilong tambaran,*" one said. *Tambaran* are ancestor spirits. It seemed they had some kind of statue or image, which they kept in the village cult house.

The next morning, Gorecki could hardly wait to finish his coffee, anticipating that we were going to be shown an important ancient artifact. The cult house proved to be a two-story wooden building with a tin roof, the only such "Western" style building in the village of mostly sago-leaf thatched dwellings. Meeting us there, one of the elders took a key out of the folds of his lava-lava and unlocked the door. The single room on the lower floor was completely empty. We climbed the narrow ladder leading to the upper floor; that room too was bare, except for a battered wooden trunk set against one wall. Once again, a key was extracted from the lava-lava folds and then inserted into the trunk's keyhole.

The trunk was filled with what looked like a bunch of old garments. The cult leader fumbled around with them, extracting an object wrapped in a dirty rag. Gorecki was now nearly beside himself with anticipation. As the last fold was lifted, the elder's hand cradled a tawdry-looking plastic Christmas tree ornament of a Santa Claus, bearing traces of once having been painted a golden color.

"Eet eez nothing but a fucking Father Christmas!" exploded Gorecki. Furious, he turned and dashed down the ladder and out of the cult house. "Never mind the Australian," I said. "Tell me about this. Why is it important to you?" They said that it had been found behind the village, at a sacred spring, by a young boy who had special powers to communicate with the spirits of Dead Land Fifty. To them, it was a sign that the ancestors were trying to send the much-desired cargo. Enlightened, I thanked the cult leaders for sharing this special object with me, watching as it was rewrapped in its rag and reverently placed back into the locked trunk.

We did find some interesting archaeological sites over the next couple of days, including a cluster of petroglyphs in a small stream valley, which exhibited human faces deeply pecked into the boulder surfaces. The face motifs reminded me of anthropomorphic designs on the Lapita pottery I had dug up at Talepakemalai. But there was no way to date these petroglyphs or tell if they had been carved by the people who had made the Lapita pots.

After three days on Lavongai, we made our way back to Kavieng. I flew to Port Moresby, sharing the news of our Lapita discoveries with Pam Swadling and Johnny Saulo at the National Museum. Stopping off in Honolulu for a couple of days on my return to Seattle, I showed a few of the most significant finds that I had hand-carried to Yosihiko Sinoto and other former colleagues at the Bishop Museum. They were stunned at the beauty of the delicate face designs on the Lapita potsherds. There was no doubt in my mind that I would have to return to uncover more of what was hidden in the sands of Talepakemalai.

CHAPTER FOURTEEN

The Secrets of Talepakemalai (Mussau Islands, 1986–1988)

During the gray Seattle winter of 1986 I made preparations for a return expedition to Mussau. With support from the National Geographic Society's Committee on Research and Exploration I would be able to take two graduate students along as field assistants. I invited Marshall Weisler—who had worked with me in Hawai'i—and Terry Hunt to join me in Mussau. We would need our own boat to travel between Mussau's small islets, so I purchased a Metzler "Maya-S" twelve-foot inflatable dingy. Powered by a 4 hp Mariner outboard, it was just big enough to carry five people and gear (Fig. 14.1).

In late August, Weisler, Hunt, and I arrived in Port Moresby, flying to Kavieng on New Ireland several days later. There I reacquainted myself with John Aini (our guide in New Hanover), who was stationed at the local PNG Fisheries Research Station. Aini agreed to join us in Mussau to help make a reference collection of fish skeletons and conduct a survey of the fishing methods used by the Mussau people.[1]

One logistical problem confronted us: how to obtain gasoline to run the Mariner outboard. There was no gasoline available on Eloaua, and regulations prohibited bringing gasoline on the Talair plane. Fortunately, I was able to put a fifty-five-gallon drum of fuel on the *Tikana*, a small boat headed up to Mussau. A few days after we arrived, the *Tikana* came close offshore, and its crew tossed the drum into the ocean (gasoline being lighter than water, the drum floated). We lashed a rope to the drum and towed it in over the reef!

On August 29 the Talair twin-engine six seater, with 620 kilos of gear and supplies lashed in place (including the inflatable boat), took off for Eloaua. About halfway through the flight I looked over at Terry Hunt, who seemed unusually happy. Unbeknownst to me, just before boarding Hunt had opened my backpack, which held a fifth of good Scotch whisky, and proceeded to chug a third of the bottle. Hunt did not like Scotch, but he had a terrible fear of flying, especially in small planes.

The plane skidded through a bumpy landing on the rough coral runway. As we pulled up to the windsock—the only navigational aid at the Eloaua "airport"

Figure 14.1. The author driving his inflatable "Maya-S" boat up the Malle Channel off of Eloaua Island, Mussau, in 1986.

(there is not even a shelter)—I could see my friends awaiting us. Jumping down from the plane I shook hands all around, introducing Weisler and the tipsy Hunt. Eager hands helped carry our boxes of supplies to Ave Male's compound. That evening the members of the "Giaman Club" assembled to sip their weak tea and tell tall tales. It felt good to be back on Eloaua.

I asked Male to put out the word that we wanted to hire as many as ten workers to assist us. Although the Eloaua islanders live off the food from their gardens and the fish they catch, they still need money to buy clothing, tools, and kerosene, as well as for other uses, such as sending children to school in Kavieng. In 1985 all of my workers had been men, because only men had shown up when I put out a call for workers. I assumed that this would again be the case. On the day after our arrival, however, a delegation from the village Women's Committee appeared. "*Mipela meri save hatwok olsem man,*" Naomi Kavi told me. ("We women work just as hard as men.") Impressed by their insistence on gender equality, I agreed to hire equal numbers of men and women. Although the women did not want to dig (they felt this was men's work), they proved to be sharp-eyed screeners.

With our mixed-gender crew of eager diggers and sifters, we set to work in the area where I had found the anaerobically preserved house posts in 1985. Once again, as soon as we were below the island's shallow freshwater lens, the pit began to fill with water. This time, I came equipped with two hand-operated marine bilge pumps to keep up with the underground flow. Overnight the excavation would fill up like a small swimming pool, so the first hour of every day was devoted to pumping the pit dry.

We followed the stratigraphic layers horizontally as we opened up new squares to the south and east, until twenty-four square meters had been opened up at Area B (Fig. 14.2). More wooden post bases appeared, forming two alignments joining at a corner with three stout posts. These posts had once supported two sides of a stilt house that had stood over the shallow lagoon. Radiocarbon dates from the prior season's excavation—some on the preserved wooden post bases—told us that the house dated to between 1400–1200 BC.[2]

This stilt house had not been an ordinary dwelling. Much of the pottery—discarded from the former house platform—bore intricate decorations, in the classic dentate-stamped Lapita style. There were flat-bottomed dishes with lacy geometric designs on their flaring sides; pedestals with elaborate cutouts; and cylinder stands with motifs made from a combination of dentate stamping and carving the wet clay, all filled in with white lime highlighting the designs. Many of the motifs depicted stylized human faces, with almond-shaped eyes, long noses, and what looked like "flame" headdresses (Fig. 14.3). This was not an assemblage of everyday, utilitarian pottery. These vessels had required skill and much labor to produce: They must have been intended for special ceremonial uses.[3]

Along with the pottery were hundreds of whole and fragmentary rings made from cone shell tops and from *Tridacna* clam shell, pendants of pearl shell, beads of orange-colored *Spondylus* shell, drilled sharks' teeth, and small round disks of chambered *Nautilus* shell. The *Nautilus* shell disks, two of which form a perfectly matched pair, may have been inlaid "eyes" for an anthropomorphic image in fiber or barkcloth. We found hundreds of sharp flakes of obsidian, imported from quarries in Manus and New Britain. There were also human bones—part of a cranium, a mandible, and a femur—possibly the bones of respected elders once kept in ancestor bundles wrapped in barkcloth or basketry.

Figure 14.2. The completed excavation of Area B at the Talepakemalai Lapita site, Eloaua, Mussau, in 1986. The hoses were used to pump out the groundwater. The dark objects in the floor of the excavation are the anaerobically preserved bases of wooden house posts.

The most striking artifact of all was found along the north-south alignment of the wooden posts. A member of the Giaman Club, Bauwa Sagila, first exposed the little bone object while scraping away at the waterlogged sands with his trowel. About six inches long, the heavy piece of porpoise bone was lying face down. I watched as Sagila carefully removed the sand and then plotted the object's position. He picked the bone up between thumb and forefinger, turning it over and

Figure 14.3. Part of a large ceramic cylinder stand as it was exposed in the Talepakemalai excavation; note the intricate dentate-stamped designs.

exposing it to sunlight for the first time in more than three thousand years. A delicately carved representation of a human face stared back at us. "*God bilong ol Lapita!*" (The Lapita God!), Bauwa exclaimed. This beautiful stylized figurine, carved from the bone of a porpoise, may have represented a sea deity. Its two short peg-like legs suggest that it might have been mounted on a wooden shaft. Perhaps it tipped a wand carried by a Lapita priest or chief.

The Area B stilt house, standing over the shallow lagoon at Talepakemalai, must have served a special function in this Lapita village; perhaps it was a place where ceremonies were held or possibly a men's house, a structure found in many Oceanic societies where men conduct rituals, worship ancestors, and pass down traditions.

More prosaic objects also came out of the waterlogged sands. There were thousands of bones of fish as well as of birds, reptiles, and even chickens and pigs—the remains of feasts that had been celebrated at this special house. There were mollusk shells by the kilo: oysters, clams, cones, whelks, and other kinds of shellfish harvested from Eloaua's reefs. Most intriguing were the well-preserved seeds of plants. Normally, such vegetal remains do not survive in Pacific archaeological sites, but the anaerobic, waterlogged conditions at Talepakemalai preserved them in the thousands.

Archaeologists debated whether the Lapita people practiced horticulture, like their later Polynesian descendants. The more than 10,000 plant remains we recovered at Talepakemalai were a "smoking gun," demonstrating that the Lapita people cultivated a diversity of tree crops.[4] In addition to coconut shells, we found the seeds or other parts of twenty-four different tree crops, including Tahitian Chestnut, the Vi Apple, and *Canarium* almond. We also found a stalk of kava, the pepper plant used ritually throughout Polynesia and parts of eastern Melanesia.

By late September it was time to close down the Talepakemalai excavation. I was needed back at the Burke Museum. Hunt and Weisler would stay on for six more weeks to excavate at other sites, including the smaller Lapita sites on Eloaua and Emananus that we had briefly tested in 1985. We visited those sites and made an excavation plan.

One question that had been puzzling me was where the clay used to make all of the Lapita pots had come from. Eloaua Island, composed of coral and upraised reef limestone, lacks clay entirely. Some of the villagers, however, told me that clay could be found near a village called Tanaliu, about thirty kilometers up the eastern coast of "Big Mussau," the main island. I decided to organize a trip to Tanaliu to see if we could obtain samples from this clay source (see Map 6).

The trip to Tanaliu required a larger craft than my little Metzler inflatable. Ave Male offered the use of *Two Mile*, his sleek dugout powered by a 25 hp outboard

(Fig. 14.4). As dawn broke Male guided *Two Mile* out through the pass; by mid-morning we reached Tanaliu. Several of the Tanaliu men guided us through the jungle to reach the exposure where I filled some plastic bags with the orange-red clay, which we would later analyze to see if this had been a source of potting clay used on Eloaua. On the way, we passed some promising looking rockshelters. Weisler proposed that he return to excavate them. I agreed with this plan, because it would be useful to obtain an archaeological sequence from the main island. The Tanaliu people were happy to provide a house for Weisler to use, knowing that he would employ them to help with the digging.

By now it was late in the afternoon; Male wanted to return before dark, because getting *Two Mile* across the reef could be tricky. Departing Tanaliu, we rounded Cape Forster, Mussau's westernmost point. Male's brother John spotted a flock of birds farther out to sea. The seabirds were in a feeding frenzy, plunging into the water after a school of tuna. Despite the fact that the sun would soon set, Male turned the canoe out to sea; the possibility of catching several large tuna was irresistible. For the better part of an hour we chased the birds and the tuna school as *Two Mile* cut through the open ocean swells, salt spray soaking us. Pull-

Figure 14.4. Preparing the dugout canoe *Two Mile* for a trip to Tanaliu Village, Mussau, in 1986. In the background is the main island of "Big Mussau" with its stair-step topography of ancient, uplifted limestone terraces.

ing in a couple of yellowfin tuna with our trolling lines, we watched one of the most magnificent sunsets I have ever seen ignite the western sky. Reluctantly, Male turned and headed back toward Eloaua. I was amazed that he could navigate in the dark, but he brought *Two Mile* right up off Eloaua's reef. We shouted until someone in the village heard us, bringing out a kerosene lantern to signal Male so he could take us through the narrow pass.

In early November 1986, Hunt and Weisler returned to Seattle. Unpacking all of the collections in my Burke Museum laboratory, I took stock of what we had recovered. Between the 1985 and 1986 field seasons at Talepakemalai, there were more than 60,000 potsherds, several thousand obsidian flakes, and about 800 non-ceramic artifacts, as well as 22,000 vertebrate bones—all needing to be cataloged, identified, and analyzed. Before leaving for Mussau I had submitted a proposal to the National Science Foundation (NSF), requesting funds to hire three graduate research assistants and to cover the costs of radiocarbon dating and specialized laboratory work; the NSF had funded my proposal and we were ready to go to work.

One of the first tasks was to figure out the source—or sources—of the Mussau Lapita pottery. In his earlier work in the Santa Cruz Islands in the eastern Solomons, Roger Green had shown that Lapita communities were linked by trading networks. They imported clay from one island and temper (the rock or shell inclusions added to the clay to make a pot stronger) from another, combining these materials in village workshops. Then, the fired pots might be traded to yet another community. I wondered whether the Lapita people on Eloaua had participated in a similar exchange network. Geochemical analysis of the pottery would provide critical evidence for such trade or the exchange of pottery or the raw materials from which the pots were manufactured.

Terry Hunt wanted to take up the geochemical analysis of the Mussau pottery as the topic for his doctoral dissertation; I provided him with one of the research assistantships that NSF had agreed to fund. Hunt selected a sample of Talapakemalai potsherds, examining and sorting them into groups based on fabric and temper. These groupings were then refined under a binocular microscope. Finally, Hunt used an electron microscope equipped with an energy-dispersive x-ray fluorescence (XRF) microprobe to obtain precise chemical signatures of the different groups of pottery.

Hunt's results were fascinating.[5] In the oldest parts of the Talepakemalai site the pottery had been made from as many as twelve unique kinds of clay. One of the groups matched the Tanaliu clay source, but the clay used in other pots must have come from elsewhere in the Bismarck Archipelago. In the upper layers, the number of distinct clay source groups declined to six and then just three. These findings suggested that at first the Lapita people in Mussau had participated in an exchange network linking many different communities. Several centuries later, the number of communities in this network had declined by about half. Eventually, the network shrunk to just a few communities.

The thousands of obsidian flakes were another indication that the Mussau Lapita people had been part of an extensive exchange or trade network. Obsidian does not occur in Mussau; within the Bismarck Archipelago it is found only in the Manus Islands (west of Mussau) and on the Willaumez Peninsula on New Britain Island. Another graduate student, Melinda Allen, went to work on the obsidian along with other rocks (such as chert and volcanic oven stones). Knowing that the Manus and New Britain obsidians had different specific gravities, we used a heavy liquid called sodium metatungstate to separate flakes from the different sources according to a specific gravity "cut point." Allen would place each obsidian flake into a beaker of the calibrated heavy liquid; depending on whether the flake floated or sank, its probable source could be discerned. Then I sent a selected sample of these flakes to the Australian Atomic High Energy Commission where their chemical composition was precisely analyzed using a method called PIXE-PIGME. Through these analyses we discovered that at first obsidian from both New Britain and Manus had been imported to Mussau; later in time, most of the obsidian was imported from Manus alone. This was more evidence that the geographic range of the Lapita trade networks had retracted over time.

I also wanted to advance our understanding of the Lapita subsistence economy. Virginia Butler, a graduate student doing an interdisciplinary PhD between archaeology and ichthyology, compared the Mussau archaeological fishbones to the reference collection I had made with John Aini's help. Identifying the bones to genus and species, Butler found that most of the fish taken by Lapita people were inshore species, although there was some evidence for offshore trolling. I sent the nonfish bones to my former Bishop Museum colleague Alan Ziegler, who identified the remains of fruit bats, snakes, lizards, birds, turtles, and pigs.

My basement laboratory in the Burke Museum hummed with activity as we worked away on the Mussau collections throughout the 1987–1988 academic year. I kept thinking, nonetheless, that the waterlogged sands of Talepakemalai had not yet given up all their secrets. Drawing upon the accumulating results, I made the successful case in a new proposal to the National Science Foundation for funding for a third expedition to Mussau.

For this third expedition, I was joined by Dana Lepofsky, who conducted an ethnoarchaeological study of plant use in Mussau,[6] and by Jason Tyler, an undergraduate who had worked with me in American Samoa. An Australian marine biologist, Carla Catterall, also met up with us in Mussau. Talepakemalai was full of tons of marine mollusk shells. I wanted to know whether centuries of mollusk harvesting on Eloaua's reefs had affected the mollusk populations and reef ecology. Catterall had studied the ecology of *Strombus* mollusks in New Guinea. Assisted by her student Mike Ritchie, Catterall agreed to survey Eloaua's reefs and mollusk populations.

Arriving on Eloaua in mid-September 1988, the routine was by now familiar, as we settled into Ave Male's comfortable cluster of huts. But almost immediately, I sensed that something was different in the village. Male seemed worried, as did a number of the other elders. When I asked Male and his brother John what was bothering them, they told me that some of the young men had formed a gang, influenced by movies (some pornographic) they had seen on the Korean ships that were transporting hardwood timber logged from Big Mussau. These teenagers thought that possessing a human skull would give them powers over the village girls, who would then be unable to resist their sexual advances. Male told me that the boys had already desecrated one recent grave. He was terrified that they would try to exhume the body of his own father, who had passed away the year before and was buried a short distance behind Male's house. Male had taken to sleeping next to the grave every night, with a kerosene lantern, as a deterrent.

These problems were symptomatic of a breakdown in social order throughout Papua New Guinea. The capital of Port Moresby had become a dangerous place, with a strict curfew from dusk to dawn to curtail the "rascals," gangs of unemployed young men. But even in remote Eloaua things were not as they had been just three years earlier. The problems could be traced to the colonial era. In the 1930s, American missionaries had undermined the authority of Mussau's traditional chiefs. Now, under the influence of Western media and other contacts with the outside world, the young people rejected the church. There was no central authority that could maintain a sense of moral order.

Despite this looming sense of uncertainty, our team set to work at Talepakemalai, opening another block excavation at Area B to obtain one final sample of pottery. Then, we cut a long transect through the jungle, extending across the low-lying terrain that had once been a shallow reef flat. I wanted to find the edge of the old stilt-house village. We dug test pits every ten meters, using our hand-operated bilge pumps to keep the pits dry.[7]

As we dug steadily north along the transect, the pottery coming from the excavations began to change. At eighty meters from the old beach ridge there were almost no sherds with the classic Lapita dentate-stamped designs. Instead, the potsherds here were decorated with incised lines in simple geometric patterns. The pots themselves had thin walls (made by the paddle-and-anvil technique in which the pliable clay is beaten between a wooden paddle and a cobble) and were well fired.

I opened up two blocks of four square meters each (Area C), again coming upon a cluster of wooden house posts, the remains of ancient stilt houses. Radio-carbon dates later showed that the houses had been built between 1100 and 800 BC. Area C was the last phase at Talepakemalai, after the village had shifted sea-ward. By the time the Area C houses were constructed, the former men's house at Area B had been abandoned and collapsed, its posts buried by the accumulating sands of the beach ridge. Meanwhile, the islanders had changed their manner of making and decorating their pots. The incised pottery of Area C represented the late, final phase in the Lapita sequence at Mussau.

While we were digging at Area C, marine biologists Catterall and Ritchie went out every day in my Metzler inflatable boat, mapping the Eloaua reefs and sam-pling the populations of mollusks and other invertebrates. In the evenings we all labored together under the light of our pressure lanterns, measuring thousands of mollusk shells recovered from the excavations. It was tedious work, using cali-pers to determine the lengths and diameters of *Strombus, Cypraea, Anadara,* and other mollusk shells.

When all of these data were analyzed, it turned out that the hypothesis of human impact on the island's marine ecology was not supported. Apparently, the marine resources of Eloaua's extensive reefs and lagoon were so rich that the exploitation of mollusks by the small human population had not had an appre-ciable impact. The changes over time in the overall frequency of certain mollusk species could be better explained by alterations in the reef's ecology caused by the drop in sea level, such as expansion of sea-grass beds and decreases in areas with coral heads. This was a good lesson in how science progresses—by posing hypotheses and then rigorously testing them with empirical data.

Male's father's grave did not get desecrated during our 1988 stay, but other events made me uneasy. There was an attempted rape in the village. Then, a Ko-rean merchant who was buying *Trochus* shells while visiting Palakau Village was attacked by one of the youth gangs. It was with some trepidation that I departed Eloaua at the end of October, leaving Lepofsky to carry out her ethnobotanical study of tree cropping on the island and Tyler to excavate a pottery site on nearby Boliu Island. Fortunately, by then we had been joined by Nick Araho, a young Papua New Guinea archaeologist. I trusted Araho to keep a watch out for the safety of Lepofsky and Tyler. Luckily, there were no further incidents.

I knew that it was going to take several years to catalog and analyze all of the material from Talepakemalai, let alone write up the results. The troubling condi-tions in Eloaua made me reluctant to return there with students. And I would soon be leaving the University of Washington to take up a new position at the University of California at Berkeley (see Chapter Sixteen). For all these reasons, it was time to call a halt to fieldwork in Mussau.

The Mussau project was the largest and most complex that I had yet undertaken, involving more than twenty collaborators and the expenditure of about a quarter-million dollars in research funds. Out of it came more than a dozen scientific articles, a book (*The Lapita Peoples*),[8] and the first of a projected three-volume monograph series. In these publications I have presented some answers to the questions that we posed about the Lapita cultural complex and its key role in the early history of Oceania.

For one thing, we now know that both Jim Allen and Roger Green were right—and wrong—in the theories they were arguing over in Cook's Bar in Dunedin (see Chapter Thirteen). The Bismarcks had been the "Lapita homeland," but not quite in the way Allen had envisioned. Rather than evolving "in situ" in these islands over thousands of years, the Lapita culture had emerged over about two centuries in the late second millennium BC. Austronesian-speaking peoples had arrived in their outrigger canoes from Southeast Asia, meeting, interacting, and intermarrying with indigenous "Papuan" populations whose ancestors had settled in the Bismarcks during the Pleistocene, as long ago as 37,000 years BP. Roger Green later summed up this process of ethnogenesis—the creation of a new culture—with his "Triple-I Model" of Lapita origins.[9] The I's stand for *intrusion, innovation,* and *integration.* Lapita was a synthesis of new and old—pottery, pigs, and root crops brought by the intrusive Austronesians in their sailing canoes, integrating with local populations who had already discovered the local obsidian sources, domesticated certain kind of tree crops, and were intimately familiar with the local environments. The innovative Lapita culture that emerged on Eloaua and other islands of the Bismarcks between 1500–1300 BC was then poised to burst out of this southwestern corner of the Pacific that we call Near Oceania, to explore and discover for the first time the islands of Remote Oceania, stretching east and south of the Solomons.

Twenty-five years after we backfilled the last test pit at Talepakemalai, I am still working away on the rich Lapita finds from Mussau. Scarlett Chiu, a former Berkeley student and now a researcher at Taiwan's Academia Sinica, has been working with me to create a database that will make this collection available to researchers anywhere in the world via the Internet.[10] When the details of our analyses of the Mussau pottery, obsidian, artifacts, and faunal and floral materials are published in the next few years, the research I began thirty years ago will be complete. Archaeology can be painstakingly slow. But then I remind myself that the little "Lapita god" lay buried in the sands of Talepakemalai for three thousand years, waiting to be discovered.

CHAPTER FIFTEEN

Hawaiki, The Polynesian Homeland (Manuʻa Islands, 1986–1989)

Not long after returning from my first trip to Mussau in 1985, I received a letter from Stan Sorenson, the director of the Historic Preservation Office in Pago Pago, American Samoa. His office had received funds from the U.S. National Park Service, Sorensen wrote, to be used for an archaeological survey. This seemed like a good opportunity to expand the research in Western Polynesia that I had begun with my expeditions to Futuna and ʻUvea in 1974 and to Niuatoputapu in 1976. I told Sorensen that I would like to explore the three small islands—Taʻū, Ofu, and Olosega—that make up the Manuʻa group at Samoa's eastern extremity. Yosihiko Sinoto and Bill Kikuchi of the Bishop Museum had reconnoitered the islands in 1962 but were disappointed in the lack of early sites. I thought that perhaps the islands would be worth a second look. I made plans for a trip to Manuʻa in the summer of 1986. Terry Hunt, from the University of Washington (UW), would assist me. Sorensen promised to make the necessary contacts with the Manuʻa chiefs before we arrived in Samoa.

When we arrived in Pago Pago, I asked Sorensen about the arrangements for our work in Manuʻa. Had the chiefs given their permission? And what were the arrangements for our lodging? Sorensen evaded my questions; it was apparent that the laid-back, former Peace Corps volunteer turned bureaucrat had not fulfilled his promise. The next day we attended a meeting of the American Samoa Historic Preservation Advisory Council. Worried and despondent, I could barely concentrate as I sat through the long, boring meeting in the stifling hot room. Nothing had been done to prepare the way for us. I had no political contacts in Samoa, which meant starting from scratch. As the meeting adjourned, one of the local Advisory Council members introduced himself. "I'm John Kneubuhl," he said. "We met briefly on Easter Island during the Congress a couple of years ago." I vaguely recalled having had a drink with him in the hotel bar on Rapa Nui.

Kneubuhl was hardly dressed like someone you expected to be on a government advisory panel. Tall, tanned, in his late sixties, and missing a couple of teeth, he wore a floral print lava-lava, a rumpled aloha shirt, and flip-flops on his feet.

His surname suggested German ancestry (the Germans had controlled Samoa in the colonial era), but his facial features told me he was also part Samoan.

"From what I gather, Stan hasn't done much to facilitate your project," Kneubuhl said drolly. "Hardly," I muttered. "He promised to handle local permissions and lodging for us, but it seems that he never bothered to contact the chiefs in Manu'a."

"Do you have plans for this evening?" Kneubuhl asked. I said we did not. "Do you have a car?" I replied that we had a rental. "OK. Let's go out to my place at Tafuna. We can talk about your situation over a good meal." As yet ignorant of Kneubuhl's pedigree—which traced back to the first English missionaries in Samoa who had married into a line of prominent Samoan chiefs—I was dubious that this man in a fraying shirt who did not even have a car could do much to help us. But he was entertainingly eccentric and interested in Samoan history; a dinner at his house could not hurt.

On the way out to Tafuna, Kneubuhl directed me to pull in to a little market. "We need some supplies," he said. He filled the shopping cart with a dozen quart bottles of Vailima beer and a fifth of Johnny Walker Scotch and then tossed in a large leg of lamb. I started to reach for my wallet, but Kneubuhl had already pulled a wad of fifty-dollar bills out of a fold in his lava-lava. The way the Samoan clerk at the counter respectfully addressed him hinted that I was dealing with someone of status.

At Tafuna, we turned down a concrete driveway bordered by lush tropical gardens. An imposing mansion stood on the right. "My brother's place," he said. We continued down through the expansive estate, pulling up at an old, rambling wooden house with a big verandah, right out of a Somerset Maugham story. It had belonged to his parents and was once quite grand but had seen better days. The house suited Kneubuhl.

"Dotty," he called out to a slender woman in the kitchen, "we've got guests for dinner." Dorothy Kneubuhl greeted us warmly. He enthusiastically told Dotty, "You and Patrick here are both Punahou graduates." John and Dorothy had been sweethearts at Punahou School, where he had been sent to be educated in the 1930s (Fig. 15.1).

While Dotty concocted a delicious feast (with the aid of several Tongan women whom I learned were retainers of this old-style chiefly household), Kneubuhl poured glasses of beer. Bookshelves holding moldy Bishop Museum *Bulletins* and other anthropological works lined the walls of the living room, whose floors were covered in *lauhala* mats. Kneubuhl told me how, while attending Punahou and living with the Judd family in Honolulu, he would visit his "uncle" Te Rangi Hiroa at the Bishop Museum. Hiroa had personally tutored young Kneubuhl in Polynesian anthropology.

Figure 15.1. John and Dotty Kneubuhl in their garden at Tafuna on Tutuila Island, American Samoa.

After finishing Punahou, Kneubuhl studied English literature at Yale, taking courses with Thornton Wilder. Graduating toward the end of World War II, he joined Naval Intelligence, serving in the western Pacific. After the war he married Dotty. They moved to Hollywood, where Kneubuhl became a scriptwriter in the booming television industry. Among the series that he wrote for were *The Fugitive, Gunsmoke,* and *Hawaii Five-O.* After twenty years of this fast-paced life he woke up one day and said to Dotty, "Pack your bags. We're going home to Samoa." Now he was living the noblesse oblige life of a Polynesian chief and writing plays, his passion.[1]

After a huge meal and emptying the bottle of Scotch, we spent the night sleeping it off at Kneubuhl's house. The next morning he made us coffee and breakfast and then said, "Now let's get to work." I realized that Kneubuhl had been testing

me, wanting to know who I really was and the strength of my commitment to
Polynesian anthropology. Getting in the car, we drove to the Fono or assembly
of chiefs of American Samoa. Kneubuhl took us straight to the office of High
Chief Aolaolangi Soli, governor of Manu'a. Soli telephoned Paopao, hereditary
chief of Fiti'uta Village on Ta'ū Island. "Chief Paopao will meet you at Ta'ū and
you will be his guests there," Soli told us. "I hope your project in Manu'a is successful. If you have any further needs, don't hesitate to call me."

As High Chief Soli had promised, Fiti'uta Village's chief Paopao was there to meet
our Manu'a Air plane when we landed on Ta'ū Island. Chief Paopao and his wife
graciously offered to lodge us in their house (Fig. 15.2). After discussing our proposed research agenda with the elders in the village guest house, Paopao told me
that he wanted to take us to Saua, a narrow coastal plain lying under the shadow
of Ta'ū's high mountain. But, Paopao stressed, we must go there before the first
light of morning.

Elsewhere, I have told the story of how Paopao took Terry Hunt and me, in
the pre-dawn darkness the following morning, to the beach at Saua.[2] We stepped
out of his truck into the salty air, guided down a sandy path to the beach by the
roar of the surf crashing on the reef. The eastern sky was becoming distinctly
lighter. Arriving at the beach crest, Paopao motioned for us to sit on the soft coral
sand. He began to speak:

If you are going to work in Manu'a, and want to understand our history,
you must know about this place, Saua, and about our great creator god,
Tangaroa. It was here, in Manu'a, that the sun first rose in the eastern
sky. It was here that Tangaroa created the world and the first man.

Tangaroa, as I already knew, was the first of the great Polynesian gods, the one
who had with enormous effort pushed his parents—Sky Father and Earth
Mother—apart from their eternal embrace, thus creating space for the World.[3] In
Western Polynesia, Tangaroa was the supreme creator god, who had fashioned the
first human from clay. In other Polynesian groups to the east, including Hawai'i,
Tangaroa joined Tāne, Tū, and Rongo as one of a pantheon of great deities. Here
on the beach at Saua, with the east wind in my face and the surf rushing relentlessly toward us over the reef crest, Paopao, hereditary chief of Fiti'uta, was sharing with me a tradition that extended back more than two thousand years, to the
time of the original Hawaiki, the ancient Polynesian homeland.

As the dawn's reddish-golden rays streamed skyward from behind a low-lying
cloud bank, Paopao continued his account of how Tangaroa, having created the

Figure 15.2. Chief Paopao and his wife in front of the meeting house,
Fiti'uta Village, Ta'ū, American Samoa.

World, at first found only the vast, lonely expanse of waters, *Moana*. Taking the
form of the migratory golden plover (*Pluvialis fulva*), known as *tuli* in Samoan,
Tangaroa flew far and wide, searching for land but finding none. So Tangaroa
caused the islands of Samoa, Tonga, and those of Fiti (Fiji) to the west to emerge
from the watery vastness. And on the island of Savai'i, he caused a boy and a girl—
Sava and I'i—to be born. Thus, here in Hawaiki, Tangaroa created the human race.

We sat for a long time on the Saua beach as the dawn melted away to the
humid warmth of a tropical morning. A solitary curlew waded in the foamy

water at the foot of the beach. I was deeply touched by Paopao's tale of Tangaroa, by the fact that this proud chief wanted us to appreciate his Polynesian point of view. Too often, Western scholars and scientists have discounted Polynesian histories and traditions. Yes, some of these were "merely" mythology, but then what civilization is not founded on its own great mythic traditions? Just as the Greeks had Zeus and Ares, and the Romans Jupiter and Mars, so the Polynesians had Tangaroa and Tū. To get to the core of a culture, one can do no better than to start with myth.

Although Hawaiki is deeply ingrained in Polynesian myth and tradition, it is more than just a mythic place. Ancestral Polynesian culture developed out of the small populations of Lapita voyagers who first reached Tonga and Samoa around 900 BC. Geographically, this Polynesian homeland of Hawaiki included the Tongan chain stretching south to north from Tongatapu up through the Ha'apai and Vava'u island groups, to tiny Niuatoputapu as well as Samoa, Futuna, and 'Uvea. By around 500 BC the culture of the Lapita people who settled these islands had adapted and changed such that we can distinguish a distinct Ancestral Polynesian culture marked by new kinds of pottery, adzes, and other artifacts. The Ancestral Polynesians had given up decorating the pottery with dentate-stamped designs; it now consisted of plainware jars and bowls. Instead of using the large *Tridacna* clam shells for their adzes, the Polynesian descendants of the Lapita people had learned to work the dense basalt found at quarries in Samoa, 'Uvea, and other volcanic islands in the region. At the same time, a new Proto Polynesian language was taking shape along a dialect chain that linked these islands. New words reflecting the changing economic and social lives of these people were added to their vocabulary while old words were lost. Over more than a thousand years in these Western Polynesian archipelagoes, the unique characteristics of Polynesian language and culture gradually took shape. Much later, toward the end of the first millennium AD, when Polynesian voyagers sailed eastward once again to discover Tahiti and the other islands of Eastern Polynesia, they would remember this ancestral homeland—this Hawaiki—glorifying it in myth and chant.

The 1986 reconnaissance in Manu'a was more rewarding than I could have hoped. We recorded stone house platforms and star mounds in the jungles of Ta'ū, Olosega, and Ofu.[4] Most exciting was a buried site on Ofu containing pottery, the first ceramic site recorded in the Manu'a group. The discovery was serendipitous: The Public Works Department had bulldozed a small depression into the coastal plain at To'aga for a garbage dump. I climbed down into the pit to see what the dozer might have exposed beneath the surface. In the eight-foot wall of the trench a grayish-brown cultural layer was sandwiched between underlying beach sands and clay eroded from the steep hillside nearby. Terry Hunt put down a one-meter test pit close by, recovering a handful of thick, coarse pottery sherds in the buried layer. A *Turbo* shell with the pottery gave a radiocarbon date of 28 BC to AD 108.[5] I thought that expanded excavations at To'aga might lead to more deeply buried and perhaps even older sites.

I returned to Ofu in 1987 with Hunt and a small team of University of Washington students. From prior experience, I knew that the coastal zones of volcanic islands such as Ofu often changed significantly over time. Early human occupations on island coasts are often buried under sand and coral rubble thrown up by storm surges, or under volcanic soil and debris eroded off of steep mountain slopes (Fig. 15.3). An island archaeologist must be prepared to dig, sometimes deeply, to find what he or she is seeking.

With machetes, we cut a swath through the bush from the shore running inland, right up to the base of the steep mountain. Then, as I had done in Niuatoputapu and Tikopia, we began to dig test pits along this transect. The first few pits in the middle of the sandy plain turned up stone flakes and a piece of a

Figure 15.3. The beach fronting the To'aga site on Ofu Island is one of the most beautiful in the South Pacific.

basalt adz, shellfish and fishbones, and carefully laid gravel pavements of old house floors. But no potsherds.

We had now reached the talus slope at the foot of the steep mountain; the ground consisted of clay rather than sand. We laid out a test unit and began to dig. The compact clay interspersed with rock and small boulders, all washed down from the steep mountain slopes, made for difficult digging. At about a meter down, we broke through the clay and were back into coral sands, stained gray with ash and flecked with small pieces of charcoal from fires that had burned in ancient earth ovens. My eye caught a glimpse of a reddish-brown potsherd in the sifting screen, a fragment of a fired clay bowl made by one of the potters of ancient Hawaiki.

Soon we had dozens of potsherds, along with a fishhook made of *Turbo* shell and a beautifully polished adz of basalt. We expanded the test pit, opening up a T-shaped trench, seven square meters in all, accumulating more potsherds, fish-hooks, and stone tools (Fig. 15.4). We had discovered a major, buried archaeologi-

Figure 15.4. The author recording the stratigraphy in the deep excavation at Toʻaga, on Ofu Island. The dark, upper layer consists of clay and boulders eroded from the steep mountain-side, which buried the older, pottery-bearing cultural deposits.

cal site at To'aga. Charcoal samples would later be radiocarbon dated to about 500 BC, a few centuries earlier than the deposits near the garbage dump.[6]

One final field season at To'aga in 1989 seemed warranted. On the way through Pago Pago to Ofu I visited John Kneubuhl again, suggesting that he come over to Ofu and see for himself what we were digging up in our test pits. When I told him that we would be there for my birthday, he promised to fly out for a visit.

This time I laid out transects across the entire two-kilometer-long coastal flat at To'aga.[7] We dug test pits along six separate transects, correlating the stratigraphy between units. I already knew that the oldest cultural deposits would be found closest to the mountain; they had formed when the coastal plain was narrower, during a period of higher sea level. But these early deposits were also the most deeply buried.

In Test Pit 28 on the inland end of Transect 5, we slogged through more than two and a half meters of thick, sticky clay clinging to large basalt boulders that had tumbled down from the mountainside. Our Samoan helpers pried out the rocks with heavy iron crowbars, barely able to lift the largest boulders out of the deep pit. Seven feet down, we hit pale brown, charcoal-flecked sand marking the ancient habitation layer. The potsherds—of a thin, fine ware—included a rim with an impressed lip as well as several with an orange-red slip, characteristic of early Samoan pottery. Although we did not find sherds with telltale dentate-stamped Lapita designs, the radiocarbon date from Test Pit 28 would later tell us that this layer dated to the early first millennium BC, probably only a century or two after the first Lapita voyagers discovered these islands.

As promised, John Kneubuhl flew over from Pago Pago to join in my birthday celebration. Dressed in his usual lava-lava and aloha shirt, Kneubuhl carried a tattered vinyl suitcase. At Manu'a Peau's house in Ofu Village where we were lodging, he tossed the suitcase on the kitchen table, unzipping it to reveal two legs of lamb wrapped in foil, a jar of Dotty's homemade mint sauce, and a bottle of good Scotch. "Your birthday dinner," Kneubuhl proclaimed. It was a birthday feast I will never forget. Sadly, it was the last time I would enjoy Kneubuhl's company; he passed away in 1992.

Our three seasons of fieldwork at To'aga revealed many aspects of life in ancient Hawaiki. Fourteen radiocarbon dates gave us a precise chronology. People had first settled on the narrow coastal plain of Ofu around 800 BC. The layers containing pottery continue until about AD 500; more recent layers lack any pottery. Pottery had been a hallmark of the Lapita culture, with its distinctive "tattooed" designs. But soon after the first Lapita voyagers settled the Hawaiki homeland, their pottery began to change. First to go were the elaborately decorated vessels. Undecorated plainware continued to be made with local clay for several centuries. But over time, the pottery began to decline in quality. The simple bowls became thick walled and coarse in texture. The pots were fired in low heat, making them susceptible to breaking. Late Polynesian plainware from the upper layers at To'aga is crude, an art form in the final stages of decay. Then pottery ceased to be produced at all. When Europeans showed up in the Pacific, no Polynesians produced pottery.

Why did the early Polynesians give up such a useful material art? The answer probably lies in gradual social changes, rather than in material necessity. Lapita pottery, with its elaborate decorations, played an important social and ceremonial role. It was never significant in Polynesian cuisine, because the earth oven was the principal means of cooking food, and the function of holding water or cooked food could be served equally well by containers of coconut shell and carved wooden bowls as by fragile pottery. It is likely that, in ancient Hawaiki, the Lapita descendants transferred the ritual role of pottery to other kinds of objects, such as barkcloth and fine mats. Lapita pottery designs also appear as tattoo motifs and on Polynesian barkcloth. For all of these reasons, it seems that the Lapita descendants who became the first Polynesians gradually lost interest in making pottery. Nonetheless, the intricate designs originally gracing the surfaces of Lapita pots continued through time as motifs on barkcloth, mats, and tattooed bodies.

Our excavations at To'aga, combined with digs that Jack Golson, Roger Green, and other colleagues had carried out on the larger islands of Western Samoa, opened a window onto the world of the first Polynesians. But that window could only open so far, limited as archaeology is to the material, physical world of ancient artifacts, fishbones, earth ovens, and postholes. The methods of archaeology did little to shed light on the social and political organization of the ancient Hawaiki people or the nature of their religious beliefs and rituals, because they left few if any material traces. Yet archaeology is not the only branch of anthropology with the ability to look back into the past. The systematic, controlled comparison of both language and culture can also reveal historical patterns.

In 1985, Roger Green came to visit me in Seattle. Over cocktails in our Ravenna home, Green mentioned that he had been reading *The Cloud People,* a new book by American archaeologists Kent Flannery and Joyce Marcus.[8] I told him that I, too, had been reading the book, intrigued by the way that Flannery and Marcus used a combination of archaeological, linguistic, and ethnographic evidence to reconstruct the cultures of the ancient Zapotec and Mixtec peoples of Mesoamerica, including such seemingly ephemeral topics as religion and ideology.

"You know, Pat, we can apply the same approach in Polynesia," Roger told me, "but we can do it even better." Sipping his wine, he continued, "Our knowledge of the historical divergence of the Polynesian languages is much more complete than what Flannery and Marcus have available for the Uto-Aztecan languages." Green was referring to the work of historical linguists such as the late Bruce Biggs of New Zealand's Auckland University, who had painstakingly reconstructed the speech of the Ancestral Polynesians—their Proto Polynesian language—in remarkable detail. More than four thousand Proto Polynesian words had been defined. Knowing the vocabulary of the Ancestral Polynesians provided a starting point for understanding their world.

The idea was appealing. Green and I started to work on an article demonstrating how one could bring together varied strands of evidence from archaeology, historical linguistics, and comparative ethnography to trace the evolution and divergence of Polynesian cultures. For example, every Polynesian society has a word for "chief," hereditary leader. In Hawai'i it is *ali'i*, in Tonga it is *'eiki*, and in Easter Island *ariki*. Comparing these words and the regular sound shifts involved, a linguist can reconstruct the original Proto Polynesian word *ariki* (the asterisk denotes that it is a reconstruction). Thus we know that in ancient Hawaiki, leaders were called *ariki*. But what kind of power did they exercise? To answer this question, one needs to carefully compare the role and status of chiefs in all of the Polynesian societies to find what is commonly shared. Widely shared traits are likely to be old, inherited from the ancestral culture, whereas traits found only in one or a few islands are most likely later innovations. When we applied this method, it became clear that the *ariki* of Hawaiki had inherited their status through patrilineal succession and that they had been ritual as well as secular leaders.

Our article demonstrating this multipronged approach to historical anthropology, "History, Phylogeny, and Evolution in Polynesia," was published in the international journal *Current Anthropology* in 1987.[9] It provoked considerable debate, partly because many archaeologists (especially outside of the United States) were not familiar with the methods of historical linguistics. They preferred to stick to the potsherds and stone tools that are the backbone of archaeology. In science as in daily life, people are often suspicious of something they do not fully understand.

In our *Current Anthropology* essay Green and I had only sketched the potential of what we were calling the "triangulation method" within historical anthropology. We based this term on an analogy with surveying, in which the location of a point is "triangulated" from several other points whose coordinates are known. Aspects of Ancestral Polynesian culture could be triangulated with data from archaeology, linguistics, and ethnography. Green and I met again in the fall of 1993, in California where I had relocated. Over a leisurely lunch in Napa Valley's *Mustards* restaurant, we hatched a plan to expand our provocative article into a book. The project would take eight years to complete, as our initial plans for a "little essay between covers" grew into a book of 375 pages. The final draft was completed while I held a fellowship at the Center for Advanced Study in the Behavioral and Social Sciences at Palo Alto in 1997–1998. In 2001, *Hawaiki, Ancestral Polynesia: An Essay in Historical Anthropology* was published by Cambridge University Press.[10]

By combining the reconstructions of Proto Polynesian language, the material record of archaeology, and the insights from comparative ethnographies of Polynesian cultures, Green and I were able to gain a much richer understanding of the world of the first Polynesians. Theirs was a *social* world, with lineages whose names traced back to ancestors, and governed by priest-chiefs and other specialists. People resided in small groups called *kainga*, each controlling a house site and adjacent area of garden land. This word continues to be used in some Polynesian societies to this day, as on Rapa Nui. In Hawai'i, the Proto Polynesian *kainga* eventually became 'āina (the ancient k going to 'and the ng sound merging with n), the Hawaiian word for land. A larger kind of social group in ancient Hawaiki was called the *kainanga*, the branched "ascent group" made up of the descendants of a founding pair of ancestors. The *kainanga* groups were those headed by the *ariki, or priest-chiefs.

Rituals also governed the world of ancient Hawaiki, another aspect of the ancient culture that can be brought to light through triangulation. People's lives were regulated by an annual cycle of ceremonies linked to the seasonal rhythms of this tropical region. Theirs was a world in which ceremonies were held to honor the ancestors, in which libations of kava were poured while chanting genealogies that extended back to Tangaroa. Using our phylogenetic approach, Green and I reconstructed these ephemeral, nonmaterial aspects of ancient Hawaiki. We showed that the Ancestral Polynesians possessed a lunar calendar of thirteen months, whose names indexed the rainy season, the time to plant yams, and the spawning of *palolo* worms on the islands' reefs. The people recalibrated this lunar calendar each year (to keep it in sync with the solar year) through careful observation of the rising and setting of the star cluster Pleiades, which they called Mata-liki ("Little Eyes").

In *Hawaiki, Ancestral Polynesia*, Green and I sought to tease out a more inclusive, a more nuanced, a more textured history than could be revealed by the trowel alone. The world of ancient Hawaiki was not just a material one of potsherds and stone adzes, fishbones, and earth ovens. We demonstrated, I believe, the power of a holistic anthropological approach that incorporates linguistics, ethnography, and archaeology. Unfortunately, *Hawaiki, Ancestral Polynesia* has been less widely cited than Green and I had hoped. It seems that in this day of ever-increasing academic subspecialization, the integrative "four-field" approach that once was at the core of American anthropology has become a thing of the past. This is to be greatly regretted.

CHAPTER SIXTEEN

Fiat Lux
(Berkeley, California, 1989–)

On an overcast Seattle afternoon in April 1988, I walked out of the Burke Museum, headed for Padelford Hall, which then housed the administrative offices of the College of Arts and Sciences. The University of Washington (UW) campus was in spring splendor, the rhododendrons blooming. Striding along, I reflected on the events leading up to my pending meeting with Dean Joe Norman. As director of the Burke Museum I had worked hard to transform the sleepy institution—long neglected under Quimby's "don't bother them and they won't bother you" policy—into a center for teaching, research, and public outreach. The Burke was receiving NSF research grants, students used the collections daily, and public membership had grown sevenfold. The *Chinasaurs* exhibit had drawn huge crowds.[1]

Despite these successes, the university had not increased the Burke's tiny operating budget. The more we raised external funds, the more the dean seemed to think that the museum could be self-sufficient. I saw things differently, believing that the university should reward our entrepreneurship by increasing its support, allowing the museum to become a centerpiece for the university. But it seemed that my vision was not shared by those in Padelford Hall.

The previous autumn I had attended the American Anthropological Association's annual meeting in Chicago. These meetings are where department chairs and search committees scope out candidates for academic jobs. Bill Simmons, chair of the Anthropology Department at the University of California, Berkeley, had phoned to ask if I would join a few of his colleagues for drinks in his hotel suite. I knew that Berkeley was searching for a senior Old World archaeologist. When I joined Simmons and a few others for cocktails later that evening, they asked if I would submit my application.

In March, Simmons called again to tell me I was on Berkeley's short list. I visited the campus to give the expected job talk and meet with faculty and students. I was up against an impressive list of competitors, including Rhys Jones from Canberra, John Parkington from Cape Town, and Doug Price from Wisconsin, all important figures in Old World archaeology. My lecture was to be given in the Gifford Room on the second floor of Kroeber Hall, named after

Edward W. Gifford who had discovered the site of Lapita in 1952. Perhaps this was a good omen. My lecture would relate the finds I had made in my Mussau expeditions; backed up with slides of the excavations and artifacts, I hoped my talk would impress (this was still the pre-PowerPoint era, when we illustrated our lectures with projected slides). Simmons introduced me briefly. As I passed him on the way to the podium he whispered hoarsely, "Knock 'em dead, Pat."

The following week the Anthropology Department faculty recommended my appointment as a full professor at Berkeley. I was excited but not quite certain that I was ready to leave Seattle and the Burke. I told Simmons I would give him an answer in a few days. Now it was up to Dean Joe Norman whether or not I left Washington for Berkeley.

Norman's secretary ushered me into the dean's cramped office. I had met here many times with Norman's predecessor, Ernest Henley, a straight shooter whom I respected but who had recently returned to research and teaching in physics. Norman, a professor of chemistry who had recently succeeded Henley, seemed tentative and unsure of himself.

"I'll get right to the point," I began. "Berkeley has made me an offer of a professorship. I'm tempted to take it. But I could be persuaded to stay at UW." Norman said he was willing to match any salary that Berkeley offered.

"It's not about my salary, Joe. It's about the museum's inadequate budget. For three years now we've shown what the museum can do. For decades the university starved the museum. The base budget hasn't been augmented in years." Norman fidgeted in his chair. He reiterated his willingness to match an offer from Berkeley but said he could not increase the Burke's budget.

"I'm sorry to hear that," I replied, standing up and extending my hand for what would be our last handshake. The meeting had lasted no more than a couple of minutes. There was no point in exhausting myself for an institution that was not committed to supporting excellence. In addition, I had become dissatisfied with the way Robert Dunnell dominated the archaeology program at UW; his rigid adherence to one narrow theoretical paradigm was intellectually stifling. I decided then and there to accept the offer from the University of California at Berkeley, one of the world's preeminent centers of teaching and research.

Simmons and I agreed to start my new appointment at Berkeley effective January 1, 1989. I would take the large collection of Lapita pottery and other artifacts from Mussau with me, because their analysis would have to continue at Berkeley. Two of my graduate students, Dana Lepofsky and Marshall Weisler, decided to transfer to Berkeley so I could continue to mentor them.

I never regretted the decision to leave UW and the Burke. Nonetheless, this was a bittersweet time because my wife Debra and I were also drifting apart. She had completed her PhD at the University of Hawai'i but had been unsuccessful in finding an academic appointment. The constant stress from my workload at the museum probably contributed to our situation. Debra liked the Northwest and decided that she did not want to move to California. While we remained friends (as we are to this day) the handwriting was on the wall—my first marriage was headed for divorce.

Founded by the famous Alfred Kroeber in 1901, Berkeley's Anthropology Department was one of the nation's first and most respected.[2] As at Yale where I had been trained, Berkeley emphasized a "four field" approach combining archaeology with social anthropology, physical anthropology, and linguistics. Berkeley's Anthropology Department claimed more faculty as members of the prestigious National Academy of Sciences (NAS) than any other anthropology department in the country. These faculty included George Foster, Elizabeth Colson, F. Clark Howell, Brent Berlin, Gene Hammel, and Desmond Clark. It was intimidating but stimulating company.

At Berkeley I reconnected with George Dales, my former undergraduate advisor at Penn from 1968–1971. Dales had left Penn for Berkeley some years later and was now a senior professor in the Department of Near Eastern Studies. Tragically, only a year or so after I arrived at Berkeley, Dales was struck with prostate cancer. He fought off the disease bravely but succumbed in April 1992. Before he died, Dales gave me his expensive Hasselblad camera with its superb Zeiss lenses. I have used this camera since throughout my fieldwork in the Pacific, often thinking of Dales.

The archaeology group at Berkeley was in the midst of a transition. In 1983, Glynn Issac (whose Old World archaeology position I was taking) had left Berkeley for Harvard, followed by the retirements of J. Desmond Clark in 1986 and John Howland Rowe in 1988, leaving only Ruth Tringham and James Deetz as active archaeology faculty. But two years earlier, Berkeley had appointed Meg Conkey, followed the next year by Kent Lightfoot. With my appointment there would now be five archaeologists. Deetz was a leader in historical archaeology, Tringham worked in Eastern Europe on Neolithic age settlements, Conkey specialized in Ice Age archaeology in France and Spain, and Lightfoot was developing a new program in California historical archaeology. Deetz was content to focus on his research, but the "gang of four," as the rest of us sometimes called ourselves, got along well both academically and socially. Sometimes doing academic business while soaking in Tringham's hot tub at her San Francisco house (the rumors about the California lifestyle were true), we revamped the curriculum and the graduate program in archaeology.

Although they had officially retired, Desmond Clark and John Rowe were actively engaged in research, coming to their offices at the Archaeological Research Facility every day. Rowe sat in on my first seminar on ceramic analysis (probably wanting to check out the competence of Berkeley's newest faculty member). Rowe had made his career with painstaking analysis of South American pottery and did not trust radiocarbon dating, whose results did not completely conform to his ceramic chronology. Desmond Clark was world renowned for his many excavations in Africa. Clark and his wife Betty often held cocktail parties at their home in the Berkeley hills. With their Old World British manners, they were gracious and charming hosts. Betty Clark drank bourbon on the rocks out of a large silver chalice. When I once asked her what brand of bourbon she preferred, Betty answered, poker-faced, "The cheaper the better."

Also at Berkeley—relatively newly arrived from Cambridge University—was the respected coral reef geomorphologist David R. Stoddart. With our mutual interest in tropical island ecosystems, we soon found an occasion to meet for lunch at Berkeley's Faculty Club. When I arrived after giving my morning lecture, I found Stoddart at the bar, already into his second gin-and-tonic. Stoddart insisted we consume two carafes of wine during our long lunch. In spite of his predilection for drink, Stoddart was incredibly prolific, with often brilliant insights into island systems.[3]

When I arrived at Berkeley, my new lab was just an empty room in the basement of the Archaeological Research Facility. During the several months that it took to establish the new lab, I decided to return to my 1974 ethnoarchaeological notes from Futuna. I had never published my Yale dissertation, and much of my data on Futunan agriculture remained untapped. Looking over my field notes—in the light of additional experience I had gained from work in Tonga and Tikopia—I decided to write a book about how agricultural systems engage with the political economy to drive sociopolitical evolution. I enthusiastically started writing *The Wet and the Dry: Irrigation and Agricultural Intensification in Polynesia.* Drawing primarily on my Futunan material, but also bringing in comparative case studies from other islands, I argued that the most aggressive, warlike political structures in Polynesia arose not in regions where irrigation dominated but in the dryland zones. The book was published by the University of Chicago Press in 1994. I am pleased that it has had considerable influence on the thinking of other researchers regarding the respective roles of irrigation versus intensive dryland farming.

Much of my energy that first spring went into setting up my new laboratory in the two-story, red brick Archaeological Research Facility, a former fraternity house. I transformed the basement rooms into labs where we could do serious geoarchaeology—thin-sectioning basalt adzes and potsherds to determine their petrography and hence places of origin—as well as conventional artifact analysis. One room became the Oceanic Archaeology Laboratory (OAL), where I have now worked together with several generations of my students for more than a quarter-century.

Late one April morning, as we were unpacking and organizing the Lapita collections in the OAL, the phone outside my lab rang. "It's for you, Professor Kirch," said the student who answered, handing me the handset.

"Pat Kirch? This is Frank Hole of Yale. I'm calling from Washington, DC." I knew Hole from my graduate student days when I had taken his seminar on the ancient Near East. I had not a clue why he was calling me now. "As chair of the Anthropology section of the National Academy of Sciences I'm pleased to tell you that earlier this morning you were elected a member of the Academy. Congratulations."

I was speechless. There is virtually no higher honor in American science than to be elected to the National Academy of Sciences (NAS). Because only seventy-two scientists can be elected in any given year (in all fields of science), many deserving researchers never receive this honor; some are in their seventies or even eighties before they are elected. Still shy of my thirty-ninth birthday, I was the newest member of the Berkeley faculty to join that distinguished club and the youngest anthropologist ever to be elected to the NAS.

At the next faculty meeting Simmons produced several bottles of champagne and proposed a toast. He was proud that his efforts to recruit me to Berkeley had paid off even more handsomely than he had anticipated. Although I would soon be elected to the American Academy of Arts and Sciences, and a few years later to the even more elite American Philosophical Society (founded by Benjamin Franklin), it is my election to the NAS that I regard as one of the proudest moments of my career. I only regret that Yoshio Kondo did not live to see his apprentice receive this high honor.

When I flew to Washington DC, the following spring, in April 1990, to be inducted into the National Academy of Sciences in its impressive neoclassical building on the National Mall, I was accompanied by a new girlfriend. Thérèse Babineau worked for Berkeley's Hearst Museum of Anthropology. Following a summer flirtation at the department's mailboxes I got up my courage to ask her out to the San Francisco Opera. I was more taken by the lovely woman at my side than by Dame Kiri Te Kawana's sterling performance in *Capriccio*. We became inseparable and would marry a few years later.

For twenty-five years, Berkeley has been my academic home. During this time I have served as director of the Archaeological Research Facility, chair of the Anthropology Department, director of the Hearst Museum of Anthropology, and chair of the Academic Senate's Budget Committee and of its Committee on Privilege and Tenure. These administrative stints allowed me to interact with deans, vice chancellors, associate vice chancellors, and three Berkeley chancellors, giving me insights into the workings of this remarkable institution. Though lacking the huge endowments of Harvard, Princeton, or Stanford, Berkeley competes directly with those and other top universities. In a recent *London Times* survey, Berkeley was ranked as the fifth most prestigious university in the world by academic reputation. Without the same deep pockets of its peers, how has Berkeley managed to maintain its status? The most important factor, in my view, has been Berkeley's insistence on hiring and retaining the very best scientists and scholars. I have been approached twice by private universities (the University of Pennsylvania in 1995 and Yale in 2007) with offers to join their faculties. Each time Berkeley made the effort to retain me, awarding me an endowed chair (the Class of 1954 Professorship) in 1995 and agreeing to a joint appointment with the Department of Integrative Biology in 2007 (important because my research interests had diversified from anthropology to include ecology and evolution).

A key factor in Berkeley's success is the faculty's insistence on shared governance. Appointments, tenure decisions, and promotions are not the exclusive purview of department chairs and deans, as is the case in many universities. Berkeley's Academic Senate plays a strong role in these personnel matters, providing a critical check and balance. Drawn mostly from the university's own ranks, Berkeley's deans and vice chancellors have served time "in the trenches"; they understand the faculty's concerns and needs. In my time, deans such as Gerry Mendelsohn and George Breslauer (who later became executive vice chancellor and provost, respectively) have been a pleasure to work with.

For four years, I served as director of Berkeley's Phoebe A. Hearst Museum of Anthropology. The Hearst Museum's collections are vast, containing more than two million objects, and include superb holdings from ancient Egypt, Peru, and the classical world, as well as specimens acquired through the research expeditions of Berkeley faculty, including those of Edward Gifford to Fiji, New Caledonia, and Yap. Unfortunately, like too many university museums the Hearst has been chronically underfunded. I did persuade the Hearst Foundation to give one million dollars toward conservation of the core collections, but my plans for an expanded exhibition gallery never came to fruition.

Most of my energies though, have been focused on my teaching and research. I greatly enjoyed having Berkeley undergraduates work in the Oceanic Archaeology Laboratory, gaining practical research experience. Many of the graduate students I mentored have gone on to academic careers in Pacific archaeology:

Marshall Weisler at the University of Queensland, Dana Lepofsky at Simon Fraser University, Pia Anderson at the American University of Sharjah (United Arab Emirates), Peter Mills and Kathy Kawelu at the University of Hawai'i in Hilo, Jennifer Kahn at William and Mary University, Scarlett Chiu at Academia Sinica in Taiwan, Mark McCoy at Southern Methodist University, and James Flexner at the University of Sydney. Others, including Julie (Endicott) Taomia, Sidsel Millerstrom, and Lisa Holm, have pursued careers in archaeology outside of traditional academic institutions.

On several occasions I thought that circumstances might take me back to Hawai'i. One was in 2000 when Donald Duckworth resigned as CEO (the old title of director having been abandoned) of the Bishop Museum. I was interviewed by the "head hunters" hired by the museum's trustees, but I withdrew when I was told that they had voted to move the museum out of its historic campus in Kalihi to Kaka'ako. I wanted no part of such a foolish move. (The trustees later reversed that decision.) In 2009 and again in 2014 I had discussions with administrators at the University of Hawai'i about a faculty appointment at Mānoa, but financial crises quashed those possibilities. I remained at Berkeley, racking up frequent flyer miles as I traveled regularly back and forth to Hawai'i and the farther-flung islands of the South Pacific. My home may be California, but my heart resides in the islands.

CHAPTER SEVENTEEN

The Gathering Place of Men (Mangaia, Cook Islands, 1989–1991)

Settling into my new academic home at Berkeley in early 1989, I decided to shift the course of my research. Up until then, I had focused on the islands of the western Pacific—Futuna, Niuatoputapu, and Manu'a in Western Polynesia, the Polynesian Outliers of Anuta and Tikopia, and Mussau in the Bismarck Archipelago. In these islands I had sought the deep roots of the Polynesians in the Lapita cultural complex as well as the later rise of Ancestral Polynesian culture in the Hawaiki homeland. But now there were new intellectual problems I wanted to tackle.

Anthropologists divide the vast Polynesian triangle into two distinct regions, Western and Eastern Polynesia. Western Polynesia—consisting of Tonga, Samoa, Futuna, 'Uvea, Tokelau, and Niue—is the original Polynesian homeland. It was in Western Polynesia that the Proto Polynesian language and Ancestral Polynesian culture developed out of its Lapita ancestor (see Chapter Fifteen).

For almost two thousand years, the Ancestral Polynesians stayed within this Western Polynesian homeland. But late in the first millennium AD, colonizing groups of Polynesians expanded across the central eastern Pacific. What inspired this unprecedented migration is not entirely clear, although the development of sophisticated double-hulled, deep-water voyaging canoes was certainly instrumental. Between about AD 900 to 1100, groups of Polynesians discovered and settled the Cook, Society, Tuamotu, Marquesas, and Gambier Islands (Mangareva). Then they radiated out to find and colonize the even more far-flung islands of Rapa Nui, Hawai'i, and New Zealand, reaching the last of these by AD 1250. The archipelagoes and islands that were settled during this incredible diaspora make up Eastern Polynesia.

The distinction between Western and Eastern Polynesia goes beyond simple geography.[1] Although sharing many patterns in common, the Western and Eastern branches of Polynesian societies each exhibited distinctive traits. For example, to the original creator god of Tangaroa (known in Western Polynesia) the early Eastern Polynesians added three primary gods: Tū, Tāne, and Rongo. Ceremonial places also varied—in Western Polynesia *malae* were open plazas where kava ceremonies were performed, whereas in Eastern Polynesia *marae* were usually enclosed courts with altars and uprights (or images) at one end. Eastern Polynesian cultures also uniquely shared certain material culture traits, such as the ways that they manufactured barkcloth or made their fishhooks.

However, the cultural and social diversity that arose in Eastern Polynesia—following the diaspora between AD 900–1250—offers anthropologists a remarkable opportunity to study how human societies change and evolve. The great biologist Ernst Mayr once pointed out that, to study evolution—whether biological or cultural—we should seek out "experiments of history." The diversification of dozens of Eastern Polynesian societies over about eight hundred years, in a variety of island ecosystems, provides an unparalleled opportunity for such controlled comparison.

One of the new research questions that I wanted to pursue was this: How had the arrival of Polynesians on islands that previously lacked humans (or large terrestrial vertebrates other than birds) affected these pristine ecosystems? My work on Futuna, Tikopia, and Niuatoputapu had given me insights about how humans transformed island landscapes. Pacific biogeographers such as Raymond Fosberg argued that remote islands were inherently vulnerable when their isolation was shattered.[2] What kinds of changes did the arrival of Polynesians initiate? On the flip side of the coin, how had the varied island environments of Eastern Polynesia influenced the evolving Polynesian cultures? Some islands had extensive reefs and lagoons; others lacked these resources. Some offered valleys suitable for irrigation, whereas others only had older, nutrient-poor soils. I would have to investigate both problems simultaneously, because on islands nature and culture are inseparably intertwined. In scientific parlance, humans and their environments were "dynamically coupled."

To carry out such a research program, I would have to enlist the collaboration of scientists in other fields. By the 1980s, archaeology was becoming a multidisciplinary endeavor, with specialists in zooarchaeology, archaeobotany, and geoarchaeology who focused on animal bones, plant remains, and stone artifacts, respectively. My earlier work in the western Pacific had mostly been done single-handedly or with one or two student assistants. In the future, I would need to put together multidisciplinary teams to investigate collaboratively the dynamically coupled human and natural systems on the islands of Eastern Polynesia (Map 7).

Some days you just get lucky. One such memorable day was July 20, 1989. I was riding in the back of a rusting Toyota pickup truck driven by Ma'ara Ngu, our guide on Mangaia, southernmost of the Cook Islands. Following a little-used dirt track in Veitatei District, we passed through second growth and abandoned banana gardens toward the inner escarpment of the *makatea,* a ring of upraised reef

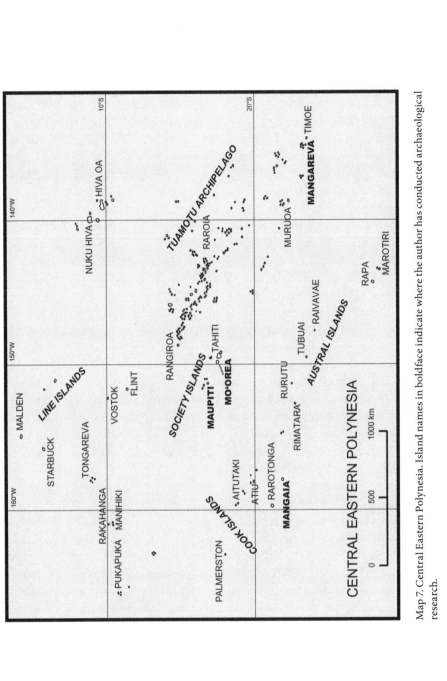

Map 7. Central Eastern Polynesia. Island names in boldface indicate where the author has conducted archaeological research.

limestone that encircles the island. Ngu told us that this was the only route to Lake Tiriara, whose sediments we wanted to sample in order to extract pollen and reconstruct the island's history of vegetation change.

I dodged low-hanging *Hibiscus* branches as Ngu negotiated the rutted track. Nearby, the *makatea* escarpment rose twenty-five meters above us, its whitish-gray facade pockmarked with solution caves where the limestone had dissolved away during earlier stages of tectonic uplift. The dark shadow of a large overhang in the cliff face caught my eye. I banged on the roof of the cab. "Maʻara! Dave! Can you stop for a minute? I want to check out something," I yelled to Ngu and David Steadman, sitting in the cab. Steadman, the world's expert on the biogeography of eastern Pacific birds, was my collaborator on this new project.

Jumping out of the truck, I grabbed a machete and slashed a rough path through the second growth toward the dark shadow in the looming cliff. Soon I was at the base of the huge overhang, towering overhead. The sheltered space had a dry dirt floor about a meter higher than the surrounding terrain. Rockshelters such as this one, where the overhanging cliff offers protection from the rain, were preferred living sites for ancient people. The elevated floor of the shelter suggested that the underlying sediments had most likely accumulated over centuries of use. I paced the shelter's floor, calculating that it had a usable area of about 225 square meters, enough to house an extended family or two.

I asked Ngu what the name of the place was. "Tangata-tau," he said. "It means the place where men gathered. In my father's day the people used to bring the oranges here when they were collecting them for export to Rarotonga. But it hasn't been used for a long time." I told Ngu that it was likely that Tangata-tau had been used well before his father's time, even before the missionaries had arrived on Mangaia. I had a gut feeling that I had just discovered one of those sites that archaeologists never forget all their lives.

The Mangaia Project had resulted from my meeting David Steadman at the Burke Museum several years earlier. Steadman was doing a postdoc at the Smithsonian Institution, learning the fine points of avian skeletal anatomy and bird taxonomy; his passion was the birds of the South Pacific. Together with the Burke's curator of ornithology, Sievert Rohwer, Steadman organized an expedition to the Cook Islands in 1987. After returning, Steadman proposed that we collaborate on Mangaia. He had found many bones of extinct birds in the island's limestone caves. Had the loss of Mangaia's bird fauna been a consequence of Polynesian occupation? It seemed likely, but more data were required.

Reading up on Mangaia's geography and ethnography, I became fascinated.[3] With a land area of about fifty-two square kilometers, Mangaia is a relatively small island, though much bigger than Tikopia or Niuatopuapu. A ring of upraised limestone reefs, the *makatea*, surrounds a twenty-million-year-old deeply weathered volcanic cone in the island's center. Deep lateritic soil mantles the volcanic cone, covered in fire-resistant *Dicranopteris* fern and scrub *Pandanus*. Six small valleys furrow the old volcanic cone, their streams ponding against the *makatea* where the fresh waters had eroded caverns through the permeable limestone.

At the base of each valley there are small lakes or swamps. The Mangaians in precontact times had converted this swampy ground to irrigated taro fields, the primary source of their staple taro (Fig. 17.1). In *Mangaian Society*, Te Rangi Hiroa reported that, before the arrival of the London Missionary Society in the 1820s, the Mangaians had fought a succession of wars for control of these irrigated fields. Hiroa's portrayal of traditional Mangaian society was disturbing. Warriors terrorized the common people; cannibalism and human sacrifice were said to have been commonplace. Hiroa's account reads like a description of institutionalized thuggery. On Mangaia, it appeared that severe environmental constraints had channeled social evolution in a direction favoring overt force.

I realized that the taro swamps and small lakes would be ideal sediment traps, catching soil eroded off of the volcanic slopes, and thus a perfect environment for taking deep sediment cores. The successive layers of silt, clay, and peat could be

Figure 17.1. View of the Tamarua Valley, Mangaia. The valley floor is covered in artificial taro pondfields, the main source of food for the ancient Mangaian population. Note the fern-covered hillsides inland of the taro fields.

dated by radiocarbon. From samples of sediment, a palynologist (specialist in pollen grains) could extract microscopic pollen encapsulated within the layers and then identify and quantify the different species of plants represented. This would allow the reconstruction of a history of gradual—or sometimes abrupt—changes in the vegetation surrounding the swamp. A pollen history from Mangaia's swamps would tell us whether the fernlands covering the central volcanic cone were natural or whether they had come about through human land use.

Steadman and I invited John Flenley of the University of Hull, England, to be our project palynologist. I wrote a successful proposal to the National Geographic Society's Committee on Research and Exploration, requesting funds for an expedition to Mangaia in the summer of 1989. Our plan was to combine archaeology with avian paleontology and palynology to unravel the island's history of Polynesian occupation and land use.

Dave and Jenny Steadman, Melina Allen (a University of Washington grad student), and I flew to Mangaia from Rarotonga on the once-a-week plane on July 18, 1989. We settled into the government's Guest House, an old wooden building situated on the *makatea* bluff overlooking Oneroa Village. Nga Teaio, a gregarious middle-aged woman, kept the place spick-and-span, while serving up breakfast and dinner. Teaio's dinners usually consisted of boiled taro and a pot of stewed mutton neck rings imported from New Zealand.

We needed a truck to transport our team and equipment over the few rough, dirt roads that traverse the island. Fortunately, Ma'ara Ngu was willing to work with us as well as drive us around in his venerable pickup. Ngu, a towering, broad-shouldered man who had played rugby until a knee injury took him out of the game, had worked in New Zealand as a welder but had moved back to Mangaia to raise his kids. Skilled with his hands, Ngu could solve any practical problem that arose during fieldwork. Ngu and his Maori wife, Diane, became close friends as well as valued helpers in our work.

As is usual in Polynesia, we rose early. Teaio had coffee, biscuits, butter, and jam on the table before the sun rose. By 7 a.m. Ngu would drive up with his truck, accompanied by Sonny and Maru whom we had hired to help us excavate. We would spend the day at the rockshelter, returning in the late afternoon to shower, sip a pre-dinner whisky, and partake of another of Teaio's filling if rather boring meals.

Flenley and his students flew in the following week to begin the lake coring work. I had met Flenley at the International Congress on Easter Island in 1984, but I had never worked with him in the field. I was a bit alarmed when the two young British undergrads stepped off the plane, one of whom, Frances, was holding her teddy bear. "Teddy-baarrr," Frances told me, "goes with me *everywhere*." Yikes, I thought to myself, I hope you are not going to be holding onto that stuffed bear on the raft while you are trying to pull up a sediment core.

The next morning Steadman, Allen, and I were up early as usual, having our coffee and breakfast. Flenley's students appeared, but there was no sign of their professor. By now Ngu and the others had arrived, with everyone talking loudly in the Guest House's living room. There was no way Flenley could not have heard us, because his bedroom was separated from the living room by only a thin curtain. Steadman was getting agitated about this delay in heading out to the field. Just then an arm pushed the curtain aside and Flenley appeared, wearing a silk dressing gown and stocking cap, like an apparition out of Edwardian England. "I say," he calmly remarked, "is breakfast ready?" I thought Steadman was going to go ballistic, but it was all I could do to keep from laughing out loud.

While Flenley and his students cored Lake Tiriara, Steadman and I dug in the spacious rockshelter (Fig. 17.2), starting with a one-meter test pit in the shelter floor. You are always "digging blind" in the first test pit, not knowing what you will encounter or how deep the deposits will be. After peeling off the upper layer with historic period glass and iron, I started digging into some ashy lenses full of charcoal and thousands of well-smashed fragments of marine shell. Each thin lens probably represented a cooking and feasting event.

I was now down sixty to seventy centimeters into a grayish deposit with less shellfish and more bone. Several fishhook fragments made from *Turbo* shell turned up, along with adz flakes and coral files. At the sifting screens, Steadman was picking through the tiny scraps caught in the 1/16-inch mesh. "OK! Wow, look at this," he called out, holding up a small, well-preserved bone between his thumb and forefinger. I got out of the test pit to have a look. "What is it, Dave?" I asked, knowing that it did not look like fish and certainly was not dog or pig. "The tibiotarsus of an extinct fruit dove, in the genus *Ptilinopus*," Steadman confidently replied. I had no reason to doubt him; he had paid his dues studying thousands of comparative skeletons in the Smithsonian's storerooms.

More bird bones appeared as I dug deeper through the ashy sediment. After several more hours the blade of my trowel exposed the top of a reddish-orange layer—decomposed limestone that formed the shelter's original, natural floor. My trowel flicked up several bones, which I handed to Steadman. There were bones of seabirds, frigates, and shearwaters, as well as those of land birds, including a flightless rail and more fruit dove bones. The pre-occupation stratum proved to be chock full of bird bones, along with some bones of the Polynesian-introduced Pacific rat, *Rattus exulans*. The presence of the rat bones showed that people were

Figure 17.2. The Tangata-tau rockshelter on Mangaia Island during excavation. This spacious shelter contained occupation deposits spanning the entire course of Mangaian history.

already on the island at the time that the bird bones were deposited. Over the next several weeks we expanded the initial test pit into a five-meter trench. In all, we would recover more than 200 bird bones, along with about 10,000 other bones of fish and fruit bats, as well as those of Polynesian-introduced dogs and pigs.

Meanwhile, Flenley and his students were having success at the lake. Working from a raft constructed of four truck tire inner tubes and a couple of sheets of plywood, they had taken a fifteen-meter-long sediment core from Lake Tiriara. This was deeper than we had dared to hope for, suggesting that it might span a considerable time period. Each one-meter segment was carefully protected in rigid plastic sleeves, labeled as to depth and orientation, ready to be air freighted to Flenley's laboratory at Hull.

A few months later, when we had received our radiocarbon dates and Flenley had analyzed the pollen samples from the TIR-1 core, Steadman and I sat down to review the results of our first expedition to Mangaia.[4] The trench in the Tangata-tau rockshelter had produced one of the best faunal sequences then known from any island in Eastern Polynesia. The deepest layers (dating to around AD 1000–1200) had yielded lots of bird bones, not only from nesting seabirds but also from many kinds of land birds, some of which were now extinct on the island. The upper layers had very little bird bone, showing that something had happened to greatly reduce the biodiversity of birds on the island during the period that the Polynesians had occupied it.[5]

The sediment core from Lake Tiriara and Flenley's analysis of pollen grains contained within the layers of lake mud offered a likely explanation for this loss of biodiversity. The core went back 5,800 years, well before any humans lived on the island. The older sediments contained pollen of indigenous and endemic trees, such as *Ficus* and *Weinmannia,* leaving no doubt that the volcanic cone was once covered in a pristine forest. Then, around 1,500 years ago according to the radiocarbon dates, something happened.[6] The forest trees disappeared, to be replaced rapidly by a fire-adapted association of ferns and scrub *Pandanus.* The timing of this change strongly implicated the arrival of colonizing Polynesians. With much of the island's original forest gone, the native bird populations no longer had the habitats needed to support their populations.

Steadman and I knew that the Mangaia story was too rich to leave at this; another field season was called for. Using our initial results as the "hook," we drafted a successful proposal to the National Science Foundation for more fieldwork in 1991.

Before we returned to the island, however, the Tangata-tau rockshelter produced yet one more startling find. Jon Hather, a young British archaeobotanist, was working as a postdoc at the Australian National University in Canberra, fine-tuning methods for identifying different root crops from carbonized tubers (what is technically called *parenchyma*) found in archaeological contexts. Hather asked if he could visit my lab to examine carbonized plant remains from sites I had excavated. When he arrived at Berkeley, I brought out some bags of charcoal from Tangata-tau. He immediately recognized some of the charcoal as charred parenchyma and asked if he could take the specimens back to the Institute of Archaeology in London. There, he would be able to examine the anatomical structure of the parenchyma under a scanning electron microscope, allowing him to discriminate taro from yam, giant swamp taro, or sweet potato.

Shortly after returning to London, Hather informed me that these specimens—from the bottom layers of the Tangata-tau rockshelter—were of sweet potato. I was stunned. Unquestionably of South American origin, sweet potatoes were cultivated in the islands of Eastern Polynesia at the time of Captain Cook's voyages. However, some scholars had suggested that the plant had been introduced by Spanish explorers such as Mendaña. Others, especially Doug Yen, argued that Polynesians had crossed the Pacific to South America, bringing the crop back with them.

The scraps of carbonized sweet potato parenchyma from the Tangata-tau rockshelter were a "smoking gun" in support of Yen's hypothesis. There was no way that these sweet potato tubers, dated to ca. AD 1100–1300, had come via the Spanish, who did not enter Pacific waters until the late sixteenth century. I realized that we had the first undeniable evidence of Polynesian contact with South America in pre-Columbian times.[7]

In late May 1991, everything was ready for our return to Mangaia. The swamp coring and pollen work would be continued by Joanna Ellison, a Berkeley graduate student in geography. My two new graduate students, Pia Anderson and Julie Endicott, would help in the survey and excavations, gaining field experience. To analyze the fishbones from Tangata-tau, I invited zooarchaeologist Virginia Butler to join us. Jon Hather would also be part of the team, making botanical collections so that he could identify the carbonized plant remains from the excavations. Finally, my girlfriend Thérèse Babineau, a photographer, planned to join us to photograph the island and our excavations.

On the way to Rarotonga, I stopped off in Honolulu to attend the Seventeenth Pacific Science Congress, where Terry Hunt and I chaired a day-long symposium on "Environmental and Landscape Change in Prehistoric Oceania." We wanted to bring together archaeologists and natural scientists with interests in human impacts on island ecosystems. A few years later the collected essays were published under the title *Historical Ecology in the Pacific Islands*.[8]

On June 7, seven hundred kilos of baggage and gear were loaded onto our chartered Air Rarotonga aircraft for the forty-minute flight to Mangaia. Ma‘ara and Diana Ngu greeted us, the old pickup looking even more battered but still running. After a few days at the Guest House, we moved into an empty house up on the *makatea,* relieving us of the daunting prospect of eating Teaio's boiled taro and mutton rings for two full months.

Ellison began by re-coring Lake Tiriara to check the results that Flenley had obtained in 1989. Then, she moved systematically around the island, coring every swamp and pond. By cross-checking the stratigraphic sequences in each valley, Ellison confirmed that the Veitatei sequence was not unique; the same changes had occurred across the entire island. After returning to Berkeley, Ellison would date selected core samples and extract pollen from two of the longest cores, elaborating the record of vegetation change that Flenley had first outlined.[9]

Ellison's work confirmed that, prior to Polynesian settlement, a pristine rain forest had cloaked Mangaia's central volcanic hill. Soon after Polynesian arrival, the interior slopes were cleared and burned, as people practiced shifting cultivation. But the old age of the underlying rocks—and their severe lack of nutrients—prevented the native forest from recovering. Instead, the hillsides became covered in a fire-resistant mix of fern and scrub *Pandanus.* After this, agriculture would have to be limited to the valley bottoms and swampy areas, where the soils were richer and could support continuous cropping.

While Ellison was busy with the coring, the main team went to work in the Tangata-tau rockshelter. Beginning from the cleaned-up sidewalls of our 1989 trench, we peeled back the complex succession of layers and fine lenses. Rockshelters such as this—where people lived in a relatively confined space over many centuries—tend to have complex stratigraphic sequences; Tangata-tau was no exception. I used a Harris Matrix to keep track of the complex vertical and horizontal relationships between the nineteen discrete stratigraphic zones and more than fifty individual "features" such as pits, earth ovens, and hearths.[10]

Opening a large block of squares against the shelter's rear wall, we came upon early deposits representing a period when the site had been used as a primary habitation. One or more families had cooked their daily meals in the earth ovens we uncovered; the scraps of their meals were incorporated into the sooty dirt of the floor. Some of the occupants had been expert stone tool craftsmen, leaving hundreds of basalt flakes as they knapped adzes. We found a dozen or so finished adzes, beautifully polished, and a score or more adz roughouts ready for grinding. Other craftsmen worked at carving out fishhooks from pearl shell, using files of branch coral. People had also been tattooed within the shelter: We found eight tattooing combs of varying sizes.

Steadman and Butler were delighted with the faunal remains they were recovering in the fine-mesh sifting screens. More than seven hundred bird bones represented seventeen species of native land birds and twelve species of seabirds. Most of the bird bones came from the deeper, older layers. The fishbones were even more abundant, totaling nearly 32,000 specimens. Mostly these specimens represented smaller reef fish, but there were also bones of freshwater eels that had been captured in the nearby lake.

When the missionaries arrived in the 1820s, there were no pigs on Mangaia, but the people said they had once possessed them. The archaeological record bore out this claim. We found more than two hundred pig bones, concentrated in the lower and middle layers. Apparently, the first Polynesians to settle the island brought pigs (as well as dogs) with them, raising them for some centuries. But prior to European contact they had exterminated the pigs, probably because it was too "costly" to feed them. On a small island, pigs have to be kept penned or they will devastate the gardens. And when food supplies are tight, feeding taro or sweet potatoes to pigs becomes a luxury that hungry stomachs may not tolerate.

The faunal sequence from Tangata-tau revealed a history of gradually intensifying pressure on food resources, what archaeologists call "resource depression." First, there was the decimation and in some cases extinction of the many species of land birds and seabirds that had originally populated the island, reducing one potential food source. Second, the sizes of fish being caught became smaller over time; the early layers had larger fish, whereas the upper layers yielded fishbones with much smaller jaws. These changes were also evident in the shellfish. The sizes of *Turbo* shells, for example, an important food item, steadily decreased over time, reflecting harvesting pressure. In all, the story is one of an island ecosystem under serious pressure from its human population. All this evidence brought to mind Te Rangi Hiroa's account of contact-era Mangaian society, with its constant wars and competition over limited areas of irrigated taro.

My previous fieldwork had been on isolated islands such as Anuta and Tikopia, where ancient lifestyles were still preserved, or in Futuna and Niuatoputapu where, in spite of Western contact, traditional social and political structures remained largely intact and people farmed and fished more or less in the old ways. On Mangaia, in contrast, I was witness to the profound effects of a century and a half of missionization and acculturation. There were no thatched *fale,* the Mangaians having adopted wooden or concrete houses with tin roofs. Everyone dressed in Western clothes; there were even such modern institutions as a post office. The island's three villages (Oneroa, Tamarua, and Ivirua), which each centered around its large Congregational church, were themselves nineteenth-century developments; originally people had lived in dispersed hamlets near the taro fields. Some families still cultivated a few of the irrigated taro fields, but mostly they lay abandoned. Our Mangaian friends consumed more rice and tinned foods than they did homegrown produce or fish.

The London Missionary Society, under the direction of Rev. John Williams, had first attempted to land Christian missionaries from Tahiti on the island in 1823, but Mangaian warriors had forced them back to the ship. The following year two Tahitian converts, Davida and Tiere, gained a foothold. By 1825, Davida had converted part of the population, including the high priest Numangatini. In February 1828, a vicious battle ensued between Christian and pagan factions, with the Christians emerging victorious. As Hiroa wrote in an unpublished history of the advent of Christianity on Mangaia:

> In the substitution of Jehovah for Rongo, a clash occurred between different cultures. The Mangaian social system was so interwoven with the religious system that it was impossible to root out the Mangaian gods without destroying other institutions that had been evolved for the guidance and government of society. In order to substitute, the new religion had to destroy its opponent.[11]

Davida became Mangaia's new high priest and his church the most influential social and political institution.

We attended Sunday services at the imposing Oneroa church with its massive stone and coral-lime mortar walls, constructed in 1891. The service and its rituals continue the Congregationalist traditions of the London Missionary Society. Men, dressed in long pants and black coats over starched white shirts, sit on the right side of the aisle, while women, decked out in flowing white dresses and large-brimmed hats, sit on the left with the younger children. The hymns, sung a cappella style in the Mangaian language, reverberate throughout the massive sanctuary.

Davida and his successors worked tirelessly to stamp out cultural practices that they associated with the heathen religion. Traditional dancing, singing, and tattooing were banned, as was kava drinking. Today, instead of the communal socializing of men around a kava bowl as I had so pleasantly experienced in Futuna and Niuatoputapu, male friends periodically go on drinking binges. They call this practice "going to the bucket." A man brews up enough bush beer—a concoction of sugar, water, and the juice of locally grown oranges or other fruit—to fill a fifty-five-gallon drum. When the mash has fermented, he calls his friends together who then literally sit around a bucket of the sweet liquor, inebriated for the several days it takes to consume the drum's contents.

Walking along Oneroa's back roads, Steadman and I were once called to join such a group. The three drunken middle-aged men loudly insisted that we join them around the plastic bucket in the side yard of the host's house. Dipping the single, sticky glass into the bucket, our host filled it to the brim and urged me to drink it down in one gulp. After several rounds the low alcohol content had only a mild effect on my mental faculties, but the not entirely fermented sugary liquid was making me belch queasily. After an hour or so Steadman and I feigned drunkenness, pleading that we had to go sleep off the effects. Our hosts reluctantly let us leave; they were still at it the next afternoon.

Yet not all of the old manners had entirely disappeared. We gradually discovered that deep-seated animosities between ancient tribal groups on the island—tracing back to the pre-Christian times of endemic warfare over the limited taro lands—still lurked in the shadows. When I suggested to some Oneroa Village friends that we might spend some time in Tamarua Village to work on sites there, they looked at me aghast. "You can't stay in Tamarua," they protested. "Those people are nasty, they smell, and they will steal from you." On a later occasion, one of the Tamarua folks said to me, "Why are you living in Oneroa? The people there are nasty, they smell, and they are stealing from you." And both the Oneroa and Tamarua groups claimed that the Ivirua villagers were even worse! Rugby games between teams of young men from the three villages are a real blood sport, playing out the old tensions inherited from their ancestors.

Although the history of what happened in Mangaia was most fully evidenced at Tangata-tau, we obtained additional evidence from several other sites. One was a large rockshelter in Keia District, called Ana Manuka. Unlike Tangata-tau, this was a specialized site, containing exclusively the remains of earth ovens and human bones. The bones were charred, evidence of having been cooked in the ovens. Later excavations in this shelter by Steadman showed that dozens of humans, including women and children, had been "processed" there.[12] I have little doubt that Ana Manuka once witnessed the gruesome practice of cannibalism.

Another site dating to the period when war and social terror were rampant on Mangaia was a large cavern in Tamarua District, called Tau Tua. Our guides told us that it had served as a refuge during times of war, with people retreating into this nearly impregnable cavern. The entrance sits seven meters up a sheer limestone face, inside a much larger cave that opens onto the Tamarua taro swamp. Our guide scaled the slippery face barefoot, his toes gripping fissures in the rock. Arriving at the entrance he then let down ropes so we could haul ourselves and our equipment up into the cavern. Exploring the branching chambers, which flowing water had once eroded out of the limestone, we found a miniature village, including house platforms, a small *marae* or temple, and cooking areas with earth ovens (Fig. 17.3). Radiocarbon dates on the oven charcoal showed that the refuge cave had been used in the century prior to European contact.

Our 1991 expedition to Mangaia, with its interdisciplinary team of specialists, produced a huge amount of data on Mangaian precontact history, land use, and ecological change. It would take many years in various laboratories for all of the results to be analyzed; indeed, I still have not fully published all the data from Tangata-tau. But the outline of what transpired on Mangaia over about eight

Figure 17.3. Mapping the interior of the Tau Tua limestone cavern in 1991. This difficult-to-access cave was used as a refuge during intertribal wars on Mangaia.

centuries is clear.[13] What made Mangaian history different from that of Tikopia or some other small Polynesian islands was that the island of Mangaia was inherently vulnerable to human disturbance. About twenty million years old, Mangaia's deep lateritic earth had all its rock-derived nutrients leached out. Once the first inhabitants cleared and burned the forest through shifting cultivation, allowing the thin soil to be eroded away, the forest could not rejuvenate.

Within a few centuries at most, Mangaia's population was no longer able to plant gardens on the hillslopes. They had to confine their agriculture to the narrow valley bottoms, totaling a mere 2 percent of the island's land area. Fights broke out between families over control of these precious taro lands. Meanwhile, the once abundant land and seabirds had been decimated, partly through hunting and partly through large-scale reductions in their nesting habitats. The narrow fringing reef came under constant pressure, with smaller and smaller fish and shellfish available for the taking.

By late prehistory, this combination of factors resulted in a "socio-ecosystem" in which there was relentless pressure on resources and competition for limited arable land; as a result, people often went hungry. The old Polynesian system of social organization based on hereditary rank had broken down, giving way to one in which charismatic leaders and their gangs of warriors seized control. The oral traditions recorded by Te Rangi Hiroa recount no less than forty-two wars fought for control of the taro lands and hegemony over the island. To the victorious went the irrigated lands, while the defeated tribes were banished to the *makatea* to eke out a living growing sweet potatoes in small pockets of dirt between the limestone pinnacles. The weak and unsuspecting were likely to be seized as sacrifices to Rongo, the Janus-faced god of war and taro—or worse, consumed at cannibal feasts as in the Ana Mauka rockshelter.

The deep history of Mangaia is disturbing. It speaks to the darker side of human nature, when circumstances beyond their control forced people to behave in ways that they would otherwise find abhorrent. Yet what happened on Mangaia in the late period is not unique within Polynesia. Similar scenarios are evidenced from Mangareva, Easter Island, and parts of New Zealand. There is a lesson lurking in these "microcosms of history," if we care to heed it. It is a lesson about the balance between population and resources, about the fragility and vulnerability of natural systems, and about the terrifying ways that people can behave when their backs are up against the wall.

CHAPTER EIGHTEEN

Kahikinui, "Great Tahiti" (Kahikinui, Maui, 1995–2000)

On a hot afternoon in August 1993 I drove a rented Jeep along the rutted road heading east from ʻUlupalakua along the arid southern slopes of Haleakalā, eastern Maui's majestic 10,000-foot volcano. My fiancé Thérèse Babineau and I were collaborating on a photographic book about Hawaiian archaeological sites. I was heading toward Kahikinui, one of the twelve ancient districts (*moku*) of Maui. Kahikinui is what the Hawaiians call *kuaʻāina*, "back country," a dry, leeward zone where life was harsh. Kahikinui's last indigenous occupants had abandoned their home sites and sweet potato fields in the late 1890s, after Portuguese ranchers started running cattle in the district.

As the unpaved road skirted the cinder cones of the Lualaʻilua Hills, I pulled the Jeep off the road, next to a pit crater where molten lava fountains had once erupted. "Follow me," I yelled over the howling wind. Picking my way between thorny lantana bushes, I led Thérèse down the twenty-foot scarp to the crater floor. Hidden behind the gnarled branches of an aged ʻohe tree, we entered a small rockshelter, scrambling over lava boulders to emerge on the shelter's dusty floor. Protected from the wind, it was eerily quiet.

"This is one of the sites where I dug with Peter Chapman on the Bishop Museum's Kahikinui project back in 1966," I told Thérèse. "Our team spent a week excavating in this earthen floor. We uncovered a small hearth, surrounded by lots of midden and artifacts."[1]

The Bishop Museum's 1966 Kahikinui project was the first settlement pattern survey in Hawaiʻi, having been inspired by Roger Green's new approach (see Chapter Two). I had been a member of the team supervised by Peter Chapman, recording more than five hundred archaeological sites over a two-month field season. Suffering from ill health, Chapman never completed his Stanford dissertation on the results. For years, it had been in the back of my mind to return to Kahikinui and finish the work that we had begun in 1966.

Thérèse and I climbed out of the crater and back into the wind. Gazing to the east, toward distant Kaupō, I could make out a structure on a prominent ridge about two miles away. I recognized this as the ruins of a Catholic chapel, St. Ynez, dating to the 1830s. Pardee Erdman, owner of ʻUlupalakua Ranch, had told me that the St. Ynez ruins had recently been taken over by Native Hawaiian activists. A vast, uninhabited land of more than 22,000 acres, Kahikinui is part of the Hawaiian Home Lands, set aside in 1920 by the U.S. Congress. Kahikinui had been leased throughout the twentieth century to cattle ranchers, but the grassroots activists wanted Kahikinui returned to the Hawaiian people.

A few minutes later we pulled up next to the St. Ynez ruins, its basalt and coral mortar walls cleared of the *koa haole* and lantana that had engulfed them in 1966. A plywood roof covered the ruin, creating a sheltered meeting place. A sign proclaimed "Ka ʻOhana o Kahikinui." Two flagpoles stood at the wall corners. From one pole fluttered the flag of the Hawaiian Kingdom while the other held that of the United Nations; poignantly, both were flying upside down, the universal sign for distress.

Approaching the entrance, Thérèse and I saw a middle-aged Hawaiian woman seated at a table within. Greeting us with a warm "Aloha," Kawaipiʻilani Paikai introduced herself as a member of Ka ʻOhana o Kahikinui (Fig. 18.1). Paikai patiently described the tragic history of the Hawaiian people, how the monarchy had been overthrown, how so many Hawaiians had lost their lands. She gestured with a sweep of her arm toward the lava slopes above us, undulating toward the high summit of Haleakalā. "Thousands of Hawaiian once lived on these lands," she stated emphatically.

"I know," I replied. "I have a detailed archaeological map that shows about 550 of those ancient sites." Paikai's eyes fixed on me. For a few seconds she did not say anything. Then she asked, "Who are *you?*" I was obviously not the typical *haole* tourist.

After explaining that I was a *kamaʻāina*, a locally born archaeologist who worked in Hawaiʻi and Polynesia, I told Paikai about the Bishop Museum research in 1966. "You need to come back to Maui," she said. "The information you have can help us in our struggle to regain access to these lands." I nodded in agreement. The three of us walked around the *puʻu* on which the ruins of St. Ynez sit, built upon the foundations of an even more ancient *heiau*. Paikai chanted an *oli*. In the distance, a rainbow formed out of the mist descending from Kaupō Gap, arching out over the point of Ka Lae o ka ʻIlio.

More than a decade had passed since the rainy summer of 1982, when I had mapped and excavated in Oʻahu's Anahulu Valley. Since then my fieldwork had taken me to Mussau in search of the Lapita homeland and to Mangaia in the Cook Islands. I longed to get back to Hawaiʻi, to launch a new archaeological project somewhere in my home islands. That afternoon in Kahikinui, chatting with

Figure 18.1. Kawaipiʻilani Paikai at the entrance to the stone ruins of St. Ynez Church in Kahikinui, 1993.

Kawaipiʻilani Paikai and watching the rainbow arch over Kaupō, I knew what that project would be.

In January 1995 I took two Berkeley graduate students, Cindy Van Gilder and Kathy Kawelu, to Kahikinui for a two-week reconnaissance. We revisited sites I had mapped in 1966, rechecking the old field data. A renewed project was definitely feasible. Little was known about the archaeology of eastern Maui, despite the fact that its vast leeward slopes had, in the words of Edward Craighill Handy, once been the "greatest continuous dry planting area in the Hawaiian Islands."[2]

Here was an opportunity to investigate an intact leeward *moku,* an entire district, running from the coast up the steep slopes of Haleakalā.

The summer of 1995 found our team back on Maui. I rented a house in the little ranching town of Makawao for our field quarters; each day we made the hour-long drive out to Kahikinui. We added another five hundred sites to the archaeological inventory for Kīpapa. Toward summer's end Van Gilder and I tested some promising habitation sites (Fig. 18.2), showing that there was ample potential for her dissertation research on Kahikinui *kauhale.*[3]

As I re-engaged with Hawaiian archaeology through the Kahikinui project, I was thinking a lot about the nature of late precontact Hawaiian society. In the 1960s and 1970s anthropologists classified societies along a spectrum of increasing complexity—from small-scale bands to tribes, chiefdoms, and finally to states. Bands were characteristic of hunting-and-gathering peoples, whereas tribal organization was often found among pastoralists or simple farming peoples. Chiefdoms emerged with more intensive agriculture and the larger populations these

Figure 18.2. Berkeley students excavating at a habitation site in the Kīpapa uplands, Kahikinui.

practices could support. In chiefdoms, leadership was typically hereditary, passed down within higher ranked kinship groups. The Polynesian societies were thought to be typical chiefdoms. Indeed, influential scholars such as Elman Service and Morton Fried used ethnographic accounts of Polynesian societies to define the chiefdom level of social evolution.[4] Contact-era Hawaiian society was usually taken to represent the most complex level of chiefdom development.[5]

But I had started to harbor doubts about the way Hawai'i was pigeonholed in these "neo-evolutionary" schemes. My colleague Robert Hommon had argued that late precontact Hawaiian societies were what he called "primitive states."[6] In states, authority becomes highly centralized, usually with the implied threat of force to back it up. At first I was skeptical of Hommon's thesis that Hawaiian society had crossed the boundary between chiefdoms and states, but the evidence from Kahikinui was causing me to rethink this position. Marshall Sahlins, in our joint Anahulu research, had also commented that Hawaiian societies differed from other Polynesian groups:

Everything looks as if Hawaiian society had been through a history in which the concepts of lineage—of a classic Polynesian sort, organizing the relations of persons and tenure of land by seniority of descent—had latterly been eroded by the development of chiefship. Intruding on the land and people from outside, like a foreign element, the chiefship usurps the collective rights of land control and in the process reduces the lineage order in scale, function, and coherence. Of course, no one knows when, how, or if such a thing ever happened.[7]

Perhaps, I mused, in the final centuries before European arrival, Hawaiian society had passed a critical threshold to become a set of "archaic states," invoking the term used by my colleagues Joyce Marcus and Gary Feinman to describe initial forms of state-level societies that emerged out of complex chiefdoms. Early states were ruled by divine kings who traced their descent back to the gods, backed up by a formal priesthood and by the control of land, tribute, and armed force. These characteristics were also exhibited by contact-era Hawaiian society.

Sahlins' claim—"no one knows when, how, or if such a thing ever happened"—posed a challenge I could not ignore. I drafted a successful research proposal to the National Science Foundation (NSF) with the title, "The Dynamics of Economic and Sociopolitical Structure in Late Prehistoric Hawai'i: An Emergent Archaic State." I proposed to investigate several lines of evidence from Kahikinui to test the hypothesis that Hawai'i had gone through a transformation from chiefdom to archaic state prior to European contact. Little did I realize that I was embarking on an intellectual voyage that would last longer than a decade.

During the spring of 1997, while working in Kahikinui, my students and I took a break from our digging and flew to Līhu'e, Kaua'i, for the annual meeting of the Society for Hawaiian Archaeology (SHA). I had been invited to give the keynote speech and wanted to use the occasion to address some disturbing trends in Hawaiian archaeology.

Over the course of the 1980s and 1990s, archaeology in Hawai'i had shifted from an academic endeavor to for-profit consulting, what was now called "cultural resource management," CRM for short. In theory, CRM protects and preserves the islands' archaeological heritage. In practice, consulting firms often cut corners to satisfy the demands of their developer clients, not always meeting professional standards. Many Native Hawaiians had come to regard archaeologists as "hired hands" of the developers. In 1993, I listened to a group of Hawaiians protest at the SHA meetings on Moloka'i. Standing at the back of the conference room, they shouted, "Stop the Digging!" Archaeology was increasingly viewed as intrusive, invasive, at odds with Hawaiian cultural values. This negative view was summed up in a comment made to my student Kathy Kawelu, while she was interviewing Hawaiians about their perception of archaeologists: "Archaeologists are pimps, they are whoring for money, and that's why we hate them."[8]

I was troubled that the Bishop Museum—where I first learned the craft of archaeology and had worked for a decade—shouldered much of the blame for this negative view of archaeology. In the mid-1980s, the museum was under contract from the state's Department of Transportation (DOT) to survey sites in the path of the H3 freeway, intended to connect Pearl Harbor with the U.S. Marine Corps air base at Kāne'ohe. Highly controversial, the H3 project was the subject of multiple lawsuits until it was pushed through Congress by Hawai'i's influential senator Dan Inouye.

The museum's H3 project started out well enough. But in October 1991, museum CEO Donald Duckworth abruptly fired Paul Cleghorn and Aki Sinoto (son of Yoshiko), who had been overseeing the work, replacing them with newcomers from the Mainland with no experience in Hawai'i or Polynesia.[9] Rumors circulated that Duckworth was diverting funds from the multimillion dollar contract to support other museum operations. I never found out whether that was true or not, but the quality of the museum's archaeological work certainly suffered.

In March 1992 Barry Nakamura, a museum historian, went public with the story that the museum was suppressing evidence of a Hale o Papa or "women's temple" in the highway's path. Denying the allegations, the museum abruptly fired Nakamura. A group of Hawaiian women soon occupied the putative Hale o Papa, vowing to remain until the DOT altered the freeway route. Two prominent Hawaiian professors at the University of Hawai'i, Haunani Kay Trask and Lilikalā Kame'eleihiwa, accused the museum of a "scholarly snow job." Trask demanded that "all anthropology and archaeology on Hawaiians should stop. There should be a moratorium on studying, unearthing, slicing, crushing, and analyzing us."[10]

On a balmy evening at the Kaua'i Community College, I delivered my SHA keynote speech to a packed auditorium. After reviewing how earlier generations of archaeologists had contributed to our knowledge of Hawaiian culture and history, I turned to the current situation. I did not attack the CRM archaeologists, as some thought I might. For better or worse, they were a product of market forces and ineffective government regulation.

Instead, I focused on what I felt had become a vacuum sucking the heart out of archaeology in Hawai'i: the lack of academic and intellectual leadership. My comments about the University of Hawai'i (UH) were brief. I noted that their faculty had benignly neglected Hawaiian archaeology, preferring to work in the Marquesas or Fiji. My main target was the Bishop Museum's abdication of responsibility for quality research in Hawaiian archaeology. Despite the expenditure of $17 million in taxpayer dollars on the H3 archaeology contract, I pointed out that the museum had yet to produce a single report.[11]

At the conclusion of my speech, the audience rose in a standing ovation. But not all of the responses were so laudatory. A few days later, Prof. Michael Graves of the University of Hawai'i—who had not been present at the Kaua'i meeting—unleashed an Internet broadside accusing me of being an intruding "neocolonialist" malihini (newcomer) sticking my nose into places it did not belong. (I found that ironic considering that I had been born and raised in the islands while Graves was the true malihini.) Some in the Native Hawaiian community also thought that I had been unduly criticizing them. Clearly, I had touched some raw nerves.

Fortunately, things began to change for the better over the next decade. Graves started a long-term project in Kohala, putting the University of Hawai'i back in the forefront of Hawaiian archaeological research. A few years later, the university started a master's program in applied archaeology, preparing students for CRM work. The University of Hawai'i at Hilo, under the leadership of Peter Mills (who had been trained at Berkeley), started to actively recruit Native Hawaiian students into archaeology. As a result of these and other efforts, the reputation of archaeology among Native Hawaiians has improved significantly. Most importantly, many Native Hawaiians have become practicing archaeologists, integrating Hawaiian protocols into their work and asking new questions inspired by Hawaiian cultural traditions. The Bishop Museum, sadly, has never regained the leadership role it once played in Hawaiian archaeological research.

The incessant east wind hit me square in the face as I stood next to an altar of stacked lava cobbles in the northeast corner of a *heiau*. A priest had once placed branch coral as dedicatory offerings on this altar in the first decade of the seventeenth century. Number KIP-405 in our archaeological site inventory of Kahikinui, this temple was dubbed by me "Wiliwili Heiau," after a gnarled old *wiliwili* tree growing out of the foundation stones (Fig. 18.3). Wiliwili Heiau occupies a knoll atop a prominent ridge of ʻaʻā lava that I had named "Heiau Ridge," because upon it were clustered not just site KIP-405 but also no less than five other temples. Heiau Ridge was a kind of acropolis, situated in the upland core of Kīpapa.[12]

Figure 18.3. Mapping "Wiliwili Heiau" (site KIP-405) atop "Heiau Ridge" in Kahikinui. *Wiliwili* trees (*Erythrina sandwicensis*), endemic to the Hawaiian Islands, shed their leaves in spring and summer when they burst forth in beautiful red and orange blossoms.

Struggling to remain upright against the strong gusts, I looked out across Heiau Ridge. I could see the stacked walls of a square temple enclosure about seventy-five meters away. A short distance to the west I could make out another well-built stone wall. Pointing to the prominent structure, I shouted over the wind to the Berkeley students standing next to me: "We'll start digging that site this morning. It's KIP-117, the only habitation site on Heiau Ridge. It was probably the house of the priest who officiated at these temples."[13]

No one had ever excavated the house of a priest, a *kahuna*. Of course, we could not be certain that this structure had been occupied by a priest until we tested this hypothesis with empirical evidence. But it seemed likely, given that only a *kahuna* would have lived in the middle of a temple complex. Signaling for the students to follow, I made my way down the boulder-strewn slope toward the house site.

It was the spring semester of 1999. Over the past four years we had completed the settlement pattern survey of Kīpapa and the adjacent land section of Nakaʻohu, with more than 1,300 sites recorded. The data had been integrated into a geographic information system (GIS) database, a technology now becoming standard in archaeological research. We had excavated in a dozen habitation complexes throughout Kīpapa. More than one hundred radiocarbon dates from these complexes, as well as agricultural and temple sites, showed that Kahikinui was first settled in the fifteenth century, with the population gradually building up to a maximum in the eighteenth century, just prior to Captain Cook's arrival.

Arriving at the KIP-117 structure, we put down our gear and began to clear away the thorny lantana, exposing a well-built terrace of ʻaʻā cobbles and boulders constructed to the east of a low outcrop. High stone walls bounded the terrace on the north and east; a perpendicular wall marked off a rectangular room where the main dwelling once stood. Later that day we started to excavate the floor deposits, concentrating in the room defined by the high walls. Sidsel Millerstrom exposed a low stone alignment dividing the room into two spaces as well as a slab-lined hearth. Peeling away the gravelly earth with her trowel, Millerstrom worked closer to the high wall along the room's west side. There she made a remarkable discovery: a cache of sixty-seven black basalt and ninety-seven white coral water-worn pebbles. They had probably all been contained within a small basket or gourd container, which had long since rotted away. My first thought was that they were gaming pieces for *kōnane*, a Hawaiian game resembling checkers. But I recalled that, according to Samuel Kamakau, Hawaiian priests known as *kahuna hāhā* diagnosed illnesses using a "table of pebbles" (*papa ʻiliʻili*). Perhaps the *kahuna* who dwelt here had been a medicinal practitioner.

Another fascinating find was a lava stalactite. There are no lava tubes with stalactites that I know of in Kahikinui, although some may exist high in Haleakalā

Crater; many can be found on Hawai'i Island, home of the volcano goddess Pele. Had this priest traveled to one of these volcanoes to pay homage to the fiery deity, bringing home this stalactite as a memory of his journey? Other finds hinted that the priest, or possibly someone who lived with him, was an expert wood-worker. We found a small basalt adz, of the kind used to carve wooden images, and two abraders of coral that might have been used to smooth or finish such wooden sculptures.

I asked my colleagues Peter Mills and Stephen Lundblad at the University of Hawai'i, Hilo, to analyze a selection of basalt artifacts from KIP-117 using the x-ray fluorescence technique. They reported to me that some of the flakes came from sources well beyond Maui, including from the large quarry on Mauna Kea on Hawai'i Island. They sourced one particular flake to O'ahu, in the vicinity of Kailua. Had the priest or one of his craftsmen traveled to O'ahu bringing back an adz? Or, had the piece arrived here at the end of a "down the line" series of exchanges? Whoever lived here had a social network that extended well beyond Kahikinui.[14]

The faunal remains from the priest's house included the bones of young dogs and pigs, mostly from the head and forequarter regions of the body, portions called *hainaki* and typically given to priests. There were also bones of forest birds, including *moho* and *kioea,* both native honeyeaters taken for the black and yellow feathers that have associations with Kū, god of high forests and mountains. The occupants of the house had received parrotfish, wrasses, convict tangs, trigger-fish, and other fish; sea urchins (*wana*); and the prized black-footed *'opihi,* as well as a large kind of cowrie. These foods were most likely taken to the priest as presents by the people of the *moku,* in exchange for his services in maintaining the temples and making the prayers and sacrifices necessary to ensure the continued fertility of the land.

Heiau Ridge and the larger settlement complex of which it is a part must have played a key role in the annual ritual cycle of Maui's emerging archaic state in the seventeenth and eighteenth centuries. From its temples the priests awaited the acronical rising of Makali'i, when the Pleiades star cluster was first visible in the fading twilight of sunset. This would mark the onset of the Makahiki season, during which the sweet potato crops matured and the Lono priests collected tribute for the king. The rites performed under the watchful eyes of the *kahuna* assured the growth of the crops. And when the sacrifices had been made, the *maka'āinana* rejoiced with hula performances on a nearby high *kahua* platform.

When I returned in 1995 to continue the research in Kahikinui, the grassroots Native Hawaiian group Ka 'Ohana o Kahikinui was beginning to negotiate with the Department of Hawaiian Home Lands for long-term leases that would allow them to reoccupy these lands. An act of Congress in 1920 created the Hawaiian Home Lands, the brainchild of Prince Jonah Kūhiō Kalaniana'ole Pi'ikoi, then Hawai'i's territorial representative. Kūhiō thought that if lands were made available to the Hawaiians to farm or to ranch, they would leave the urban ghettos of O'ahu and return to a wholesome lifestyle. Although part of the Hawaiian Home Lands, for decades Kahikinui had been leased to *haole* ranchers. The Department of Hawaiian Home Lands considered the land too marginal for Hawaiians to live on. Ka 'Ohana o Kahikinui believed otherwise; when the general lease for Kahikinui District came up for renewal, they organized to return the *moku* to Hawaiian hands.[15]

The group coalesced around the charismatic leadership of Mo Moler, a Vietnam veteran and former firefighter, electing him as its president. I first encountered Moler in July 1995, when I arrived with my Berkeley students to spend the summer months mapping sites in the Kīpapa uplands. We sat in the shade of the plywood-roofed ruin of St. Ynez church, "talking story" for a couple of hours. Moler, his Native Hawaiian ancestry evident in his rugged facial features and piercing dark eyes, told me that relations with the Department of Hawaiian Home Lands had improved lately. At first the department had rebuffed their efforts, regarding them as trespassers, but the group had been persistent. They asked to be the unofficial caretakers of Kahikinui, a vast land that Hawaiian Home Lands had no staff to police or look after. They were prepared to *mālama ka 'āina*, take care of the land. As Moler put it, Ka 'Ohana's philosophy was "No means yes, and yes means go!" If they got no for an answer they pushed ahead anyway, and when they got a yes, they really went for it.

Later that summer the Hawaiian Home Lands chairman, Kali Watson, and several commissioners arrived to make a site visit, the first time that the governing board had actually seen Kahikinui. During a tour of Kīpapa, Moler insisted that Chairman Watson ride in my Jeep, knowing that I would point out the hundreds of ancient house sites and *heiau*. Moler reasoned that once Watson saw the archaeological evidence for ancient Hawaiian occupation of the district, the commission could not claim that Hawaiians were incapable of living on the land again.

Over the next few years I watched as the 'Ohana successfully pushed their agenda, eventually getting Hawaiian Home Lands to agree to a program of ninety-nine-year leases on twenty-acre lots where those who wanted to could live in an off-the-grid manner. Meanwhile my students and I developed close friendships with several Ka 'Ohana families, including Lehua and 'Aimoku Pali, Harry and Chad Newman, and Donna and Leon Sterling. They helped us search out archaeological sites and clear them of thorny lantana. On other occasions we camped out with them at the little bay of Niniali'i, going night fishing for *'ō'io*. Modern Hawaiians, these friends of ours, who had jobs in Kahului or Lahaina, nonetheless cared deeply about their cultural traditions. Lehua and 'Aimoku Pali, especially, were respected *kūpuna,* custodians of their ancestral practices. They taught my students that there is more to anthropological archaeology than just mapping old rock walls, that the Hawaiian culture—changed as it may be—is still vibrant and proud of its traditions.

Some might have thought Kahikinui an odd choice in which to investigate the rise of archaic states in ancient Hawai'i. Kahikinui was a *kua'āina,* or "backwater" district (literally "back of the land"); the Hawaiian oral traditions had no references to chiefs ever dwelling in these marginal lands. But I was convinced that I had chosen the right place to investigate the rise of archaic states in ancient Hawai'i. Being ecologically marginal Kahikinui had not suffered from the effects of nineteenth- and twentieth-century land development; the archaeological landscape of an entire *moku,* or district, was intact. More importantly, I thought that the radical shifts in economic production, land tenure, religious organization, and social structure that accompanied the transition to archaic states would likely be reflected more clearly in such outlying *kua'āina* lands than in the "salubrious core regions" frequented by the chiefs. As chiefs became kings, as they reached out to integrate entire island domains, the new economic, religious, and political structures would have left their imprint on the archaeological landscape of more marginal regions such as Kahikinui.

These changes would have been especially evident in the temple system. In archaic states, secular and religious authority typically merge and become centralized as the power of kings is validated by their claims of divine descent. State cults managed by a formal priesthood become the means of collecting tribute. A major change in Hawai'i from chiefdoms to states should be reflected, I thought, in an elaboration of the temple system.

In 1929, pioneering Bishop Museum archaeologist Winslow Walker rode through Kahikinui on horseback, recording the ruins of eighteen *heiau.*[16] But it was clear that Walker had missed many temples, including the largest of all: a site in the uplands that we labeled KIP-1010. I now have recorded sixty structures in Kahikinui that I believe to have been *heiau,* more than three times the number reported by Walker. The most common *heiau* type, accounting for one-third of all the temples in the *moku,* goes by the epithet "notched," a term coined by Walker. In plan view, these *heiau* form a square with a notch taken out of one corner. There are six wall segments, rather than just four as there would be in a square or rectangular enclosure. Internally, notched *heiau* usually have a lower court and a slightly elevated court where we find offerings such as branch coral and water-worn *'ili'ili* pebbles.

After the notched forms, the most common Kahikinui *heiau* type is the square enclosure, distinguished from house sites by its larger and better constructed walls, cardinal wall orientations, and often branch coral offerings. Sometimes this type has internal architectural features, such as a small paved platform in one corner (the foundation for an *'anu'u* tower) or a stone-lined pit for sacrificial offerings.

A third kind of *heiau* I call the "elongated double-court" form. This is a fairly large temple, often oriented toward the summit of Haleakalā, although one double-court temple faces east. It has two rectangular courts, defined by enclosing core-filled stone walls that are separated by a low division or terraced step.

Other *heiau* consist of platforms or terraces, lacking enclosing walls. One platform in Nakaaha, on a prominent *'a'ā* lava ridge, consists of a rectangle about five by six and a half meters, the surface carefully paved with *'a'ā* clinkers. At the eastern end of the pavement two *'a'ā* cobble uprights represent deities. If you sit in the center of this platform—as a *kahuna* would have on his *lauhala* mats—the twin uprights frame a natural *'a'ā* outcrop to the northeast, on the adjacent ridgeline. The outcrop stands at the rising position of Pleiades, the star cluster called Makali'i by the Hawaiian priests, whose acronitic rising at sunset marked the commencement of the Makahiki.[17]

Along the Kahikinui coastline we encountered another type of ritual structure—small shrines dedicated to Kū'ula, the deity of fishermen. These shrines were called *ko'a,* a word that means "coral" or "coral head" and also refers to fishing grounds or places offshore where fish abound. A *ko'a* is a small structure, usually consisting of a small enclosure or platform, that stands out from other sites because it is covered in large quantities of coral heads and broken coral branches. Many of them, such as a *ko'a* at Makee in Auwahi, also have a phallic, water-worn upright representing Kū'ula.

Documenting the distribution and architectural variation of Kahikinui *heiau* was a critical step in my research design. But to understand how the temple system had developed temporally—and especially how this evolution related to the transition from chiefdom to archaic state—called for precise chronological control. One afternoon during the late 1990s I was chatting with two geologist colleagues at the Berkeley Faculty Club. "It's so frustrating dealing with radiocarbon dates from the last few centuries," I grumbled. "The calibration curve has so many wiggles. We end up with multiple possible ages. It's impossible to tie anything down with much precision."

I had mentioned that many *heiau* had corals on them, apparently placed on the altars as offerings. "Why not use the uranium/thorium method of radiometric dating?" Carl Swisher suggested. "It would work well with your corals. It's far more precise than radiocarbon dating. What's more, you won't have to deal with thorny calibration issues."

I was aware of uranium/thorium (U/Th) dating but thought that it was useful primarily for older corals, such as those found in fossil reefs. "Can you apply U/Th to young corals like we have in Maui?" I asked. Swisher's reply stunned me: "Sure. We can date corals right down to ones only a decade old. And we can probably give you error ranges of less than ten years." Dates with error ranges of just a few years? It was an archaeologist's dream.

Why the ancient Hawaiian priests placed coral heads, or more often simply branches knocked off of such coral heads, on the altars of *heiau,* or placed them in *heiau* wall fill during construction, is not clear. Scattered references in the sources on Hawaiian traditions hint at the ritual significance of coral, which may have been symbols of the god Kāne. Because coral bleaches to pure white after exposure to sunlight, it might also have been a symbol of Lono, whose color is white. We will never rediscover the full meaning of branch corals to the ancient Hawaiians, but we know that the priests carried these offerings from the ocean to the *heiau* to be incorporated into walls and platforms.

Soon after my conversation at the Berkeley Faculty Club, I began to collaborate with Warren Sharp of the Berkeley Geochronology Center on the application of U/Th dating to the *heiau* corals from Kahikinui. The U/Th method is similar to radiocarbon in that it involves calculation of an age based on the steady decay of an unstable isotope. Living corals take up uranium, which is abundant in seawater. After the coral dies, the uranium decays at a constant rate to ^{230}thorium. By measuring the ratios of these elements—in parts per million in his mass spectrometer—Sharp could calculate the time since the coral's death. The error range on his age estimates was typically just a few years.

Sharp ran an initial series of U/Th measurements on corals from seven *heiau* sites. When we met over lunch in the Faculty Club to discuss the results I was taken aback. We already had a large sample of radiocarbon dates spanning four centuries from AD 1400 until European contact. I expected that the new coral dates would display a similar range, just with tighter error spans. But the numbers on the spreadsheet that Sharp handed me were all closely clustered. "Warren, it looks like all of these corals were collected and placed on the *heiau* altars within the span of just a few decades. Is that right?" A careful lab scientist, Sharp replied, "Yes, and we've run the analyses multiple times to double-check the results. I'm very confident of these numbers."

I ran my eyes down the column with the calculated dates: site KIP-405, an upland agricultural *heiau,* had an age of AD 1596±4 years; KIP-1010, the largest *heiau* in the *moku,* had coral dating to AD 1574±10 years; a coastal temple in Auwahi, AUW-11, was the youngest of the set, at AD 1629 ± 4 years. Other dates fell within this same time span of no more than sixty years and quite possibly as short as thirty years.

"These were all placed on the altars within the lifetime of one or two of Maui's rulers," I mumbled. "What's that?" Sharp inquired. I told Sharp that I had recently been reading Abraham Fornander's history of the Hawaiian *ali'i*. The end of the sixteenth century had been a period of major political change; this was the same time frame referenced by the coral dates.

According to Fornander who used a genealogical chronology, Pi'ilani and his son Kiha-a-Pi'ilani unified the island of Maui between about AD 1570 and 1610. Our dates from the corals placed as dedicatory offerings on *heiau* ranged between AD 1570 and 1620. This could not be mere chance. We were witnessing a period when—after consolidating the formerly independent chiefdoms of east and west Maui—the Pi'ilani rulers initiated the construction of a system of *heiau* around the island. *Heiau,* after all, were essential to the ritualized control of production and of tribute collection. Sharp and I put that hypothesis forward in 2005 in the prestigious journal *Science*.[18]

Not everyone accepted our conclusions. Some thought that we might be dating a kind of "fad" when people decided to place branch corals on *heiau* altars. To counter this critique, more dates would be necessary. Sharp and I obtained a grant from the National Science Foundation to date more corals on Kahikinui *heiau*. We collected another forty specimens from temple sites throughout Kahikinu and nearby Kaupō. This time we included corals that had been placed inside of walls at the time of construction. We knew those corals, which we called "architecturally integral," had to date the actual building of the *heiau* foundations.

When Sharp handed me the chart on which he had plotted the new set of dates, a broad smile broke out across my face. Although there were three or four dates in the fourteenth century, the largest number of dates appeared between AD 1550–1650. Without doubt, the reigns of Pi'ilani and Kiha-a-Pi'ilani had seen a major phase of *heiau* construction throughout the *moku*.

Altogether, I have spent more than fifteen years conducting archaeological research in Kahikinui, the longest running project I have ever directed. Initially, I thought I would be able to accomplish my goals in just two or three field seasons, but each time I was drawn more deeply into that dramatic landscape. The more I learned, the more new questions arose. I have told the stories of those long years of fieldwork, as well as of the efforts of Ka 'Ohana o Kahikinui to regain access to their Native Hawaiian lands, more extensively in my book *Kua'āina Kahiko: Life and Land in Ancient Kahikinui*. Kahikinui will forever hold a special place in my *na'au*.

CHAPTER NINETEEN

Forbidden Peninsula
(Kalaupapa, Moloka'i, 2000)

No place in Hawai'i has a darker history than Kalaupapa, a forbidding, wind-swept peninsula on windward Moloka'i. Cut off from the world by 2,800-foot-high cliffs, Kalaupapa became in the 1860s a place of banishment for those beset with the feared *ma'i pākē*, leprosy. The hardships endured by those forcibly sent to Kalaupapa in the first decades of the Kalawao settlement and the aid provided by those who dared to live among them—Father Damien and Sister Marianne especially—have inspired histories, novels, and motion pictures.[1]

I had made a one-day visit to Kalaupapa in 1993, when National Park Service (NPS) archaeologist Buddy Neller showed my Berkeley colleague Kent Lightfoot and me around various sites he was recording. I was struck by Kalaupapa's potential for archaeological research, resolving someday to return to this enigmatic place with its richly textured history. That opportunity came in 1999 when Robert Hommon, in charge of NPS archaeology in the Pacific region, told me that the National Park Service would welcome archaeological research at Kalaupapa.

What intrigued me was the great diversity of micro-environments that were packed into the ancient Ko'olau District of windward Moloka'i. In striking contrast with Kahikinui—where the vast leeward slope of Haleakalā consists of relatively young, arid lava flows (see Chapter Eighteen)—windward Moloka'i displays a diversity of landscapes (Fig. 19.1). Within the space of less than six linear miles, extending east to west as the frigate bird flies, there are the spectacular deep valley of Waikolu; the dry valley of Wai'ale'ia; the peninsula with its broad, gentle slopes of recent lava flows; and finally the "landshelf" of Nihoa, a tiny block of land that juts into the stormy windward waters.

I arranged for five of my students (all seasoned fieldworkers from Kahikinui) to join me in Kalaupapa in August 2000. NPS Superintendent Dean Alexander informed me that we would have to bring in all our own food and supplies. "Also, if you get injured, they won't treat you in the settlement hospital," Alexander had said. "You'll have to go back up 'Topside' for medical treatment." We planned out our meals, using as much dehydrated food as possible. "What about beer for after work?" my six-foot-tall Hawaiian student Solomon Ka'ilihiwa asked. "No way," I

Figure 19.1. The isolated peninsula of Kalaupapa is cut off from the rest of Moloka'i by sheer cliffs rising several thousand feet. This view was taken from the slopes above the old Kalawao settlement, looking eastward down the windward coastline toward Waikolu, Pelekunu, and Wailau Valleys.

replied. "It weighs far too much. But there is a little bar run by one of the patients. It's open for a few hours in the afternoons. Hopefully they'll sell us some beers."

On August 11 we flew from Kahului, Maui, on a chartered Pacific Wings turboprop to Kalaupapa. The pilot took off into the stiff wind, making a left turn toward Moloka'i. Flying at about 2,500 feet, we crossed the channel. Hālawa Valley came into view; I nostalgically gazed down at the sand dune where I had excavated in 1969–1970. Rounding the northeast tip of Moloka'i, the spectacular windward cliffs—the highest sea cliffs in the world—stretched out in front of us. Stunning waterfalls cascaded down between Hālawa and Wailau Valley. Beyond Wailau lay Pelekunu Valley, followed by Waikolu Valley and then the forbidden peninsula itself.

Superintendent Alexander greeted us at the simple, open-sided shed that passes for an airport terminal. "Aloha, Pat. Let's go into the settlement and get you guys registered with the Health Department. Then I'll show you your quarters." We drove along the narrow road, passing the hundreds and hundreds of tombstones attesting to the generations of patients who had been banished to and then died on this isolated peninsula. The settlement itself is a motley mix of architectural styles—board-and-batten wooden houses, surplus Quonset huts from World War II, nondescript concrete structures—all showing signs of neglect and decay. At the administration building we were given a list of regulations that governed life in Kalaupapa. One of these was "No 'Opihi Picking." The right to collect the juicy limpets that cling to the rocky shorelines was reserved exclusively for the patients. The frown on Solomon Kaʻilihiwa's face showed his disappointment. Our lodgings would be in a Quonset hut that had once served as a dormitory. The other occupants were the settlement's antisocial Portuguese electrician and a somewhat loony handyman who liked to make "smoothies" out of moldy old carrots rotting in the refrigerator.

We began our exploration of the park's archaeological landscapes with a reconnaissance into Waikolu Valley, the westernmost of four great valleys that slice into the East Molokaʻi mountains. Descending a badly rutted trail to the mouth of Waiʻaleʻia Valley, we continued for a kilometer and a half along the narrow beach between Waiʻaleʻia and the mouth of Waikolu. It was an eerie feeling to hike in the shadow of the nearly 3,000-foot-high cliff, knowing that an unexpected earthquake might bring down a deadly shower of boulders. I was relieved when, an hour or so later, we arrived at the mouth of Waikolu Stream.

I waded into the icy cold water, clambered up the eastern bank, put my boots back on, and began to explore the broad alluvial flat. I soon realized that we were walking over a series of rectangular terraces, separated by low earthen bunds, the remnants of loʻi or taro pondfields. Exploring inland I found the ʻauwai or irrigation channel, then scrambled up a steep slope, making my way through a tangle of guava, Christmas berry, and sisal. On a gently sloping shelf overlooking the terraced flat we found the overgrown stone walls of ʻAhina Heiau, up to two meters high, originally reported by J. F. G. Stokes in 1909.[2]

I knew from historic records that the settlement pattern of Waikolu was likely to have been dominated by irrigation systems, such as that in Hālawa farther to the east. On a second visit we recorded a vertical, wave-cut face in the coastal alluvium with alternating dark black and reddish-yellow layers. These were reduction and oxidation zones, representing different periods of pondfield irrigation. Charcoal flecks recovered from the deepest of the pondfield soil layers were radiocarbon dated to AD 1240 to 1280.[3] This date is one of the oldest for irrigation in the archipelago, informing us that people were attracted to Waikolu and similar wet valleys within a couple of centuries after initial Polynesian arrival.

In contrast with Waikolu, the "dry" valley of Wai'ale'ia was a disappointment. Flash floods had torn up much of the valley floor. There were a few small sites with historic period glass bottles and rusted iron pots or tools. Some of these sites might have been the residences of *kōkua*, "helpers" of the Kalawao lepers during the early days of the settlement.

Nihoa, a landshelf one and a half miles west of Kalaupapa peninsula, proved to be far more interesting. About 0.4 miles long, the landshelf resulted from a massive landslide that brought the entire mass crashing down from the cliffs almost to sea level. When we told some of the Kalaupapa residents that we were going to hike out to Nihoa they looked at us like we were *pupule*, crazy. Even patients who had lived in the settlement all their lives had never been there.

Rising at dawn, we began the long trek to Nihoa, making our way along the steep boulder beach, whose rocks range from cobbles a foot or two in diameter up to massive boulders the size of a shipping container. About halfway out to Nihoa, leaping from one boulder to another, as my boot hit the basalt surface of the target stone it rolled, throwing me forward, my heavy pack propelling me as I crashed into several jagged rocks. Thankfully, no bones were broken. But a large patch of skin on my right shin had been torn away by the rough surface, exposing the underlying muscle. Sidsel Millerstrom and Sharyn Jones, who had seen me go down, helped bandage the wound.

Unlike lush Waikolu, Nihoa was windswept and arid; a small stream cascading down the cliff on the eastern end provided the only evident source of freshwater. Yet everywhere we looked there were sites, including house terraces and the low stone walls of a dryland agricultural field system. A site cluster near the center of the landshelf was covered in shellfish midden and basalt flakes from chipping stone adzes. Farther to the west a well-faced set of terraces was probably a *heiau*. We came upon an extensive grove of old *milo* trees (*Thespesia populnea*), prized by the Hawaiians for carving calabashes, as well as stands of *kamani* (*Calophyllum inophyllum*), another prized hardwood. Perhaps the people who had lived on Nihoa had been specialist wood carvers. Parts of Nihoa were also covered in the largest *noni* (*Morinda citrifolia*) plants I have ever seen; groves of *hala* (*Pandanus tectorius*) hung over the cliffs. Later I encountered this line in a sacred hula chant recorded by Nathaniel Emerson: "Ah, the perfume of Nihoa's pandanus exhales!"[4]

After the Nihoa adventure, we turned our attention to the peninsula proper, where the archaeological landscape was dominated by a grid of closely spaced stone walls. I had first noticed these walls from the air when flying in some years earlier. They clearly demarcated the plots within an extensive dryland agricultural system. I selected an area along the peninsula's eastern side where the vegetation was low and we could make out row upon row of stone field walls, running at right angles to the incessant easterly wind. We surveyed a transect 150 meters wide from the coast running inland about 700 meters, mapping the parallel agricultural walls about one to two feet high, some of which were spaced just four to six feet apart. Dispersed among this grid of densely packed walls we discovered nearly forty other features, mostly stone shelters and residential enclosures. This transect gave us the first clear picture of what the Kalaupapa landscape had once looked like: an intensively cultivated dryland field system with small clusters of houses (*kauhale*) dispersed among the sweet potato gardens. Later work by my student Mark McCoy would show that the field walls began to be constructed around the fifteenth century AD.

That Kalaupapa was so suitable for intensive sweet potato farming is due to its unique geology. The peninsula consists of lava outpourings from Kauhakō Crater that erupted about a half-million years ago, long after the main mass of the East Molokaʻi mountains had already been eroded and the high sea cliffs formed. Because the Kauhakō lavas are still young, they possess a high level of rock-derived nutrients, especially phosphorus. With these rich soils and an annual rainfall of between sixty and eighty inches, the peninsula was ideal for growing sweet potatoes.

Meanwhile, my injured leg had become a concern. The skin was missing over a sizable part of my shin. I changed the dressing every day, but the wound was not responding to the topical antibiotics in our limited medical kit. Due to the Health Department's arcane rules, the settlement's hospital would not treat me. I phoned Dr. Emmett Aluli, an old friend from the days when I had worked at Kawela (see Chapter Ten). Aluli urged me to fly up to "Topside" for treatment. I decided that the rest of the crew deserved a break as well and booked us on the small plane for Saturday morning.

Early Saturday morning we made the short flight to Hoʻolehua Airport. Aluli had told me to meet him at the Mitchell Paoli Center in Kaunakakai, where he was attending a community meeting regarding Hawaiian sovereignty issues. Taking a break from his meeting, Aluli took one look at my festering leg wound and said, "Pat, a few more days and we might be looking at amputation." He immediately wrote out prescriptions for some potent antibiotics and ointment used for burn victims. Fortunately, my leg began gradually to heal. But to this day I bear a large scar as a memento of that hike to Nihoa.

After spending the weekend visiting Hālawa Valley and enjoying a memorable dinner with Emmett Aluli and his partner Davianna McGregor at their home in Hoʻolehua, we flew back down to Kalaupapa. One final objective remained. In 1966, Richard Pearson, then a young assistant professor at the University of

Hawai'i, had tested a rockshelter near Kaupikiawa Point. A charcoal sample from the rockshelter's base had later been radiocarbon dated to AD 1000–1140, one of the oldest dates for Moloka'i Island.[5] But was the date valid?

We relocated the rockshelter, formed by the partial collapse of a lava tube in one of the last lava flows from Kauhakō Crater. Cutting a path through the *naupaka* obscuring the low overhang, I scrambled down the rubble slope into the cool darkness of the tube's interior. As my eyes adjusted to the dim light, I could make out the rectangular depressions where Pearson and his students had dug their test pits.

Not wanting to disturb the site more than necessary, we cleaned up the sidewalls of Pearson's old pits, recorded the stratigraphy, and then cut small 20-by-20 centimeter "columns" into the cleaned faces, using them to obtain samples for faunal and floral analyses and for radiocarbon dating.[6]

After we returned to my Berkeley lab, Sharyn Jones identified the shellfish and fishbones, also finding some bones of the Native Hawaiian bat (*Lasiurus cinereus*), a rare find. James Coil analyzed charcoal fragments from the different layers, showing how the vegetation surrounding the site had changed over time. The deepest sediments contained charcoal with abundant fragments of native dryland trees and shrubs. In the intermediate deposits, after the rockshelter had become a fishermen's camp, the charcoal was dominated by shrubs and grasses typical of a disturbed landscape. These deposits also included fragments of economic plants such as *kukui* and breadfruit. The uppermost sediments reflected the postcontact period when ungulates grazed the peninsula and the vegetation consisted mostly of grasses.

We obtained three new radiocarbon dates from the Kaupikiawa shelter. The earliest one—from the deeper layer with evidence of native dryland forest—dated to about 650 years ago, roughly the fourteenth century. Thus, the site was not quite as old as had been thought. The main occupation deposits dated to the Late Expansion and Proto-Historic periods of Hawaiian history, when the field system was developed.

Although it was one of the shortest field projects I have undertaken, the work at Kalaupapa was challenging and exciting. We not only documented the incredible range of settlement patterns and adaptations to diverse environments along windward Moloka'i but also our reconnaissance at Kalaupapa set the stage for two subsequent archaeological studies. Beginning in 2001 my graduate student Mark McCoy spent several summers mapping and excavating on the Kalaupapa peninsula, producing a detailed chronology of the development of this agricultural landscape.[7] As McCoy was completing his field research another doctoral student, James Flexner, arrived at Berkeley to do historical archaeology. Flexner also spent several summers exploring the ruins of the early leprosy colony at Kala-wao, adding greatly to the understanding of everyday life during the years that Father Damien ministered to the banished lepers.[8] On the basis of my field re-search in 2000 and the subsequent studies by McCoy and Flexner, Berkeley's Oceanic Archaeology Laboratory made important contributions to both the pre-contact and historic archaeology of Moloka'i's "forbidden peninsula."

CHAPTER TWENTY

Belly of the Stonefish
(Moʻorea, Society Islands, 2000–2010)

In January 1924, the four-masted schooner *Kaimiloa* dropped anchor in ʻŌpūnohu Bay on Moʻorea, second largest of the Society Islands. Its owner, Medford R. Kellum, a wealthy capitalist from Florida, was on a round-the-world cruise with his family. From *Kaimiloa*'s afterdeck, Kellum took in the magnificent landscape surrounding the calm, deep bay. A broad valley extended inland, cloaked in forests of Tahitian Chestnut interspersed here and there with lighter colored patches of fernland (Fig. 20.1). The spectacular volcanic peaks of Tohi-veʻa and Moua-roa, shrouded by swirling mists, backstopped the valley's amphitheater head. Kellum soon learned that the ʻŌpūnohu Valley was for sale by the French colonial authorities; he immediately bought it as a wedding present for his son Medford Kellum Jr. and his bride Gladys Laughlin. The young couple would soon build a modest house on the shore of ʻŌpūnohu Bay, spending their lives together in this idyllic setting.

This South Seas romance also influenced the course of Polynesian archaeology. When the *Kaimiloa* had arrived in Honolulu in May 1923, Bishop Museum director Herbert Gregory convinced Kellum to take a group of museum scientists along on the cruise. The trip through the Line Islands did not go well as the scientists' demands conflicted with Kellum's notion of a pleasure cruise. Arriving in Tahiti, Kellum kicked the scientists off the *Kaimiloa*. Kellum had taken a liking, however, to young Kenneth Emory, who had helpfully developed motion pictures of the Kellum clan in the ship's darkroom. Kellum gave Emory a parting gift of $1,500, sufficient for a year of archaeological fieldwork in the then unexplored Society Islands. Emory was soon exploring the depths of the ʻŌpūnohu Valley, guided by locals to a cluster of *marae* or temple sites in the shadow of Tohi-veʻa.[1] In the ensuing months, Emory not only recorded temple ruins throughout the Society Islands but also met and married a local French Tahitian *belle*, Marguerite.

In their home on ʻŌpūnohu Bay, Gladys Kellum and her husband Medford Jr. raised a daughter, Marimari. During his periodic expeditions to the French Polynesian Tuamotu Islands and Mangareva during the 1920s and 1930s, Emory

Figure 20.1. Mt. Rotui looms over the 'Ōpūnohu Valley and Bay, Mo'orea Island.

kept up his contacts with the Kellums. Influenced by her parents' connection with Emory and the Bishop Museum, young Marimari Kellum decided to become an archaeologist. In the early 1960s she assisted Yosihiko Sinoto during his fieldwork at the important Hane Dune Site on Ua Huka Island in the Marquesas. I first met Marimari Kellum in 1965, when she was studying for her master's degree at the University of Hawai'i.

But there is more to the intertwined story of the 'Ōpūnohu Valley, the Kellum family, and archaeology. In 1961 Roger Green, then a Harvard graduate student, was seeking a location to conduct a settlement pattern study in the Society Islands. Emory suggested that Green have a look at the 'Ōpūnohu. Uninhabited and thick with archaeological sites, the valley proved to be ideal for Green's fieldwork. Green spent months mapping hundreds of house terraces, *marae* enclosures, council platforms, and other structures in the 'Ōpūnohu. This first application of the settlement pattern approach changed the course of archaeological research throughout the Pacific.[2]

On October 12, 1996, my wife Thérèse and I stepped off an Air New Zealand 747 into the floral-scented air of a warm Tahitian night. En route to the second International Congress of archaeologists on Rapa Nui, we had arranged to meet up in Tahiti with Roger Green and his wife, Valerie. Although I was by now a seasoned veteran of Pacific archaeology, this was the first time that I had set foot on that fabled isle at the center of South Seas lore. During the years that I had worked at the Bishop Museum, Yoshihiko Sinoto regarded French Polynesia as "his" territory. I had been too busy with my expeditions to Western Polynesia to consider intruding onto Sinoto's turf.

The next morning the four of us took the ferry from Papeʻete to Moʻorea. Packed into a tiny rented Citroën, we drove through Maharepa and around Paopao Bay to the University of California's Richard Gump Research Station. My graduate student Dana Lepofsky had carried out her dissertation project here in the early 1990s, investigating ancient agricultural practices in the ʻŌpūnohu Valley.[3] I was now thinking of launching a new project, building on Green's and Lepofsky's research. The facilities available at the Gump Station could provide critical logistical support.

After dropping our bags off at the Gump Station we headed to ʻŌpūnohu Bay, pulling in to Marimari Kellum's estate, where her parents had built their modest house decades earlier. We strolled through the famous gardens lovingly planted by her father, down to the jetty extending into the bay. Kellum pointed out a stonefish (nohu) camouflaged among the seaweed-cloaked rocks. "The name ʻŌpūnohu means 'belly of the stonefish,'" she said. "The bay is full of them." I made a mental note not to go swimming there. A puncture from a stonefish's hypodermic dorsal spines can be fatal.

Standing on the rickety jetty, Green waxed nostalgic about his fieldwork forty years earlier. "Sometimes I would be returning from a long day mapping in the valley, sailing toward Papetoʻai village in our outrigger canoe," Green reminisced. "Medford would walk out on the jetty, hailing us. It was a sign to come over for a refreshing cocktail before going back to the village."

After some Hinano beers in the old board-and-batten Kellum house (the timbers had been brought from Honolulu on the Kaimiloa), we piled back into the Citroën for a drive up the ʻŌpūnohu Valley. Before he passed away, Medford Kellum had deeded the valley to the Territory of French Polynesia as an archaeological preserve. Except for an agricultural school, most of the valley remained cloaked in deep glades of Tahitian Chestnut. We stopped to look at the cluster of marae that Emory had first recorded in 1925: Marae Tetiʻiroa, Marae Ahu o Mahina, and Marae Afareʻaito (Fig. 20.2). Green's excavations at Marae Ahu o Mahina were one of the very first efforts to put Polynesian ceremonial architecture into a firm chronological framework.

Green coaxed the underpowered Citroën up the winding switchbacks to a viewpoint perched on a narrow ridge under the towering mountain peak of Tohiveʻa. The entire ʻŌpūnohu Valley, as well as the adjacent Paopao Valley to the east,

Figure 20.2. Marae Ahu o Mahina, in the Tupauruuru branch of the 'Ōpūnohu Valley. The stepped *ahu* of this *marae* is characteristic of the late period in the Society Islands, when the 'Oro cult was expanding and chiefs were vying for power.

spread out before us. Between the two deep bays the pyramidal mountain of Rotui rose into the clouds, its striated lava cliffs reputedly studded with burial caves. Green's white beard fluttered in the wind as he gazed over terrain he had lovingly explored in his youth. After quietly absorbing the view—his mind no doubt flooded with memories—Green turned toward me. With a dramatic sweep of his arm, he proclaimed, "I give you the 'Ōpūnohu." I knew that this was an invitation as well as a challenge. Carry on the work that I began, Green was telling me. The 'Ōpūnohu has so much more to reveal to you and to your students.

It took several years to put things in motion for a project in the 'Ōpūnohu Valley. At Berkeley, I had taken on a new graduate student, Jennifer Kahn. With prior field experience in Hawai'i and the Marquesas Islands, Kahn wanted to investigate Polynesian household archaeology. Just the person, I thought, to tackle the settlement landscape of the 'Ōpūnohu Valley.

In spite of its central place in Eastern Polynesia, Tahiti and the Society Islands had not been nearly so well studied by archaeologists as Hawai'i, the Marquesas, Rapa Nui, or New Zealand. Yet like Hawai'i, the Society Islands had one of the most complex, hierarchical social and political systems in Polynesia. When the first European explorers showed up there in the late eighteenth century, they encountered a hotbed of chiefdom polities vying for hegemony. The highest ranked chiefs alternated between wars of conquest and building great pyramidal temples at which human sacrifices were offered to 'Oro, the god of war.

In 1769, during a tour around Tahiti, Captain James Cook was shown the newly constructed temple of Mahaiatea at Papara. The *marae* had been built for the installation of the high chief Teri'irere. Cook was astounded by this "enormous pile, certainly the masterpiece of Indian architecture," with eleven steps (each four feet high) to its pyramidal *ahu,* faced with cut and polished coral blocks. In true Enlightenment fashion, Cook carefully measured the base of the pyramid at 267 feet long and 87 feet wide.[4] Such accounts from the early period of European contact were fascinating, but how and over what time period had this complex sociopolitical system developed? Only archaeology could provide the answers to these questions.

I wrote a successful research proposal to the Wenner-Gren Foundation in New York, requesting support for a project on household archaeology in the 'Ōpūnohu. In 1999, Kahn and I made an initial trip to Mo'orea to lay the groundwork for what would become her dissertation research. We met with Gré Tahiata, a soft-spoken man from Tubuai in the Austral Islands, who was in charge of the valley. Tahiata gave us free rein to do whatever we wanted. More importantly, he and his wife Paulette soon "adopted" Kahn in the classic Polynesian style, their daughter Marta and son Taufa becoming helpers in Kahn's fieldwork.

Over three field seasons from 2000 to 2002, Kahn opened up large-scale excavations of three household complexes, seeking subtle differences in subsurface architecture and in the distribution and density of stone tools, clues that could tell us about activity spaces and functions of the structures. I visited Kahn during each field season, assisting her by using my plane table to map the sites. The stone architecture of the 'Ōpūnohu Valley was different from that of Hawai'i, making extensive use of stacked prismatic dikestones that gave the walls a crisp, angular appearance. In spite of the inevitable mosquitoes and periodic tropical downpours, I enjoyed mapping the moss-encrusted enclosures, platforms, and alignments.

I had become interested in the concept of the "house society," originally proposed by the famous French social anthropologist Claude Lévi-Strauss.[5] Lévi-Strauss observed that in many societies around the world—including those of Polynesia—the "house" was not merely a physical dwelling but was also a fundamental unit of kinship. The Tikopia were a classic case of such a *société-à-maison,* with lineages carrying the house name down through time. The house thus had a persistence extending over multiple generations. Those affiliated with a house acquired rights to land, to other kinds of material property, and even to nonmaterial possessions such as ancestral deities and particular rituals. Roger Green and I, in our *Hawaiki* book, had argued that house societies were an essential component of Ancestral Polynesia (see Chapter Fifteen). Kahn made the house society concept a key part of her dissertation research, and we collaborated on an article published in 2004 in the French *Journal de la Société des Océanistes,* further developing the application of the house society model to Polynesian archaeology.[6]

One site complex (ScMo-170/-171) situated on a broad ridge in the upper valley nicely exemplified the house society mode of social organization. At the bottom of the ridge a small *marae* functioned as the group temple. Moving up the ridge we found several stone-faced terraces and then three distinct rectangular houses (*fare haupape*) of the kind known to have been commoner dwellings. At the top of the ridge, set slightly apart from the rectangular houses, a large round-ended house (*fare pote'e*) occupied a stone-paved terrace. The residence of the highest ranked member of the house group, this dwelling had a specialized adz workshop attached to it. Radiocarbon dates showed that the complex had been used from the mid-fifteenth century until European contact.

This initial foray into the archaeology of the 'Ōpūnohu only whetted our appetites. After Kahn received her PhD from Berkeley in 2005,[7] we wrote a successful research proposal to the National Science Foundation (NSF) to investigate the spatial organization of communities within the valley. We would work at both a micro-level consisting of dwellings and residential clusters and a macro-level of monumental architecture and its spatial distribution, integrating the two datasets to model community-level social relations.

I shifted the lumbering Land Rover into four-wheel low gear, then crossed the first of two fords over the Amehiti Stream. In the open rear, our crew of eight young Tahitian men and women were chatting away. A low-hanging *pūrau* branch bounced off the top of the cab, eliciting peals of laughter. "*Patrique! Fait attention!*" Ha'amoi yelled from the back. Mud oozed out from around the tires as I struggled to keep the heavy vehicle from slipping into the deep ruts. Holding my breath, we entered the second ford, mossy cobbles clinking beneath the tires. Past the treacherous fords, I followed the slippery track deep into the Amehiti branch of the 'Ōpūnohu.

Roger Green had surveyed only part of this western branch of the great valley back in 1961, mapping sites on the lower slopes. In 2006, Kahn had discovered two extensive site complexes in the deeper recesses of the Amehiti. Now, in August 2007, with our new NSF funding in hand, we could investigate these ruins in detail.

I pulled the Land Rover over at a small clearing. Beyond this point the track became impassable because of the incessant rains that kept the lateritic clay as slippery as axle grease. The crew tumbled out, grabbing machetes, survey gear, and day packs. We smeared on mosquito repellent and then made our way single file along a rough foot path into the jungle. The trail led a short distance up a muddy slope past birds' nest ferns and hanging lianas, a babbling stream on our right, under a towering canopy of stately Tahitian Chestnuts.

After a few minutes we arrived at Kahn's excavation, a level terrace cut into the hillslope and buttressed on the downslope side with a sturdy retaining wall of basalt cobbles. On the terrace, a curbstone alignment of basalt cobbles indicated where a rectangular house had once stood. The well-trained Tahitian crew took up their positions, some grabbing trowels to begin scraping down the earthen house floor, others lashing sifting screens to their wooden tripods, anticipating the first bucket loads of dirt.

Leaving Kahn in charge of the excavation, I continued past the house terrace, crossing the stream deeper into the narrow ravine, with a tripod slung over my right shoulder balanced by the wooden alidade box in my left hand. Accompanying me was my good friend John Holson from Berkeley, a cultural resources management (CRM) archaeologist who had volunteered to help out with the 'Ōpūnohu mapping. In a cleared space in front of an imposing platform of stacked basalt boulders, I located the red-and-white chaining pin that marked the position of yesterday's survey station. The platform was a *marae,* indicated by two rows of three upright prismatic slabs, each representing a deity or ancestor, to whom prayers had once been addressed. Kahn had found a *ti'i* or anthropomorphic stone sculpture on the platform, lying face down in front of the uprights.

Setting up the tripod and plane table over the chaining pin, I began to map with my aging but trustworthy Gurley telescopic alidade, while Holson held the stadia rod on different features. I still preferred to map using this optical method that I had first been taught by Lloyd Soehren in 1965. Not only is this method accurate but it also allows you to draw the stones and architecture of the features as you map them. Some think that GPS and digital technology have replaced the plane table and alidade, but this is not the case. In fact, it was next to impossible to use GPS in the higher recesses of the 'Ōpūnohu Valley. The towering cliffs and thick forest canopy usually hid the satellite signals, whereas the cloud cover and rain further degraded the signals when they did come in. I did use GPS to get position fixes when possible, but it was much more efficient and accurate to map the complex stone features with the plane table.

We were working on a cluster of dispersed house sites and several *marae,* focused around a small set of irrigated agricultural terraces. Water still flowed through the terraces, bubbling up from the spring that originally attracted people to this location high in the valley. They had built their *marae* just above the spring, no doubt making offerings and prayers to assure the persistence of the life-giving waters. Over several generations this "house" of related kinsfolk had flourished and grown, until several dwellings surrounded the irrigated fields.

Later that field season we moved to another site complex, on a higher ridge across the stream, with a zone of fertile soil where people had grown their crops in dryland terraces. Numerous dryland terraces had been built on an ancient landslide of rock and debris that had tumbled down from the surrounding cliffs. As I later discovered when working on Moʻorea with soil scientist Oliver Chadwick, such "debris flows" with their nutrient-rich eutrophic soils were sought after by the Polynesians for garden plots. They would rework the boulders and stones into terrace walls, planting their crops in the small level spaces.

The settlement pattern on this broad ridge with its dryland terraces consisted of a mix of residential and ritual structures.[8] At the top of the ridge stood the principal *marae,* with six uprights of prismatic stone. Below it were several broad, well-faced terraces; Kahn's excavations suggested these terraces had been used for community-wide feasting. Farther down the slope were agricultural terraces interspersed with residential sites on small flat areas around the margins of the garden zone.

Our fieldwork in the upper Amehiti area gave us a good idea of the residential landscapes and community organization in the ʻŌpūnohu Valley during the last century or two prior to European contact. But we also wanted to understand how the valley's impressive ceremonial architecture had developed. What role had these monumental structures played in the evolution of late precontact Moʻorean society, when the island's chiefs were at war with neighboring Tahiti, when the cult of ʻOro was sweeping through the archipelago? For our 2008 field season, therefore, we decided to focus on the valley's most extensive ceremonial complex. Perhaps there we would find the answers to our questions.

The Tupauruuru ceremonial complex includes fourteen *marae* or temple enclosures, along with dozens of smaller shrines, terraces, and house foundations clustered in a dry swale between two broad ridges capped with immense boulders, the remnants of ancient landslides.[9] Human skulls and bones tucked here and there in crevasses under the giant boulders testified to the *tapu* nature of the place. Rising from the western ridge, the massive crown of a sacred banyan tree towered above the surrounding forest of *māpē* and *mara* trees.

I was fascinated by the architectural details of the Tupauruuru *marae.* Most of the enclosures, constructed of stacked basalt cobbles topped with prismatic dikestones, exhibited cornerstones of cut-and-dressed tuff or scoria, chosen for its reddish color—red being associated with the gods. The most sacred part of the *marae* was the *ahu* or altar, a rectangular platform at one end of the *marae* court, usually freestanding but in some cases attached to the rear wall of the enclosure. Some *ahu* facades incorporated cut-and-dressed blocks of *Porites* coral, arranged in rows, alternating with rows of dark gray prismatic dikestone.

An especially large *marae* (site ScMo-124J) downslope from the big banyan tree with its impressive aerial roots boasted the most impressive *ahu*. This altar once had two steps incorporating *Porites* coral blocks, topped with a large basalt upright. Another *marae* (-124T) although small in scale, had a facade of uniformly pecked basalt cobbles, carefully fitted together (Fig. 20.3), marking this *marae* as one dedicated to the 'Oro cult and worshipped by the highest ranked chiefs.

While I mapped the Tupauruuru complex, Kahn opened up test excavations in and around the *marae*. It was slow going, surveying in the dim light under the towering canopy of Tahitian Chestnut trees, cutting sight lines through tangles of *pūrau*. I surrounded myself with smoking mosquito coils to ward off the hordes waiting to suck my blood and possibly give me dengue fever. But capturing the architectural details was essential to putting these *marae* into a temporal sequence.

Figure 20.3. The enclosing wall of *marae* -124T at the Tupauruuru ceremonial complex is constructed of pecked stone cobbles of uniform size. This architectural style is associated with the 'Oro cult.

We had recently developed a chronology for *marae* on Moʻorea Island, using the high-precision uranium/thorium (U/Th) method that I had pioneered with Warren Sharp in Hawaiʻi (see Chapter Eighteen). The previous summer, Sharp and I had visited all nineteen *marae* in the ʻŌpūnohu Valley that had coral incorporated into their *ahu*. With a portable Makita saw, we sliced off small samples of *Acropora* or *Porites* corals used as facing slabs, or in larger *marae* as fill, taking these to Berkeley for dating in Sharp's geochronology laboratory. We also collected coral samples from the island's three largest coastal *marae:* Nuʻurua, Nuʻupure, and ʻUmarea. These *marae,* with impressive stepped *ahu* rising four to five meters above the ground, had been identified by Kenneth Emory in 1924 as the ritual seats of the island's highest-ranking lineages. These huge *marae* were in use when Captain Cook arrived in the Society Islands.

After Sharp finished analyzing the U/Th content of the coral samples in his laboratory, I compared the resulting dates with the architectural variations revealed by my mapping. When I put the *marae* in a relative sequence based on their architectural features—a method archaeologists call *seriation*—it closely matched the absolute sequence of U/Th dates.[10] The three oldest *marae* in our sample, dating to the early seventeenth century, had simple *ahu* raised just 20 or 30 centimeters above the court. Their low platforms were faced with *Acropora* "fan" coral set on edge. *Marae* dating to the mid-seventeenth century had more substantial *ahu* with platforms closer to a meter high and incorporating blocks of cut-and-dressed *Porites* corals. This more elaborate kind of *marae* construction was typical of the Tupauruuru complex.

The greatest elaborations in *marae* architecture occurred in the early to mid-eighteenth century when stepped *ahu* appeared, as did the use of pecked volcanic cobbles, architectural elaborations associated with the ʻOro cult. The ʻOro war cult had spread from the leeward islands of Borabora and Raʻiatea to Moʻorea and Tahiti during the late seventeenth and early eighteenth centuries. The leading chiefs of Tahiti and Moʻorea had then adopted ʻOro worship, which included human sacrifice as well as elaborate investiture ceremonies involving red feather loincloths (*maro ʻura*). Our precise coral dating of *marae* architecture on Moʻorea—including the construction of the coastal *marae* with their massive *ahu*—reflects the ascendancy of this religious cult and the increased competition between chiefly lineages for political hegemony.

In September 2009, I returned to Moʻorea to spend a few weeks with students from Berkeley's Integrative Biology Department who were carrying out independent research projects in island ecology and biogeography. (In keeping with my expanding research interests in ecology, I had recently taken up a dual appointment as professor of integrative biology and of anthropology.) At the beginning of October, Kahn arrived from Honolulu to join me. As we sat chatting, watching the sun set over Moʻorea's lagoon, our conversation turned to Roger Green, whose health we knew was failing. In August, Green had phoned me to say that he had been diagnosed with an aggressive form of cancer; the prognosis was not good.

Green had been a mentor to both of us. In 1969 Green had placed me, a mere freshman at Penn, together with graduate students Tom Riley and Gil Hendren in the Hālawa Valley. Later we collaborated on our *Hawaiki* book, of which he was so proud. When Kahn began to work in the ʻŌpūnohu in 2000, Green similarly reached out to her, helping fund her dissertation research through a private foundation he established.

The following day Kahn and I hiked up to the Tupauruuru complex. Leaving the trail, we made our way through tangles of *ʻieʻie* vines and *pūrau* to arrive at an overgrown cluster of *marae* enclosures lying directly below the towering cliffs. Green had found and mapped these temples in 1961. As we cut away the obscuring vegetation and measured the walls, I imagined young Roger Green in this place, directing his Tahitian assistants.

As the afternoon wore on heavy clouds obscured the peaks looming above us. The wind whistled through the crowns of majestic *mara* trees. Heavy raindrops thudded onto my clipboard. The place was alive with agitated energy. Were the spirits of Tupauruuru aware that, in far-off Aotearoa, the man who had brought their ancient *marae* to light lay dying? A strong gust knocked me off balance. I heard a cracking sound; a thick *mara* branch crashed down through the canopy next to me. "Let's get out of here," I called over to Kahn. Once it started to pour the streams would turn to torrents, possibly trapping us in the valley for the night. Slipping and sliding we made our way through the undergrowth down to the trail as the thunder pealed and sheets of rain drenched us.

Two days later, on October 4, 2009, Roger Green passed away. I like to think that as his spirit passed out of his body in Aotearoa it flew like a frigate bird across the wide ocean, *moana*, swooping down one last time over the ʻŌpūnohu, the place he loved so dearly. Then it would have flown on to his special spirit world, his Hawaiki.

CHAPTER TWENTY-ONE

Roots of Conflict
(Hawai'i and Maui, 2001–2009)

In early February 2001, the National Science Foundation (NSF) put out a call for proposals under a new program, Biocomplexity in the Environment, which would support research on "dynamically coupled human and natural systems." The program seemed to be a perfect fit with the research I had already been conducting on the relationships between people and island ecosystems, especially in Mangaia and Hawai'i. Moreover, it was generously funded. Why not submit a proposal, I asked myself. Nothing ventured, nothing gained.

Knowing that a successful application would have to be multidisciplinary, I immediately thought of Peter Vitousek across San Francisco Bay at Stanford University. I had met Vitousek—who, like me, grew up in the islands—during a sabbatical year at the Center for Advanced Study in the Behavioral Sciences at Palo Alto in 1996–1997. Vitousek worked on the flow of nutrients in Hawaiian ecosystems, something we could link to my own work on ancient Hawaiian agricultural systems.

I telephoned Vitousek and asked him, "Peter, have you seen this call for proposals in NSF's new program on human and natural systems?"

"Yes," came the reply. "I was just getting ready to call you myself." The two of us had already bandied about vague ideas of future collaboration. Now that a funding source was evident, we agreed to pursue the opportunity.

NSF's new Biocomplexity in the Environment program called for "quantitative modeling," meaning we would need someone who could bridge empirical fieldwork with theoretical models and computer simulation. Vitousek suggested that I contact Shripad Tuljapurkar, a population biologist about to join Stanford's Biology Department. As ignorant of Polynesian archaeology as I was of mortality and fertility schedules, Tuljapurkar was nonetheless intrigued by the larger issues of human population and landscape interaction that we wanted to tackle. Meanwhile, Vitousek called Oliver Chadwick, a "renegade" soil scientist at the University of California, Santa Barbara, who studied Hawaiian soils. A knowledge of Hawaiian soils would be critical to understanding how the intensive Hawaiian farming systems had operated.

I wanted to focus on Kahikinui, where over six years I had built up a database on Hawaiian land use and agriculture. Vitousek suggested that we also include the Kohala District of Hawai'i Island, where he and Chadwick had both been working. Kohala's broad leeward slopes had once been thickly inhabited by Native Hawaiians. As a Hawaiian proverb states, "*Le'i o Kohala i ka nuku na kānaka*" (Covered is Kohala with men to the very point of land).[1]

I was aware of Kohala's potential for studying traditional Hawaiian agriculture and land use. In 1968, Richard Pearson of the University of Hawai'i had discovered that a vast dryland field system once extended over leeward Kohala, which was densely planted in sweet potatoes, dryland taro, sugarcane, and other crops. This flourishing agricultural system was indelibly inscribed over the Kohala landscape by a reticulate grid of closely spaced, low stone-and-earth embankments bounding ancient fields. The field embankments were crosscut by curbstone-lined trails that run up- and downslope delineating *'ili* and *ahupua'a* boundaries.[2] Covering roughly sixty square kilometers, the Kohala field system is one of the most remarkable archaeological landscapes in all of Polynesia (Fig. 21.1).

Paul Rosendahl had mapped part of this grid of ancient garden walls and trails, along with residential features, in upland Lapakahi, for his University of Hawai'i doctoral dissertation. Rosendahl showed me—when I visited him in the field in the early 1970s—how the stone-and-earth embankments sometimes ran under, but at other times abutted with, the curbstone-lined trails.[3] I incorporated this Lapakahi evidence in my 1984 book *The Evolution of the Polynesian Chiefdoms*, using Rosendahl's map to define several phases of development in Kohala's agricultural landscape.[4] I showed how an early pattern of a few large fields was transformed over time into one with more fields of smaller and more uniform size, a process known as agricultural *intensification*, or increased production per unit area. Such intensification, I argued, was linked to the rise of stratified polities in Hawai'i. As the landscape was divided into a grid of increasingly uniform parcels, the *konohiki* or land managers were able to control production—and the collection of surplus—more efficiently.

In the late 1990s, Michael Graves of the University of Hawai'i had recommenced fieldwork in Kohala. Technological advances in global positioning (GPS) and geographic information systems (GIS) made it possible for Graves to survey on a larger regional scale. Teaming up with Thegn Ladefoged, an expert in GPS and GIS applications in archaeology, Graves investigated the field system over large parts of leeward Kohala.[5] Knowing of their work, Vitousek and I invited Graves and Ladefoged to join our project.

Our team drafted the NSF proposal, which focused on the intensive dryland agriculture that had underwritten the staple economies of the emerging archaic

Figure 21.1. The Kohala field system, covering sixty square kilometers, consists of a reticulate grid of earthen and stone embankments demarcating ancient sweet potato and taro fields, crosscut by stone-lined trails. A small part of the system is visible here, from the summit of Puʻu Kehena, as the late afternoon sun creates shadows behind the low embankments.

states of Hawaiʻi and Maui Islands in the centuries leading up to European contact. We argued that the development of these rain-fed agricultural landscapes was a key to understanding how Hawaiian society had been transformed from complex chiefdoms to archaic states. We would combine field studies of the agricultural systems and their "biogeochemical gradients" with computer simulations of agricultural production.

We argued that the lessons to be learned in Kohala and Kahikinui had implications beyond local history. Hawaiʻi was a kind of "model system," we wrote, for investigating linkages among population, land, intensive agriculture, and sociopolitical organization. The processes that had driven intensification and sociopolitical change in ancient Hawaiʻi might be broadly applicable to many other parts of the world. In short, Hawaiʻi was a microcosm of the world.

Our proposal, "Human Ecodynamics in the Hawaiian Ecosystem, 1200 to 200 Years before the Present," had to be approved by research administrators at five universities, a minor bureaucratic feat. I was sure that the competition for this major program would be stiff, steeling myself for a decision of "reject and resubmit." To our surprise and delight, four months later we were informed that the review panel had ranked our proposal as one of the highest. With a budget of $1.4 million it was by far the largest research grant I had ever received. Now, the challenge was to show that our multidisciplinary team could deliver the goods.

The two Jeeps crawled up a rarely used four-wheel drive track on the steep lava slopes below Puʻu Pane, a cinder cone perched at 3,900 feet in the Mahamenui region of Kahikinui. Sitting next to me was soil scientist Chadwick. Driving the Jeep behind us was Chadwick's postdoctoral student Tony Hartshorn. For the past few days we had been digging soil pits spaced out along two transects over the Kahikinui landscape. One transect—which Chadwick called our "chronosequence"—ran at an elevation of about 1,500 feet, allowing us to sample a variety of lava flows of different ages, holding elevation (and hence also rainfall) constant. Dave Sherrod of the U.S. Geological Survey had given us a copy of his map showing the ages of these flows. The second transect, the one we were now working on, was a "climo-sequence" running from the coast to the uplands, all on the same 226,000-year-old lava flow. It would show the effects of elevation—and increasing rainfall—on soil development, holding geological age constant.

Over the hum of the Jeep engine, Chadwick and I chatted about our sampling strategy. "I want to get as high up on the old Kula surface as we can this morning," Chadwick told me. "We got some good samples yesterday near the coast and in the intermediate zone. If we can sample a location up where the fog drip has a daily effect, we'll be able to determine how soils of the same age develop in relation to water input."

I nodded in agreement. "I'll get us as high as this road goes. Then we'll have to hike up the slopes on foot."

"How far upslope have you guys found evidence for Hawaiian habitation and cultivation?" Chadwick asked.

Over a number of years of walking the rugged lava landscape of Kahikinui, I had determined that the Native Hawaiian population had been densely concentrated in a zone between about 400 and 600 meters' elevation. "The main zone of intensive land use starts to peter out around 2,000 feet elevation," I replied. "Above that you get occasional small features, and virtually nothing at all above 3,000 feet."

Just why Hawaiian land use in Kahikinui had been narrowly concentrated in a band between 400 and 600 meters had been puzzling me. The reason for a lack of cultivation and permanent habitation *below* about 400 meters seemed obvious:

the lack of water, either for growing crops or for other human needs. But why had people not moved farther up the mountain slopes, above 900 meters? Fog drip and rainfall increase as one moves higher up the face of Haleakalā. Sweet potato, a crop originally domesticated in the Andes of South America, readily tolerates low nighttime temperatures. So why had the Hawaiian population not expanded farther inland, up to say 1,500 or even 2,000 meters? Had the process of inland expansion been truncated by the devastating effects of Western contact? Or was something else responsible?

Chadwick seemed to be reading my thoughts. "Over in Kohala," he said, "I've found that there is a nonlinear relationship between rainfall and soil nutrients. Instead of just declining gradually as rainfall increases, soil nutrients hit a threshold—an invisible cliff—at about 1,500 mm of annual rainfall. Above that rainfall level leaching increases dramatically and soil nutrients plummet."

"Right, Oliver," I responded. "I remember the diagram you showed us when the team met in Kohala earlier this year. It really looks like that threshold closely matches the upper limit of the Kohala field system. I hope that the soil samples Peter is collecting in Kohala this summer will allow us to see whether the field system had reached its physical limits to expansion."

The jeep track was about to cross a ravine where periodic flash floods had cut into the lava slope. The track was little used, and the tire ruts were partly obscured by thick lantana. Always cautious, I made sure I could see bare rock ahead for my vehicle's tires to grip onto. The Jeep lurched as I crossed the dip, but we made it over without mishap.

A couple of seconds later I heard the metallic crunch of steel on lava. Looking in my rear-view mirror I could see Hartshorn's Jeep stopped at a peculiar angle, the left front lower than the right. He had driven a few inches too far to the left, into the obscuring clump of lantana that hid a three-foot dropoff. The chassis of Hartshorn's vehicle rested on a lava shelf with the left wheel spinning in the air. It took us an hour to gather up lava rocks and build a platform under the wheel and then jack up the vehicle so he could get it back onto the track again. Fortunately, no serious damage was done.

We spent the rest of the day digging the last soil pit of our climo-sequence transect. That evening, over glasses of wine at the ʻUlupalakua Ranch field house, we continued our discussion about the interactions between rainfall and the geological age of the lava flows that Hawaiian farmers had cultivated. When Chadwick had started his research into Hawaiian soil genesis, he had not been thinking at all about ancient Hawaiian land use. He simply wanted to understand how soils develop over time. He was curious about the fundamental physical and chemical processes involved. The sequence of "pedogenesis" or soil formation that his field and laboratory research had unveiled, however, was now proving to be of critical significance in our efforts to explain why Hawaiian farmers had intensified their field systems across the mid-elevation slopes of leeward Kohala and in a similar band across the face of Haleakalā on Maui.

The key was the relationship between rainfall—which is correlated on the leeward sides of islands with elevation above sea level—and the geological age of the island surface. Given a lava flow of the same age, rock-derived nutrients in the soil that forms on the flow surface are progressively leached out as rainfall increases. Conversely, with a given rainfall level, soils on younger flows will have a higher nutrient value than those on older flows, where there has been more time for leaching to occur. In addition, rainfall was an essential variable for dryland (rainfed) farming. Sweet potato, for example, needs at least 760 mm of rain per year to grow but does not do well if rainfall is much higher than about 1,270 mm. Dryland taro prefers a somewhat higher rainfall range, up to as high as 2,500 mm annually.

"It seems that the Hawaiian farmers were looking for the right combination of soils and rainfall," I mused, sipping my wine as I looked out at Kahoʻolawe Island, illuminated by the light of a nearly full moon. "Kind of like Goldilocks," I said. "Not too old, not too wet, but *just* right."

Chadwick chuckled. "Yeah. They were after the sweet spot."

Over the next two years, our team teased out the relationships among soils, rainfall, and the archaeological evidence for intensive cultivation in Kahikinui and Kohala. Chadwick and Hartshorn's analyses of the soil samples from our Kahikinui transects showed that the Hawaiian farmers had indeed found the "sweet spot" that ran right across the face of Haleakalā, between about 400 and 600 meters' elevation.[6] Edward Craighill Handy had called this "the greatest continuous dry planting area in the Hawaiian Islands."[7] Vitousek summed it up during one of our team meetings: The Hawaiians were "farming the rock," he said. Not the youngest rock, of course, but lava flows of the right age that had abundant nutrients, located within the right rainfall range.

The sweet spot running across the face of Maui's great volcano was not uniform in its soil properties. The best soils for sweet potato cultivation were on lava flows with ages of between about 25,000 and perhaps 100,000 years. Younger surfaces, such as the 10,000-year-old Alena flow, were simply too rocky, with little fine sediment in which sweet potato tubers could grow. In contrast, older flows such as the 226,000-year-old Kula surface, which makes up most of the land in the eastern part of Kahikinui, had good tilth (workability) but significantly reduced nutrients. Although easy to work with using a digging stick, those older soils would not have supported intensive cropping, year after year.

These results went a long way toward explaining the settlement pattern that my doctoral student Lisa Holm had uncovered in her survey of two large tracts in Mahamenui and Manawainui in eastern Kahikinui.[8] Unlike Kīpapa, where habitation sites and *heiau* were densely concentrated on lava flows of between 25,000 and 50,000 years old, in Holm's survey areas sites were far fewer and more dispersed. This suggested a lower population density on the older land surfaces. Radiocarbon dates from Holm's test pits confirmed that eastern Kahikinui had not been farmed until roughly the final century prior to European contact. Aware that these older soils were not as fertile (something they may have discovered through trial and error), the Hawaiian farmers avoided them until the crunch of growing population finally made it necessary to expand onto those lands.

Over in Kohala, Vitousek had collected soil samples along five parallel transects running from *mauka-to-makai* across the Kohala field system. Plotting out the values for soil nutrients in relation to the ancient field system, it became clear that the Kohala farmers had likewise found their sweet spot for sweet potato farming. The *makai* edge of the field system closely followed the 750 mm rainfall isohyet; below this it would have been too dry to grow *'uala*. The field system's upper boundary corresponded with rainfall of between 1,500–2,000 mm, the "threshold" where soil nutrients drop off precipitously.

The implication was obvious: The Hawaiians in Kohala had extended their vast field system over the full extent of terrain suitable for intensive agriculture, pushing the system to its geographic limits.[9] This confirmed what I had long suspected but had not been able to prove—that by around AD 1600 "nearly all suitable land" on Hawai'i Island had been brought under intensive cultivation, not only in Kohala but also in other regions such as Kona and Ka'ū.[10] Having reached the limits of dryland cultivation, I surmised that the Hawaiians worked these field systems harder and harder during the seventeenth and eighteenth centuries, partly driven by increasing chiefly demands for tribute, especially in the form of sweet potatoes and pigs.

Our new evidence indicated that the field systems had been heavily intensified during the two centuries prior to European contact. In Kohala our team dug trenches across field embankments, obtaining samples from open field plots and from undisturbed soils capped by the stone-and-earthen embankments. Vitousek and his student Molly Meyer analyzed pairs of soil samples from under the embankments and in the fields, finding that the samples from the cultivated plots had significantly reduced nutrient values.[11] Hartshorn, Chadwick, and I found similar evidence for nutrient depletion in intensively gardened areas in Kahikinui.[12] This quantitative evidence supported my hypothesis that yields—and most likely available surplus—had been declining on Hawai'i and Maui Islands prior to European contact. Such declining surplus could have been a major impetus to inter-island conflicts. Hawaiian oral traditions indicated that wars between the islands became increasingly common in the seventeenth and eighteenth centuries, especially between the Hawai'i and Maui kingdoms.

Not all of the Hawai'i Biocomplexity Project's work was focused on soils. Tuljapurkar and his postdoc Charlotte Lee developed a computer model of sweet potato production in the Hawaiian field systems. Computer modeling allows one to run thousands of simulations, exploring how slight differences in rainfall or variations in soil nutrients would have affected crop yields. The simulations gave us a better idea of the spatial variation within the sweet spot of the Kohala field system, revealing differences between its core and marginal parts. 'Uala production would have varied substantially from year to year, depending on rainfall. In wet years farmers could have expanded their gardens *makai,* whereas in drier years only the higher elevation gardens would have yielded crops. To deal with this risk, the Hawaiian farmers had used a "bet-hedging" strategy, planting crops at both lower and higher elevations, a strategy that matched their territorial pattern of long, narrow *ahupua'a.*

In 2004 we published our initial conclusions in the international journal *Science.* Observing that intensive, rain-fed field systems such as those of Kohala and Kahikinui were largely confined to the geologically younger islands of Hawai'i and Maui, whereas the older islands such as O'ahu and Kaua'i boasted large areas of irrigated taro lands, we wrote:

> The resulting contrast in the agricultural bases of societies on the younger versus older islands (rain-fed dryland versus irrigated wetland) influenced the archipelago-wide pattern of sociopolitical complexity that emerged late in Hawaiian prehistory. In comparison to irrigated wetlands, dryland agricultural systems are more labor-intensive, yield smaller surpluses, and are more vulnerable to climatic perturbations—features that probably contributed to the development of the aggressive and expansive chiefdoms that arose on the younger islands.[13]

In other words, the very nature of Hawaiian sociopolitical organization was closely linked to the agricultural potential of older and younger landscapes. Other articles presented the details of the Kahikinui investigations and the computer simulations.[14]

With these publications in prestigious journals our team confidently reapplied in late 2004 to NSF's Biocomplexity Program for a second phase of research. But in spite of all the successes of our first phase, NSF turned us down. The NSF administrators wanted "new" projects, they said. To me this reflected the short-sightedness of government bureaucrats, abandoning a productive research endeavor before its full potential had been achieved. Fortunately, during a meeting at NSF headquarters in Washington, DC, the director of a different program, Human Social Dynamics, approached Vitousek, encouraging us to submit a proposal. In late 2006 we received funding through that program for another three years of research.

It was important to delve more deeply into the relationships between the demography of Kohala's ancient farmers and the process of agricultural intensification. This required getting a better handle on the long-term history of population growth and obtaining information about how the region's economy had operated at the household level. I suggested that we apply the approach of "household archaeology," which I had pioneered in Kahikinui. By sampling residential sites in Kohala, we would be able to estimate the number of households over time; their relative status; their access to marine resources, domestic pigs, and dogs; and other aspects of their social and economic life. This new research direction also pushed Tuljapurkar and his team to develop new theoretical models linking agricultural production with the key variables of human demography, fertility, and mortality. Theory would meet history when we attempted to test the predictions from these models with our archaeological data.

In early 2007, around the same time that we received word that the NSF would support another three years of our project, I was faced with a major career decision. Yale University had discreetly approached me, asking whether I would leave Berkeley to join its Anthropology Department. There were both "push" and "pull" reasons to take this overture seriously. While Berkeley had been suffering from declining financial support from the State of California, privately endowed Yale was hiring top faculty and building new facilities. Yale was willing to equip a state-of-the-art laboratory designed to my specifications.

I had also become disillusioned with the way in which the sociocultural anthropologists at Berkeley had jumped onto the "postmodernist" bandwagon. The older cohort of scientifically oriented anthropologists who had once put Berkeley in the top academic ranks—scholars such as Elizabeth Colson, Brent Berlin, Gene Hammel (all members of the National Academy of Sciences), and others—had retired. Those now in control no longer regarded anthropology as a holistic science of human evolution and culture. Instead, they viewed the goal of anthropology as the "critique of science." One senior Berkeley professor went so far as to inform his graduate students that *nothing* written prior to 1986 (the year in which George

Marcus and James Clifford published an influential postmodern critique of ethnography[15]) was worth reading! How absurd, I thought to myself when I heard this, to dismiss out-of-hand the incredibly rich and nuanced ethnography of someone like Raymond Firth, whose writings on the Tikopia had been such an inspiration to me during my own fieldwork. Or the writings of Bronislaw Malinowski, Ward Goodenough, or even Marshall Sahlins, to name just a few scholars whose cumulative research provides the foundation for our understanding of Oceanic cultures. Although my archaeology colleagues at Berkeley had not gone quite this far, some were also flirting with postmodern, "interpretive" approaches. I found it disturbing when I heard from the graduate student teaching assistants that some of these colleagues denigrated or mocked scientific archaeology and an evolutionary approach in their lectures.

I phoned Berkeley's Dean of Social Science, George Breslauer, telling him we needed to meet. A respected political scientist, Breslauer was aware of the intellectual tensions in anthropology. In his cramped Campbell Hall office I told Breslauer of the Yale offer and of my frustrations at Berkeley. "You're one of our stars, Pat," Breslauer told me. "We don't want to lose you. Would you be happier in another department?" I decided to pursue the opening Breslauer had just broached.

Ever since the Mangaia project (see Chapter Seventeen), and increasingly with the Hawai'i Biocomplexity Project, my research had become closely entwined with that of colleagues in ecology, palynology, botany, paleontology, and related fields. I met with David Lindberg, a senior professor of paleontology in Berkeley's Department of Integrative Biology. Over coffee at the Free Speech Cafe, Lindberg urged me to shift my faculty position over to Integrative Biology. "We're very open intellectually," Lindberg told me. "I think my colleagues would be happy to have you join us."

I arranged to give an afternoon lecture to the Integrative Biology faculty and students. Soon after they voted unanimously to make me a full member of their department. I politely informed Yale that I was declining its offer. In the end, I decided to retain a 25 percent appointment in the Department of Anthropology, because I still had graduate students housed there. I also kept my lab in the Archaeological Research Facility. But the appointment in Integrative Biology allowed me to develop new courses, such as Human Biogeography of the Pacific and a worldwide review called Holocene Paleoecology: How Humans Changed the Earth. I also became a member of the team-taught intensive field course in Geomorphology and Biogeography of Tropical Islands, taking small groups of students to the Richard Gump Research Station on Mo'orea Island in French

Polynesia. I am grateful that even as anthropology was becoming increasingly narrow-minded and antiscience, my colleagues in the biological sciences were happy to open up their department to an anthropologically trained archaeologist.

The morning United Airlines flight from San Francisco to Kona descended low over 'Upolu Point on its final approach to Keāhole. From my window I could see the red cinder cone of Pu'u 'Ula'ula, along with Kamilo Bay to the south. It was early June 2007. A few days earlier our team had begun work there; I wondered what they were finding.

Julie Field met me at Keāhole Airport. I tossed my bags in the back of the Ford F150 pickup and hopped into the cab. I had hired Field as a postdoc under the new NSF grant; her task was to lead the excavations in Kohala. Field, who had finished her PhD at the University of Hawai'i the previous year, was eager to apply our strategy of household archaeology in Kohala.

"I think you're going to like the site we're digging," Field said as we headed up the Ka'ahumanu Highway toward Kohala. "It's a stone enclosure with adjoining U-shaped structure that might have been a canoe shed. There's some branch coral on it. I think the enclosure might have been a fishing shrine."

"Or, maybe a men's house," I replied. "Or both. Those functions weren't necessarily mutually exclusive."

Arriving in Makiloa ahupua'a, Field put the Ford into four-wheel drive and headed down a rutted track. A few minutes later Field pulled up next to a grove of kiawe trees. It was baking hot there on the leeward coast, an abrupt transition from the foggy Bay Area I had left a few hours earlier. The dry air sucked the moisture from my skin. I slathered on sunscreen, then walked over to see what Kathy Kawelu was finding. Kawelu had recently finished her dissertation under my direction at Berkeley and was helping Field with the excavations. Kneeling in a test pit inside the enclosure, Kawelu pointed to the outlines of a stone-lined fire pit. She pointed out the pieces of branch coral set on and into the walls, likely evidence of ritual use.[16]

Getting out of the test pit, Kawelu dumped the contents of a plastic bucket into her screen, shaking it vigorously. The powdery sediment rapidly passed through the 1/8-inch mesh, a size considered standard in archaeological work. I could see many mollusk shells in the screen, along with some basalt flakes. There were *Nerita, Drupa,* and *Cypraea* shells, as well as fragments of the prized 'opihi limpets (*Cellana*). But no fishbones. "Have you been recovering much fishbone, Kathy?" I asked, puzzled.

"None at all," came the reply. "That's crazy," I said. "We're just a few feet from the shore. There ought to be fishbone in this deposit."

"Well, we haven't found any so far, Uncle Pat." Kawelu, born and raised in Keaukaha, Hawai'i, like many Native Hawaiians had fit me into her "fictive kinship" system, calling me "Uncle."

"Wait a minute. Lift up that screen. I want to take a look at the dirt pile." I poked at the dirt with a *kiawe* twig. Sure enough, there were a few tiny fishbones, so small that they had passed right through the sieve. "Look at this," I said, handing Kawelu a tiny bone just a few millimeters across. "It's the pharyngeal grinding plate from a parrotfish. But it's so small that the whole fish can't have been longer than my hand." *Uhu* are often a foot to two feet in length, so we were dealing with the remains of really small fish here.

"OK, on the way back to the field house this afternoon we're going to stop at the hardware store to buy some window screen," I told Field. "That's the only way we are going to get an adequate sample of these tiny fishbones."

With our new sieves fitted with window screen, we started recovering lots of tiny fishbones—more than 84,000 of them before we were finished—along with abundant mollusk and sea urchin remains. The Hawaiians inhabiting leeward Kohala had heavily exploited their inshore marine environment. Barely a half-million years old, the Kohala coastline, with its low, rocky cliffs indented here and there by small bays, lacks a true reef. Coral heads dot the offshore rocky bottom, providing food for herbivores such as parrotfish and wrasses. But the biomass that can be supported on this kind of incipient reef is much lower than for a more mature reef such as is found along the leeward coast of Moloka'i or around much of O'ahu and Kaua'i.

The large population that had once occupied leeward Kohala, supported primarily by the intensive cultivation of sweet potatoes, had to depend largely on this immature reef ecosystem for its supply of protein. The farmers did raise pigs and dogs—we found the bones of these domestic animals in our excavations—but most of those animals were destined for the households of the *ali'i* and *konohiki* or were consumed at special temple ceremonies. For their daily *i'a*, their flesh food to accompany their staple *'ai* of sweet potato and taro, the commoners had to harvest fish and shellfish. With a population that likely exceeded twenty thousand in the century prior to Captain Cook's arrival, the pressure on leeward Kohala's delicate inshore marine ecosystem was intense.

The minute fishbones in the Makiloa men's house were just the first of many discoveries that we made over the course of three summers of fieldwork between 2007 and 2009. We sampled household sites in two areas, each with both coastal and inland components. One set of sites was located in the adjacent *ahupua'a* of Kaiholena and Makeanehu. Tuljapurkar and Lee's computer model indicated that these *ahupua'a* were within the central core of the Kohala field system, with the most productive lands and least risk of crop failure due to drought. Our second set of sites was in the Kalala, Makiloa, and Pahinahina *ahupuaʻa*, near the southern margins of the field system where the risks of periodic drought were greater. Comparing household sites between the core and the periphery of the field system, we hoped to see differences in the local economies. After Thegn Ladefoged and his students from the University of Auckland conducted GPS surveys of the archaeological features within each sample area, Field and I selected sites to excavate. By the end of the 2009 field season we had dug in fifty-seven precontact residential features, sufficient to give us a statistically valid sample of house sites in two study areas.

While Field and I worked on the household excavations, Tuljapurkar and his team fine-tuned their new models linking agricultural food production to key variables in human demography, especially fertility and mortality. Central to their work was the concept of "food availability."[17] When the Hawaiians had first settled an area such as leeward Kohala, population density was low and land was freely available. The main limiting factor to food production would have been available labor to clear, plant, and tend the fields. Several centuries later, after the population had grown to thousands of individuals, suitable land for farming—not labor—was now the limiting factor. Thus, as population density increased and the limiting factor shifted from labor to land, food availability would have decreased, as more and more mouths had to be fed on a finite amount of arable land. Another way of putting this is that over time people became increasingly hungry more often. And as food availability decreased, feedback loops would have affected women's fertility at the same time that they increased the death rate among the most vulnerable: infants and the elderly.

Tuljapurkar's postdoc Cedric Puleston ran computer simulations using the new models. I was fascinated by the nonlinear trends they projected. Such nonlinearity is, after all, what makes the study of "dynamically coupled" human and natural systems so intriguing. The model simulations predicted that population growth in an area such as leeward Kohala would have initially followed an exponential growth rate, with population sizes doubling over short time intervals. Simultaneously, the food availability ratio would have declined, following a negative exponential curve. As the food ratio approached and then dropped below a value of 1 (the equilibrium point at which the population replaces itself without growing or declining), the negative consequences for fertility and mortality would have kicked in, slowing the rate of population growth dramatically. Although this may have kept the population in balance with the agricultural system's capacity to produce food, the final outcome would have been a population constantly on the margins of hunger.

Mulling over these results, I recalled the Hawaiian *moʻolelo* or traditions that spoke of repeated attempts by the Hawaiʻi and Maui kings to break out of their island kingdoms, to conquer new lands where their people would have better farming land and resources. I had long been intrigued by the fact that it was the Maui and Hawaiʻi polities that had been the most aggressive and warlike in precontact Hawaiʻi. I thought that our new models revealed some of the complex dynamics that lay behind this political history.

Field's painstaking excavations in the sample of household sites allowed us to test Tuljapurkar's and Puleston's computer simulations. Radiocarbon dates from a series of habitation sites confirmed that there had been exponential population increase in leeward Kohala over a 400-year period. The maximum population had been reached between AD 1650–1800, just prior to European contact.[18] But within the core of the field system (the Kaiholena-Makeanehu area) the population reached its peak earlier, by about AD 1650. Continued population growth had been absorbed by expanding the Kohala system into marginal zones, including the Kalala-Makiloa-Pahinahina area to the south. The intensive agricultural system of Kohala had, in its late stages, been pushed to its limits.

The theoretical models that we tested in Kohala with empirical, archaeological data were not just academic exercises. In fact, they are central to a debate that has raged in Western intellectual circles ever since Thomas Malthus published his provocative *Essay on the Principle of Population* in 1798.[19] Malthus observed that, whereas the natural reproductive potential of humans is geometric—as in the series 1, 2, 4, 8, 16—the ability of food production systems to increase output is arithmetic, as in 1, 2, 3, 4, 5. All things being equal, human population growth will inevitably outstrip our ability to feed the exponentially increasing mouths. Using European history as his gauge, Malthus argued that disease, starvation, pestilence, and ultimately war were the forces that kept human numbers in check. Malthus's *Essay* had a major influence on Charles Darwin's thinking, contributing to the latter's theory of natural selection.

But Malthus always has had his detractors, those who argue that human creativity and innovation can blunt the Malthusian "scissors" as they slice away the excess population. Economist Ester Boserup argued in her widely read 1965 book, *The Conditions of Agricultural Growth*, that population growth was in itself a powerful force driving agrarian innovation.[20] Her theory seemed to be borne out by the so-called Green Revolution in which high-yielding rice, wheat, and other crop varieties developed through new genetic technology dramatically boosted world harvests (until those gains leveled off, as they now have). The debate over the limits to population growth was most famously played out in the 1980 wager between Stanford ecologist Paul Ehrlich (author of *The Population Bomb*) and economist Julian Simon.[21] That Simon won the $1,000 bet emboldened many conservative economists, strengthening their anti-Malthusian views.

Our Hawai'i Biocomplexity Project research in Kohala and Kahikinui tested the Malthus-Boserup models with empirical data spanning four centuries in the "model system" of Hawai'i. Both Malthus and Boserup were partly right and partly wrong. Malthus's insight that the human potential to reproduce outstrips the pace of agricultural production is correct. At the same time, humans do have an amazing capacity to innovate. In Kohala, this capacity was evident in the highly intensive field system that the Hawaiian farmers developed over more than sixty square kilometers. But there *are* limits to innovation. The Hawaiians were discovering those limits in the late eighteenth century, as their soils were increasingly depleted of nutrients, as they pushed their fields to the maximum. Their chiefs sought solutions in wars of conquest and territorial acquisition. There are lessons in the story of what transpired in late precontact Hawai'i if we care to heed them—lessons from the model system of the Earth's most isolated archipelago.

In the late 1960s, Roger Green's settlement pattern approach moved archaeology in Hawai'i and the Pacific out of an older "culture history" paradigm, launching a new period of research into island societies. The Hawai'i Biocomplexity Project in a similar way took Hawaiian archaeology to a new level, creating another paradigm shift centered on the dynamic interactions between human populations and their ecosystems. Our team demonstrated how multidisciplinary research—with archaeology as a core integrating discipline—can develop and test models with implications that extend beyond the histories of individual islands. It is not too much to claim that the linkages among population, agriculture, food, and society that the Hawai'i Biocomplexity Project has addressed are directly relevant to problems that have beset humanity for the last ten thousand years and that will become even more crucial in the decades that lie ahead.

CHAPTER TWENTY-TWO

The Sun Sets at Ana Tetea
(Mangareva Islands, 2001–2014)

From the pressurized cabin of the Air Tahiti turboprop cruising at 20,000 feet, the sparkling bands of coral reefs encircling Marokau and Ravahere atolls in the central Tuamotu Archipelago looked like strings of pearls cast on shimmering blue velvet. We would soon land for refueling at Hao atoll and then continue on to Mangareva, the most southeasterly island in French Polynesia. Also known as the Gambier Archipelago, Mangareva consists of fourteen small volcanic islets all enclosed within a single barrier reef and lagoon.

Almost seven decades earlier, when the only way to travel between these islands had been by boat, the Bishop Museum's chartered sampan *Islander* had made the same voyage, from Tahiti via the Tuamotus to Mangareva. During my youthful apprenticeship with Yoshio Kondo I had been steeped in the lore of the museum's 1934 Mangarevan Expedition (see Chapter Two). It was on the *Islander* that Kondo had met malacologist and expedition leader C. Montague Cooke Jr., whose life's desire had been to collect the endemic land snails of the remote islands of southeastern Polynesia. When the *Islander* arrived at Mangareva on May 23, 1934, Cooke and the other scientists accompanying him soon had their hopes dashed. Cooke later wrote that "Mangareva proved to be the most disappointing place on our entire trip . . . . All the endemic forests have disappeared, and with them the native fauna." Nonetheless, Cooke found sediments containing abundant subfossil land snail shells. Cooke surmised that "these fossil beds . . . represent lowland fauna that probably existed after the arrival of the Polynesians."[1]

Also participating in the Mangarevan Expedition were ethnologist Te Rangi Hiroa and archaeologist Kenneth Emory. Hiroa gleaned what he could about traditional cultural practices from a population that had been oppressed for a century by Catholic missionaries.[2] For his part, Emory was as disappointed in the poverty of Mangarevan archaeology as Cooke had been in the devastation of the island's biota. Emory complained about "the complete disappearance of all important structures in the Mangarevan group," due to the zeal of the infamous Père Laval, who had ripped up stones from the island's *marae* to build his cathedral at Rikitea and other churches.[3] Emory did discover some rockshelters, especially on the uninhabited islet of Agakauitai, that contained evidence of ancient Polynesian occupation. But unfamiliar with stratigraphic excavation and lacking the yet-to-be-invented method of radiocarbon dating, Emory merely shoveled out the shelters' deposits in a crude hunt for fishhooks and adzes.

A quarter-century later, in 1959, Roger Green arrived in Mangareva for his first Polynesian fieldtrip, having been sent there by Harry Shapiro of the American Museum of Natural History in New York. On Kamaka and Aukena Islands (Map 8), Green dug in several rockshelters. Carefully following the stratigraphic layers that Emory had ignored, Green put the different kinds of fishhooks and adzes into a chronological sequence. Using the then-new radiocarbon dating method, Green determined that Mangareva had been settled by at least AD 1200.[4]

Now, in November 2001, I was on my way to pick up where Green had left off. With me were Eric Conte of the Université de Polynésie Française, Atholl Anderson of the Australian National University, and Marshall Weisler of the University of Otago in New Zealand. During a conference on the status of archaeology in French Polynesia that Conte and I had organized at the Gump Station on Mo'orea the previous year, the newly appointed minister of culture, Louise Peltzer, asked us what we regarded as the highest priority for new research. We had pointed to Mangareva, and Minister Peltzer agreed to fund a month of fieldwork. I especially wanted to unravel the history of human-environment interactions that had most likely created the devastated ecosystem witnessed by the Mangarevan Expedition in 1934.

We had chosen November and December because this was the only time we could all get free of our academic duties. Unfortunately, this proved to be the rainiest time of the year in Mangareva, when the Intertropical Convergence Zone sags southward and engulfs the islands. Each day we would return from our surveys thoroughly soaked from the incessant rain squalls. The cramped A-frame cabin we shared at Benoit and Bianca Uari'i's *pension,* littered with sweat-soaked clothes that would not dry, smelled like a high-school locker room. Nonetheless, we were finding little pieces in a larger puzzle that would eventually take me more than a decade to put together.

We began by coring along transects in Rikitea, the main village, looking for buried sites. The main population center when Europeans arrived in the early nineteenth century, Rikitea boasts a wide coastal plain backed by fertile mountain slopes fronting the protected lagoon. It was the ideal place for the first Polynesians to have settled. Unfortunately, what was probably ideal for the island's first settlers remained the best place for the modern population to concentrate. Today, Rikitea—the administrative center and main village of the Gambier Islands—is

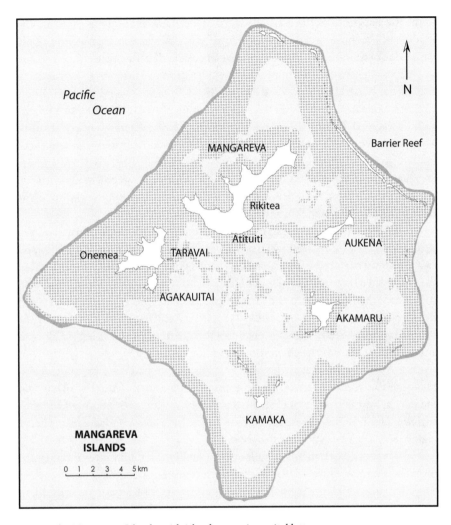

Map 8. The Mangareva Islands, with island names in capital letters.

home to a little more than one thousand people. A concrete surfaced road runs the length of the village; on either side of the road are neatly kept compounds with wooden or concrete houses, interspersed with a few small stores, along with the medical clinic, gendarmerie, *Mairie* (Mayor's offices), and so forth. Not exactly an ideal landscape to search for archaeological remains.

The bit of our auger did bring up charcoal from a layer near the cathedral, later radiocarbon dated to AD 1160–1220. Clearly, there once had been early settlements in the Rikitea area. But the densely packed modern houses, outhouses, sheds, and roads in Rikitea made it nearly impossible to find open spaces to excavate. We would have to look elsewhere for undisturbed evidence of early settlement.

Across the island at Atiaoa, in Gatavake District, we discovered a promising rockshelter.[5] Our test pit exposed layers filled with fishbone and shellfish. Charcoal from an earth oven would later give us a date of AD 1280–1300. In a nearby valley I mapped the remains of an irrigation system and some house platforms. More evidence of once intensive land use turned up at Atituiti, on the southern flank of Auorotini (Mt. Duff), Mangareva's highest peak. There we found stone-faced terraces, the remnants of an intensive horticultural system, along with terraced house sites. I had to use sheets of waterproof plastic vellum on my plane table so that I could map the ruins in the incessant rain.

At Atituiti we came across an imposing square *paepae* or platform, twenty-three meters on a side, well faced with large basalt boulders on the north and east. The level surface of the *paepae* was paved with smooth, flattish cobbles; in the center sat a large rectangular boulder, perhaps weighing a half-ton (Fig. 22.1). It had been hauled up onto the *paepae,* probably for use as a seat. Emory had mentioned such "stone seats" (*'akapua*) used by chiefs and priests. When the British explorer Beechy visited Mangareva in 1826, the island's "king" led him to a stone seat in front of the chief's house at Marau-Tagaroa.[6]

The Atituiti *paepae* was the largest structure we had seen on Mangareva. Mapping the boulder facade with my plane table and alidade, I realized that the *paepae* was laid out along cardinal directions. When not obscured by invasive Java plum trees, the *paepae* originally must have commanded a magnificent view over Mangareva's southern lagoon.

As I trudged back to Rikitea along the muddy track that afternoon, I kept thinking that the name—Atituiti—sounded familiar. A couple of years earlier, while writing my *Hawaiki* book with Roger Green (see Chapter Fifteen), I had reviewed the ethnographic literature on Polynesian calendars and timekeeping, including Père Laval's account of how the Mangarevan priests had calibrated their lunar calendar by observing the solstices. Elsewhere in Polynesia timekeeping was done by observing the rising and setting of the star cluster Pleiades, Mataliki in Polynesian. It was essential to recalibrate the lunar calendar each year to keep it in sync with the solar year. I now remembered that I had seen the name Atituiti in Laval's account of Mangarevan observation of the solstice.

Benoit Uari'i had a copy of Père Laval's book on ancient Mangareva at the *pension.* Pulling the tome off the bookshelf, I searched for the passage that I vaguely remembered. On page 213 I found the text where Laval described how Atituiti had been an observatory where the priests watched the annual winter solstice.[7] The

Figure 22.1. The massive stone seat on the paved surface of the *paepae* at Atituiti, Mangareva. Here the priests sat to observe the solstice sunset and to predict the coming breadfruit harvest.

priest, Laval wrote, had been seated on a large, flat stone, watching the setting winter sun as it appeared to sink into the mountain peak on the islet of Agakauitai. At the foot of the high cliff below the peak was a burial cave, Ana Tetea, where the mummified bodies of two famous chiefs, Te Akarikitea and Te Akarikipagu, had lain.

During my years of fieldwork in Kahikinui, I had come to appreciate that the Hawaiian priests had been close observers of the heavens, using *heiau* as sites for astronomical observations (see Chapter Eighteen). Now in Mangareva we had stumbled upon another site that evidenced Polynesian astronomical practices. Over a dinner of sashimi and rice served up by Bianca, I shared Laval's passage about Atituiti with my companions. They agreed that the *paepae* likely had some special significance, but not everyone was willing to admit that it might have been the solstice observatory described by Laval. Eric Conte, especially, was dubious.

Unfortunately, the field of archaeoastronomy, the study of ancient people's astronomical knowledge and practices as revealed through archaeology, has attracted so much unscientific speculation by amateur practitioners that many scholars regard it as the realm of crackpots. I could see that it was going to take more careful work to support my hypothesis that the Atituiti *paepae* was indeed the ancient solstice observatory described by Laval.

Toward the end of our trip, we made plans to visit Kamaka Island, where Roger Green had first excavated in 1959. Tihoni Reasin, then the fourteen-year old son of an American photographer who had married into a French Polynesian family, had accompanied Green on that expedition. Reasin's family had inherited uninhabited Kamaka from a maiden aunt whose French father, a pearl trader, had purchased the islet in the nineteenth century. Later, Reasin returned to Kamaka to live—a sort of Mangarevan Robinson Crusoe—in a cluster of houses partly within the rockshelter that he and Green had named "Kitchen Cave."

I met Reasin in 2001 when he came over from Kamaka to visit Rikitea Village. When I told him that Green had been my mentor, Reasin agreed to our reopening the old excavations on Kamaka. Arranging boat transport there with a pearl farmer, we found that the heavy rains had flooded the floor of Kitchen Cave. So we turned to a smaller rockshelter, Green's site GK-2, digging the backfill out of Green's test pit and then excavating a column through the sediments. Although this excavation was limited, it allowed us to reexamine the site's stratigraphy and obtain charcoal from the different layers to date the age of the deposits.

Flying out of Mangareva several days later, I gazed down at Kamaka as the turboprop circled and climbed toward Tahiti. Emory might have been disappointed with Mangarevan archaeology in 1934, but I realized that we had barely scratched the surface.

In August 2003 Eric Conte and I returned to Mangareva, again funded by the French Polynesian ministry of culture. My first priority was to investigate the Atituiti *paepae* to determine whether it had indeed been the solstice observatory mentioned by Père Laval. After settling in at Benoit and Bianca's *pension*, we began work at the *paepae*. We dug a three-meter trench into the platform's western side, but there was no datable charcoal in the fill. Next we cleaned off a nine-square-meter area adjacent to the stone seat, exposing the pavement. Digging into the sediment beneath and between the paving stones, I found carbonized pieces of candlenut shell, *Pandanus*, and some *ti* stem, all plants used by the Polynesians. We later radiocarbon dated the *ti* to AD 1430–1470, well before European contact.

While the excavations were ongoing, I took precise compass bearings from the *paepae* to prominent points on the several islets visible from this vantage point on the slopes of Auorotini. A priest seated on the stone slab in the middle of the platform would have had an unobstructed view over the Mangareva lagoon from due east (90°) to about 260°, just short of due west, a perfect viewplane for solstice observations.[8]

Laval had written that from the Atituiti "observatory" the austral summer solstice was marked by the sun setting into the high cliff of Ana Tetea on Agakauitai. I took sightings from the *paepae* to all of the landmarks visible on the islets from Akamaru to Taravai, recording their azimuth and altitude to within 0.5 degrees, which allowed me to calculate the declination of each point. These could be compared to the declination of the setting sun during the austral summer solstice, a value that I calculated using an astronomical software program. On December 21, 1834 (the year that Père Laval arrived in Mangareva), the sun would have set at a declination of -23.2, the same declination of the cliff of Ana Tetea. Indeed, from the priest's position on the *paepae,* the solar disc would have merged with the tip of Agakauitai Island. This convergence can hardly have been coincidence; I was convinced that we had indeed discovered the Atituiti solstice observatory.

There was a second piece of confirming data. Laval had mentioned that at midday on the austral winter solstice the high peak of Auorotini—which looms over Atituiti—casts its shadow onto a place called Te Rua Ra, "The Pit of the Sun." Observing this shadow, the priest would declare, *"Kua noʻo te ra i to te rua"* (The sun has come to rest in its pit). Calculations showed that on June 21, 1834, the sun, as viewed from the *paepae,* would have passed for about twenty minutes behind the peak of Auorotini, casting its shadow over Atituiti. Te Rua Ra was either the *paepae* or very close to it.

Why had the Mangarevan priests been so keen to observe the summer and winter solstices from Atituiti and similar observatories? The obvious reason was to annually recalibrate their lunar calendar. But Laval gives another reason, deeply linked to the Mangarevan economic system. The priests paid close attention to the way in which the sun arose from the horizon, whether it "detached crisply" or appeared to be enveloped in a "humid vapor." If the latter, the priests predicted that there would be rain and an abundant breadfruit harvest. But if the sun detached itself sharply from the horizon, drought was forecast, and a warning went forth that famine might ensue.

Confirming that the Atituiti *paepae* had been one of Mangareva's ancient solstice observatories was a high point of our 2003 expedition, but it was not our only significant discovery. After completing the work at Atituiti, Conte and I reconnoitered Agakauitai and Taravai Islands. Tiny Agakauitai was unoccupied, whereas Taravai had but three people living on it. On an unusually calm day, we circled both islands in a small boat, landing to make forays inland and examining rockshelters at the base of the cliffs. Putting in at a small bay called Onemea, on Taravai's southwestern coast, we tied the boat to a fallen coconut tree trunk and waded ashore. A steeply rising sand dune, mostly covered in *Pandanus* and *Hibiscus* shrubs, had been eroded at its base by periodic storm surges. Pulling out my trowel, I scraped away at the meter-high bank, revealing flecks of charcoal as well as pieces of shell and bone. The midden deposit looked like it might repay a test excavation.

We returned to Onemea for two days, digging two 1-meter test pits. The first pit, just inland of the eroded bank, produced only fire-cracked rock, some shell, and a little bone. We then moved to the top of the sand dune, about eighteen meters inland. Here the deposit was darker, with more charcoal. Then, the sediment abruptly changed color from dark gray to a reddish yellow. This sand, which seemed to be the original surface of the dune before people had started to live on it, was packed full of well-preserved bird bones. There were wing bones, leg bones, and a complete beak or rostrum. I immediately thought of the Tangata-tau rockshelter on Mangaia, where the deepest levels had also been thick with bird bones (see Chapter Seventeen). I collected a sample of charcoal from a thin lens at the interface between the beach sands and the gray cultural deposit, wondering whether the site might date back to the period of first Polynesian settlement.

A few months later, I received the results of accelerator mass spectrometry (AMS) radiocarbon dating from the Beta Analytic lab in Miami, Florida. The charcoal from the thin lens was dated to AD 945–1030. A second date, from one of the well-preserved bird bones, gave an identical age. These two samples confirmed that the Onemea sand dune dated to the time of initial Polynesian expansion into the southeastern Pacific.

The bird bones from Onemea were a significant discovery, because seabirds only occur in low numbers in Mangareva today. I sent the 153 bird bones from Test Pit 2 to Trevor Worthy and Alan Tennyson, avian specialists at the Te Papa National Museum in New Zealand. About one-third of the bones belonged to a species of petrel, in the genus *Pseudobulweria*. These seabirds are extremely rare in French Polynesia today. Yet at the time that Polynesians colonized Taravai these petrels were seemingly the most common species. There were also many bones of the Christmas Island shearwater (*Puffinus nativitatis*), the red-tailed tropicbird (*Phaethon rubricauda*), and the white tern (*Gygis alba*), along with less frequent bones of a few other seabirds. Although most of the bones were from seabirds, there were a few fragments of *Ducula*, a genus of large fruit pigeons, historically unknown in Mangareva. The fruit pigeon bones hinted that Mangareva, like other islands of tropical Polynesia, might once have been the home of endemic land birds.

Clearly, Onemea held important clues about what had happened in Mangareva to so decimate the islands' flora and fauna, leading to the extreme disappointment experienced by the 1934 Mangarevan Expedition scientists. But we would need to expand the excavations to obtain a larger sample and to date the site more thoroughly. Once again, Mangareva was calling me back.

Two years later, in August 2005, Conte and I again made the four-hour flight to Mangareva, accompanied by his graduate students, Emilie Dotte and Christelle Carlier. The Wenner-Gren Foundation for Anthropological Research in New York had agreed to fund this expedition. We arranged to stay in a small house owned by Mateo, a pearl farmer on the eastern side of Taravai Island. His half-brother Timeo Tu had an aluminum skiff powered by a 25 hp motor; it would allow us to get to Onemea each day.

The accommodations were rustic but adequate. There was rainwater from a tank, and we cooked on a kerosene stove. We took turns bathing out of a barrel of rainwater. The worst part of making the trip to the outhouse near the beach was avoiding Tu's pet geese, Romeo and Juliet. Romeo, very protective of his mate, had a nasty habit of charging and pecking at your feet. After I learned to arm myself with a broom, Romeo and I reached a cautious détente.

At Onemea, we cut a transect inland through the dense *purau* and then dug a series of test pits into the dune. These tests showed that the richest deposits were those near our 2003 Test Pit 2, the one that had produced the rich haul of bird bones. I laid out a one-by-three-meter trench, which Dotte and I excavated while Conte and Carlier dug more test pits to the west and east.[9]

Dotte and I dug for several days through the dark gray cultural deposit, with its intercutting pits and earth ovens, as well as some thin lenses of charcoal representing burn events. Carrying the buckets of dirt to the beach, we wet-screened the sediment through fine mesh to catch the thousands of small fish and bird bones. There were smaller numbers of bones from the Polynesian-introduced Pacific rat and, surprisingly, some pig bones. Pigs had not been present on Mangareva when Europeans arrived, but clearly they had once been raised on the islands. As in Mangaia and Tikopia, pigs had been eliminated prior to European arrival, probably due to competition with their human owners for the island's limited carbohydrate foods.

Approaching the reddish-yellow sands of Layer III, we began to find lots of bird bones, just as we had in 2003. In the top of Layer III, bird bones became abundant; we recovered more than one thousand of them during our 2005 excavations. These bones were again mostly of seabirds, but there were a few bones from the extinct pigeon and some of an extinct fruit dove. I was also finding thousands of tiny shells of endemic land snails, the kinds that malacologist Cooke had sought in 1934 but that are now entirely extinct in Mangareva. These native snails had clearly once been abundant at Onemea.

I needed to ascertain whether Layer III, so rich in bird bones, was a natural deposit or if it had accumulated after the arrival of the Polynesians. Excavating carefully down into the reddish-yellow sands, I found a dikestone flake and several fire-cracked oven stones, along with rat bones and the shells of a land snail called *Allopeas gracile*. Both the rat and the snail had been carried by the Polynesians as stowaways on their voyages. Also embedded within Layer III was a thin lens of carbonized material. Examining the fragments later under my microscope in Berkeley, I saw that they were burned fragments of *Pandanus* matting. These finds revealed that people had been present when the bird bones accumulated at the top of Layer III. This was confirmed when we examined the bird bones in my laboratory. Almost 90 percent of the bones exhibited fractures deriving from human butchering and eating. Large numbers of birds had been cooked and eaten at Onemea in the years following Polynesian settlement.

Radiocarbon dates confirmed that people first started visiting Onemea around AD 950, feasting on the nesting seabirds. Later, in the mid-fourteenth century, the dune surface had been used as a fishing camp, resulting in the dark gray Layer II midden containing a number of pearl-shell fishhooks.

After nearly three weeks of digging we were ready to close the excavations, satisfied that Onemea had opened a window onto the earliest period of Mangarevan history. On what was to be our second to last day, a strong *maragai* wind came up from the southwest. By early afternoon the coconut palms were swaying dramatically. Sand blowing up the dune slope blasted my eyes as I struggled to draw the stratigraphy in the main trench. Finishing my diagram, I told Conte that we should call it a day. We gathered up our tools and packs. Everyone climbed into the skiff, I cast off the line, Tu started the outboard, and we headed out of the bay.

Driven by the *maragai* wind, the deep lagoon off Taravai was running a three- to four-foot swell. With the wind hailing from sub-Antarctic waters, it was cold. We wrapped our parkas tight around us, waiting for the boat to round Taravai's northern point, bringing us into calmer lee waters. Just as we were about to make the turn, the outboard engine cut out. Tu frantically tried to restart it, without success. I could sense the worry on his furrowed face. "What's wrong?" I asked. "It's frozen," he replied. Then he sheepishly added, "I haven't put any oil in the engine for two years."

The strong wind and running swell were pushing us away from the island. The ebb tide would pull us toward the barrier reef's western pass just a few miles distant. I was terrified at the prospect. We had no radio, no flares, no food, and almost no water. If we were swept out through the pass it might be a day or two before anyone realized we were missing. A search-and-rescue attempt would have to originate far away in Tahiti. The chances of survival until someone found us—if they ever found us—were dim.

As these thoughts raced through my mind I spotted two spades that we had tossed into the boat. Grabbing one and handing the other to Conte, I shouted, "Paddle as hard as you can. If we're lucky we can get into the lee of Taravai."

For a half-hour we paddled furiously with the iron spades, which though hardly designed for this purpose worked fairly effectively. Exhausted, we brought the skiff into the shallows near the island's north end. Here Tu propelled us using a wooden pole, pushing against the coral bottom. The boat glided along past inlets and cliffs until we rounded the northeast point. But once again we faced into the *maragai* wind and could not make headway.

"We have to leave the boat here," Tu told us. Wading ashore on a little beach, we secured the boat's line to a *Pandanus* tree. Darkness had fallen. Because there are no roads or foot paths around Taravai, we would have to wade in chest-deep water around the rocky headlands, then follow the small beaches between them. Wearing only a pair of Teva sandals, I worried about stepping on a sea urchin spine or a stonefish, but there was little choice.

Nearly an hour later and still only halfway back to the village, I heard the sound of an outboard engine coming toward us, slowly. Then I caught the beam of a flashlight sweeping across the water. One of the few other occupants of Taravai, Edouard Sanford, had become concerned when he did not see our boat return. I was never more grateful than when Sanford extended his hand to haul my exhausted and shivering body into his boat.

The next day Sanford took us over to Onemea so we could complete the backfilling. Then we towed Tu's skiff with the frozen engine back home. After a couple of days in Rikitea we were on the Air Tahiti flight to Tahiti, with the Onemea collections in the cargo bay. My third expedition to Mangareva had concluded successfully, but I shuddered to think how narrowly we had averted disaster.

After our 2005 expedition my attention for the next few years turned to Mo'orea's 'Ōpūnohu Valley (see Chapter Twenty). But in 2011 Jennifer Kahn and I launched an ambitious four-year project, with National Science Foundation (NSF) funding. It not only included Mo'orea, as well as Maupiti in the Society Islands, but also leveraged the work I had done in Mangareva. We called the project "Vulnerability and Resilience in Island Socio-Ecosystems." The plan was to compare the development of Polynesian societies on three island ecosystems of different sizes, geological ages, and varied marine and terrestrial resources. We hypothesized that Moʻorea, the geologically youngest and largest ecosystem, would likely have been the most resilient to human impacts. In contrast, Maupiti and Mangareva, which have small land areas and are between five to six million years old (hence with soils that might be nutrient depleted), were likely to have been more vulnerable to human impacts. But the more extensive marine resources of Mangareva might have given it greater resiliency than Maupiti.

The project began in the summer of 2011 with work on Moʻorea. The following summer was divided between fieldwork on Maupiti, directed by Kahn, and renewed excavations in Mangareva. For this fourth field season, I wanted to return to a small rockshelter on Agakauitai that I had briefly tested with Conte in 2003. I thought the shelter, called Nenega-Iti, might fill in a gap in the Mangarevan sequence not covered by the Onemea site. I also hoped to get back to Kamaka Island to visit Tihoni Reasin and reopen Roger Green's large Kitchen Cave.

We spent a month in Mangareva, mostly digging in Nenega-Iti on Agakauitai (Fig. 22.2). Joining me were Conte's former student Guillaume Molle, my graduate student Jillian Swift, and a Berkeley undergrad, Rose Guthrie, as well as Jennifer Kahn for several weeks. Edouard Sanford—who had rescued us that dark night off Taravai—had built a comfortable house across from Agakauitai. He and his wife Denise graciously hosted us.

Nenega-Iti proved to be more deeply stratified than Conte and I realized from our initial test pit in 2003. The deposits extended down nearly one and a half meters, with two cultural layers separated by a thick zone of red clay that had washed down from the steep hillside. In the upper layer we found nine whole adzes.[10] The lower layer overlapped in time with the deposits at Onemea and, like the latter, contained numerous bird bones, especially near the base. When we later finished identifying all of the bones in my laboratory, it was clear that the frequency of bird bones was highest at the bottom of the lower cultural layer. A precipitous decline in the number of bird bones over time was matched by a significant increase in the number of rat bones. Rats were probably a major predator on the eggs and fledglings of the nesting seabirds. Charcoal samples from the cultural layers also revealed major changes in the island's vegetation over time. Early on, large indigenous trees dominated, whereas in the upper deposits the charcoal consisted mostly of Polynesian-introduced plants.

After completing the Nenega-Iti excavations we were finally able to get to isolated Kamaka for a few days. It turned out that part of Kitchen Cave (so named because Green and his crew cooked their meals there in 1959) was undisturbed. Digging a one-meter test pit against the rockshelter's wall, we were excited to see that continuous cultural deposits extended down more than one and a half meters. The faunal remains—mostly fishbone and shellfish, and some bird

Figure 22.2. Agakauitai Island, Mangareva. The Nenega-Iti rockshelter lies at the base of the cliffs below the rocky peak.

bones toward the base—were incredibly rich and well preserved. I knew I would have to return one more time.

After studying the materials from our Kitchen Cave test pit in my Berkeley lab I realized that we had barely tapped the potential of that large rockshelter. I resolved to return to Kamaka to open up a larger excavation and included funds for it in a grant proposal to the National Science Foundation in 2013. The new project, "Socio-Ecosystem Dynamics of Human-Natural Networks on Model Islands," would build upon the results of the work that Kahn and I had been doing on Mo'orea, Maupiti, and Mangareva. We would collaborate with ecologists Jennifer Dunne and Neo Martinez, combining our archaeological data with cutting-edge computer techniques to model island foodwebs over time. NSF's program, Dynamics of Coupled Natural and Human Systems, agreed to fund the program.

In July 2014 I made the Air Tahiti flight to Mangareva for the fifth time, accompanied by Guillaume Molle, and my graduate students, Jillian Swift and Alex Baer. As the Air Tahiti plane descended low over the lagoon on its approach to Totogiegie airstrip I could see Kamaka out the window. The sea was flat and glassy; the islands looked brown and parched. This was unusual weather for the southern winter, but it meant that our boat crossing to Kamaka would be smooth. In Rikitea Village that afternoon we purchased supplies and then were treated to a barbeque dinner by Tihoni Reasin's son Tehotu.

The following morning we loaded up Tehotu's aluminum "barge" (homemade in Rikitea) for the hour-long trip across the lagoon. As Tehotu deftly navigated his way through the narrow reef passage along the eastern cliffs of Kamaka I saw Tihoni Reasin waiting on the beach. He was expecting us, excited at the prospect of having guests for a few weeks in his homestead nestled between the sand dune and Kitchen Cave. A tense moment ensued when a rogue wave swept Reasin's little dog Styx—excitedly swimming out to greet the arriving visitors—under the barge. Fortunately, Styx emerged a few seconds later none the worse for her experience.

After unloading our gear and supplies through the surf and hauling everything up the grassy path under towering coconut palms, we settled down into Reasin's comfortable compound (Fig. 22.3). Over coffee in the rustic kitchen, we mused that it had been almost fifty-five years to the day since Tihoni Reasin had set foot on Kamaka with Roger and Kaye Green.

After digging with Green at Kamaka in 1959, Reasin attended school in Hawai'i. He returned to Kamaka in 1963 to shoot the foreign goats that were devastating the island's vegetation and to plant fruit trees; he moved to the island permanently in 1981 with his wife Moeata and two-year old son Tehotu. A daughter, Raruna, soon followed. Tihoni and Moeata raised their children on the tiny island. Reasin first built an open-sided kitchen just in front of the rockshelter and

Figure 22.3. Tihoni Reasin's cluster of houses lies within the overhang of Kitchen Cave, a rock-shelter occupied by Polynesians for hundreds of years.

then a sleeping house and shower room right into the cliff itself. A small "library" (Reasin is an avid reader) soon followed, along with a little schoolhouse where Te-hotu and Raruna were home-schooled.

I laid out my sleeping bag in the "library" (fending off a swarm of angry wasps that emerged from their nest behind some old *National Geographic* magazines), while my students set up their quarters in the former schoolhouse. Molle chose the side room off the kitchen to lay out his bedding.

Eager to begin work, that afternoon we laid out a grid of four 1-meter squares adjacent to our 2012 test pit and then began removing the backfill from the old unit. The next morning we started digging down into the dark-gray layers of the rockshelter, rich in charcoal, fishbones, limpet shells, and other refuse from centuries of occupation. Before long the first fragment of a pearl-shell fishhook appeared in Swift's sifting screen.

For most of its history, Kitchen Cave served as a temporary camping place for fishermen. In all, we would recover sixty pieces of pearl-shell hooks during our two-week excavation. But during the later period of Mangarevan history Kamaka seemed to have become a refuge for one or more family groups fleeing the increasing warfare and violence on the larger islands. They lived off of breadfruit, sea-almonds, and coconuts growing in a few small, steep valleys on Kamaka's eastern slopes, augmented with fish and shellfish. One occupant mentioned in the oral traditions collected in 1934 by Hiroa was the famous warrior Mori-a-tararoa. In a speech addressed to the paramount chief of the Ati-kura tribe, Mori-a-tararoa metaphorically referred to the shortage of food in Mangareva, saying, "Look inside my stomach. All you will see are the legs of land crabs from the rocky promontories of Kamaka."[11] Sorting through the greasy midden sands of Kitchen Cave, I encountered the smashed claws of hermit crabs, some of which were likely eaten by Mori-a-tararoa and his group (Fig. 22.4).

Figure 22.4. Sifting the midden sands of Kitchen Cave through fine mesh I found, among the scraps of bone and shell, the crab legs referred to in Mori-a-tararoa's famous speech.

Our team soon settled into a routine, rising with the sunrise, having our breakfast of coffee and biscuits, and then digging and screening all day. I was happy to let Molle do the digging because he is well trained in the French techniques of "*archéologie fine*," tracing out the subtle contours of ancient oven pits, living floors, and other features. Along with Swift and Baer I worked the 2 and 3 mm mesh screens, recovering small bits of fish, rat, and bird bone. As I sorted through the buckets of soil, I silently mused how far our techniques had come from my student days with Kenneth Emory, when we had screened through ¼-inch mesh, throwing away most of the faunal remains in a hunt for fishhooks. Green had also used coarse mesh in 1959 and probably missed many smaller fishhook fragments.

When the fading afternoon light made it impossible to continue work, Reasin would begin preparing the shower, a contraption consisting of a large bucket hoisted on a block-and-tackle suspended from the rockshelter ceiling. Two large, well-blackened kettles of water were heated over a hot fire of *miro* wood. When the kettles were boiling Reasin poured the water into the bucket, mixing it with cold rainwater from a barrel. After the bucket was hoisted aloft, the ancient brass shower head (from a camping shower that once belonged to Reasin's father) affixed to the bottom of the bucket released a gentle flow of warm water, sufficient to rinse away the day's accumulation of grime.

Later, we would sit on the grassy dune enjoying the sunset. Lesser frigate birds often swooped overhead in an aerial display, accompanied by fairy terns that nest in the *miro* trees next to the kitchen. The view across the lagoon to the pinnacle islet of Makaroa and beyond to Taravai and Mangareva is one I shall never forget (Fig. 22.5). Once darkness fell we would sit around flickering kerosene lamps in the tiny kitchen, eating dinner and sharing tales. Tucking myself into my sleeping bag, I was lulled to sleep by the wind in the *miro* trees and the scuttling of hermit crabs in the fallen leaves outside, going about their nightly business in their adopted *Turbo*-shell homes.

The days passed as we dug ever deeper into the rockshelter deposits. Rainy weather then set in, and it became difficult to see in the rockshelter's dim light. Reasin brought out a portable Honda generator and jerry-rigged a couple of electric light bulbs so Molle could continue to discern the subtle color differences between ash lenses and fire pits (Fig. 22.6). After two weeks we reached the base of the cultural deposit at 1.8 meters below the surface. Beneath it there were only compacted silt and rock that had fallen over eons from the cave roof. Radiocarbon dates from charcoal just above the original cave floor would later reveal that the site had first been inhabited around AD 1300.

The day before we were scheduled to leave, the weather was sunny and calm, but as fate would have it the wind picked up during the night. Reasin phoned his

Figure 22.5. The stunning view from Kamaka Island. Rocky Makaroa islet occupies the center; to its left is Taravai Island and to its right is Mangareva Island.

son-in-law Dada in Rikitea Village to discuss the situation. (Although life on Kamaka is still primitive, cell phones get reception!). The lagoon was running a big swell with a lot of wind chop, making it dangerous for Dada's small boat to attempt the crossing. Fortunately, the mayor's office agreed to send the *Tokani,* a larger boat used to ferry passengers from the airport to Rikitea. The *Tokani* towed Dada's skiff, and while the larger craft stood offshore Dada made two runs through the surf to pick us up. My adrenaline was pumping as we plunged into the water, ferrying our gear out through the surf to the skiff. This time Reasin tied up little Styx with a rope to prevent her from joining in the fray. With the surf buffeting us I quickly shook Reasin's hand, thanking him for all his help and hospitality, then hauled myself over the skiff's gunwale. Tihoni Reasin is truly one of the most intriguing personalities I have met in my many years in the South Seas; it was a great pleasure to share his little island for a few weeks.

Our excavations at Onemea, Nenega-Iti, and Kitchen Cave left no doubt that Taravai, Agakauitai, Kamaka, and other islands within the Mangareva lagoon had once been home to abundant populations of seabirds. Petrels, terns, noddies, tropicbirds, and other species all nested here, nourished by an endless supply of pe-

Figure 22.6. The 2014 excavation in Kitchen Cave. Tihoni Reasin, on the right, strung up electric lights powered by his portable generator, allowing Guillaume Molle to continue digging when rainy weather set in.

lagic fish in the offshore waters. Based on what we know of other island rookeries, Mangareva's seabird populations may have numbered into the hundreds of thousands or even millions of birds. The land snails, along with the bones of the pigeon and fruit dove, testify that Mangareva's islands also supported a rich endemic biota, as on other southeastern Polynesian islands. What happened to change this pristine ecosystem into the deforested landscape witnessed by the Mangarevan Expedition scientists in 1934?

We believe that in pre-Polynesian times, the vast seabird populations performed a critical ecological role in the Mangareva ecosystem. With an age of five to six million years, Mangareva's soils were largely depleted of rock-derived nutrients, especially phosphorus. The seabirds served as nutrient transferors, fishing at sea and depositing their guano on the land, fertilizing the terrestrial ecosystem. When the Polynesians arrived, their activities immediately started to reduce the size of the seabird populations. Large numbers of the naive birds, never having faced a human predator, were effortlessly taken for food, as witnessed by the rich bone deposits at Onemea and in the lowest layers at Nenega-Iti and Kitchen Cave. The Polynesian-introduced Pacific rat may also have preyed on their eggs or fledglings; numerous rat bones were present in all of the archaeo-logical deposits. The birds' nesting grounds were further disturbed as people cleared forest for gardens, lit fires, and burned off the hillsides. Within a couple of centuries, the seabird populations had been decimated, restricted to the small-est islets and steepest cliffs.

With the birds' key ecological function of supplying nutrients disrupted, the native forests that had been the habitat for pigeons and fruit doves, along with the diminutive land snails, could not regenerate. The hillsides and ridge crests came to be covered in a few species of fire-resistant plants that can tolerate poor soils, especially *Miscanthus* grass and *Dicranopteris* fern, along with scrub *Pandanus*. Only in the tiny valley bottoms were the soils rich enough to support bread-fruit orchards and taro gardens. Thus here, as in Mangaia, people began to fight with each other over control of the limited arable land. Te Rangi Hiroa described how, in the late period before the arrival of Europeans, there was no centralized political control, with each island consisting of its own tribe, fiercely defending these resources. Warriors such as the fierce Mori-a-tararoa held out on the small islets such as Kamaka. Only the abundant fish and shellfish of Mangareva's exten-sive lagoon and reefs saved them from the more extreme conditions of Mangaia.

A fascinating footnote to this history is that when Captain Beechy and other explorers arrived in Mangareva in the 1820s, they found the island lacking in large canoes. Instead, the islanders traveled between islets on rafts of *Hibiscus* logs. De-forestation had been so thorough that no large hardwood trees remained that were suitable for hewing out canoe hulls. One consequence of this lack of oceangoing canoes was that the remote islands of Pitcairn and Henderson, to the southeast of Mangareva, became completely cut off and isolated. Mangare-van voyagers had once supplied those tiny outposts with food, trading for Pitcairn's prized adz rock and Henderson's bird feathers. With this lifeline cut, the occupants of Pitcairn and Henderson abandoned their islands or perished, leaving them as unoccupied "mystery" islands at the time of first European discovery.[12]

CHAPTER TWENTY-THREE

Kekaulike's Kingdom
(Kaupō, Maui, 2003–2013)

During my Kahikinui fieldwork in the late 1990s (see Chapter Eighteen), I would often gaze eastward toward Kaupō, where in the late afternoon rainbows would appear in the mist blowing around from Hāna and Kīpahulu. Sometimes, at the end of a long week of mapping or digging, we would drive the narrow, pothole-studded road down to Nuʻu Bay on the western side of Kaupō. There we would jump from the ruins of the old inter-island steamship landing into the dark waters, washing off the day's encrusted dirt. After swimming, as we shared beers from a cooler, I would often light a cigar, and we would "talk story" as the sun descended over Lualaʻilua Hills.

Inland from Nuʻu Bay the landscape was reputed to be rich with archaeological sites. My longtime friend and respected Hawaiian *kupuna* Charles Pili Keau had told me this. Keau belonged to a tradition of Hawaiian scholars, including Theodore Kelsey, Henry Kekahuna, and Rudy Mitchell, who—although lacking academic degrees—were deeply knowledgeable about Hawaiian history, culture, and archaeology. Kenneth Emory introduced me to Keau in 1971; we worked together on my Bishop Museum team surveying sites at Kapalua on Maui. Later, we traveled together to Kahoʻolawe on one of the first legal access visits of Protect Kahoʻolawe ʻOhana. Keau mentored me in Hawaiian ways of "asking permission" before entering onto a *heiau* or other ancient place; his practice was not that of formal chant and protocol (as is often the case today) but of silently and respectfully entering into a personal dialogue with the ancestral spirits of the place. It is a practice I have continued to this day.

In the late 1970s, Keau worked with the Bishop Museum's Maui Island field team on a statewide archaeological inventory. It was during that survey that Keau first encountered the archaeological riches of Nuʻu. Whenever I would see Keau on my visits to Maui, he would remind me in his pidgin accent, "Pat, you gotta go study Nuʻu. I know you like Kahikinui. But Nuʻu got plenty *heiau*, house sites all up and down the mountainside." I would always reply, "OK, Uncle Charlie, after my Kahikinui work *pau,* I go check ʻem out."

In 2002 while I was on Maui with my wife Thérèse, I phoned Keau to find out how he was doing. He told me, "Pat, we bought Nuʻu. You gotta come take a look."

"What do you mean, you bought Nuʻu?" I asked. I had never thought of Keau, who lived modestly, as someone having the means to purchase an entire *ahupuaʻa*.

"Kaupō Ranch put Nuʻu up for sale," Keau explained. "My daughter Bernie and my son-in-law Andy got some loans. We bought it. All the way from the highway to the top of Haleakalā." They had put in a well and water system in order to replant the native *koa* forests and do sustainable ranching and farming—and, of course, to protect the archaeological sites so dear to Keau's heart, on their new Nuʻu Mauka Ranch.

The next day Thérèse and I drove out to Nuʻu to have a look for ourselves (Fig. 23.1). We met up with Keau and his family at a newly constructed cabin near the well, which was pouring out crystal clear water. Keau thrust out his big weathered hand in greeting; our eyes met. I had not seen him in a couple of years, and I was struck by how he had visibly aged. Sitting on the cabin steps with his dog "Little Boy," Keau told me that his health was failing. "I suck wind," he said, referring to his emphysema. But this was not going to prevent him from showing me the sites for which he was now the *kahu*. We piled into a couple of ATVs for a trip up the rough, unpaved track leading *mauka*.

Throughout the afternoon Keau showed us one impressive site after another. In 1929 Winslow Walker had recorded Kaʻiliʻili and Halekou *heiau* as well as ʻOheʻohenui, a large terrace set into the face of a massive *ʻaʻā* flow.[1] Walker had called ʻOheʻohenui a *heiau*, but I wondered whether it might have been a chiefly residence. At the road's end, about 1,600 feet above sea level, we climbed up onto a lava outcrop to enjoy the spectacular view all the way to the Lualaʻilua Hills of Kahikinui.

It had been a glorious day and Keau had worked his magic on me; I was convinced that I needed to come back. It would be informative, I mused, to compare the settlement patterns of Kaupō with those of Kahikinui that I had already researched so thoroughly. Although still leeward, Kaupō is considerably wetter than Kahikinui, and the great Nāholokū fan of younger lavas that flowed out of the Kaupō Gap provided rich soils for sweet potato cultivation.

Rather than launch another big, NSF-funded project, I decided to tackle Nuʻu slowly, in small increments. Andy and Bernie Graham graciously offered to make the little cabin available for our use. Our first systematic survey started in 2003 with an area to the west of ʻOheʻohenui, and we continued our survey work in 2004. Then, in May 2005 I heard from the Grahams that Charlie Keau had passed away. One of his last wishes was that the archaeological work at Nuʻu continue. His ashes were scattered high on the slopes at Nuʻu, the *ʻāina* that he so dearly loved.

Since 2005 I have made dozens of field trips to Nuʻu, accompanied by my students and often by my good friend, archaeologist John Holson. The work of

Figure 23.1. View of the Nuʻu landscape looking toward the rim of Haleakalā and Kaupō Gap. Younger lavas and mud flows emanating from Kaupō Gap provided nutrient-rich soils in which the Hawaiian farmers cultivated sweet potato and dryland taro. I have explored the archaeological sites of this region for more than a decade.

finding and recording more than four hundred sites has served as an excellent training opportunity for my students. Alex Baer has used Nuʻu as a base from which to explore other parts of Kaupō, whereas Kirsten Vacca is excavating in Nuʻu habitation sites. It will be a few more years before we finish all that I would like to accomplish at Nuʻu. Meanwhile, every time I walk that rugged landscape, I feel Charlie Keau's presence, watching over us.

Kaupō, today a sleepy ranching community, was one of twelve districts (*moku*) of Maui's ancient kingdom. Around AD 1710, almost seven decades before British captain James Cook broke the sea barrier that had isolated the Hawaiian archipelago from the rest of the world, Kaupō was the royal seat of King Kekaulike.[2] Revered to this day by Hawaiians on Maui, Kekaulike was a descendant of the great Piʻilani, who first unified the island kingdom around AD 1570.

Kekaulike was an *aliʻi akua*, literally a "god-king." In the hierarchical society of late precontact Hawaiʻi, the highest ranked chiefs or *aliʻi* traced their genealogies back to the gods, practicing *pi'o* (arched) marriages between brother and sister, or between half-siblings, to concentrate their bloodlines. Kekaulike married his half-sister Keku'iapoiwanui to produce a sacred heir, Kamehameha-nui. Similar royal incest had been practiced by the pharaohs of Egypt and by the Inca of Peru, other ancient societies that anthropologists classify as "archaic states." The Hawaiian god-kings were considered so sacred (*kapu*) that they could not be gazed upon by commoners; hence they often traveled at night, to avoid being seen by commoners who then had to perform the *kapu moe* (prostrating taboo), lying facedown on the ground. A stolen glance at the passing god-king, resplendent in cloak and helmet of rare red and yellow bird feathers, could bring instant death from the warrior guard.

Samuel Mānaiakalani Kamakau, in *Ruling Chiefs of Hawai'i,* tells us that in the early 1700s Kekaulike, having moved the royal seat from Hāna to Kaupō, was "engaged in building *luakini* heiaus for his gods."[3] Success in war required the dedication of a *luakini* to Kū, the war god. Kekaulike, who had his sights set on the conquest of Hawai'i Island, across the rough 'Alenuihāhā Channel, assembled a formidable army and fleet of war canoes, ready to be launched from the bay of Mokulau. One of the *luakini* temples built by Kekaulike, Lo'alo'a, is well known to archaeologists. An imposing rectangular stone platform with a basal area of 44,800 square feet and a terraced front rising 30 feet from the ground, Lo'alo'a took countless hours of human toil to construct.

But Kamakau tells us that Kekaulike also dedicated a second temple, Pōpōiwi. In 2009, I decided to have a look at Pōpōiwi for myself. My grad student Alex Baer had already started his doctoral research in Kaupō. Before Baer departed to spend the summer surveying sites in Kaupō, I pointed out the location on a map where the ruins of Pōpōiwi should lie, obscured by thick Christmas berry and other invasive plants. "See if you can hack your way into that brush and find the main temple walls," I told Baer. "When I come out to visit later in the field season, I'd like to map the site." Baer promised to take a look.

Some weeks later Baer met me at Kahului Airport. The first thing I asked was if he had found the ruins of Pōpōiwi. "You bet," he grinned. "You are going to be amazed at the size and extent of that site." A couple of hours later, Baer pulled the Jeep up a narrow dirt road. Dank foliage hung over the rutted track; the humid air was thick with hungry mosquitoes. Slathering on repellent and picking up our machetes, Baer and I plunged into the tropical vegetation, following a narrow trail he had cut.

Soon we came into a more open space, where an aged candlenut tree shaded out the other vegetation. Looming up in front of us was a massive stone rampart, its rocks green with moss undisturbed for centuries. "My God," I half-muttered under my breath. "This thing is huge." Baer suppressed a chuckle, saying, "This is just one of the outer terraces. Wait until we get up on top of the main structure."

For several hours Baer, his student assistant Kris Hara, and I explored the ruins of Pōpōiwi, which cover roughly two continuous acres overlooking the bay of Mokulau where Kekaulike's war fleet had beached. Baer and Hara had hacked much of the undergrowth away from the main walls and terraces. Later, we would begin the laborious task of mapping the structure. For now, I just wanted to explore this site, linked in tradition with one of Maui's most famous divine kings. We made our way up onto two expansive courtyards, paved with thousands of basket-loads of water-rounded pebbles hauled up from the beach. Baer tapped my shoulder and said, "Come over here, you've got to see this feature."

Ducking under low-hanging branches and clambering over a stone wall, we emerged on a small, well-paved terrace overlooking Mokulau Bay. Here the ceaseless easterly winds kept the wiry vegetation down to a few feet. I climbed out onto a kind of rampart supported by a massive stone facing that descended down the steep slope. The facing angled away from me like a sharp inverted V—one might say like the prow of a Polynesian canoe—with the point of the V facing directly toward Hawai'i Island. Struggling to keep from being blown over by the strong gusts, I pulled out my sighting compass. The V-shaped rampart pointed almost exactly to the bearing of Waipi'o Valley on Hawai'i Island. Waipi'o was the royal seat of the divine kings of Hawai'i Island, arch-rivals and at the same time the blood relatives of Kekaulike. We knew from Kamakau's account that it was here that Kekaulike launched his fleet for the conquest of Hawai'i. Was this special terrace—with the V-shaped rampart directed at Waipi'o—a place where Kekaulike himself had once sat, cross-legged on fine mats, gazing at his goal, plotting his strategy?

That evening, after a well-earned meal of barbequed Maui grass-fed steaks, Baer, Hara, and I sat on the porch of the Nu'u cabin. Enjoying the spectacular stars, we engaged in a kind of informal seminar. "Hawai'i," I said, pausing to take a long draw on my cigar, "is the last place on earth where a true archaic state emerged."

Hara asked what I meant by an archaic state. "An archaic state is one that was ruled by divine kings, like Kekaulike. They had formal priesthoods and distinct commoner and elite classes," I replied.

Baer challenged me: "But most anthropologists and archaeologists have classified Hawai'i as a complex chiefdom, not an archaic state. That's what Marshall Sahlins and Tim Earle claimed in the books we read in your seminar at Berkeley."[4]

"Correct, Alex. I used to believe that as well. But my research in Kahikinui convinced me otherwise. Now I'm writing a book called *How Chiefs Became Kings.*

It lays out the argument for why late precontact Hawaiian society should be considered a group of archaic states, rather than chiefdoms." As the evening wore on and the fire's embers dimmed, we continued to talk about how new research was changing our ideas about how Hawaiian society had evolved over eight centuries.[5]

I worked on *How Chiefs Became Kings* for the better part of a decade; the book was published in 2010.[6] I had floated the idea of Hawaiian archaic states in a keynote address to the Society for Social Anthropology in Oceania in Vancouver in 2000. In the audience was French anthropologist Maurice Godelier, who invited me to visit him at the École des Hautes Études en Sciences Sociales in Paris. In May 2002, I presented my thesis to audiences in Paris and Marseille; there was less resistance than I had anticipated. My French colleagues were intrigued, peppering me with questions.

At first I planned to draw upon ethnohistoric accounts of contact-era Hawaiian society and then trace the transformation from chiefdom to state through the Hawaiian archaeological record. But as I worked away, something unexpected happened. I began to delve into a third source of information, one that archaeologists in Hawai'i had too frequently overlooked. These are the accounts of traditional histories, the *mo'olelo*, that were passed down orally from generation to generation, eventually to be put into written form by Hawaiian scholars in the nineteenth century. Among the most famous of those scholars were Samuel Kamakau and Davida Malo. The Swedish magistrate Abraham Fornander, who married a Hawaiian chiefess and learned the Hawaiian language, was also a great compiler of *mo'olelo*.

Anthropologists have tended to regard the *mo'olelo* as myths or legends, rather than as history based on the actions and deeds of real historical persons. For example, the account of 'Umi-a-Līloa, the commoner-born king who overthrew his *pi'o* half-brother and unified the kingdom of Hawai'i for the first time, was recounted by folklorists such as Martha Beckwith and Padraic Colum as a fine story but not a real history.[7] The brilliant scholar Valerio Valeri likewise regarded the 'Umi-a-Līloa *mo'olelo* as a legend that revealed key structures of Hawaiian society.[8]

In my earlier Tikopia research I had discovered that the oral traditions of the wars between Nga Ariki, Nga Ravenga, and Nga Faea could be linked to material signposts in the archaeological record (see Chapter Nine).[9] And in Kahikinui, using precise dating of coral offerings, we had found that the expansion of the *heiau* system between about AD 1570 to 1630 corresponded with the reigns of Maui kings Pi'ilani and his son Kiha-a-Pi'ilani (see Chapter Eighteen). Fornander, and several scholars after him, had shown that the *moʻolelo* could be tied to an internally consistent chronological framework based on the genealogies of the chiefly lines.[10] Thus, these oral histories do not just "float" timelessly.

Pulling the three hefty volumes of *Fornander's Collection of Hawaiian Antiquities* along with Kamakau's *Ruling Chiefs of Hawaiʻi* down from my bookshelves, I spent months poring over the texts.[11] As I read through the detailed accounts of the births, marriages, deaths, wars, and other affairs of the *aliʻi* of the seventeenth and eighteenth centuries, I realized that this was the stuff of history, not legend. To be sure, some oral traditions have doubtless been elaborated or modified over time. Nonetheless, the genealogically linked histories of Hawaiian chiefs going about their social and political affairs offered a critical, *insider* perspective on Hawaiian history.

Marrying the indigenous history of the Hawaiian *moʻolelo* with the material evidence of archaeology gave me a more nuanced perspective on how Hawaiian society had changed dramatically over about four centuries from complex chiefdom to archaic state. By AD 1400, four centuries after the archipelago was first discovered by Polynesian voyagers, the Hawaiian population had densely occupied the most ecologically favorable regions, especially those valleys with permanent streams amenable to irrigation. Then the population began to expand into the drier, leeward regions, including the vast slopes of Kohala and Kona on Hawaiʻi Island as well as Kahikinui and Kaupō on Maui. Although not as productive as the irrigated zones, the fertile volcanic soils of these leeward slopes produced good yields of sweet potato and dryland taro. Bringing these leeward regions into production not only allowed the population to keep growing but also provided the surplus that the chiefs could use to fuel their political aspirations. In Kaupō, Alex Baer and I discovered extensive rock walls and embankments of an intensive field system covering several square kilometers, a system that had provided the surplus that Kekaulike needed to support his warriors and attendants.[12]

As these leeward regions were developed and the population grew to encompass tens of thousands of people, the *aliʻi* increasingly competed for status and power. Fine gradations between *aliʻi* arose, ultimately resulting in nine distinct ranks of elites. At the same time, distinctions between the *aliʻi* and the common people became marked.

In Hawaiʻi, commoners are called *makaʻāinana*, a word that Roger Green and I had traced to its deep roots in Ancestral Polynesian society (see Chapter Fifteen). The ancient word *mata-kāinanga*, from which the Hawaiian *makaʻāinana* derived, originally meant the descendants of a common progenitor, who held land in common. But whereas the original word referred to a group of kinfolk who shared a common territory and held rights to farm that land, the new word indexed the common people who worked the land and paid tribute to their chiefs. The right to work the land was now subject to taxation.

The greatest change setting Hawaiian society off from its Polynesian relatives was the new system of land tenure. In most Polynesian societies, access to land was controlled by membership in a hereditary social group (such as a *mata-kāinanga*). But in contact-era Hawai'i the land tenure system was based on *ahupua'a* territories held by the prominent chiefs. Each *ahupua'a* was overseen by a *konohiki* or manager, who made certain that the commoner families worked their plots and provided labor to communal projects, such as repairing the ir-rigation works. Surplus food and other goods provided by the *maka'āinana* supported the chiefly households and the king's establishment.

This fundamental transformation in Hawaiian society—the shift from com-plex chiefdom to archaic state—occurred between the late sixteenth and early sev-enteenth centuries. According to the royal genealogies it was then that Pi'ilani and his son Kiha-a-Pi'ilani consolidated the Maui kingdom. At the same time on Hawai'i Island, 'Umi-a-Līloa defeated his half-brother Hākau, launching wars of conquest against the previously independent chiefs of the island. 'Umi-a-Līloa and Kiha-a-Pi'ilani were linked through the marriage of Kiha's sister Pi'ikea to 'Umi. Thereafter, the royal houses of Maui and Hawai'i elaborated the practices of di-vine kingship and vied for ultimate control of the archipelago.

About a century after Pi'ilani unified Maui, his descendant Kekaulike gazed out from Pōpōiwi across the foamy 'Alenuihāhā Channel to plot his conquest of Hawai'i. Kekaulike launched his war canoes from Mokulau, descending unsus-pected upon the Kona District of Hawai'i. The Maui forces devastated the agri-cultural fields and cut down the stately breadfruit trees in the Kona uplands. Then warriors under the command of Alapa'inui, the Hawai'i Island king, counterat-tacked, forcing the Maui troops back to their canoes. Fleeing north along the Kohala coast, the Maui warriors cut down all the coconut trees; they slaughtered any commoners in their path, seizing their possessions.

Kekaulike's battered forces returned to Mokulau in Kaupō, where the king of-fered sacrifices to Kū at his *luakini*. But Alapa'inui, incensed by the cowardice of the Maui invaders, crossed the channel with his own fleet, taking the war to Kaupō. Kekaulike was seized with a violent illness, which the Hawaiians called *ka maka huki lani* or "eyes drawn heavenward." Kekaulike fled Kaupō, leaving the kingship to his sacred son Kamehamehanui, Alapa'inui's own nephew (the new king's mother Keku'iapoiwanui being Alapa'inui's brother). Alapa'inui then called off his war of revenge.

In *How Chiefs Became Kings* and in my more recent book, *A Shark Going Inland Is My Chief,* I sought to integrate archaeology with the indigenous perspective of the Hawaiian oral traditions.[13] Sometimes I wonder why it took me so long to engage with the *moʻolelo*, given their significance for our understanding of Hawaiian history. But then, like anyone, I partly was a product of my times. My early teachers and mentors—Emory, Sinoto, and Green—regarded those indigenous sources as myth or legend, not the stuff of scientific inquiry. Eventually, I discovered their importance for myself and have been greatly enriched as a consequence.

CHAPTER TWENTY-FOUR

Reflections

A half-century has passed since I sat down with Yoshio Kondo in his Bishop Museum malacology lab, on the cusp of my apprenticeship in science. I could scarcely have anticipated where the journey—a physical and intellectual voyage whose excitement and highlights I have tried to convey in the pages of this book—would take me. In this final chapter, I reflect on some of the big changes that I have witnessed along the way—changes in archaeology as an academic discipline and in the questions that archaeologists ask about the past, changes in archaeological practices, and changes in the institutions that support archaeological research. I also reflect on how our knowledge and understanding of what happened in the deep past of Polynesia have been transformed over the past five decades of research and scholarship.

In the early 1960s archaeology was in the final stage of its "culture history" phase.[1] Since the late nineteenth century, archaeologists had labored to construct cultural sequences for different regions of the world. Their primary tool for chronology building was "seriation," the ordering of sites according to the waxing and waning of artifact styles, especially pottery. But radiocarbon dating, invented by Willard Libby in 1947, changed everything.[2] The painstaking comparison of artifact types—formerly the key to chronology but now no longer needed—rapidly faded. Why labor over the details of fishhook or adz typology when the age of a site could be determined in a physics lab?

When as a student I first joined in the Bishop Museum's archaeology program, Kenneth Emory and Yosihiko Sinoto were digging for artifacts with which to establish cultural sequences for Eastern Polynesia. They compared the shapes and details of fishhooks, adzes, and ornaments from different islands, seeking to uncover the sequence of migrations in the Pacific. When they found similar artifacts on different islands, these finds were deemed to indicate a connection between the people who had made them. Roger Green shifted Polynesian archaeology away from this artifact-centered approach to a more encompassing study of past island societies, applying the settlement pattern method.[3] Green had learned about settlement patterns from Gordon Willey at Harvard.[4] Settlement pattern archaeology was the advance guard of what would soon come to be known as the New Archaeology.

The New Archaeologists' mantra, in Lewis Binford's classic words, was "archaeology is anthropology or it is nothing."[5] Archaeologists would now strive to be ethnographers of the past, reconstructing ancient economies, social and political organizations, trade networks, and religions. Along with the new emphasis on settlement patterns, archaeologists became as interested in animal bones and fishbones, charcoal, and seeds as they had once been in classifying artifacts. Inspired by advances in the emerging field of ecology, archaeologists wanted to know how people had interacted with their environments, and for this the evidence of faunal and floral remains was essential. Culture came to be seen less as a mental template for behavior than as "man's means of adaptation." The New Archaeology inspired our research in Moloka'i's Hālawa Valley in 1969–1970.

The New Archaeology, however, was never a unified paradigm. Some advocated an explicitly "scientific" approach, emulating experimental sciences such as physics and chemistry.[6] Their goal of discovering "laws" of human behavior was doomed to failure, in the end only producing what Kent Flannery famously called "Mickey Mouse laws," such as that a heavy stone artifact will eventually work its way downslope.[7] A more productive school followed the model of such historical sciences as paleontology and evolutionary biology, focused on long-term processes of change while taking account of contingency and chance. This approach gradually solidified into what became known as "processual" archaeology, the rubric with which a large number of archaeologists—myself among them—identify.[8]

Within processual archaeology there are nonetheless distinct theoretical schools. My own approach has been that of *cultural evolution,* the idea that cultures, like species, evolve and differentiate over time. This is in keeping with Darwin's view of evolution as "descent with modification." It requires, as Stephen Jay Gould once asserted, that we discriminate between cultural traits that have been passed down through time ("homologous" traits) and those that have arisen independently in response to similar circumstances ("analogous" traits).[9] But cultural evolution is not identical to biological evolution; it has a distinctly Lamarckian element due to humans' ability to transmit information through language and culture, rather than strictly by means of a genetic code (i.e., DNA). Humans also do not just passively adapt to their environment: They actively alter and change the surrounding environment to suit them. Evolutionary biologists have recently termed this kind of behavior "niche construction."[10] Although we now know that many species construct their niches, *Homo sapiens* has taken this ability to an extreme.

I spent a lot of time thinking about cultural evolution in the late 1970s, summarizing my developing approach in a long essay, "The Archaeological Study of Adaptation," published in 1980.[11] In 1984 I put theory to work in *The Evolution of the Polynesian Chiefdoms*,[12] a book that drew extensively on my fieldwork in Tikopia, Futuna, and Niuatoputapu, as well as Hawai'i. I sought to demonstrate how the varied Polynesian cultures had gradually evolved and differentiated from a common ancestral culture over nearly three millennia. Several kinds of processes were at work, including adaptation to varied island environments, population growth and pressure, human-induced changes to natural resources, the intensification of agriculture, and competition and warfare. The book has stood the test of time; three decades later it remains in print. According to Google Scholar, it is my most cited work.

In 1987, Roger Green and I—building on earlier proposals by Kim Romney and Evon Vogt—advocated an explicitly "phylogenetic approach" to cultural evolution.[13] A phylogeny is a family tree; thus, a phylogenetic approach seeks to establish the branching pattern of historical relationships among a group of cultures that descended from a common ancestral culture. To accomplish this we made use of a "triangulation method" that applied independent datasets—from archaeology, historical linguistics, and ethnography—to reconstruct the earlier stages in a cultural phylogeny, such as Ancestral Polynesian culture (see Chapter Fifteen). Unfortunately, our use of historical linguistic methods was off-putting to some narrowly trained archaeologists. Our 2001 book, *Hawaiki, Ancestral Polynesia*, did not have the impact that we hoped it would.[14] Perhaps a future generation more comfortable with multidisciplinary research will rediscover our message and further advance the power of phylogenetic reconstruction using triangulation.

Although cultural evolution has dominated Polynesian and Pacific archaeology, there have been other competing voices. My colleague Matthew Spriggs has advocated a Marxist perspective within archaeology.[15] In the 1980s, I too engaged with Marxian anthropology and archaeology, finding it useful for thinking about "the social relations of production," their "mystification" through religion and ideology, and class struggle in stratified chiefdoms and archaic states. But I regard Marxist theory as a supplement to, rather than replacement for, a cultural evolutionary approach. I feel similarly about the *Annales* school that was fashionable for a time, drawing inspiration from the French historians Marc Bloch, Le Roy Ladurie, and the great Fernand Braudel, whose "wavelength" theory of historical cycles is truly inspiring.[16] I read their works, gaining insights. But I always returned to my own carefully considered evolutionary paradigm.

In the 1990s, postmodernism—originating in the "deconstructionist" approaches of some humanities scholars—began to make inroads into the social sciences. In archaeology this trend was sometimes called "post-processualism" and was closely associated with Ian Hodder and his followers. Their goal—at least in some of their more extreme manifestos—was to overturn empirical processualism.[17] Postmodernism is a slippery beast, difficult to pin down precisely. But its more rabid forms are both antiscientific and ultra-relativist. Archaeological postmodernists have advocated archaeological excavation as "theater," proposed that we dig round rather than square holes, and claimed that all "stories" of the past are equally valid. This is not science. Science is a self-correcting system in which one returns repeatedly to the empirical data—the "hard" evidence—to test and if possible reject one's hypotheses. Contrary to what the postmodernists claim, not all stories of the past are equally valid, because only a few of them actually account for the evidence.[18]

To be sure, science, like any endeavor, is to some degree a "social construction." A reasonable amount of critical reflection on one's practices can help expose hidden bias. But I have steadfastly resisted the more extreme forms of postmodernism that end in hyper-reflexivity. Following that path only leads one—like the apocryphal Foo-Bird—in ever-tighter and convoluted circles of self-criticism until you fly up your own arse and disappear. Or, simply put, your work becomes irrelevant to all but a handful of likeminded postmodernists. Most archaeologists saw the pitfalls along the postmodernist path and turned back. Unfortunately, a significant segment of American social anthropology has now embraced postmodernism, making it increasingly unlikely that the kind of cross-disciplinary research that Marshall Sahlins and I pioneered in our *Anahulu* study will be emulated any time soon.[19]

In the 1950s and early 1960s, the questions asked by Pacific archaeologists were largely the same ones that had engaged earlier generations from James Cook and Dumont d'Urville to William Ellis, Abraham Fornander, Edward S. C. Handy, and Te Rangi Hiroa. Where had the Polynesians originated? How had they managed to discover and settle the far-flung islands of the eastern Pacific? When had their remarkable voyages taken place?

Yet culture historians such as Kenneth Emory and Yosihiko Sinoto were *not* asking other questions, such as the following: Had the social and political organization of Polynesian societies changed over time? At what rate had island populations grown; had they reached or exceeded the carrying capacities of their island environments? How had island agricultural systems and fishing techniques adapted to the differences in the terrestrial and marine ecosystems across the Pacific? Why were warfare and cannibalism so evident on some islands but not on others? These were the questions that an anthropologically informed archaeology needed to address.

Why were such questions—central to an archaeology that regards itself as a branch of anthropology—not on the research agendas of Emory or Sinoto, Heyerdahl or Ferdon, Duff or Gifford? Perhaps these scholars felt that they first had to address the age-old puzzle of Polynesian origins, to establish the basic chronology of human migrations into the Pacific. But another, deeply ingrained assumption held them back. It was the view, inherited from an earlier generation of ethnologists, that the Polynesians had come into the Pacific with their culture fully formed. As Gifford once put it, "Tropical Polynesia has yielded only the early phase of the local cultures which were flourishing at the time of discovery."[20]

Of course, nothing could have been further from the truth. The Polynesians did not migrate into the Pacific sui generis. They descended from the Lapita people, whose culture was quite different from that of the Polynesians of Captain Cook's time. Among other things, the Polynesian descendants of the Lapita people had completely forgotten about the art of pottery making. Ancestral Polynesian culture evolved from this Lapita ancestor over more than a thousand years in the Western Polynesian homeland. In the late first millennium AD, small groups in newly invented double-hulled voyaging canoes explored eastward, discovering the archipelagoes of Eastern Polynesia. Once again, a rapid series of innovations led to cultural change, so that the new Eastern Polynesian colonies diverged from those of the Western Polynesian homeland. But this was only the beginning, not the end of cultural evolution on the far-flung islands from Aotearoa to Hawai'i, and to Rapa Nui. In every island group the founding populations grew; their fishing technologies and agricultural practices adapted to local conditions; their natural ecosystems were transformed; and their social, political, and religious institutions evolved and differentiated. In spite of these changes, however, all of the Eastern Polynesian cultures retained certain patterns in common, which is why we can recognize them as "sister" cultures all deriving from the same ancestral group.

One of the first archaeologists to ask such new questions about the long-term evolution of Polynesian cultures was Robert Carl Suggs. His work on the Marquesan island of Nuku Hiva in the late 1950s, although rooted in an older culture history paradigm (he used fishhook seriation to build a chronology), was informed by modern anthropological theory.[21] Suggs wrote with sophistication about how the early Marquesans had adapted to their environment, how their population had grown during the "Expansion" Period, and how this growth in turn led to competition for land and warfare. He drew upon Irving Goldman's then-new theory of "status rivalry," suggesting that this rivalry was materialized in megalithic architecture and statuary in the Marquesan "Classic" Period. Suggs's four-phase sequence for Nuku Hiva was based not so much on artifact changes as on fundamental processes of cultural evolution.

Although Suggs posed provocative questions he was held back by his tools, which were still those of culture history, based on the excavation of a few artifact-rich sites. (The still-primitive radiocarbon dating of the 1950s also provided Suggs with dates that resulted in a chronology that we now know to have been too long.) Roger Green's settlement pattern archaeology was what the field needed to move forward, taking us away from a narrow focus on artifact-rich sites to looking at entire landscapes and the ways that human activities had been configured on them. Douglas Yen, coming into Pacific archaeology from ethnobotany, gave us more tools to address the new questions.[22] He challenged archaeologists to think ecologically about the evolution of Pacific cultures. I still recall the excitement of his graduate seminar at the University of Hawai'i in the spring of 1970, when he had us debating such then-controversial works as Ester Boserup's *The Conditions of Agricultural Growth*.[23]

Paradigm shifts in science are hard to see when you are in the midst of them. But I believe that the questions we are asking today have once again shifted. The change has been not so much away from asking questions about cultural evolution but about how the cultures and societies of the Pacific *co-evolved* with their ecosystems. We are now talking, at our academic conferences, about the evolution of "socio-ecosystems."[24] This is a big advance, but additional efforts are still needed to break down the academic barriers between the social and natural sciences. At the risk of displaying some hubris, I believe that the Hawai'i Biocomplexity Project has helped push this new way of asking questions about the "dynamically coupled" interactions between island peoples and their environments over long time spans (see Chapter Twenty-One). Island cultures did not simply "adapt to" an environmental canvas; they transformed their ecosystems at the same time that their cultures responded to changes they had set in motion. Everything was linked, often through complex, nonlinear pathways.[25]

New ways of thinking about island systems require new concepts and tools. The idea of island socio-ecosystems acknowledges that societies and ecosystems cannot meaningfully be studied apart from each other. The concepts of "vulnerability," "resilience," and "sustainability" come into play here as well, as does the provocative (if perhaps still somewhat vaguely formed) theory of "panarchy" put forward by Lance Gunderson, C. S. Holling, and others.[26] These concepts are helping us ask new questions about how Pacific island societies co-evolved with their ecosystems as well as making the work of archaeologists more relevant than ever to the role and impact of *Homo sapiens* in that all encompassing socio-ecosystem we call Earth.

Over a half-century, I have witnessed enormous advances in the methods and practice of archaeology. In the 1960s radiocarbon dating was still primitive. I recall

Kenneth Emory telling me to collect the biggest pieces of charcoal I could find for radiocarbon dating. Little did he suspect that doing so was biasing our samples toward old-growth wood! In the 1980s, in the Waimea-Kawaihae and other projects (see Chapter Ten), we developed techniques for botanically identifying species of carbonized wood, allowing us to select and date only short-lived plants, eliminating the "old wood" problem. This led to the discovery that many early Eastern Polynesian sites were not as old as Emory, or Suggs, or Sinoto had once thought. Even the date for my Hālawa Dune Site on Molokaʻi (see Chapter Three) had to be revised.[27] These advances in radiocarbon sample selection led to a revolution in our understanding of when Eastern Polynesia was settled. Instead of voyagers from Western Polynesia arriving in the Marquesas around 150 BC as Suggs thought based on his dates from Haʻatuatua, we now believe that central Eastern Polynesia was first settled between AD 900–1100.

The techniques of radiocarbon dating, along with our appreciation of the complexities of ^{14}C calibration, have also improved dramatically. Accelerator mass spectrometry (AMS) reduced standard error ranges to thirty to forty years, whereas atmospheric and marine calibration curves allowed us to convert ^{14}C dates to calendar years. Bayesian statistical analysis of radiocarbon dates refines our chronologies with information from stratigraphic sequences. In short, today's radiocarbon dating is nothing like the primitive chronology building of my youth.

Another exciting advance is the highly precise uranium/thorium (U/Th) dating method, which Warren Sharp and I pioneered with our work on corals in Hawaiian *heiau* (see Chapter Eighteen). Using coral dating, David Burley has pinpointed the age of the first Lapita settlement in Tonga to 2838 ± 8 years before present.[28] U/Th dates from *marae* on Moʻorea Island allowed Sharp and me to show that temple architecture in the Society Islands evolved dramatically within less than two centuries (see Chapter Twenty).[29] I fully expect that continued application of the U/Th method will in time yield unprecedented control over Polynesian chronologies.

Stunning technological advances have also been achieved in the analysis of rocks used by Polynesians to manufacture stone tools. I remember Bill Kikuchi at the Bishop Museum trying to tackle this problem in the late 1960s, comparing petrographic "thin sections" cut from adzes with samples from known quarries, using a polarizing light microscope. But the method was too crude to discriminate among basalts with similar compositions. Frustrated, Kikuchi shelved the project. By the early 1990s newly developed instrumentation such as x-ray fluorescence (XRF) could determine the elemental composition of rocks in parts per million. While studying with me at Berkeley, Marshall Weisler applied XRF to adzes from different parts of Polynesia. We showed that adz flakes from Tangata-tau on Mangaia originated from Samoa.[30] Recently, Peter Mills and Steven Lundblad at the University of Hawai'i at Hilo have unraveled broad archipelago-wide patterns of adz production and exchange in Hawai'i, based on thousands of high-precision analyses. Bill Kikuchi, had he lived to see these results, would have been thrilled.

The list of technological advances goes on: analysis of the isotopic composition of bones, revealing aspects of diet; extraction and sequencing of ancient DNA from human skeletal remains and from the bones of rats, dogs, pigs, and chickens, opening windows onto the genetic relationships of populations of people as well as their commensal animals; global positioning systems (GPS) to precisely record site locations; geographic information systems (GIS) to digitally analyze spatial relationships; and LiDar mapping to reveal landscapes obscured by vegetation, to name just a few.

But without doubt the greatest technological change I have witnessed over the course of my career is the digital revolution, driven by Moore's Law, which dictates an exponential increase in the power of computing devices. Early in my professional career, we still typed article and book manuscripts by hand, corresponded by mail (neither the Internet nor e-mail existed), drew maps and other graphics by hand with pen and ink, took photographs with cameras loaded with film, cataloged artifacts and systematized data using card files, and surveyed with optical instruments (such as my beloved plane table and alidade). Today, everything is digitized and computerized; we carry entire libraries and databases around with us on our laptops, something unimaginable even thirty years ago.

I jumped on the digital bandwagon along with everyone else, buying a Kaypro-4/84 computer in 1984 and never looking back (see Chapter Ten). These technological advances have doubtless enhanced productivity. Yet I harbor a certain nostalgia over the loss of some of the old practices. Receiving mail from scholars in other countries—opening airmail envelopes decked out with colorful stamps—was something to be savored in a leisurely fashion. Not so with the incessant barrage of e-mail that occupies ever-increasing chunks of my time. Likewise, I used to take great pleasure in inking my maps by hand at the drafting table—there was a certain "Zen" to hand cartography that is not replicated with Adobe Illustrator. I miss these departed ways of doing things and feel sorry that a younger generation will never experience them.

All of these technological advances also come with strings attached, one of which is increased specialization. When I was in graduate school, one trained to be an archaeologist, within a geographic area of interest. One student might be more interested in pottery, another in stone tools, but everyone was expected to master the principal methods and techniques. Four decades later, our students self-identify as zooarchaeologists, geoarchaeologists, archaeobotanists, or spatial archaeologists (using GIS), not as "jack-of-all-trades" archaeologists. Each subfield now has its own specialized journals and an ever-expanding literature, accompanied by its own technical jargon.

Gone are the days when a lone archaeologist—Robert Suggs, or Roger Green, or Pat Kirch—could step off a boat and "do" the archaeology of Nuku Hiva, 'Upolu, or Tikopia. Now we arrive in teams of four or five—or more—digging together but taking our fishbones, plant remains, and rock samples off to separate laboratories for analysis. The cost of research rises, while coordinating these teams during the long, drawn-out period of post-excavation analysis becomes increasingly challenging. The gains in information we extract about the past are presumably worth the cost and effort. But again I admit to having a certain nostalgia for the old days.

There have been other changes in the practice of Pacific archaeology. In the post–World War II era, Polynesian archaeology was largely the domain of White male researchers from elite universities or museums in the United States, New Zealand, and Australia. In the early 1980s, Pacific islanders began to be recruited for the first time into academic programs in archaeology. Today, the number of indigenous archaeologists in the Pacific has finally become significant. In Hawai'i, Kehau Abad, Kathy Kawelu, and Keku'ewa Kikiloi all have PhD degrees in archaeology; many more Native Hawaiians are engaged in cultural resources management (CRM) archaeology or are in academic degree programs. Other archaeologists hailing from Pacific island communities include Herman Mandui, John Muke, and Nick Araho in New Guinea; Lawrence Foanaota in the Solomon Islands; Jacques Bole and André Ouetcho in New Caledonia; 'Epi Su'afoa in Samoa; Hinanui Cauchois and Paul Niva in Tahiti; and Sergio Rapu and Sonya Haoa in Rapa Nui, to name just a few.

Indigenous archaeologists inevitably change the questions that we ask about the past. Intimately connected with their natal communities, these scholars bring a strong commitment to engage with the descendants of the peoples whose history we study.[31] The entry of Native Hawaiians into archaeology has helped reverse the negative perceptions that inspired my Kaua'i keynote speech in 1997 (see Chapter Eighteen). To now witness archaeologists at the annual meeting of the Society for Hawaiian Archaeology learning the cultural protocols and chants to be used before entering or leaving a *wahi pana* is a marvelous thing. Even more inspiring has been hearing the presentations of the young Native Hawaiian scholars in Kelly Ueoka's internship program. With so many young, enthusiastic Kanaka Ma'oli entering the field, I know that the future for archaeology in Hawai'i is bright.

In the mid-1960s, archaeology in Hawai'i was the exclusive purview of the Bishop Museum and the University of Hawai'i (UH). The lone exception was Ed Ladd, then employed by the National Park Service to restore sites at Hōnaunau National Historical Park. Bishop Museum's Emory and Sinoto dominated the scene, supported by junior staff such as Lloyd Soehren, Bill Kikuchi, and Marion Kelly. At UH Mānoa, Richard Pearson was getting his feet wet in Hawaiian archaeology, although his first commitment was always to East Asia.

By the time I officially joined the Bishop Museum staff in 1975 the institution had ramped up its archaeology program. Patrick McCoy and Paul Rosendahl were among the PhD archaeologists; Doug Yen was deeply involved as well. Steve Athens and Tom Riley were soon hired to direct the museum's contract archaeology program. At the university in Mānoa, P. Bion Griffin and David Tuggle joined the faculty, running the field school at Lapakahi started by Pearson and Roger Green. The State of Hawai'i had also established a Historic Preservation Office, at first housed within the Division of State Parks but soon to become its own division.

Hawaiian archaeology was rapidly changing. Responding to the demand for contract archaeology, archaeologists were setting up shop as independent consultants, giving rise to the emerging field of CRM. The post-statehood shift in Hawai'i from a plantation- to a tourism-based economy spurred the demand for archaeological work. Among those who established consulting firms in the late 1970s and early 1980s were Stephen Athens, Bill Barrera, Francis Ching, Hallett Hammett, Robert Hommon, and Paul Rosendahl. Many others would soon join them. Today, the State Historic Preservation Division's website lists twenty-six consulting firms doing archaeological work in the islands.

The increased dominance of CRM in Hawai'i over the past thirty years can be summed up in terms of "the good, the bad, and the ugly," to borrow the title of Sergio Leone's famous Western. The good: More archaeological work has been accomplished—supported by a vast expenditure of private and public monies—than was ever dreamed of by the older research institutions. The bad: Most of this archaeological work is reported only in limited, photocopied "gray literature" reports. The results are all too rarely published in scholarly journals, let alone synthesized for the public at large.

Now for the ugly part, which has two aspects. First, responding to their bottom line, some CRM practitioners regularly cut corners, failing to meet minimal professional standards. Sites are overlooked in too rapid surveys, documentation is substandard, and potentially significant contributions to our understanding of Hawaiian history go unnoticed. Second, the products of all this archaeological work—the original data and the collections of artifacts and specimens—are not being cared for. There is a huge "curation crisis" in Hawaiian archaeology. Field notes, photographs, artifacts, and radiocarbon samples are rotting in garages and storage lockers around the state, with no coordinated plan for long-term preservation. The irreplaceable record of Hawai'i's past is in danger of disappearing out of sheer neglect.

Institutional support for research-oriented archaeology in Hawai'i (as opposed to CRM archaeology) has also diminished. One year after arriving at the Bishop Museum in 1984, director Donald Duckworth fired many members of the museum's research staff, including Patrick McCoy and Marion Kelly. The remaining archaeologists were reorganized as an "applied research" group, with the goal of bringing in lucrative CRM contracts. But when the federal H3 highway contracts expired a few years later, the applied research group was disbanded. The demise of research at the Bishop Museum has not been limited to archaeology. In 1981, the museum employed twenty-eight researchers holding PhD degrees, and 50 percent of the museum's staff were engaged in research or collections-based activities. In 2011, the museum employed just eight PhD scientists; only 20 percent of the staff worked in research or collections.[32]

In 2011 I traveled to Kuala Lumpur to attend the Twenty-Second Pacific Science Congress, where I was being honored with the Herbert E. Gregory Medal for Distinguished Service to Science in the Pacific.[33] The Gregory Medal, created in 1961, is named for the Bishop Museum's second director, who organized the first Pan-Pacific Scientific Congress in Honolulu in 1920 and strategically put the museum in the forefront of Pacific research in the 1920s and 1930s. The list of hundreds of scientists attending the Kuala Lumpur meeting, in fields ranging from archaeology to zoology, did not include a single researcher from the Bishop Museum. The museum had not even sent an official representative. The irony was poignant.

It is easy to forget that museum collections are the fruits of field research, that the labels in exhibit cases depend upon the knowledge created by the scientists laboring behind the scenes. When a museum ceases to engage in research, ceases to add to its collections, and ceases to pursue the frontiers of knowledge, it becomes static, fossilized, trapped in an older era. Such institutions eventually become mere "museums of museums," quaint mementos of a bygone era. I hope that this will not be Bishop Museum's fate; I have too much aloha for the institution that laid the foundations for modern archaeology and natural history in the Pacific—and, as my mentor Kondo would have reminded me, too heavy a personal debt (what the Japanese call *on*) for the opportunities Bishop Museum gave me, launching me on my career. I hope that the Bishop Museum's leaders will yet muster the vision to restore the institution's proud tradition of research, of not just exhibiting knowledge but also of creating it. Future generations in Hawai'i and the island nations of the Pacific will be the beneficiaries.

With all of these changes in the theory, methods, and practices of archaeology, what have we learned about the Polynesian past over the past five decades? What advances have we made in our understanding of the histories of these island cultures? Pondering these questions, I pulled from my bookshelf Robert Carl Suggs' *The Island Civilizations of Polynesia*, published in 1961, skimming the yellowing and brittle pages.[34] Suggs' book was the first updating of Polynesian prehistory since Hiroa's *Vikings of the Sunrise* (1939),[35] incorporating exciting results of the post–World War II resurgence of archaeology. I had read Suggs' book as a fourteen-year old in 1964. His writing inspired my budding career in archaeology.

To conclude this chapter, I have chosen five examples from Suggs' book as a way to assess how far we have progressed in our understanding of the Polynesian past over the last half-century. I hasten to add that this is in no way intended as a criticism of Robert Suggs, for whom I have the greatest admiration. He was at the cutting edge of research in 1961, and he helped move Polynesian archaeology in new directions.

Archaeological knowledge of Southeast Asia, the New Guinea region, and island Melanesia was in its infancy when Suggs drafted his chapter, "Out from Asia," which traces the migrations of the "Malayo-Polynesian speaking groups," what we now call the Austronesians. For Melanesia, Suggs had to rely almost exclusively on the pioneering excavations of Berkeley's Edward Gifford. The term "Lapita" appears but once in Suggs' book, when he mentions the "unusual pottery" from Koné on New Caledonia, then recently dated by Gifford to about 800 BC. Suggs' brief comment about Lapita is amazingly prescient: "This pottery appeared in small quantities on unexcavated sites in Fiji and *may ultimately attain increased archaeological importance*" (emphasis added). Lapita has indeed attained prominence as the founding culture throughout island Melanesia east of the Solomons and on into Fiji and Western Polynesia. A topic that took up just three sentences in Suggs' book is now at the core of our understanding of Pacific prehistory.

My second example concerns the movement of early Polynesians out of the Western Polynesian homeland (Suggs used the Polynesian name Hawaiki for this homeland, as did Roger Green and I years later) into central Eastern Polynesia. Based on his excavations at Ha'atuatua on Nuku Hiva, Suggs believed that this event had occurred "in the second century B.C." Comparing the handful of potsherds from Ha'atuatua with Golson's pottery from Vailele in Samoa, Suggs drew a direct connection between Samoa and the Marquesas. (This was a radical shift from Te Rangi Hiroa's view that Tahiti had been the center of Eastern Polynesian settlement.) But we now know that Suggs' dating for this initial Marquesan settlement was at least one thousand years too old. The error was not his fault; it was due to the primitive nature of radiocarbon dating in the 1950s, especially the lack of control over dating old wood, such as driftwood, which grew and died (and then floated around the Pacific) for centuries before it was finally burned by colonizing islanders. We now know that Polynesians arrived in the Marquesas not much earlier than AD 900. This later settlement date greatly shortens the time span over which the Marquesans—and other Eastern Polynesian cultures—subsequently evolved their unique variants of Eastern Polynesian culture.

My third example is the evolution of ritual architecture, *marae,* in the Society Islands. In 1961 nothing was known of subsurface archaeology in this central archipelago. Quoting Suggs: "As I write, however, Dr. Douglas Oliver and Mr. J. [*sic*] Green of Harvard University are in Tahiti, preparing to undertake some excavations in Raiatea and Moorea." He was referring, of course, to Roger Green's seminal settlement pattern survey of the 'Ōpūnohu Valley. Absent direct evidence of how Tahitian *marae* had developed over time, Suggs fell back on Kenneth Emory's pre–World War II hypothetical sequence of temple development, from simple to complex.[36] Influenced by his own work in the Marquesas, Suggs assumed that Emory's temple sequence of temple development required a long chronology.

Suggs proposed that Emory's "Intermediate" type of *marae,* with an enclosed court and platform *ahu,* "often faced with dressed coral blocks," appeared between AD 1000–1100. Then, according to Suggs, "from the fourteenth century on, the development of temple architecture in Tahiti was rapid and spectacular, evolving the structures known as the Coastal *marae.*" Today, with the insights into *marae* chronology that Warren Sharp and I obtained from U/Th coral dating in the 'Ōpūnohu Valley, we know that the sequence of temple development described by Suggs occurred over a mere two centuries. The valley's oldest and simplest *marae* date to the fifteenth century, whereas the "Intermediate" and "Coastal" forms did not arise until the seventeenth and eighteenth centuries. Suggs was correct in claiming that the development of Society Islands ritual architecture was "rapid and spectacular," but he had no idea of just how rapid this evolution really had been.

My fourth example revolves around Suggs' views of the theories of Norwegian adventurer Thor Heyerdahl and his ideas about how the sweet potato came into the Pacific. Suggs devoted a chapter of his 1961 book to "the Kon-Tiki myth." Heyerdahl had pointed to the fact that the Eastern Polynesian cultures of Easter Island, New Zealand, and Hawai'i extensively cultivated the sweet potato, which many botanists thought had been domesticated in South America. And, Heyerdahl noted, the Polynesian word for this tuber crop, *kumara, 'umara,* or *'uala,* was suspiciously similar to the word used by the Quechua people of South America for sweet potato, *kumar.* Suggs was dismissive of this linguistic evidence: "This is similar to maintaining that Coca-Cola originated in Arabia because Arabians now use the word." Citing botanist Elmer D. Merrill as his authority, Suggs claimed that the sweet potato was "probably of African origin." Yet just as Suggs was writing, Douglas Yen was studying sweet potato variation across the Pacific. Yen's research would soon support a South American origin of the crop. At the 1961 Pacific Science Congress in Honolulu, Yen presented his evidence, arguing that "Polynesian contact" with the coastal peoples of Peru or Chile resulted in the plant's transfer into the Pacific.[37]

Four decades later, a wealth of genetic and archaeological data leave no doubt that the sweet potato was indeed domesticated, as Heyerdahl thought and Yen's work confirmed, in South America.[38] That the sweet potato came from South America, however, did not mean that Heyerdahl's theory of the South American origins of the Polynesians was correct. Quite the contrary, all the evidence points to Polynesian seafarers reaching the shores of South America and taking the *kumara* (along with its name) back to Polynesia with them. My own discovery of carbonized sweet potato tubers in the Tangata-tau rockshelter (see Chapter Seventeen) was just one contribution to this history of the sweet potato and its spread in the Pacific.

My final example comes from Suggs' chapter "North to Flaming Hawaii." Drawing upon Emory and Sinoto's excavations at South Point and elsewhere in Hawai'i, Suggs put the initial settlement of the archipelago at "approximately A.D. 120 ± 120 years, earlier than even Emory expected." Suggs identified the source of the first settlers to Hawai'i as Tahiti, based on the nature of the early "total tool assemblage." As Suggs summed it up, "The Hawaiian Islands were discovered and settled by a large expedition from Tahiti in the second century after Christ." The culture represented by the enigmatic ruins on remote Nihoa and Necker islands to the northwest of Kaua'i was taken to be representative of this early period. Then, in the fourteenth century, contact with Tahiti resumed with the famous voyage of Pā'ao, "resulting in an influx of new ideas," including changes in the forms of temple architecture.

Emory and Sinoto would soon revise their theory of initial settlement of Hawai'i from Tahiti, after Sinoto's excavations on Ua Huka in the Marquesas showed that early Hawaiian artifacts were closer to Marquesan forms than those found in the Society Islands. Then, Roger Green demonstrated that the Hawaiian language contained elements of both the Marquesic and Tahitic branches of

Eastern Polynesian. This led to a two-stage model of Hawaiian settlement, first from the Marquesas and only later from Tahiti, one that has garnered support from genetic studies of the Polynesian rat. Most strikingly, the date for Polynesian arrival in the Hawaiian Islands is now considered to be around AD 1000, centuries later than Suggs—basing his interpretation on Emory's dating of what must have been old driftwood from the Puʻu Aliʻi sand dune—had claimed in 1961.[39]

These five examples highlight just how much our understanding of the Polynesian past has advanced since Suggs wrote *The Island Civilizations of Polynesia* in 1961. Suggs, like all of us, worked with available evidence, struggling to make a coherent and credible account of it all. But as the great evolutionary biologist Ernst Mayr famously wrote, science is a self-correcting system.[40] Over time, we discover and correct our mistakes, we recognize where bias has unduly influenced our thinking, we fill in our gaps in knowledge. In the process, our understanding deepens. The greatest gratification of a life in science is in seeing such understanding of the world unfold.

The act of writing one's memoirs—of committing a life to ink on paper—has an unsettling finality about it. I sometimes ask myself whether my career in Polynesian archaeology has come to an end. Are there no more islands to explore, no new sites to map with my plane table and alidade (or now record with my GPS), no new discoveries to make? No, I resolutely tell myself. There is still so much to do, so many new questions that cry out to be addressed—not to mention the backlog of unfinished projects simmering on the back burner. I still need to complete the analysis of the Lapita pottery from Mussau, to write a full account of the excavations at Tangata-tau, and to author a detailed monograph on household archaeology in Kahikinui. Then there are other topics that I would like to delve into, such as an inquiry into why cannibalism arose in some Polynesian societies, whereas ritualized human sacrifice occurred in others. A comparison of Polynesian ritual architecture is also on my list.

One of my fondest memories is of a lunch I shared with the great evolutionary biologist Ernst Mayr at the American Philosophical Society meeting in Philadelphia in 1999. As a newly elected member of that august society founded by Benjamin Franklin, I was stewarded around by my old mentor Ward Goodenough. Goodenough introduced me to Mayr, and the three of us sat down with our sandwiches at a table in historic Philosophical Hall. After responding to Mayr's questions about my own research projects, I asked Mayr (who was ninety-five years old at the time) what he was working on. In his German accent he replied, "I have three books to finish before I die." He proceeded to name the titles. Several years later after Mayr died at the age of 101, I realized that he had indeed finished and published all three books. Whether fate will permit me to be as productive into my later years as Ernst Mayr only time will tell, but his was certainly a life to emulate.

Of course, my knees are not what they used to be; too many field seasons of sitting cross-legged on *Pandanus* mats and kneeling in pits for long hours while excavating have taken their toll. These days I mostly leave the digging to younger colleagues, preferring to spend my days in the field picking through the scraps of bone and shell in a sifting screen. My eyesight—after cataract surgery to undo the damage from years of intense tropical sunlight—is nearly as sharp as ever. I can find fragments of pearl shell fishhooks that younger, unseasoned eyes sometimes miss. Nor have I given up my love of plane table mapping, a technique that has yet to be adequately replaced by any digital technology. It pleases me that several of my students asked me to teach them this method, knowing that they will carry on the tradition.

There is still nothing so exciting and satisfying for me as spending my days "in the field," as we archaeologists say. Whether on the windy slopes of Nuʻu in Kaupō, or in a little skiff getting soaked with sea spray while crossing Mangareva's vast lagoon, I hope to experience the pleasures of fieldwork on Polynesian islands for some years to come. And so, to borrow a phrase from that great English archaeologist, Sir Mortimer Wheeler, I hope to be "still digging."

NOTES

One outcome of my early association with Yoshio Kondo of the Bishop Museum (see Chapter Two) was a compulsion to keep detailed field notebooks, a practice I began with my first trip to Moloka'i's Hālawa Valley in 1964. In writing this book I have consulted these notebooks and field journals extensively. Conversations with various individuals have been rendered to the best of my memory, although when recalling dialogue that occurred decades ago, some degree of creative license must be allowed for.

The old Tahitian song is from Clifford Gessler, 1937, *Road My Body Goes* (New York: Reynal and Hitchcock).

Chapter 1. *Keiki o ka 'Āina*

1. For a summary of Harold William Kirch's career in Hawai'i's orchid industry, see Patrick V. Kirch, 2003, "In Memoriam—Harold William Kirch," *Orchids, The Magazine of the American Orchid Society,* January, p. 10.

2. Mānoa's history, along with many historical photographs, is told in Mānoa Valley Residents, 1994, *Mānoa: The Story of a Valley* (Honolulu: Mutual Publishing).

3. The early history of Punahou School is recounted by Mary C. Alexander and Charlotte P. Dodge, 1941, *Punahou, 1841–1941* (Berkeley: University of California Press).

4. See Francis Haar (photographer) and Cobey Black (narrator), 1985, *'Iolani Luahine* (Honolulu: Topgallant Publishing Co.).

5. Roger Rose, 1980, *A Museum to Instruct and Delight* (Honolulu: Bishop Museum Press), recounts the founding of the Bishop Museum and includes photos of the exhibit halls more or less as they remained into the 1950s, prior to later renovations that "modernized" the galleries.

6. The history of Polynesian anthropology and archaeology, including the important role of the Bishop Museum's Bayard Dominick Expeditions, is summarized in Patrick V. Kirch, 2000, *On the Road of the Winds: An Archaeological History of the Pacific Islands Before European Contact* (Berkeley: University of California Press), pp. 20–41.

7. Peter H. Buck (Te Rangi Hiroa), 1938, *Vikings of the Sunrise* (Philadelphia: J. B. Lippincott Co.), p. 12.

8. Thor Heyerdahl, 1950, *Kon Tiki: Across the Pacific by Raft* (London: Allen & Unwin).

9. Thor Heyerdahl, 1958, *Aku-Aku: The Secret of Easter Island* (London: Allen & Unwin).

10. Willard F. Libby, 1952, *Radiocarbon Dating* (Chicago: University of Chicago Press); the Kuli'ou'ou date is reported on p. 95. See also R. E. Taylor, 1987, *Radiocarbon Dating: An Archaeological Perspective* (New York: Academic Press) for a history of radiocarbon dating.

11. The story of Kenneth Emory's long career in Polynesian archaeology is recounted by Bob Krauss, 1988, *Keneti: South Seas Adventures of Kenneth Emory* (Honolulu: University of Hawai'i Press).

12. Emory reported the Kuli'ou'ou radiocarbon date and discussed its significance in his preface to Kenneth P. Emory, William J. Bonk, and Yosihiko H. Sinoto, 1959, *Hawaiian Archaeology: Fishhooks*, Bernice P. Bishop Museum Special Publication 47 (Honolulu: Bishop Museum Press), p. ix.

13. E. W. Gifford, 1951, *Archaeological Excavations in Fiji*, Anthropological Records 13:189–288 (Berkeley: University of California Press). E. W. Gifford and D. Shutler Jr., 1956, *Archaeological Excavations in New Caledonia*, Anthropological Records 18:1–125 (Berkeley: University of California Press).

14. Thor Heyerdahl and Edwin N. Ferdon Jr., Eds., 1961, *Reports of the Norwegian Archaeological Expedition to Easter Island and the East Pacific*. Vol. 1, *Archaeology of Easter Island*, Monographs of the School of American Research 24 (Santa Fe: School of American Research).

15. Robert C. Suggs, 1962, *The Hidden Worlds of Polynesia* (New York: Harcourt, Brace, and World).

Chapter 2. An Apprenticeship in Science

1. The life and scientific contributions of Charles Montague Cooke Jr. are related by Yoshio Kondo and William J. Clench, 1952, *Charles Montague Cooke, Jr., A Bio-Bibliography*, Bernice P. Bishop Museum Special Publication 42 (Honolulu: Bishop Museum Press).

2. Regrettably, no detailed account of Yoshio Kondo's remarkable life has ever been published, although a brief biographical statement and a list of his contributions to Pacific land snail taxonomy are provided in Robert H. Cowie, 1993, "Yoshio Kondo: Bibliography and List of Taxa," *Bishop Museum Occasional Papers*, No. 32 (Honolulu: Bishop Museum Press). Kondo used to tell me that someday I should write his story under the title "Tales of a Traveling Snailsman." Perhaps in my retirement I will yet do that.

3. Patrick Vinton Kirch, MS [1965], "Halawa Valley, Molokai: A Survey of the Native Culture," Typescript, 105 pp., 15 figs., 7 tables. Original carbon copy in author's possession.

4. The 1965 fieldwork on Hawai'i Island was never published, but the excavation results were reported by Lloyd J. Soehren, "Hawaii Excavations, 1965" (MS in Library and Archives of the Bishop Museum, Honolulu).

5. Patrick Vinton Kirch, 2014, *Kua'āina Kahiko: Life and Land in Ancient Kahikinui, Maui* (Honolulu: University of Hawai'i Press).

6. For more on Roger Green and his contributions to Pacific archaeology, see Patrick V. Kirch, 2010, "Roger Curtis Green, March 15, 1932–October 4, 2009," *Biographical Memoirs of the U.S. National Academy of Sciences*, Washington, DC. (http://www.nasonline.org /publications/biographical-memoirs/memoir-pdfs/green-roger.pdf).

7. D. E. Yen, 1974, *The Sweet Potato and Oceania: An Essay in Ethnobotany*, Bernice P. Bishop Museum Bulletin 236 (Honolulu: Bishop Museum Press).

8. On "thinking in prose" see Richard Dawkins, 2013, *An Appetite for Wonder: The Making of a Scientist* (New York: Harper Collins), p. 291. On the "historical-narrative" mode of explanation in science, see Ernst Mayr, 1982, *The Growth of Biological Thought: Diversity, Evolution, and Inheritance* (Cambridge, MA: Harvard University Press), pp. 71–73.

9. K. C. Chang, 1967. *Rethinking Archaeology*. (New York: Random House).

10. Richard Pearson, Patrick V. Kirch, and Michael Pietrusewsky, 1971, "An Early Prehistoric Site at Bellows Beach, Waimanalo, Oahu, Hawaiian Islands," *Archaeology and Physical Anthropology in Oceania* 6:204–234.

11. The age of the O18 Bellows Beach site has recently been firmly established by accelerator mass spectrometry (AMS) dating of specimens originally excavated in 1967 to the period AD 1050–1209. See T. S. Dye, 2011, "A Model-Based Age Estimate for Polynesian Colonization of Hawai'i," *Archaeology in Oceania* 46:130–138.

12. G. A. Highland, R. W. Force, A. Howard, M. Kelly, and Y. H. Sinoto, Eds., 1967, *Polynesian Culture History: Essays in Honor of Kenneth P. Emory,* Bernice P. Bishop Museum Special Publication 56 (Honolulu: Bishop Museum Press).

13. Patrick V. Kirch, 1970, "Houses on Lifou, Loyalty Islands," *Journal of the Polynesian Society* 79:43–53.

Chapter 3. Moloka'i-Nui-a-Hina

1. Sally R. Binford and Lewis R. Binford, Eds., 1968, *New Perspectives in Archeology* (Chicago: Aldine). David L. Clarke, 1968, *Analytical Archaeology* (London: Methuen & Co.).

2. "A Häolé" was the pseudonym of George Washington Bates, whose engaging account of Hālawa in the early 1850s may be found in his 1854 book, *Sandwich Island Notes* (New York: Harper & Brothers).

3. Jacques Barrau, 1958, *Subsistence Agriculture in Melanesia,* Bernice P. Bishop Museum Bulletin 219 (Honolulu: Bishop Museum Press); Barrau's theory of the evolution of Oceanic agriculture is summarized on pp. 33–34.

4. For an overview of the University Museum and its contributions to world archaeology, see D. P. Winegrad, 1993, *Through Time, Across Continents: A Hundred Years of Archaeology and Anthropology at the University Museum* (Philadelphia: University Museum).

5. Edgar Anderson, 1952, *Plants, Man and Life* (New York: Little, Brown and Co.); L. von Bertalanffy, 1968, *General System Theory: Foundations, Development, Applications* (New York: George Braziller); Robert H. MacArthur and E. O. Wilson, 1967, *The Theory of Island Biogeography,* Monographs in Population Biology 1 (Princeton, NJ: Princeton University Press); Ernst Mayr, 1942, *Systematics and the Origin of Species,* Facsimile Reprint 1964 (New York: Dover Publications); Carl O. Sauer, 1967, *Land and Life* (Berkeley: University of California Press).

6. Patrick V. Kirch, 1973, "Prehistoric Subsistence Patterns in the Northern Marquesas Islands, French Polynesia," *Archaeology and Physical Anthropology in Oceania* 8:24–40.

7. Douglas E. Yen, Patrick V. Kirch, Tom Riley, and Paul Rosendahl, 1972, "Prehistoric Agriculture in the Upper Valley of Makaha, Oahu," in E. Ladd and D. E. Yen, Eds., *Makaha Valley Historical Project: Interim Report No. 3,* pp. 59–94, Pacific Anthropological Records 18 (Honolulu: Bishop Museum). I described our 1970 fieldwork in Mākaha and its significance more thoroughly in chapter 9 (pp. 147–150) of Patrick Vinton Kirch, 2012, *A Shark Going Inland Is My Chief: The Island Civilization of Ancient Hawai'i* (Berkeley: University of California Press).

8. For an account of our 1970 fieldwork in Hālawa by one of the volunteers on the project, see Victoria Nelson, 1989, *My Time in Hawaii: A Polynesian Memoir* (New York: St. Martin's Press).

9. For a preliminary account of the Hālawa dune site excavations, see Patrick V. Kirch, 1971, "Halawa Dune Site (Hawaiian Islands): A Preliminary Report," *Journal of the Polynesian Society* 80:228–236. The research objectives of the Hālawa Valley Project were outlined in Patrick V. Kirch,

1971, "Halawa Valley Project: Two Field Seasons in Retrospect," *New Zealand Archaeological Association Newsletter* 14:47–61. The final report of the Hālawa Valley Project is Patrick Vinton Kirch and Marion Kelly, Eds., 1975, *Prehistory and Ecology in a Windward Hawaiian Valley: Halawa Valley, Moloka'i,* Pacific Anthropological Records 24 (Honolulu: Bishop Museum).

Chapter 4. The Smallest Polynesian Island

1. Roger C. Green and M. M. Cresswell, Eds., 1976, *Southeast Solomon Islands Cultural History: A Preliminary Survey,* Royal Society of New Zealand Bulletin 11 (Wellington: Royal Society of New Zealand).

2. James A. Michener, 1947, *Tales of the South Pacific* (New York: Macmillan).

3. Woodford's forays to the Solomon Islands as a naturalist, before becoming the first resident commissioner of the British Solomon Islands Protectorate, are recounted in Charles M. Woodford, 1890, *A Naturalist Among the Head-Hunters* (London: George Philip & Son).

4. In 1971, the only ethnographic information available on Anuta Island was a short article by Raymond Firth, 1954, "Anuta and Tikopia: Symbiotic Elements in Social Organization," *Journal of the Polynesian Society* 63:87–131.

5. Following our expedition, Richard Feinberg carried out ethnographic fieldwork on Anuta in 1972. Richard Feinberg, 1981, *Anuta: Social Structure of a Polynesian Island* (Laie, Hawai'i: Institute for Polynesian Studies).

6. The prefixes Pu and Nau are used to signify the male and female members of a married couple, in the same way that Mr. and Mrs. are used in Western culture. The proper name of the couple is the same as that of their dwelling house; such house names are inherited.

7. Richard Feinberg, 1998, *Oral Traditions of Anuta: A Polynesian Outlier in the Solomon Islands* (New York: Oxford University Press), includes a variant of the Anutan origin tradition.

8. The results of our 1971 Bishop Museum expedition to Anuta were published in D. E. Yen and J. Gordon, Eds., 1973, *Anuta: A Polynesian Outlier in the Solomon Islands,* Pacific Anthropological Records 21 (Honolulu: Bishop Museum). See also Patrick V. Kirch and Paul H. Rosendahl, 1976, "Early Anutan Settlement and the Position of Anuta in the Prehistory of the Southwest Pacific," in Roger C. Green and M. M. Cresswell, Eds., *Southeast Solomon Islands Cultural History,* pp. 223–244. I later presented a reanalysis of the Anutan cultural sequence in Patrick V. Kirch, 1982, "A Revision of the Anutan Sequence," *Journal of the Polynesian Society* 91:245–254.

Chapter 5. *Lux et Veritas*

1. For an overview of the life and scientific contributions of K. C. Chang, see Robert E. Murowchick, 2012, "Kwang-chih Chang, 1931–2001," *Biographical Memoirs of the U.S. National Academy of Sciences,* Washington, DC (http://www.nasonline.org/publications/biographical -memoirs/memoir-pdfs/chang-kwang-chih-1.pdf).

2. Leopold Pospisil, 1963, *Kapauku Papuan Economy,* Yale University Publications in Anthropology 67 (New Haven, CT: Yale University Press).

3. Conklin's magnum opus on Ifugao agriculture, which he was working on while I was a Yale student, is Harold C. Conklin, P. Lupiah, and M. Pinther, 1980, *Ethnographic Atlas of Ifugao: A Study of Environment, Culture, and Society in Northern Luzon* (New Haven, CT: Yale University Press).

4. Patrick Vinton Kirch, 1973, *Archaeological Excavations at Kahalu'u, North Kona, Island of Hawaii,* Anthropology Department Report 73–1 (Honolulu: Bishop Museum).

5. Patrick Vinton Kirch, 1979, *Marine Exploitation in Prehistoric Hawaiʻi: Archaeological Investigations at Kalahuipuaʻa, Hawaiʻi Island,* Pacific Anthropological Records 29 (Honolulu: Bishop Museum).

6. Karl Wittfogel, 1957, *Oriental Despotism* (New Haven, CT: Yale University Press); quote regarding Hawaiʻi from p. 241.

7. Marshall D. Sahlins, 1958, *Social Stratification in Polynesia* (Seattle: American Ethnological Society).

8. Edwin G. Burrows, 1936, *Ethnology of Futuna,* Bernice P. Bishop Museum Bulletin 138 (Honolulu: Bishop Museum Press).

Chapter 6. Of Pigs and Pondfields

1. Le Rev. Père Grézel, 1877, "Grammaire Futunienne," *Revue de Linguistique et Philologie Comparée* 10:321–325, 11:33–69. Le Rev. Père Grézel, 1878, *Dictionnaire Futunien-Français avec Notes Grammaticales* (Paris: Maisonneuve et Cie).

2. J. A. J. de Villiers, Trans., 1906, *The East and West Indian Mirror, Being an Account of . . . the Australian Navigations of Jacob le Maire,* Hakluyt Society, Series II, No. XVIII (London: Cambridge University Press).

3. J.-A. Bourdin, 1867, *Vie du Vénérable P.-M. L. Chanel* (Paris: J. Lecoffre et Cie). Le Rev. Père Mangeret, 1932, *La Croix dans les Îles du Pacifique* (Lyon).

4. My ethnographic account of Futunan agriculture was published as Patrick Vinton Kirch, 1994, *The Wet and the Dry: Irrigation and Agricultural Intensification in Polynesia* (Chicago: University of Chicago Press).

5. My botanical collections were published by Harold C. St. John, 1977, "Additions to the Flora of Futuna Island, Horne Islands," *Phytologia* 36:367–390.

6. On the excavations at Tavai and other early sites on Futuna, see P. V. Kirch, 1981, "Lapitoid Settlements of Futuna and Alofi, Western Polynesia," *Archaeology in Oceania* 16:127–143. See also P. V. Kirch, "Rapport préliminaire sur les recherches éffectuées aux îles Wallis et Futuna (Polynésie Occidentale)," *Journal de la Société des Océanistes* 32:107–110.

7. I later reconstructed the traditional religious system of Futuna based on the journal of Père Chanel; see P. V. Kirch, 1994, "The Pre-Christian Ritual Cycle of Futuna, Western Polynesia," *Journal of the Polynesian Society* 103:255–298.

8. The rendering of the kava commands given here follows E. G. Burrows, 1936, *Ethnology of Futuna,* Bernice P. Bishop Museum Bulletin 138 (Honolulu: Bishop Museum Press), pp. 202–203.

9. Results of my fieldwork on ʻUvea were published in P. V. Kirch, 1976, "Ethno-Archaeological Investigations in Futuna and ʻUvea (Western Polynesia): A Preliminary Report," *Journal of the Polynesian Society* 85:27–69; and in P. V. Kirch, 1978, "Indigenous Agriculture on ʻUvea (Western Polynesia)," *Economic Botany* 32:157–181.

10. Patrick Vinton Kirch, 1975, "Cultural Adaptation and Ecology in Western Polynesia: An Ethnoarchaeological Study," Unpublished PhD Dissertation, Yale University, New Haven.

Chapter 7. The Isle of Sacred Coconuts

1. Garth Rogers, 1974, "Archaeological Discoveries on Niuatoputapu Island, Tonga," *Journal of the Polynesian Society* 83:308–348.

2. The mapping of burial mounds in Vavaʻu turned out to have interesting implications for Tongan sociopolitical organization, which were published in P. V. Kirch, 1980, "Burial Structures and Societal Ranking in Vavaʻu, Tonga," *Journal of the Polynesian Society* 89:291-308.

3. The concept of a Tongan "maritime empire" was proposed by Jean Guiart, 1963, *La Chefferie en Mélanésie du Sud* (Paris: Institut d'Ethnologie, Musée de l'Homme).

4. On the hierarchical society of traditional Tonga see Edward Gifford, 1929, *Tongan Society*, Bernice P. Bishop Museum Bulletin 61 (Honolulu: Bishop Museum Press).

5. P. V. Kirch and T. S. Dye, 1979, "Ethnoarchaeology and the Development of Polynesian Fishing Strategies," *Journal of the Polynesian Society* 88:53-76.

6. W. C. McKern, 1929, *Archaeology of Tonga*, Bernice P. Bishop Museum Bulletin 60 (Honolulu: Bishop Museum Press); the quote regarding *sia heu lupe* is from p. 20.

7. Patrick Vinton Kirch, 1988, *Niuatoputapu: The Prehistory of a Polynesian Chiefdom*, Thomas Burke Memorial Washington State Museum Monograph 5 (Seattle: Burke Museum). See also P. V. Kirch, 1978, "The Lapitoid Period in West Polynesia: Excavations and Survey in Niuatoputapu, Tonga," *Journal of Field Archaeology* 5:1-12.

Chapter 8. *Matou, Nga Tikopia*

1. M. W. Young, 2004, *Malinowski: Odyssey of an Anthropologist, 1884-1920* (New Haven, CT, Yale University Press).

2. Raymond Firth, 1936, *We, The Tikopia: A Sociological Study of Kinship in Primitive Polynesia* (New York: American Book Company). On the Tikopia economy, see Raymond Firth, 1939, *Primitive Polynesian Economy* (London: George Routledge & Sons).

3. Raymond Firth, 1961, *History and Traditions of Tikopia*, Polynesian Society Memoir 33 (Wellington, New Zealand: Polynesian Society).

4. José Garanger, 1972, *Archéologie des Nouvelles-Hébrides*, Publication de la Société des Océanistes 30 (Paris: Musée de l'Homme).

5. The traditional religion of Tikopia, including the annual ritual cycle and ceremonies performed at Marae in Uta, is described in Raymond Firth, 1967, *The Work of the Gods in Tikopia* (New York: Athlone Press); the words of the Taomatangai chant are from p. 324. The final conversion of the pagan chiefs of Ravenga to Christianity in 1955-1956 is described by Raymond Firth, 1970, *Rank and Religion in Tikopia: A Study in Polynesian Paganism and Conversion to Christianity* (Boston: Beacon Press).

Chapter 9. The Ghost of Sinapupu

1. Tikopian oral traditions are related and analyzed in detail in Raymond Firth, 1961, *History and Traditions of Tikopia*, Polynesian Society Memoir 33 (Wellington, New Zealand: Polynesian Society).

2. The results of my research into Tikopia archaeology are presented in Patrick Vinton Kirch and D. E. Yen, 1982, *Tikopia: The Prehistory and Ecology of a Polynesian Outlier*, Bernice P. Bishop Museum Bulletin 238 (Honolulu: Bishop Museum Press). Tikopia's position within the Polynesian Outliers is summarized in P. V. Kirch, 1984, "The Polynesian Outliers: Continuity, Change, and Replacement," *Journal of Pacific History* 19: 224-238. The evolution of the Tikopia long-distance exchange system is analyzed in P. V. Kirch, 1986, "Exchange Systems and Inter-Island Contact in the Transformation of an Island Society: The Tikopia Case," in P. V. Kirch, Ed., *Island Societies: Archaeological Approaches to Evolution and Transformation*, pp. 33-41 (Cambridge: Cambridge University Press).

3. E. R. Leach, 1962, "Review of R. Firth, *History and Traditions of Tikopia*," *Journal of the Polynesian Society* 71:273–276.

4. A. M. Hocart, 1929, *Lau Islands, Fiji*, Bernice P. Bishop Museum Bulletin 62 (Honolulu: Bishop Museum Press). Marshall D. Sahlins, 1981, *Historical Metaphors and Mythical Realities: Structure in the Early History of the Sandwich Islands Kingdom* (Ann Arbor: University of Michigan Press).

5. The linkages between the Tikopia traditions and the archaeological record are discussed by Kirch and Yen, *Tikopia: The Prehistory and Ecology of a Polynesian Outlier*, pp. 362–368.

6. P. V. Kirch, 1983, "An Archaeological Exploration of Vanikoro, Santa Cruz Islands, Eastern Melanesia," *New Zealand Journal of Archaeology* 5:69–113.

Chapter 10. *Aloha ʻĀina*

1. For an account of Kenneth Emory's academic career, see P. V. Kirch, 1992, "Kenneth Pike Emory, 1897–1992," *Asian Perspectives* 31: 1–8.

2. Adrienne L. Kaeppler, 1978, *"Artificial Curiosities," An Exposition of Native Manufactures Collected on the Three Pacific Voyages of Captain James Cook, R. N.*, Bernice P. Bishop Museum Special Publication 65 (Honolulu: Bishop Museum Press).

3. Patrick Vinton Kirch and D. E. Yen, 1982, *Tikopia: The Prehistory and Ecology of a Polynesian Outlier*, Bernice P. Bishop Museum Bulletin 238 (Honolulu: Bishop Museum Press).

4. Raymond Firth to Patrick V. Kirch, letter dated September 30, 1982, in Kirch personal archives.

5. For an exposé of these tightly interlocked relationships between politics and land development in Hawaiʻi, especially in the 1960s and 1970s, see George Cooper and Gavan Daws, 1985, *Land and Power in Hawaii: The Democratic Years* (Honolulu: Benchmark Books).

6. An overview of the Kawela, Molokaʻi, research results was presented in M. I. Weisler and P. V. Kirch, 1985, "The Structure of Settlement Space in a Polynesian Chiefdom: Kawela, Molokaʻi, Hawaiian Islands," *New Zealand Journal of Archaeology* 7:129–158.

7. Information on the history and programs of the Protect Kahoʻolawe ʻOhana can be found at http://www.protectkahoolaweohana.org.

8. A summary of the legal proceedings surrounding the proposed condominium project at Kawakiu is provided by Marshall I. Weisler, 1987, *A Second Look at the Archaeology of Kawakiu Nui, West Molokaʻi, Hawaiian Islands*, Report Prepared for Kaluakoʻi Corporation (Seattle: Archaeological Consulting and Research Services), pp. 1–5.

9. Jeffrey T. Clark and Patrick V. Kirch, Eds., 1983, *Archaeological Investigations of the Mudlane-Waimea-Kawaihae Road Corridor, Island of Hawaiʻi: An Interdisciplinary Study of an Environmental Transect*, Anthropology Department Report 83-1 (Honolulu: Bishop Museum).

Chapter 11. The Anahulu Valley

1. Marshall D. Sahlins, 1958, *Social Stratification in Polynesia* (Seattle: American Ethnological Society).

2. Marshall D. Sahlins, 1972, *Stone Age Economics* (Chicago: Aldine-Atherton Inc.).

3. On the Mahele and its significance see J. J. Chinen, 1958, *The Great Mahele: Hawaii's Land Division of 1848* (Honolulu: University of Hawaiʻi Press).

4. For the results of the initial study of Anahulu archaeology see Patrick V. Kirch, 1979, *Late Prehistoric and Early Historic Settlement-Subsistence Systems in the Anahulu Valley, Oʻahu*, Department of Anthropology Report 79-2 (Honolulu: Bishop Museum).

5. Patrick V. Kirch and Marshall Sahlins, 1992, *Anahulu: The Anthropology of History in the Kingdom of Hawaii*. Volume 1, *Historical Ethnography*, by Sahlins; Volume 2, *The Archaeology of History*, by Kirch (Chicago: University of Chicago Press).

6. The quote regarding Emerson's visit to Kamakea's house is from Kirch, *Anahulu*, Vol. 2, p. 88.

7. Patrick V. Kirch, Ed., *Prehistoric Hawaiian Occupation in the Anahulu Valley, Oʻahu Island: Excavations in Three Inland Rockshelters*, Archaeological Research Facility Contribution 47 (Berkeley: University of California).

8. The letters from Paulo Kanoa to Gidiona Laʻanui are discussed by Sahlins, *Anahulu*, Vol. 1, pp. 143–45.

9. Marshall Sahlins, 1990, "The Political Economy of Grandeur in Hawaii from 1810 to 1830," in E. Ohnuki-Tierney, Ed., *Culture Through Time*, pp. 26–56 (Stanford, CA: Stanford University Press).

10. The quotes from John Emerson and Ursula Emerson regarding the oppressive extraction of surplus by the chiefs are from Sahlins, *Anahulu*, Vol. 1, pp. 145–146.

11. The parable told by the schoolteacher Kaiʻaikawaha is from Sahlins, *Anahulu*, Vol. 1, p. 149.

12. The quote regarding the "modest aim" of the Anahulu project is from Sahlins, *Anahulu*, Vol. 1, p. 2.

13. The quotes regarding Sahlins' views on Hawaiian agency in history are from *Anahulu*, Vol. 1, pp. 215–216.

14. Lilikalā Kameʻeleihiwa, 1994, "Review of Kirch and Sahlins, *Anahulu: The Anthropology of History in the Kingdom of Hawaii*," *The Contemporary Pacific*, Spring, pp. 214–218.

Chapter 12. "Looking for the Lion"

1. On George Quimby's career and especially his early years, see the essays by R. C. Dunnell and D. K. Grayson, and by J. B. Griffin, in Robert C. Dunnell and Donald K. Grayson, Eds., 1983, *Lulu Linear Punctated: Essays in Honor of George Irving Quimby*, Anthropological Papers of the Museum of Anthropology 72 (Ann Arbor: University of Michigan).

2. Bill Holm, 1987, *Spirit and Ancestor: A Century of Northwest Coast Indian Art at the Burke Museum*, Thomas Burke Memorial Washington State Museum Monograph 4 (Seattle: Burke Museum and University of Washington Press).

3. Patrick Vinton Kirch, 1984, *The Evolution of the Polynesian Chiefdoms* (Cambridge: Cambridge University Press).

4. Patrick Vinton Kirch, 1985, *Feathered Gods and Fishhooks: An Introduction to Hawaiian Archaeology and Prehistory* (Honolulu: University of Hawaii Press).

5. Patrick Vinton Kirch, Ed., 1986, *Island Societies: Archaeological Approaches to Evolution and Transformation* (Cambridge: Cambridge University Press).

6. Although I was not impressed by Dunnell's arguments about a Darwinian approach to cultural evolution, I did find his treatise on archaeological systematics to be insightful, urging my students to read his classic work, Robert C. Dunnell, 1971, *Systematics in Prehistory* (New York: Free Press).

7. On the *Annales* school of history and its influence on archaeology, see A. Bernard Knapp, Ed., 1992, *Archaeology, Annales, and Ethnohistory* (Cambridge: Cambridge University Press).

8. Patrick Vinton Kirch and Terry L. Hunt, Eds., 1988, *Archaeology of the Lapita Cultural Complex: A Critical Review,* Thomas Burke Memorial Washington State Museum Research Report 5 (Seattle: Burke Museum).

9. Patrick V. Kirch, 1987, *The Burke Museum, Biennial Report 1984–86* (Seattle: Burke Museum); Patrick V. Kirch, 1989, *The Burke Museum, Biennial Report 1986–88* (Seattle: Burke Museum).

Chapter 13. The Search for the Lapita Homeland

1. Otto Meyer, 1909, "Funde prähistorischer Töpferei und Steinmesser auf Vuatom, Bismarck Archipel," *Anthropos* 4:215–252, 1093–1095.

2. E. W. Gifford and D. Shutler Jr., 1956, "Archaeological Excavations in New Caledonia," Anthropological Records 18:1–125 (Berkeley: University of California Press).

3. J. Golson, 1971, "Lapita Ware and Its Transformations," Pacific Anthropological Records 12:67–76 (Honolulu: Bishop Museum).

4. Roger C. Green, 1979, "Lapita," in J. Jennings, Ed., *The Prehistory of Polynesia,* pp. 27–60 (Cambridge, MA: Harvard University Press).

5. J. Allen and P. White, 1989, "The Lapita Homeland: Some New Data and an Interpretation," *Journal of the Polynesian Society* 98:129–146.

6. A. Pawley and R. C. Green, 1973, "Dating the Dispersal of the Oceanic Languages," *Oceanic Linguistics* 12:1–67; A. Pawely and R. C. Green, 1984, "The Proto-Oceanic Language Community," *Journal of Pacific History* 19:123–146.

7. Brian J. Egloff, 1975, "Archaeological Investigations in the Coastal Madang Area and on Eloaue Island of the St. Matthias Group," *Records of the Papua New Guinea Museum and Art Gallery* 5:15–31.

8. Background information on the 1985 Lapita Homeland Project, along with a series of initial reports by the participating research teams, may be found in Jim Allen and Chris Gosden, Eds., 1991, *Report of the Lapita Homeland Project,* Occasional Papers in Prehistory 20 (Canberra: Research School of Pacific Studies, Australian National University).

9. Preliminary results from the 1985 fieldwork in Mussau were presented in P. V. Kirch, 1987, "Lapita and Oceanic Cultural Origins: Excavations in the Mussau Islands, Bismarck Archipelago, 1985," *Journal of Field Archaeology* 14:163–180. See also C. Gosden, J. Allen, W. Ambrose, D. Anson, J. Golson, R. Green, P. Kirch, I. Lilley, J. Specht, and M. Spriggs, 1989, "Lapita Sites of the Bismarck Archipelago," *Antiquity* 63:561–586.

Chapter 14. The Secrets of Talepakemalai

1. John Aini later founded an NGO, Ailan Awareness, to help Papua New Guinea villages develop marine resource management plans. In 2012, we met once again in Berkeley when Aini was awarded the 2012 Seacology Prize.

2. Results of the 1986 fieldwork in Mussau were reported in Patrick V. Kirch, 1988, "The Talepakemalai Site and Oceanic Prehistory," *National Geographic Research* 4:328–342.

3. For a detailed discussion of Lapita pottery, including the assemblages from Mussau, see Patrick Vinton Kirch, 1997, *The Lapita Peoples: Ancestors of the Oceanic World* (Oxford: Blackwell Publishers).

4. P. V. Kirch, 1989, "Second Millennium B.C. Arboriculture in Melanesia: Archaeological Evidence from the Mussau Islands," *Economic Botany* 43:225–240. See also D. Lepofsky,

P. V. Kirch, and K. Lertzman, 1998, "Metric Analyses of Prehistoric Morphological Change in Cultivated Fruits and Nuts: An Example from Island Melanesia," *Journal of Archaeological Science* 25:1001–1014.

5. Terry L. Hunt, 1989, Lapita Ceramic Exchange in the Mussau Islands, Papua New Guinea, Unpublished PhD Dissertation, University of Washington, Seattle.

6. Dana Lepofsky, 1992, "Arboriculture in the Mussau Islands, Bismarck Archipelago," *Economic Botany* 46:192–211.

7. The excavations at Talepakemalai are reported in Patrick Vinton Kirch, Ed., 2001, *Lapita and Its Transformations in Near Oceania: Archaeological Investigations in the Mussau Islands, Papua New Guinea, 1985–88.* Vol. I, *Introduction, Stratigraphy, Chronology,* Archaeological Research Facility Contribution 59 (Berkeley: University of California).

8. Kirch, *The Lapita Peoples.*

9. Roger C. Green, 1991, "Near and Remote Oceania: Disestablishing 'Melanesia' in Culture History," in A. Pawley, Ed., *Man and a Half: Essays in Pacific Anthropology and Ethnobiology in Honour of Ralph Bulmer,* pp. 491–502 (Auckland: Polynesian Society).

10. The Lapita database can be accessed at http://lapita.rchss.sinica.edu.tw/web.

Chapter 15. Hawaiki, The Polynesian Homeland

1. Some of his plays were published in John Kneubuhl, 1997, *Think of a Garden, and Other Plays* (Honolulu: University of Hawai'i Press).

2. See chapter 2 of Patrick Vinton Kirch, 2012, *A Shark Going Inland Is My Chief: The Island Civilization of Ancient Hawai'i* (Berkeley: University of California Press); parts of the following paragraphs are adapted from this account.

3. On Tangaroa, see E. S. Craighill Handy, 1927, *Polynesian Religion,* Bernice P. Bishop Museum Bulletin 34 (Honolulu: Bishop Museum Press), pp. 115–118. The Manu'a version of the Tangaroa creation myth is given by Margaret Mead, 1930, *Social Organization of Manu'a,* Bernice P. Bishop Museum Bulletin 76 (Honolulu: Bishop Museum Press), pp. 148–156.

4. These initial discoveries in Manu'a are described in Patrick V. Kirch and Terry L. Hunt, 1988, "Archaeological Survey of the Manu'a Islands, American Samoa," *Journal of the Polynesian Society* 97:153–183.

5. Patrick V. Kirch and Terry L. Hunt, 1987, "Radiocarbon Dates from Two Coastal Sites in the Manu'a Group, American Samoa," *Radiocarbon* 29:417–419.

6. The results of this season of fieldwork at To'aga were published by Patrick V. Kirch, T. L. Hunt, L. Nagaoka, and J. Tyler, 1990, "An Ancestral Polynesian Occupation Site at To'aga, Ofu Island, American Samoa," *Archaeology in Oceania* 25:1–15. See also Patrick V. Kirch, Terry L. Hunt, and Jason Tyler, 1989, "A Radiocarbon Sequence from the To'aga Site, Ofu Island, American Samoa," *Radiocarbon* 31:7–13.

7. The final season of excavations at the To'aga site is reported in Patrick V. Kirch and Terry L. Hunt, Eds., 1993, *The To'aga Site: Three Millennia of Polynesian Occupation in the Manu'a Islands, American Samoa,* Archaeological Research Facility Contribution 51 (Berkeley: University of California).

8. Kent Flannery and Joyce Marcus, Eds., 1983, *The Cloud People: Divergent Evolution of the Zapotec and Mixtec Civilizations* (New York: Academic Press).

9. Patrick V. Kirch and Roger C. Green, 1987, "History, Phylogeny, and Evolution in Polynesia," *Current Anthropology* 28:431–456. Reprinted in S. Silverman, Ed., 1991, *Inquiry and Debate in the Human Sciences,* pp. 161–186 (Chicago: University of Chicago Press).

10. Patrick Vinton Kirch and Roger C. Green, 2001, *Hawaiki, Ancestral Polynesia: An Essay in Historical Anthropology* (Cambridge: Cambridge University Press).

Chapter 16. *Fiat Lux*

1. My accomplishments during my period as Burke Museum director are reported in Patrick V. Kirch, 1987, *The Burke Museum, Biennial Report 1984–86* (Seattle: Burke Museum) and in Patrick V. Kirch, 1989, *The Burke Museum, Biennial Report 1986–88* (Seattle: Burke Museum).

2. On the history of anthropology at Berkeley, see the virtual exhibit "Foundations of Anthropology at the University of California" organized by the Bancroft Library, http://bancroft .berkeley.edu/Exhibits/anthro/index.html.

3. For an engaging autobiographical account of Stoddart's career—including the ubiquitous drinking—see David R. Stoddart, 2001, "Be of Good Cheer, My Weary Readers, for I Have Espied Land," *Atoll Research Bulletin* No. 494, Part 12 (Washington, DC: Smithsonian Institution).

Chapter 17. The Gathering Place of Men

1. The distinction between Western and Eastern Polynesia was first made explicit by Edwin G. Burrows, 1939, *Western Polynesia: A Study of Cultural Differentiation*, Etnologiska Studier, Vol. 7 (Goteborg).

2. Raymond Fosberg, 1963, "The Island Ecosystem," in F. R. Fosberg, Ed., *Man's Place in the Island Ecosystem: A Symposium*, pp. 1–7 (Honolulu: Bishop Museum Press) and Raymond Fosberg, 1963, "Disturbance in Island Ecosystems," in J. L. Gressitt, Ed., *Pacific Basin Biogeography*, pp. 557–561 (Honolulu: Bishop Museum Press).

3. Te Rangi Hiroa related the oral traditions of Mangaia, as well as an ethnographic overview of Mangaia, in his 1934 monograph, *Mangaian Society*, Bernice P. Bishop Museum Bulletin 122 (Honolulu: Bishop Museum Press).

4. On the results of our first season of fieldwork in Mangaia see Patrick V. Kirch, John R. Flenley, David W. Steadman, Frances Lamont, and Stewart Dawson, 1992, "Ancient Environmental Degradation: Prehistoric Human Impacts on an Island Ecosystem: Mangaia, Central Polynesia," *National Geographic Research and Exploration* 8:166–179.

5. D. W. Steadman and P. V. Kirch, 1990, "Prehistoric Extinction of Birds on Mangaia, Cook Islands, Polynesia," *Proceedings of the National Academy of Sciences USA* 87:9605–9609.

6. The dates obtained from the Mangaia cores have been the subject of some controversy. Although internally consistent, the dates for the transition from native forest to fernland on the volcanic hill—associated with Polynesian colonization—appear to be as much as 500–700 years too early when compared with the dates for initial human occupation from the Tangata-tau rockshelter. The reason for this discrepancy has not been resolved but very likely it resulted from a reservoir of older soil carbon that washed into the swamp basins at the time of initial forest clearance.

7. Jon Hather and Patrick V. Kirch, 1991, "Prehistoric Sweet Potato (*Ipomoea batatas*) from Mangaia Island, Central Polynesia," *Antiquity* 65:887–893.

8. Patrick V. Kirch and Terry L. Hunt, Eds., 1997, *Historical Ecology in the Pacific Islands: Prehistoric Environmental and Landscape Change* (New Haven, CT: Yale University Press).

9. J. Ellison, 1994, "Palaeo-Lake and Swamp Stratigraphic Records of Holocene Vegetation and Sea-Level Changes, Mangaia, Cook Islands," *Pacific Science* 48:1–15.

10. Patrick V. Kirch, David W. Steadman, Virginia L. Butler, Jon Hather, and Marshall I. Weisler, 1995, "Prehistory and Human Ecology in Eastern Polynesia: Excavations at Tangatatau Rockshelter, Mangaia, Cook Islands," *Archaeology in Oceania* 30:47–65.

11. Te Rangi Hiroa (P. H. Buck), MS, "The Advent of Christianity," p. 654. Typescript with hand-numbered pages 641–705, in Archives, Bernice P. Bishop Museum, Honolulu. The manuscript seems originally intended to be published as part of Hiroa's *Mangaian Society* but was evidently removed by the museum's editor.

12. On the evidence for cannibalism at the Keia rockshelter, see D. Steadman, S. Anton, and P. V. Kirch, 2000, "Ana Manuka: A Prehistoric Ritualistic Site on Mangaia, Cook Islands," *Antiquity* 74:873–83.

13. For overviews of the prehistoric cultural sequence on Mangaia, see Patrick V. Kirch, 1996, "Late Holocene Human-Induced Modifications to a Central Polynesian Island Ecosystem," *Proceedings of the National Academy of Sciences USA* 93 (11):5296–5300; Patrick V. Kirch, 1997, "Changing Landscapes and Sociopolitical Evolution in Mangaia, Central Polynesia," in P. V. Kirch and T. L. Hunt, Eds., *Historical Ecology in the Pacific Islands*, pp. 147–165 (New Haven, CT: Yale University Press); and, Patrick V. Kirch, 1997, "Microcosmic Histories: Island Perspectives on 'Global' Change," *American Anthropologist* 99:30–42.

Chapter 18. Kahikinui, "Great Tahiti"

1. The 1966 excavations at M9 and other sites in Kahikinui were reported by Peter S. Chapman and Patrick V. Kirch, 1979, *Archaeological Excavations at Seven Sites, Southeast Maui, Hawaiian Islands*, Department of Anthropology Report 79-1 (Honolulu: Bernice P. Bishop Museum).

2. E. S. Craighill Handy, 1940, *The Hawaiian Planter*, Vol. I, *His Plants, Methods, and Areas of Cultivation*, Bernice P. Bishop Museum Bulletin 161 (Honolulu: Bishop Museum Press), p. 161.

3. Our initial results of archaeological survey and household excavations in Kahikinui are presented in Patrick V. Kirch, Ed., 1997, *Nā Mea Kahiko o Kahikinui: Studies in the Archaeology of Kahikinui, Maui, Hawaiian Islands*, Oceanic Archaeology Laboratory Special Publication 1 (Berkeley: Archaeological Research Facility, University of California).

4. Elman Service, 1967, *Primitive Social Organization: An Evolutionary Perspective* (New York: Random House). Morton H. Fried, 1967, *The Evolution of Political Society: An Essay in Political Anthropology* (New York: Random House).

5. This was the view, for example, presented by Timothy Earle, 1997, *How Chiefs Come to Power: The Political Economy in Prehistory* (Stanford, CA: Stanford University Press).

6. Robert J. Hommon, 1976, The Formation of Primitive States in Pre-Contact Hawaii. Unpublished PhD Dissertation, University of Arizona, Tucson.

7. Marshall Sahlins, 1992, *Historical Ethnography*, Vol. 1 of Patrick V. Kirch and Marshall Sahlins, *Anahulu: The Anthropology of History in the Kingdom of Hawaii* (Chicago: University of Chicago Press), p. 192.

8. Kathy Leinani Kawelu, 2007, A Sociopolitical History of Hawaiian Archaeology: Kuleana and Commitment, Unpublished PhD Dissertation, University of California, Berkeley, p. 167.

9. This controversial event was reported by Bob Krauss in the *Honolulu Advertiser*, "Two archaeologists resign in dispute at Museum," 10/4/1991; and, by Helen Altonn in the *Honolulu Star Bulletin*, "2 'quit' Bishop in management row," 10/3/1991.

10. Haunani Kay Trask, 1993, *From A Native Daughter: Colonialism and Sovereignty in Hawai'i* (Monroe, ME: Common Courage Press), pp. 172–173.

11. My keynote address to the Society for Hawaiian Archaeology was published as Patrick V. Kirch, 1999, "Hawaiian Archaeology: Past, Present, and Future," *Hawaiian Archaeology* 7:60–72.

12. These and other sites are more fully described in Patrick Vinton Kirch, 2014, *Kua'āina Kahiko: Life and Land in Ancient Kahikinui, Maui* (Honolulu: University of Hawai'i Press).

13. On the excavations at site KIP-117 see Patrick V. Kirch, Sidsel Millerstrom, Sharyn Jones, and Mark McCoy, 2010, "Dwelling Among The Gods: A Late Pre-Contact Priest's House in Kahikinui, Maui, Hawaiian Islands," *Journal of Pacific Archaeology* 1:144–160.

14. Results of the XRF analysis of stone tools from KIP-117 and other sites in Kahikinui are presented in P. V. Kirch, P. Mills, S. Lundblad, J. Sinton, and J. Kahn, 2012, "Inter-Polity Exchange of Basalt Tools Facilitated via Elite Control in Hawaiian Archaic States," *Proceedings of the National Academy of Sciences USA* 109:1056–1061.

15. I recount Ka 'Ohana o Kahikinui's struggles to gain access to the lands of Kahikinui in Kirch, *Kua'āina Kahiko*.

16. Winslow Walker, MS [1930], "Archaeology of Maui," Typescript in Archives, Bernice P. Bishop Museum, Honolulu.

17. The orientation of Kahikinui *heiau* to particular directions and their association with certain gods are discussed in Patrick V. Kirch, 2004, "Temple Sites in Kahikinui, Maui, Hawaiian Islands: Their Orientations Decoded," *Antiquity* 78:102–114.

18. P. V. Kirch and W. D. Sharp, 2005, "Coral [230]Th Dating of the Imposition of a Ritual Control Hierarchy in Precontact Hawaii," *Science* 307:102–104. See also P. V. Kirch, R. Mertz-Kraus, and W. D. Sharp, 2015, "Precise Chronology of Polynesian Temple Construction and Use for Southeastern Maui, Hawaiian Islands Determined by [230]Th dating of Corals," *Journal of Archaeological Science* 53:166–177.

Chapter 19. Forbidden Peninsula

1. One of the best histories of Kalaupapa and Father Damien is certainly that by Gavan Daws, 1973, *Holy Man: Father Damien of Molokai* (New York: Harper & Row).

2. John F. G. Stokes, MS [1909], "Heiau of Molokai," Typescript in Archives, Bernice P. Bishop Museum, Honolulu.

3. Investigations at the Waikolu pondfield site along with other aspects of our research at Kalaupapa are reported in Patrick Vinton Kirch, Ed., 2002, *From the "Cliffs of Keolewa" to the "Sea of Papaloa": An Archaeological Reconnaissance of Portions of the Kalaupapa National Historical Park, Moloka'i, Hawaiian Islands*. Oceanic Archaeology Laboratory Special Publication 2 (Berkeley: Archaeological Research Facility, University of California).

4. Nathaniel B. Emerson, 1909, *Unwritten Literature of Hawaii: The Sacred Songs of the Hula*, Bureau of American Ethnology Bulletin 38 (Washington, DC: Smithsonian Institution).

5. Marshall I. Weisler, 1989, "Chronometric Dating and Late Holocene Prehistory in the Hawaiian Islands: A Critical Review of Radiocarbon Dates from Moloka'i Island," *Radiocarbon* 31: 121–145.

6. P. V. Kirch, S. O'Day, J. Coil, M. Morgenstein, K. Kawelu, and S. Millerstrom, 2004, "The Kaupikiawa Rockshelter, Kalaupapa Peninsula, Moloka'i: New Investigations And Reinterpretation of Its Significance for Hawaiian Prehistory," *People and Culture in Oceania* 19:1–27.

7. Mark D. McCoy, 2006, Landscape, Social Memory, and Society: An Ethnohistoric-Archaeological Study of Three Hawaiian Communities, Unpublished PhD Dissertation, University of California, Berkeley.

8. James L. Flexner, 2010, Archaeology of the Recent Past at Kalawao: Landscape, Place, and Power in a Hawaiian Hansen's Disease Settlement, Unpublished PhD Dissertation, University of California, Berkeley.

Chapter 20. Belly of the Stonefish

1. The story of the *Kaimiloa* and of Emory's relationship with the Kellum family is told by Bob Krauss, 1988, *Keneti: South Seas Adventures of Kenneth Emory* (Honolulu: University of Hawaii Press). On Emory's survey of *marae* throughout the Society Islands see Kenneth P. Emory, 1933, *Stone Remains of the Society Islands,* Bernice P. Bishop Museum Bulletin 116 (Honolulu: Bishop Museum Press).

2. Roger C. Green, 1961, "Moorea Archaeology: A Preliminary Report," *Man* 61:169–173. See also Roger C. Green, 1967, "Settlement Patterns: Four Case Studies from Polynesia," in W. G. Solheim II, Ed., *Archaeology at the Eleventh Pacific Science Congress,* pp. 101–132, Asian and Pacific Archaeology Series 1 (Honolulu: Social Science Research Institute, University of Hawaii).

3. Dana Lepofsky, 1994, Prehistoric Agricultural Intensification in the Society Islands, French Polynesia, Unpublished PhD Dissertation, University of California, Berkeley.

4. On the contact-period ethnohistory of the Society Islands, see Douglas L. Oliver, 1974, *Ancient Tahitian Society,* 3 Vols. (Honolulu: University of Hawaii Press).

5. The concept of the "house society" was first presented in C. Lévi-Strauss, 1982, *The Way of the Masks.* Translated by Sylvia Modelski (Seattle: University of Washington Press).

6. Jennifer Kahn and Patrick V. Kirch, 2004, "Ethnographie préhistorique d'une 'société à maisons' dans la vallée de 'Opunohu (Mo'orea, îles de la Société)," *Journal de la Société des Océanistes* 119:229–256.

7. Jennifer Kahn, 2005, Household and Community Organization in the Late Prehistoric Society Islands Chiefdoms (French Polynesia), Unpublished PhD Dissertation, University of California, Berkeley.

8. Jennifer Kahn and Patrick V. Kirch, 2013, "Residential Landscapes and House Societies of the Late Prehistoric Society Islands," *Journal of Pacific Archaeology* 4:50–72.

9. Jennifer Kahn and Patrick V. Kirch, 2011, "Monumentality and Ritual Control in Mo'orea, Society Islands: Investigations at the Upper Tupauruuru Complex," *Archaeology in Oceania* 46:93–104. Jennifer G. Kahn and Patrick Vinton Kirch, 2014, *Monumentality and Ritual Materialization in the Society Islands: The Archaeology of a Major Ceremonial Complex in the 'Opunohu Valley, Mo'orea.* Bishop Museum Bulletin in Anthropology 13 (Honolulu: Bishop Museum Press).

10. W. D. Sharp, J. Kahn, C. M. Polito, and P. V. Kirch, 2010, "Rapid Evolution of Ritual Architecture in Central Polynesia Indicated by Precise [230]Th/U Coral Dating," *Proceedings of the National Academy of Sciences USA* 107:13234–13239.

Chapter 21. Roots of Conflict

1. Mary Kawena Pukui, 1983, *'Ōlelo No'eau: Hawaiian Proverbs & Poetical Sayings,* Bernice P. Bishop Museum Special Publication 71 (Honolulu: Bishop Museum Press), proverb 1973, p. 213.

2. Richard J. Pearson, Ed., 1968, *Excavations at Lapakahi: Selected Papers,* Hawaii State Archaeological Journal 69–2 (Honolulu: Department of Land and Natural Resources).

3. Paul H. Rosendahl, 1972, Aboriginal Agriculture and Residence Patterns in Upland Lapakahi, Island of Hawaii, Unpublished PhD Dissertation, University of Hawaii, Honolulu.

4. Patrick Vinton Kirch, 1984, *The Evolution of the Polynesian Chiefdoms* (Cambridge: Cambridge University Press).

5. T. N. Ladefoged, M. W. Graves, and R. P. Jennings, 1996, "Dryland Agricultural Expansion and Intensification in Kohala, Hawai'i Island," *Antiquity* 70:861–80.

6. P. V. Kirch, A. Hartshorn, O. Chadwick, P. Vitousek, D. Sherrod, J. Coil, L. Holm, and W. D. Sharp, 2004, "Environment, Agriculture, and Settlement Patterns in a Marginal Polynesian Landscape," *Proceedings of the National Academy of Sciences USA* 101: 9936–9941.

7. E. S. Craighill Handy, 1940, *The Hawaiian Planter*, Vol. I, *His Plants, Methods, and Areas of Cultivation*, Bernice P. Bishop Museum Bulletin 161 (Honolulu: Bishop Museum Press), p. 161.

8. Lisa Holm, 2008, The Archaeology and the 'Āina of Mahamenui and Manawainui, Kahikinui, Maui Island, Unpublished PhD Dissertation, University of California, Berkeley.

9. P. M. Vitousek, T. Ladefoged, A. Hartshorn, P. V. Kirch, M. Graves, S. Hotchkiss, S. Tuljapurkar, and O. A. Chadwick, 2004, "Soils, Agriculture, and Society in Precontact Hawai'i," *Science* 304:1665–1669.

10. Kirch, *The Evolution of the Polynesian Chiefdoms*, p. 189.

11. M. Meyer, T. Ladefoged, and P. M. Vitousek, 2007, "Soil Phosphorus and Agricultural Development in the Leeward Kohala Field System," *Pacific Science* 61:347–353.

12. A. S. Hartshorn, O. A. Chadwick, P. M. Vitousek, and P. V. Kirch, 2006, "Prehistoric Agricultural Depletion of Soil Nutrients in Hawaii," *Proceedings of the National Academy of Sciences USA* 103:11092–11097.

13. P. M. Vitousek et al., "Soils, Agriculture, and Society in Precontact Hawai'i," p. 1668.

14. For an overview of the results of the Hawai'i Biocomplexity Project, see Patrick Vinton Kirch, Ed., 2011, *Roots of Conflict: Soils, Agriculture, and Sociopolitical Complexity in Ancient Hawai'i* (Santa Fe: School for Advanced Research). See also P. V. Kirch, G. Asner, O. Chadwick, J. Field, T. Ladefoged, C. Puleston, S. Tuljapurkar, and P. Vitousek, 2012, "Building and Testing Models of Long-Term Agricultural Intensification and Population Dynamics: A Case Study from the Leeward Kohala Field System, Hawai'i," *Ecological Modeling* 227:12–28.

15. James Clifford and George E. Marcus, 1986, *Writing Culture: The Poetics and Politics of Ethnography* (Berkeley: University of California Press).

16. For the results of our first field season at Makiloa see J. Field, P. V. Kirch, K. Kawelu, and T. Ladefoged, "Houses and Hierarchy: Domestic Modes of Production in Leeward Kohala, Hawai'i Island," *Journal of Island and Coastal Archaeology* 5:52–85.

17. Charlotte T. Lee and Shripad Tuljapurkar, 2008, "Population and Prehistory I: Food-Dependent Population Growth in Constant Environments," *Theoretical Population Biology* 73:473–482. Cedric O. Puleston and Shripad Tuljapurkar, 2008, "Population and Prehistory II: Space-Limited Human Populations in Constant Environments," *Theoretical Population Biology* 74:147–160. Charlotte T. Lee, Cedric O. Puleston, and Shripad Tuljapurka, 2009, "Population and Prehistory III: Food-Dependent Demography in Variable Environments," *Theoretical Population Biology* 76:179–188.

18. J. Field, T. N. Ladefoged, and P. V. Kirch, 2011, "Household Expansion Linked to Agricultural Intensification During Emergence of Hawaiian Archaic States," *Proceedings of the National Academy of Sciences USA* 108:7327–7332.

19. Thomas Malthus, 1798 [1993 reprint], *An Essay on the Principle of Population* (Oxford: Oxford University Press).

20. Ester Boserup, 1965, *The Conditions of Agricultural Growth: The Economics of Agrarian Change Under Population Pressure* (Chicago: Aldine).

21. Paul R. Ehrlich, 1968, *The Population Bomb* (New York: Ballantine Books). On the bet between Ehrlich and Simon see http://www.stanford.edu/group/CCB/Pubs/Ecofablesdocs /thebet.htm.

Chapter 22. The Sun Sets at Ana Tetea

1. C. Montague Cooke Jr., 1935, "Report of the 1934 Mangarevan Expedition," in Herbert E. Gregory, *Report of the Director for 1934,* Bernice P. Bishop Museum Bulletin 133, pp. 33–71 (Honolulu: Bishop Museum Press), pp. 41–42.

2. Te Rangi Hiroa, 1938, *Ethnology of Mangareva,* Bernice P. Bishop Museum Bulletin 157 (Honolulu: Bishop Museum Press).

3. Kenneth P. Emory, 1939, *Archaeology of Mangareva and Neighboring Atolls,* Bernice P. Bishop Museum Bulletin 163 (Honolulu: Bishop Museum Press).

4. Roger Green's 1959 excavations on Kamaka and Aukena Islands remained unpublished for many years; late in his life he began to report on these excavations in several works coauthored with Marshall Weisler. See R. C. Green and M. I. Weisler, 2000, *Mangarevan Archaeology: Interpretations Using New Data and 40 Year Old Excavations to Establish a Sequence from 1200 to 1900 AD,* University of Otago Publications in Prehistoric Archaeology No. 19 (Dunedin: University of Otago).

5. The results of our 2001 and 2003 expeditions to Mangareva were published in Eric Conte and Patrick Vinton Kirch, Eds., 2004, *Archaeological Investigations in the Mangareva Islands (Gambier Archipelago), French Polynesia,* Archaeological Research Facility Contribution 62 (Berkeley: University of California).

6. F. W. Beechey, 1831, *Narrative of a Voyage to the Pacific and Beering's Strait, to Cooperate with the Polar Expeditions: Performed in His Majesty's Ship Blossom . . . in the Years 1825, 26, 27, 28* (London: Henry Colburn and Richard Bentley).

7. Père H. Laval, 1938, *Mangareva: l'Histoire Ancienne d'un Peuple Polynésien* (Paris: Librairie Orientale Paul Geuthner).

8. Patrick V. Kirch, 2004, "Solstice Observation in Mangareva, French Polynesia: New Perspectives from Archaeology," *Archaeoastronomy* 28:1–19.

9. Patrick V. Kirch, Eric Conte, Warren Sharp, and Cordelia Nickelsen, 2010, "The Onemea Site (Taravai Island, Mangareva) and the Human Colonization of Southeastern Polynesia," *Archaeology in Oceania* 45:66–79.

10. P. V. Kirch, G. Molle, D. Nickelsen, P. Mills, E. Dotte-Sarout, J. Swift, A. Wolfe, and M. Horrocks, 2015, "Human Ecodynamics in the Mangareva Islands: A Stratified Sequence from Nenega-Iti Rockshelter (Site AGA-3, Agakauitai Island)," *Archaeology in Oceania* 50:23–42.

11. Te Rangi Hiroa, 1938, *Ethnology of Mangareva,* Bernice P. Bishop Museum Bulletin 157 (Honolulu: Bishop Museum Press). The story of Mori-a-tararoa and his eventual departure from Kamaka in search of new lands is given on pp. 88–89.

12. M. I. Weisler, 1995. "Henderson Island Prehistory: Colonization and Extinction on a Remote Polynesian Island," *Biological Journal of the Linnean Society* 56:377–404.

Chapter 23. Kekaulike's Kingdom

1. Winslow Walker, MS [1930]. "Archaeology of Maui." Typescript in Archives, Bernice P. Bishop Museum, Honolulu.

2. On Kekaulike and his times, see Samuel Kamakau, 1961, *Ruling Chiefs of Hawai'i* (Honolulu: Kamehameha Schools Press), pp. 66–69; and, Abraham Fornander, 1880, *An Account*

of the Polynesian Race, Vol. II, *Ancient History of the Hawaiian People to the Times of Kamehameha I* (London: Trübner & Co.), pp. 211–214.

3. Kamakau, *Ruling Chiefs of Hawaiʻi,* p. 66.

4. Marshall Sahlins, 1972, *Stone Age Economics* (Chicago: Aldine); Timothy Earle, 1997, *How Chiefs Come to Power* (Stanford, CA: Stanford University Press).

5. The idea that late precontact Hawaiian society was organized as several competing "primitive states" was first broached by Robert J. Hommon, 1976, The Formation of Primitive States in Pre-Contact Hawaii, Unpublished PhD Dissertation, University of Arizona, Tucson. See also Robert J. Hommon, 2013, *The Ancient Hawaiian State: Origins of a Political Society* (Oxford: Oxford University Press).

6. Patrick Vinton Kirch, 2010, *How Chiefs Became Kings: Divine Kingship and the Rise of Archaic States in Ancient Hawaiʻi* (Berkeley: University of California Press).

7. Martha W. Beckwith, 1940, *Hawaiian Mythology* (New Haven, CT: Yale University Press); Padraic Colum, 1925, *Tales & Legends of Hawaii,* Vol. II, *The Bright Islands* (New Haven, CT: Yale University Press).

8. Valerio Valeri, 1985, "The Conqueror Becomes King: A Political Analysis of the Hawaiian Legend of 'Umi," in Antony Hooper and Judith Huntsman, Eds., *Transformations of Polynesian Culture,* pp. 97–104 (Auckland: Polynesian Society).

9. Patrick Vinton Kirch and Douglas E. Yen, 1982, *Tikopia: The Prehistory and Ecology of a Polynesian Outlier,* Bernice P. Bishop Museum Bulletin 238 (Honolulu: Bishop Museum Press), see pp. 362–368.

10. Over the years a number of scholars have compiled chronologies of the ruling chiefs of Hawaiʻi based on the genealogies, including Fornander, 1880, *An Account of the Polynesian Race,* Vol. II; Hommon, The Formation of Primitive States in Pre-Contact Hawaii; and Carolyn Kehaunani Cachola Abad, 2000, The Evolution of Hawaiian Socio-Political Complexity: An Analysis of Hawaiian Oral Traditions, Unpublished PhD Dissertation, University of Hawaiʻi, Honolulu.

11. Abraham Fornander, 1916–1920, *Fornander Collection of Hawaiian Antiquities and Folk-Lore,* T. G. Thrum, Ed., Bernice P. Bishop Museum Memoirs, Vols. IV, V, and VI (Honolulu: Bishop Museum Press); and Kamakau, *Ruling Chiefs of Hawaii.*

12. P. V. Kirch, J. Holson, and A. Baer, 2009, "Intensive Dryland Agriculture in Kaupō, Maui, Hawaiian Islands," *Asian Perspectives* 48:265–290.

13. Patrick Vinton Kirch, 2012, *A Shark Going Inland Is My Chief: The Island Civilization of Ancient Hawaiʻi* (Berkeley: University of California Press).

Chapter 24. Reflections

1. For an overview of historical trends in archaeological method and theory, see Bruce G. Trigger, 1989, *A History of Archaeological Thought* (Cambridge: Cambridge University Press).

2. For this momentous discovery, Libby was awarded the Nobel Prize in Chemistry in 1960. See Willard F. Libby, 1952, *Radiocarbon Dating* (Chicago: University of Chicago Press).

3. Roger C. Green, 1967, "Settlement Patterns: Four Case Studies from Polynesia," in W. G. Solheim II, Ed., *Archaeology at the Eleventh Pacific Science Congress,* pp. 101–132, Asian and Pacific Archaeology Series 1 (Honolulu: Social Science Research Institute, University of Hawaii).

4. The foundational work for the settlement pattern approach was Gordon R. Willey, 1953, *Prehistoric Settlement Patterns in the Virú Valley, Peru,* Bureau of American Ethnology Bulletin 155 (Washington, DC: Smithsonian Institution).

5. Lewis R. Binford, 1962, "Archaeology as Anthropology," *American Antiquity* 28:217–225.

6. The prime example of this approach is Patty Jo Watson, Steven A. LeBlanc, and Charles L. Redman, 1971, *Explanation in Archaeology: An Explicitly Scientific Approach* (New York: Columbia University Press).

7. Kent V. Flannery, 1973, "Archaeology with a Capital S," in C. L. Redman, Ed., *Research and Theory in Current Archeology,* pp. 47–53 (New York: Wiley). For an insightful critique of some aspects of the New Archaeology, see also Paul Courbin, 1988, *What Is Archaeology? An Essay on the Nature of Archaeological Research* (Chicago: University of Chicago Press).

8. For a history of the processual approach in archaeology, see Michael J. O'Brien, R. Lee Lyman, and Michael B. Schiffer, 2005, *Archaeology as a Process: Processualism and its Progeny* (Salt Lake City: University of Utah Press).

9. Stephen Jay Gould, 1986, "Evolution and the Triumph of Homology: Or Why History Matters." *American Scientist* 7:60–69.

10. F. John Odling-Smee, Kevin N. Laland, and Marcus W. Feldman, 2003. *Niche Construction: The Neglected Process in Evolution* (Princeton, NJ: Princeton University Press).

11. Patrick V. Kirch, 1980, "The Archaeological Study of Adaptation," *Advances in Archaeological Method and Theory* 3:101–156. In this article I argued that "group selection" was necessarily a key component of cultural evolution, which ran against the then-dominant paradigm of "kin selection" (made famous by Richard Dawkins' "selfish gene" hypothesis). Now, thirty-five years later, no less a giant of evolutionary theory than Edward O. Wilson has pronounced the failure of narrow kin selection theory and advocates a multi-level theory—prominently including group selection—for the evolution of eusociality. See Edward O. Wilson, 2012, *The Social Conquest of Earth* (New York: W. W. Norton).

12. Patrick Vinton Kirch, 1984, *The Evolution of the Polynesian Chiefdoms* (Cambridge: Cambridge University Press).

13. Patrick V. Kirch and Roger C. Green, 1987, "History, Phylogeny, and Evolution in Polynesia," *Current Anthropology* 28:431–456. A. K. Romney, 1957, "The Genetic Model and Uto-Aztecan Time Perspective," *Davidson Journal of Anthropology* 3:35–41. E. Z. Vogt, 1964, "The Genetic Model and Maya Cultural Development," in E. Z. Vogt and A. Ruz L., Eds., *Desarrollo Cultural de los Mayas,* pp. 9–48 (Mexico DE: Universidad Nacional Autonoma de Mexico).

14. Patrick Vinton Kirch and Roger C. Green, 2001, *Hawaiki, Ancestral Polynesia: An Essay in Historical Anthropology* (Cambridge: Cambridge University Press).

15. Matthew Spriggs, Ed., 1984, *Marxist Perspectives in Archaeology* (Cambridge: Cambridge University Press).

16. Marc Bloch, 1953, *The Historian's Craft* (New York: Alfred A. Knopf). Emmanuel Le Roy Ladurie, 1978, *The Mind and Method of the Historian,* Sian Reynolds and Ben Reynolds, Trans. (Chicago: University of Chicago Press). Fernand Braudel, 1980, *On History,* Sarah Matthews, Trans. (Chicago: University of Chicago Press).

17. Ian Hodder, 1986, *Reading the Past: Current Approaches to Interpretation in Archaeology* (Cambridge: Cambridge University Press). See also Michael Shanks and Christopher Tilley, 1987, *Re-Constructing Archaeology: Theory and Practice* (Cambridge: Cambridge University Press).

18. The critical interplay between evidence and interpretation, in a "realist" philosophy of science, was beautifully discussed by Alison Wylie, 1989, "Archaeological Cables and Tacking: The Implications of Practice for Bernstein's 'Options' Beyond Objectivism and Relativism." *Philosophy of the Social Sciences* 19:1–18.

19. Sahlins comments on what he calls "postmodern terrorism" and its effects on cultural anthropology: "One of the more poignant aspects of the current postmodernist mood is the way it seems to lobotomize some of our best graduate students, to stifle their creativity for fear of making some interesting structural connection, some relationship between cultural practices, or a comparative generalization. The only safe essentialism left to them is that there is no order to culture." In Marshall Sahlins, 2002, *Waiting for Foucault, Still* (Chicago: Prickly Paradigm Press), p. 48.

20. E. W. Gifford, 1951, *Archaeological Excavations in Fiji,* Anthropological Records Vol. 13, No. 3 (Berkeley: University of California Press), p. 189.

21. Robert Carl Suggs, 1961, *The Archaeology of Nuku Hiva, Marquesas Islands, French Polynesia,* Anthropological Papers of the American Museum of Natural History, Vol. 49, Part 1 (New York: American Museum of Natural History).

22. D. E. Yen, 1971, "The Development of Agriculture in Oceania," in R. C. Green and M. Kelly, Eds., *Studies in Oceanic Culture History,* Vol. 2, pp. 1–12, Pacific Anthropological Records 12 (Honolulu: Bishop Museum).

23. Ester Boserup, 1965, *The Conditions of Agricultural Growth: The Economics of Agrarian Change Under Population Pressure* (Chicago: Aldine).

24. C. M. Barton, J. Bernabeu, J. E. Aura, O. Garcia, S. Schmich, and L. Molina, 2004, "Long-Term Socioecology and Contingent Landscapes," *Journal of Archaeological Method and Theory* 11:253–295.

25. For more on this approach to archaeology, see the essays in Timothy A. Kohler and Sander E. van der Leeuw, Eds., 2007, *The Model-Based Archaeology of Socionatural Systems* (Santa Fe: School for Advanced Research).

26. Lance H. Gunderson and C. S. Holling, Eds., 2002, *Panarchy: Understanding Transformations in Human and Natural Systems* (Washington, DC: Island Press).

27. Patrick V. Kirch and Mark McCoy, 2007, "Reconfiguring the Hawaiian Cultural Sequence: Results of Re-Dating the Halawa Dune Site (MO-A1-3), Moloka'i Island," *Journal of the Polynesian Society* 116:385–406.

28. David Burley, Marshall I. Weisler, and Jian-xin Zhao, 2012, "High Precision U/Th Dating of First Polynesian Settlement," *PLOS One* 7(11):e48769.

29. W. Sharp, J. Kahn, C. M. Polito, and P. V. Kirch, 2010, "Rapid Evolution of Ritual Architecture in Central Polynesia Indicated by Precise ^{230}Th/U Coral Dating," *Proceedings of the National Academy of Sciences USA* 107:13234–13239.

30. Marshall I. Weisler and Patrick V. Kirch, 1996, "Interisland and Interarchipelago Transport of Stone Tools in Prehistoric Polynesia," *Proceedings of the National Academy of Sciences USA* 93:1381–1385.

31. Kathleen Kawelu and Donald Pakele, 2014, "Community-Based Research: The Next Step in Hawaiian Archaeology," *Journal of Pacific Archaeology* 5:62–71.

32. Statistics on the Bishop Museum staff in 1980–1981 are drawn from *Nature, Culture & Future: Report of Bernice P. Bishop Museum, January 1980–June 1981* (Honolulu: Bishop Museum Press, 1981). The statistics for 2011 are drawn from the museum's *Annual Report,* available online at http://www.bishopmuseum.org/images/pdf/Annual.report.pdf.

33. The Herbert Gregory Medal is awarded every four years at the Pacific Science Congress; the only other archaeologist to have been honored with the Gregory Medal was Kenneth P. Emory in 1983.

34. Robert Carl Suggs, 1960, *The Island Civilizations of Polynesia* (New York: Mentor Books); quoted passages are from pp. 70, 112, 135, 142, 143, 224, 23, 152, and 168, sequentially.

35. Peter H. Buck (Te Rangi Hiroa), 1939, *Vikings of the Sunrise* (Philadelphia: J. B. Lippincott Co.).

36. Kenneth P. Emory, 1933, *Stone Remains in the Society Islands,* Bernice P. Bishop Museum Bulletin 116 (Honolulu: Bishop Museum Press).

37. Douglas E. Yen's emerging theory on the Polynesian transfer of sweet potato to the Pacific was published in 1961, "Sweet Potato Variation and Its Relation to Human Migration in the Pacific," in J. Barrau, Ed., *Plants and the Migrations of Pacific Peoples,* pp. 93–118 (Honolulu: Bishop Museum Press).

38. Yen's "tripartite" model of sweet potato transfer from South America to the Pacific and Southeast Asia was recently reconfirmed by an innovative molecular biological study, using methods not originally available to Yen. See Caroline Roullier, Laure Benoit, Doyle B. McKey, and Vincent Lebot, 2012, "Historical Collections Reveal Patterns of Diffusion of Sweet Potato in Oceania Obscured by Modern Plant Movements and Recombination," *Proceedings of the National Academy of Sciences USA* 110:2205–2210.

39. On the dating of initial Polynesian settlement in Hawai'i, see Patrick V. Kirch, 2011, "When Did the Polynesian Settle Hawai'i? A Review of 150 Years of Scholarly Inquiry and a Tentative Answer," *Hawaiian Archaeology* 12:3–26. See also J. Stephen Athens, Timothy M. Rieth, and Thomas S. Dye, 2014, "A Paleoenvironmental and Archaeological Model-Based Age Estimate for the Colonization of Hawai'i," *American Antiquity* 79:144–155.

40. Ernst Mayr, 1997, *This is Biology: The Science of the Living World* (Cambridge, MA: Harvard University Press).

Appendix

Archaeological Books and Monographs by the Author

Note: This bibliography excludes book chapters and journal articles.

1975   Editor (with M. Kelly), *Prehistory and Ecology in a Windward Hawaiian Valley: Halawa Valley, Moloka'i*. Pacific Anthropological Records 24. Honolulu: Bernice P. Bishop Museum.

1979   *Marine Exploitation in Prehistoric Hawaii: Archaeological Excavations at Kalahuipua'a, Hawaii Island*. Pacific Anthropological Records 29. Honolulu: Bernice P. Bishop Museum.

1982   (with D. Yen), *Tikopia: The Prehistory and Ecology of a Polynesian Outlier*. Bernice P. Bishop Museum Bulletin 238. Honolulu: Bishop Museum Press.

1983   Editor (with J. Clark), *Archaeological Investigations of the Mudlane-Waimea-Kawaihae Road Corridor, Island of Hawai'i: An Interdisciplinary Study of an Environmental Transect*. Department of Anthropology Report 83–1. Honolulu: Bernice P. Bishop Museum.

1984   *The Evolution of the Polynesian Chiefdoms*. Cambridge: Cambridge University Press.

1985   *Feathered Gods and Fishhooks: An Introduction to Hawaiian Archaeology and Prehistory*. Honolulu: University of Hawai'i Press.

1986   Editor, *Island Societies: Archaeological Approaches to Evolution and Transformation*. Cambridge: Cambridge University Press.

1988   *Niuatoputapu: The Prehistory of a Polynesian Chiefdom*. Burke Museum Monograph No. 5. Seattle: Burke Museum.

1988   Editor (with T. L. Hunt), *Archaeology of the Lapita Cultural Complex: A Critical Review*. Burke Museum Research Report No. 5. Seattle: Burke Museum.

1989   Editor, *Prehistoric Hawaiian Occupation in the Anahulu Valley, O'ahu Island: Excavations in Three Inland Rockshelters*. Archaeological Research Facility Contribution No. 47. Berkeley: University of California.

1992   *Anahulu: The Anthropology of History in the Kingdom of Hawaii*. Volume 2, *The Archaeology of History*. Chicago: University of Chicago Press.

1993   Editor (with T. L. Hunt), *The To'aga Site: Three Millennia of Polynesian Occupation in the Manu'a Islands, Samoa*. Archaeological Research Facility Contribution No. 51. Berkeley: University of California.

1994   *The Wet and the Dry: Irrigation and Agricultural Intensification in Polynesia*. Chicago: University of Chicago Press.

1996   (with photographs by Thérèse Babineau), *Legacy of the Landscape: An Illustrated Guide to Hawaiian Archaeological Sites.* Honolulu: University of Hawai'i Press.

1997   *The Lapita Peoples: Ancestors of the Oceanic World.* Oxford: Blackwell Publishers.

1997   Editor (with T. L. Hunt), *Historical Ecology in the Pacific Islands: Prehistoric Environmental and Landscape Change.* New Haven, CT: Yale University Press.

1997   Editor (with M. I. Weisler and E. Casella), *Towards a Prehistory of the Koné Region, New Caledonia: A Reanalysis of the Pioneering Archaeological Excavations of E. W. Gifford.* Kroeber Anthropological Society Papers, Vol. 82, Special Edition. Berkeley: University of California.

1997   Editor, *Nā Mea Kahiko o Kahikinui: Studies in the Archaeology of Kahikinui, Maui, Hawaiian Islands.* Oceanic Archaeological Laboratory, Special Publication No. 1. Berkeley: Archaeological Research Facility.

2000   *On the Road of the Winds: An Archaeological History of the Pacific Islands Before European Contact.* Berkeley: University of California Press.

2001   (with R. C. Green), *Hawaiki, Ancestral Polynesia: An Essay in Historical Anthropology.* Cambridge: Cambridge University Press.

2001   Editor, *Lapita and Its Transformations in Near Oceania: Archaeological Investigations in the Mussau Islands, Papua New Guinea, 1985–88.* Volume I, *Introduction, Stratigraphy, Chronology.* Archaeological Research Facility Contribution No. 59. Berkeley: University of California.

2002   Editor, *From the "Cliffs of Keolewa" to the "Sea of Papaloa": An Archaeological Reconnaissance of Portions of the Kalaupapa National Historical Park, Moloka'i, Hawaiian Islands.* Oceanic Archaeology Laboratory, Special Publication No. 2. Berkeley: Archaeological Research Facility.

2002   (with Christophe Sand), *L'Expédition Archéologique d'Edward W. Gifford et Richard Shutler, Jr. en Nouvelle-Calédonie au Cours de l'Année 1952. Edward W. Gifford and Richard Shutler Jr's Archaeological Expedition to New Caledonia in 1952.* Les Cahiers de l'Archéologie en Nouvelle-Calédonie, Vol. 13. Noumea: Service des Musées de du Patrimoine de Nouvelle-Calédonie.

2004   Editor (with E. Conte), *Archaeological Investigations in the Mangareva Islands (Gambier Archipelago), French Polynesia.* Archaeological Research Facility, Contribution No. 62. Berkeley: University of California.

2007   Editor (with J. -L. Rallu), *The Growth and Collapse of Pacific Island Societies: Archaeological and Demographic Perspectives.* Honolulu: University of Hawai'i Press.

2010   *How Chiefs Became Kings: Divine Kingship and the Rise of Archaic States in Ancient Hawai'i.* Berkeley: University of California Press.

2011   Editor, *Roots of Conflict: Soils, Agriculture, and Sociopolitical Complexity in Ancient Hawai'i.* Santa Fe: School for Advanced Research.

2012   *A Shark Going Inland Is My Chief: The Island Civilization of Ancient Hawai'i.* Berkeley: University of California Press.

2014   *Kua'āina Kahiko: Life and Land in Ancient Kahikinui, Maui.* Honolulu: University of Hawai'i Press.

2014   (with Jennifer G. Kahn), *Monumentality and Ritual Materialization in the Society Islands: The Archaeology of a Major Ceremonial Complex in the 'Opunohu Valley, Mo'orea*. Bishop Museum Bulletin in Anthropology 13. Honolulu: Bishop Museum Press.

Glossary of Polynesian Words

afukere (Tikopian) The original people of the island (literally "earth sprung").

ahu (Tahitian) The altar of a temple or *marae*.

ahupua'a (Hawaiian) A traditional territorial unit, running from the ocean to the mountain-top (literally, "pig altar").

ala (Hawaiian) Road or trail.

ali'i (Hawaiian) Chief.

a matua (Futunan) The "ancient wall" that keeps pigs confined to the village area.

'anā'anā (Hawaiian) Sorcery.

alofi (Futunan, Tongan) The semi-circle of chiefs seated for a kava ceremony.

ariki, aliki (Pan-Polynesian) Chief (see *ali'i*).

aue, auwe (Pan-Polynesian) Alas! Alack! Oh dear!

'auwai (Hawaiian) An irrigation canal or ditch.

'awa (Hawaiian) The kava plant (*Piper methysticum*), used to make an infusion consumed for its psychoactive properties.

fale, fare (Pan-Polynesian) House. (See Hawaiian *hale*).

fare haupape (Tahitian) A rectangular house, occupied by commoners.

fare pote'e (Tahitian) A round-ended house, occupied by elites or used for special functions.

fau (Futunan) The *Hibiscus tiliaceous* shrub, as well as the kava strainer made from its dried and shredded bark.

fono (Tongan) An assembly or gathering of chiefs and lineage elders.

hala (Hawaiian) The *Pandanus* tree.

hale (Hawaiian) House.

hau (Hawaiian) A shrubby plant (*Hibiscus tiliaceous*) that forms thickets in wet valleys.

he'e (Hawaiian) Octopus.

heiau (Hawaiian) A temple or place of worship in ancient Hawai'i.

hīhīwai (Hawaiian) A brackish water shellfish (*Neritina granosa*).

hōlua (Hawaiian) A kind of sled used on grassy slopes or on prepared stone slides.

honi (Hawaiian) The traditional greeting of pressing noses and sharing breadth (see *ongi*).

hou'eiki (Tongan) Chief.

hula (Hawaiian) Traditional dance form in Hawai'i.

'ie'ie (Hawaiian and Tahitian) A climbing vine (*Freycinetia arborea*) in the *Pandanus* family.

'ili (Hawaiian) A land section within an *ahupua'a* territory.

kaiga (Futunan) A household group occupying a common dwelling and farming its ancestral land.

kahu (Hawaiian) Steward, guardian, caretaker.

kahua (Hawaiian) A platform, foundation, or stage, especially for hula performances.

kākū (Hawaiian) Barracuda fish.

kalauniu (Futunan) A feast prestation, consisting of a coconut leaf basket containing yams or other tubers, usually topped with a roasted pig.

kamaʻāina (Hawaiian) Native born, one born to a place (literally "land child").

kamani (Hawaiian) A large hardwood tree (*Calophyllum inophyllum*), quite rare in Hawaiʻi, found in lowland or coastal areas.

kapa (Hawaiian) Barkcloth.

katoaga, katoanga (Futunan and Tongan) Community feasts, typically accompanied by formal kava ceremonies and traditional dance performances.

kauhale (Hawaiian) A cluster of structures making up a residential complex.

kava (Pan-Polynesian) The kava plant (*Piper methysticum*) used to make an infusion consumed for its psychoactive properties. See *ʻawa*.

kī (Hawaiian) The *ti* plant (*Cordyline fruticosa*).

kiato (Anutan) The booms that attach the outrigger to a canoe.

kiokio (Tikopian) Bonefish (*Chanos chanos*) that live in the island's lake.

koa (Hawaiian) An endemic hardwood tree (*Acacia koa*); also a warrior.

koʻa (Hawaiian) A fishing shrine.

konohiki (Hawaiian) The traditional land manager of an *ahupuaʻa* territory.

koʻolau (Hawaiian) The windward side of an island.

kukui (Hawaiian) The candlenut tree (*Aleurites moluccana*).

kūpuna (Hawaiian) Grandparents, ancestors, elders. The singular form is *kupuna*.

langi (Tongan) Stone-faced burial mounds reserved for the highest ranked Tongan chiefs.

lauhala (Hawaiian) Leaves of the *Pandanus* tree, and mats woven from these leaves.

leho (Hawaiian) Cowrie shell (*Cypraea* spp.).

lei (Hawaiian) Necklace, typically of flowers but also of shells, seeds, or other materials.

liku (Tongan) The windward coast or side of an island.

loʻi (Hawaiian) Irrigated pondfield for taro cultivation.

luakini (Hawaiian) A war temple at which the king offered human sacrifices.

makaʻāinana (Hawaiian) Commoner.

makai (Hawaiian) Directional indicator, toward the ocean.

malae (Futunan) An open plaza fronting the chief's house, used for formal kava ceremonies and feast presentations.

mana (Pan-Polynesian) Spiritual power.

māpē (Tahitian) The Tahitian Chestnut tree (*Inocarpus fagifer*) which produces a large nut, edible after cooking.

mara (Tahitian) A large tree (*Neonauclea forsteri*) common in the interior of the ʻŌpūnohu Valley on Moʻorea.

marae (Tahitian and other Polynesian) A temple or place of worship.

maru (Anutan and Tikopian) Senior males who form a kind of advisory council to the chiefs.

matapaito (Tikopian) The seaward, sacred side of a house.

matapare (Anutan) The seaward, sacred side of a house.

mauka (Hawaiian) Directional indicator, toward the mountains.

milo, miro (Pan-Polynesian) A coastal tree (*Thespesia populnea*) prized for wood carving.

moai (Rapanui) The stone statues of Easter Island.

moana (Pan-Polynesian) Ocean; the deep sea.

motu (Pan-Polynesian) Island, islet, especially a small coral islet built up on the reef of an atoll.

mua (Futunan, Tongan) The adjutant or spokesman for a chief. The word also has a Pan-Polynesian meaning of "front" or "forward."

mua (Hawaiian) A men's house; a house where men ate together and made offerings to their collective ancestors.

naʻau (Hawaiian) Guts, belly, heart, the center of one's feelings.

noforanga (Tikopia) A hamlet (literally "dwelling place").

nui (Pan-Polynesian) Big, large.

ʻōhiʻa lehua (Hawaiian) An indigenous tree (*Metrosideros polymorpha*) dominant in upland forests.

ʻokipū (Hawaiian) An upland garden or shifting cultivation.

ʻolonā (Hawaiian) An endemic shrub (*Touchardia latifolia*) used to make cordage.

ongi (Anutan) The traditional greeting of pressing noses and sharing breath (see *honi*). The Tikopian variant of the term is *songi*.

ʻopihi (Hawaiian) Limpet (*Cellana exarata*), much prized for its flesh.

paepae (Pan-Polynesian) Platform, usually of stone, for a house or other structure.

pāpio (Hawaiian) The young growth stage of *ulua* fish (*Caranx ignobilis*).

patongia (Anutan) A household; those who cook and consume their meals collectively.

piʻo (Hawaiian) Royal marriage between full siblings or half-siblings, and the offspring produced by such unions.

pipipi (Hawaiian) A small sea snail (*Nerita* spp.).

poi (Hawaiian) The preferred staple starch food of Hawaiʻi, made from the pounded taro root mixed with water.

pola (Tongan) A platter or presentation of food prepared for a feast, consisting of yams, puddings, and other foods topped usually with a baked pig.

pua kenikeni (Hawaiian) A shrub or small tree (*Fagraea berteriana*) noted for its fragrant, orange, tubular flowers.

pūneʻe (Hawaiian) Couch or daybed.

pūrau (Tahitian) A shrubby plant (*Hibiscus tiliaceous*) that forms thickets in wet valleys.

renga (Anutan and Tikopian) The reddish-yellow pigment extracted from the turmeric plant (*Cucurma longa*).

rongorongo (Rapanui) Tablets incised with an indigenous script; also the name of the script.

sau (Futunan) Paramount chief or "king" of one of Futuna's two chiefdoms.

sia heu lupe (Tongan) Special mounds used for pigeon snaring, a chiefly sport.

tamanu (Anutan and Tikopian) A hardwood tree (*Callophyllum inophyllum*) used for canoe hulls (see *kamani*).

tanoʻa (Tongan) Special bowl for making and serving kava.

taoʻasu (Futunan) Informal kava drinking, usually in a chief's house in the evening.

taʻovala (Tongan) A finely woven mat worn around the loins as a sign of respect.

tapakau (Anutan and Tikopian) Floor mats of woven coconut fronds.

tapu (Pan-Polynesian) Sacred, prohibited; Hawaiian variant is *kapu*.

tatau (Pan-Polynesian) Tattoo, tattooing.

telega (Futunan) A complex of irrigated pondfields for taro cultivation.

tiki (Marquesan and other Eastern Polynesian) Anthropomorphic sculpture.

toafa (Futunan) Degraded, pyrophytic fern or grasslands.

tofiʻa (Tongan) The estate or lands of a chief.

tohua (Marquesan) A tribal dance plaza, usually surrounded by megalithic house platforms. See Hawaiian *kahua*.

tui (Futunan) A prefix before a proper name denoting a chiefly title, as in Tui Saʻavaka.

ʻuala (Hawaiian) The sweet potato (*Ipomoea batatas*), a major dryland crop in ancient Hawaiʻi.

uhu (Hawaiian) Parrotfish (*Scarus* spp.).

vaka (Anutan) Canoe.

wauke (Hawaiian) Paper mulberry (*Broussonetia papyrifera*), used to make barkcloth.

wiliwili (Hawaiian) An endemic dryland tree of Hawaiʻi (*Erythrina sandwicensis*).

Index

Note: An f following a page number denotes a figure.